"I found this book impossible to put down! A compelling theory and historical context set alongside real stories f frontline of schools and education, it offers a powerful relationships to support leadership effectiveness in schoc to the power of coaching, albeit later in life, this impress. ... . , impressive set of contributors, manages to capture the reality of leading in schools, with all its highs and lows, whilst leaving you, as the reader, clearer and more optimistic about the future. Essential reading for any school leader!"

Andy Buck, CEO Leadership Matters

"At a time when the educational system is in one of its regular states of crisis, and when head teachers are leaving the profession at a worrying rate, *Keeping Your Head* is a vital contribution to understanding leadership in schools. Writing from a sophisticated psychodynamic and systems perspective but maintaining clarity and a practical focus, the highly experienced contributors to this book offer hugely important insights into ways of managing the enormous stress of school leadership. The book will prove to be a landmark collection for those who want to understand the emotional and psychological pressures of being a school leader – and how to survive them."

Stephen Frosh, Professor of Psychology, Birkbeck, University of London

"This book reflects deeply on the experience of school leadership – both the highs and the lows. The authors explore the complex and varied pressures on leaders and the many means to mitigate them, with insight and humanity. I recommend this book to anyone interested in education and especially those making or implementing education policy."

Francis Listowel, The Earl of Listowel (PhD), Officer: All Party Parliamentary Group for the Teaching Profession; Vice Chair: All Party Parliamentary Group for looked After Children and Young People and Care Leavers

"This a great book to add to any school leader's 'go to' pile of leadership books. However, what makes this one stand out is that it talks to the reader and really gets to the heart of what it means to lead a school in such challenging times.

I read with avid interest and appreciated the current voices of school leaders reflected throughout the book. Many chapters really resonated and confirmed the belief that remarkable people lead remarkable schools – but they are human and do also need support and guidance. Having worked in a range of challenging schools as a senior leader and in two as headteacher, I truly value the shared experiences that are captured in this book.

Andrea and Emil have got under the skin of the enormity of the job, the fact that it can be an all-consuming and lonely job at times. In doing so, they offer solutions and suggestions which I think are invaluable to current and aspiring headteachers."

Evelyn Forde, headteacher Copthall School

"Everyone who knows about our schools is aware of the challenges and difficulties experienced by headteachers and other school leaders. As *Keeping Your Head* says, 'school leaders today require higher degrees of self-awareness, emotional intelligence and political literacy than ever before.' The book is in effect a manual not only for school leaders at all levels but also a range of others from school governors and inspectors to training providers. It is informed by a range of approaches from its thoroughly knowledgeable authors, including insights from the theory and practice of psychotherapy. There are numerous case studies, some of them quite emotional, and the whole work is supported by extensive research. It is hard to think of anyone needing but not yet benefitting from its advice who would fail to be helped by this book."

Professor Robert Cassen, OBE, Emeritus Professor,
London School of Economics

SUSTAINING DEPTH AND MEANING IN SCHOOL LEADERSHIP

Sustaining Depth and Meaning in School Leadership: Keeping Your Head concerns the emotional and psychological experience of school leadership—in particular, the felt experience of life as a headteacher. It describes the pressures and rewards of the role, together with some of the ways that school leaders successfully sustain and develop themselves and their teams in what has become an increasingly complex, challenging, and highly accountable role.

This book explores the personal experience of leading schools. Part I provides an overview and analysis of current and historical trends in school leadership and offers some theoretical frameworks for making sense of these. Part II then offers psychodynamic approaches to supporting and developing school leaders and the impact that trends in executive education continue to have on this. Part III looks at approaches to school leadership development more generally, including team development; influences from the business world; the growth of mentoring and coaching as a leadership intervention; the design and evaluation of leadership development programmes; and a case study on whole-system development. The final word is given to ten serving headteachers and deputies and their leadership journeys. This range of chapters, concepts, and perspectives will support school leaders to maintain an emotional equilibrium while navigating the multilayered tightrope of intrapsychic, interpersonal, and organizational dynamics inherent in school life.

Rooted in Jackson and Berkeley's belief that school leaders are likely to be at their best when they find their own unique and authentic way of taking up their leadership role, this book is an accessible, supportive, and developmental contribution for all those involved in education leadership.

Emil Jackson is a Consultant Child and Adolescent Psychotherapist, Adult Psychotherapist, and Executive Coach. His clinical and teaching base is at the Tavistock and Portman NHS Foundation Trust, where he is Head of Child and Adolescent Psychotherapy in the Adolescent and Young Adult Service. Since 2002, Emil has been involved in a wide range of coaching and consultancy across public and corporate sector organizations—from FTSE 100 companies, to global social media firms, to family businesses, to schools. Emil now works nationally and internationally with senior executives and CEOs, but he particularly values his coaching work with headteachers and senior leaders in education.

Andrea Berkeley has worked at the leading edge of education development and reform. For 14 years she was head of culturally diverse Preston Manor comprehensive in London, leading the school from a "Serious weaknesses" to an "Outstanding" Ofsted rating. She has worked for 13 years with various national organizations on the training and development of education leaders, including the National College for School Leadership and University College London Institute of Education, and during her six years as founding Dean of Development at Ambition School Leadership. Andrea now works as an executive coach and leadership consultant to headteachers and chief executives—particularly those working in challenging contexts—and also to senior executives in social enterprise and corporate sectors.

Tavistock Clinic Series

Margot Waddell, Jocelyn Catty, & Kate Stratton (Series Editors)

Recent titles in the Tavistock Clinic Series

Addictive States of Mind, *edited by Marion Bower, Rob Hale, & Heather Wood*

Assessment in Child Psychotherapy, *edited by Margaret Rustin & Emanuela Quagliata*

Childhood Depression: A Place for Psychotherapy, *edited by Judith Trowell, withGillian Miles*

Conjunctions: Social Work, Psychoanalysis, and Society, *by Andrew Cooper*

Consultations in Psychoanalytic Psychotherapy, *edited by R. Peter Hobson*

Contemporary Developments in Adult and Young Adult Therapy. The Work of the Tavistock and Portman Clinics, Vol. 1, *edited by Alessandra Lemma*

Couple Dynamics: Psychoanalytic Perspectives in Work with the Individual, the Couple, and the Group, *edited by Aleksandra Novakovic*

Doing Things Differently: The Influence of Donald Meltzer on Psychoanalytic Theory and Practice, *edited by Margaret Cohen & Alberto Hahn*

Inside Lives: Psychoanalysis and the Growth of the Personality, *by Margot Waddell*

Internal Landscapes and Foreign Bodies: Eating Disorders and Other Pathologies, *by Gianna Williams*

Living on the Border: Psychotic Processes in the Individual, the Couple, and the Group, *edited by David Bell & Aleksandra Novakovic*

Making Room for Madness in Mental Health: The Psychoanalytic Understanding of Psychotic Communication, *by Marcus Evans*

Melanie Klein Revisited: Pioneer and Revolutionary in the Psychoanalysis of Young Children, *by Susan Sherwin-White*

New Discoveries in Child Psychotherapy: Findings from Qualitative Research, *edited by Margaret Rustin & Michael Rustin*

Oedipus and the Couple, *edited by Francis Grier*

On Adolescence, *by Margot Waddell*

Organization in the Mind: Psychoanalysis, Group Relations, and Organizational Consultancy, *by David Armstrong, edited by Robert French*

Psychoanalysis and Culture: A Kleinian Perspective, *edited by David Bell*

Researching the Unconscious: Principles of Psychoanalytic Method, *by Michael Rustin*

Reason and Passion: A Celebration of the Work of Hanna Segal, *edited by David Bell*

Sexuality and Gender Now: Moving Beyond Heteronormativity, *edited by Leezah Hertzmann & Juliet Newbigin*

Short-Term Psychoanalytic Psychotherapy for Adolescents with Depression: A Treatment Manual, *edited by Jocelyn Catty*

Sibling Matters: A Psychoanalytic, Developmental, and Systemic Approach, *edited by Debbie Hindle & Susan Sherwin-White*

Social Defences against Anxiety: Explorations in a Paradigm, *edited by David Armstrong & Michael Rustin*

Surviving Space: Papers on Infant Observation, *edited by Andrew Briggs*

Talking Cure: Mind and Method of the Tavistock Clinic, *edited by David Taylor*

The Anorexic Mind, *by Marilyn Lawrence*

The Groups Book. Psychoanalytic Group Therapy: Principles and Practice, *edited by Caroline Garland*

The Learning Relationship: Psychoanalytic thinking in Education

Therapeutic Care for Refugees: No Place Like Home, *edited by Renos Papadopoulos*

Therapeutic Interventions with Babies and Young Children in Care: Observation and Attention, *by Jenifer Wakelyn*

Thinking Space: Promoting Thinking about Race, Culture, and Diversity in Psychotherapy and Beyond, *edited by Frank Lowe*

Towards Belonging: Negotiating New Relationships for Adopted Children and Those in Care, *edited by Andrew Briggs*

Turning the Tide: A Psychoanalytic Approach to Mental Illness. The Work of the Fitzjohn's Unit, *edited by Rael Meyerowitz & David Bell*

Understanding Trauma: A Psychoanalytic Approach, *edited by Caroline Garland*

Waiting to Be Found: Papers on Children in Care, *edited by Andrew Briggs*

"What Can the Matter Be?": Therapeutic Interventions with Parents, Infants, and Young Children, *edited by Louise Emanuel & Elizabeth Bradley*

Young Child Observation: A Development in the Theory and Method of Infant Observation, *edited by Simonetta M. G. Adamo & Margaret Rustin*

SUSTAINING DEPTH AND MEANING IN SCHOOL LEADERSHIP

Keeping Your Head

Edited by

Emil Jackson & Andrea Berkeley

Routledge
Taylor & Francis Group

LONDON AND NEW YORK

First published 2021
by Routledge
2 Park Square, Milton Park, Abingdon, Oxon OX14 4RN

and by Routledge
52 Vanderbilt Avenue, New York, NY 10017

Routledge is an imprint of the Taylor & Francis Group, an informa business

British Library Cataloguing-in-Publication Data
A catalogue record for this book is available from the British Library

Library of Congress Cataloging-in-Publication Data
Names: Jackson, Emil, 1969- editor. | Berkeley, Andrea, 1945- editor.
Title: Sustaining depth and meaning in school leadership : keeping your head /
Edited by Emil Jackson & Andrea Berkeley.
Description: Abingdon, Oxon ; New York, NY : Routledge, 2020. | Series: Tavistock clinic book series | Includes bibliographical references and index. | Identifiers: LCCN 2020002896 (print) | LCCN 2020002897 (ebook) | ISBN 9780367859428 (hardback) | ISBN 9780367859411 (paperback) | ISBN 9781003015901 (ebook)
Subjects: LCSH: Educational leadership—Psychological aspects. | School management and organization—Psychological aspects. | School improvement programs.
Classification: LCC LB2806 .S86 2020 (print) | LCC LB2806 (ebook) | DDC 371.2/011—dc23
LC record available at https://lccn.loc.gov/2020002896
LC ebook record available at https://lccn.loc.gov/2020002897

ISBN: 978-0-367-85942-8 (hbk)
ISBN: 978-0-367-85941-1 (pbk)
ISBN: 978-1-003-01590-1 (ebk)

Typeset in Palatino
by Swales & Willis, Exeter, Devon, UK

CONTENTS

SERIES EDITORS' PREFACE   xi

ACKNOWLEDGEMENTS   xv

ABOUT THE EDITORS AND CONTRIBUTORS   xix

Introduction
       Andrea Berkeley & Emil Jackson   1

Part I
Context and concepts for contemporary school leadership

1   Keeping your head: the unspoken realities of headship
          Andrea Berkeley   17

2   The context and challenges of contemporary school leadership
          Peter Earley & Toby Greany   41

3   Emotional factors in leading teaching and learning
          Biddy Youell   57

4   Individual, group and organizational dynamics: a
theoretical overview
Judith Bell   73

Part II
School leadership development: psychodynamic approaches

5   Executive coaching for the hidden realities of life as a
school leader
Emil Jackson & Andrea Berkeley   97

6   Leadership and governance: leadership pairs coaching
Clare Huffington   116

7   On the leading edge of learning: work discussion groups
for headteachers
Emil Jackson & Andrea Berkeley   132

8   Learning leadership: lessons from the top
Ben Bryant   151

Part III
School leadership development: trends and approaches

9   The impact of personality preferences on school leadership
Emil Jackson   173

10   Developing leaders: lessons from the business world
Barry Speirs & Andrea Berkeley   199

11   Creating coaching cultures in schools
Chris Munro, Margaret Barr, & Christian van Nieuwerburgh   226

12   Designing, managing, and evaluating school leadership
programmes
Sarah Harrison   246

13   Lessons from "The London Challenge": a whole-system
approach to leadership development
David Woods   267

Part IV
The last word

14   Talking heads: the voice of school leaders
    Andrea Berkeley et al.   285

REFERENCES   319
INDEX   336

SERIES EDITORS' PREFACE

Since it was founded in 1920, the Tavistock Clinic—now the Tavistock and Portman NHS Foundation Trust—has developed a wide range of developmental approaches to mental health that have been strongly influenced by the ideas of psychoanalysis. It has also adopted systemic family therapy as a theoretical model and a clinical approach to family problems. The Tavistock is now one of the largest mental health training institutions in Britain. It teaches up to 600 students a year on postgraduate, doctoral, and qualifying courses in social work, systemic psychotherapy, psychology, psychiatry, nursing, and child, adolescent, and adult psychotherapy, along with 2,000 multidisciplinary clinicians, social workers, and teachers attending Continuing Professional Development courses and conferences on psychoanalytic observation, psychoanalytic thinking, and management and leadership in a range of clinical and community settings.

The Tavistock's philosophy aims to promote therapeutic methods in mental health. Its work is based on the clinical expertise that is also the basis of its consultancy and research activities. The aim of this Series is to make available to the reading public the clinical, theoretical, and research work that is most influential at the Tavistock. The Series sets out new approaches in the understanding and treatment of psychological disturbance in children, adolescents, and adults, both as individuals and in families.

Sustaining Depth and Meaning in School Leadership: Keeping Your Head, expertly edited by Emil Jackson and Andrea Berkeley, focuses on the emotional, group, and organizational dynamics in leading, teaching, and learning—on the "leading edge of learning", as they put it in one of their own chapters. The descriptions on these pages—both in their own chapters and in those of a wide variety of professionals—of the prerequisites of a creative and effective learning culture vividly evoke the complexity of trying to "keep one's head" amidst the ever-changing demands of the social and political pressures on the educational system; of what it means to learn in the current landscapes—target-driven and cash-strapped as they tend to be.

The editorial focus is on the multifold pressures entailed in creating, leading, and managing a successful learning environment. The respective authors—some of them teachers themselves—take up, in their very different ways, the crucial matter of how to provide a genuine learning culture for those all-important years when children and young adults are acquiring the wherewithal not only to learn about science, history, and geography, but also about themselves, about the nature of friendship, and about the importance of loyalty, generosity, truthfulness in the current political mêlée: in short, between internal, emotional, and psychological worlds and external pressures and forces.

The editors draw on many years of their own professional knowledge and expertise and that of their contributors to illuminate the nature and the vicissitudes of emotional and cognitive development, whether in staff or student, and also the roles of being a consultant/school-leader in a wide variety of institutions, including multi-academy trusts and educational charities.

This confluence of influences goes to the heart of the leading vision and purpose of the Tavistock Clinic Series: the founding commitment to finding ways, individually, collectively, and institutionally, to offer the best possible community service despite all; the development and nurturing of a system that best serves, in this case, the educational priorities of an enlightened and thinking society. It also serves the task of identifying and supporting those situations that neglect, undermine, or abuse what could otherwise be more progressive paths. Group dynamics and personal dynamics are inseparable. The fact is that the clashes and breakdowns between the two in contemporary culture have rightly become a matter of pressing concern with respect to cultural differences, unequal opportunities—indeed, to in-built disadvantages of every kind. We Series Editors are proud that this book addresses so immediately and evocatively the depth and breadth of such concerns and demonstrates how much difference can be made by enlightened structures of management and learning. Such an examination is of immediate and pressing importance. As Robert Cassen puts it in his endorsement, ". . . the book is, in effect, a manual not only for school leaders at all levels but also for a range of others, from school governors and inspectors to training providers" —and, it has to be added, to parents, too.

ACKNOWLEDGEMENTS

This book has had a very long gestation period since its inception several years ago. At times, it felt like a leap of faith to trust that it would ever actually be completed or see the light of day. Arriving at this point is therefore a significant junction, so we would like to thank some of the people who have played a significant role in our respective journeys, both professionally and personally.

Emil Jackson

When I first embarked on my pre-clinical training in child and adolescent psychotherapy at the Tavistock Centre back in 1991, I could never have imagined how my work, interests, or career would later evolve. During my most impressionable training years, I was privileged to have had some of the best teachers, supervisors, and managers one could ever hope for—people whose wisdom, belief, and support continue to be influential in the way I think and work nearly 30 years later. In particular, this includes the late Freddie Gainza, Ricky Emanuel, Margaret Rustin, Margot Waddell, Claire Cripwell, and the late Jonathan Bradley and Hamish Canham.

I will always be grateful to Dr Maxim de Sauma, clinical director at the Brent Centre for Young People, for all the support and freedom he gave me in setting up and leading Brent Centre's schools' outreach service between 1999 and 2010. I am similarly grateful to my co-editor,

Andrea Berkeley, for trusting me to work with the students, parents, and so many of her staff at Preston Manor High School—a leap of faith for any headteacher. This innovative work, together with the support given to me by Clare Huffington and Linda Hoyle from the Tavistock Consultancy Service, served as a bridge into the world of executive coaching. As such, it has been formative in my career and the catalyst for so many unexpected and wide-ranging areas of professional development, interest, and growth, including this book. It is hugely gratifying to know that, 20 years later and 10 years after leaving my post at the Brent Centre, the joint project between Brent Centre and Preston Manor is still going strong and continuing to innovate in the way it supports staff and engages hard-to-reach young people.

My development has been influenced very significantly by the many school-based staff with whom I have worked over the past 20 years—teachers and learning support assistants, middle and senior leaders, and headteachers. It has been a source of great personal pleasure to have built so many excellent and long-standing relationships with such wonderful, wise, and inspiring people. Among these, some deserve particular thanks for their contributions to this book—directly and indirectly: Sue Lowidt, Jo Shuter, Irene Forster, Sue Howe, Rosi Jordon, Lyn Harding, Nicky Williams, Ken Warman, Jerry Collins, Sian Maddrell, Sarah Jacobs, Lira Winston, Jo Sassienie, Marc Shoffren, Yvonne Baron, Jillian Dunstan, Rebecca Abrahams, and Francis Listowel.

I am grateful to my colleagues at the Tavistock and Portman NHS Foundation Trust who supported me to take study leave to work on this book. In particular: Katie Argent, Linda Young, Justine McCarthy Woods, Catrin Bradley, Kate Stratton, Geraldine Creehan, Sheva Habel and Sally Hodges.

I would also like to thank a few of the special people who have supported me in other important ways *en route* to completing this book—whether by reading drafts of chapters, bearing with my doubts and fatigue, nourishing me with ideas renewed inspiration, or simply being there as a totally dependable support every step of the way. These include Erica Garb, Jeremy Keeley, Amelia La Spada, Ben Bryant, Ali Reardon, Charles Imber, Anthony Bor, Alexandra and Andrew Maurice.

Finally, I would like to thank my family. My parents, Rodwin and Judith Jackson, for being the most incredible secure base and role models throughout my life and for supporting me to find and pursue a career that I love and feel passionate about. My mother deserves special appreciation for her reliably insightful and rigorous critique of anything I write!

Along with my children, Eliana, Michaela, and Levi, I would also like thank my wife, Andy, for the tremendous support, love, and generosity she also always shown me throughout this project and everything I do.

Andrea Berkeley

My primary debt is to the school leaders I have worked with—and who are the inspiration for this book. Without exception, they have moved me with their moral purpose, integrity, and humility and have informed my thinking in many ways. There are so many people to thank: among them are those who deserve particular gratitude for their contributions to this book, directly and indirectly: Jill Baker, Rose Blackman-Hegan, Ellen Clarke, Sarah Creasey, Andrew English, Annie Gammon, Beth Kobel, Natali Kojik, Oli Knight, Gloria Lowe, Paddy McGrath, Trevor North, Sarah Pringle and Andrew Webster; Chong-Hao Fu and Kelly McClure of Leading Educators USA.

Publication also provides an opportunity to thank tutors, mentors, role models, and colleagues, from whom I am fortunate to have learned. The brilliant Open University made postgraduate professional qualifications feasible while my children were young. During my headship and beyond, I owe a huge debt to the great minds and practitioners of the UCL Institute of Education (IOE), The Work Foundation, the Tavistock Centre, the former National College for School Leadership (NCSL), and the Former London Challenge teams.

In praxis, I owe much to the late Dame Tamsyn Imison and the talented staff at Hampstead School, most particularly Mich Jonas and the Sixth Form and History of Ideas teams. Tamsyn gave me many opportunities to develop and lead innovation, so that, in retrospect, I realize she taught me the essentials of effective leadership.

From my headship years, I am indebted to the teaching, pastoral, and support staff of Preston Manor School, especially deputy heads Jonathan Bach, Georgina Liveras, and Steve Rigby and senior leaders John Galligan, Dan Graham, and Beth Kobel; to successive chairs of governors, Reiner Thoelke, Rob MacLachlan, Julian Granville, and Sandra Bennett, for their faith in me and judicious challenge and support; and, with affection, Janet Hobbs, for her wise counsel and loyal assistance.

I am indebted to Jay Altman, Sharath Jeevan, and Jo Owen at Absolute Return for Kids (ARK) for the opportunity to work with so many talented and altruistic young professionals with very different backgrounds from my own. I would particularly like to thank James Toop, Lucy Peyton, Sarah Harrison, and Tom Ebbut—and school leader colleagues Jenny Francis, Georgina Liveras, Beth Kobel, and David Radomsky.

In an attempt to offer me comfort during a moment of professional ennui, a colleague once said, "It may seem like we don't work in the 'real world', but our advantage is that we will always know what it feels like to be a child, what a teenager is doing and thinking, what preoccupies twenty-, thirty- and forty-year-olds—and those approaching retirement." The greatest pleasure of professional life continues to be intergenerational collaboration and learning. For that I would like to thank colleagues and friends who have enriched and extended my thinking on leadership and organizational psychology more recently Catriona Horey, Catrina Plastow, Carina Saner, Andy Buck and colleagues at RSAcademics. Particular thanks to Laurence Barrett and Andy Buck—and to Sophie James for her insight, grace and wit.

I would also like to thank some special people who have supported my professional and personal development in important ways: Clare Huffington, John Simpson, Max Blustin, and Sarah Harrison, without whose encouragement and help this book would not have been completed. Most importantly, a special thank you to Iain Oswald.

Finally, I would like to acknowledge my late father, Constantine Vitalis, an autodidact who left school at 13 himself but who gave me a life-long love of learning and intellectual opportunities way beyond the boundaries of our times, means, and class; my daughters Xanthe and Zoe, for their inspiration and tolerance; and, most importantly, my husband Peter, whose love, unfailing support, wit, and humour has sustained me throughout my career.

Emil Jackson and Andrea Berkeley

Finally, we would both like to thank all the contributing writers for their thoughtfulness, grace, and openness to our many editorial suggestions and for being incredible, and incredibly patient, partners throughout this journey. We are also grateful to each other for the support, encouragement, and occasionally robust nudges we have both needed from each other, especially when we felt despairing and/or stuck along the way.

We would like to acknowledge Dr Maxim de Sauma for his key role in establishing the initial pilot partnership with Andrea and Preston Manor High School, back in 1998. We are grateful to Eric and Klara King for their expert editorial contribution, and to Peter Berkeley for his work on the front cover. And special appreciation is due to Margot Waddell, Kate Stratton, and Jos Catty—the Tavistock Series' Editors—who have been so generous with the encouragement and feedback they have given us, and the patience they have shown us as we passed each new deadline.

Thank you!

ABOUT THE EDITORS AND CONTRIBUTORS

Editors

Andrea Berkeley has 40 years' experience in education, including 14 years as head of North London secondary, Preston Manor, where she led her school from "Serious weaknesses" to "Outstanding" Ofsted rating. Following headship, she has engaged with the development of school leaders with several organizations, including the National College for School Leadership, The London Leadership Strategy and University College London Institute of Education. Her most recent leadership role was with ARK, where she supported the CEOs and directorate of The Future Leaders Trust and Teaching leaders—now Ambition Institute graduate school—from their inception, in designing the leadership curriculum for aspiring heads and middle leaders working in challenging contexts and growing the programmes nationally. Her international consultancy includes Russia, Sweden, Singapore, the Middle East, and extensively in the United States. Andrea is also an accredited executive coach, consultant and facilitator, coaching trainer, and supervisor who, while continuing to support school and academy trust leaders, also works in corporate and not-for-profit sectors with board members, senior executives and their teams. She takes great pleasure in combining her depth of understanding about people, interpersonal relationships and group dynamics to help clients develop the insight and confidence to maximize their potential in ways they hadn't anticipated possible.

Formerly a school governor, trustee of a young people's counselling service and advisory board member of Leading Educators USA, she is currently a trustee of The StARTed Foundation, which supports young talent in the performing arts, and a pro bono coach with On Purpose, a social enterprise that develops leaders for purpose-driven businesses.

Emil Jackson is a Consultant Child and Adolescent Psychotherapist, Adult Psychotherapist, and Executive Coach. His clinical, teaching and management base is at the Tavistock & Portman NHS Foundation Trust, where he is Head of Child and Adolescent Psychotherapy in the Adolescent and Young Adult Service. Emil is also an accredited executive coach and coaching supervisor. Since 2001, he has been involved in a wide range of coaching and consultancy across public and corporate sector organizations—from FTSE 100 companies, to global social media firms, to family businesses to schools. Specializing in executive coaching, Emil now works nationally and internationally with senior and board-level executives, but he particularly values his coaching work with headteachers. Emil is also experienced in MBTI (Myers–Briggs Type Indicator)—a personality instrument he has used extensively with middle and senior leaders. Emil has been working in or with schools and school leaders since 1999, when he began to develop a special interest and expertise in the application of work discussion groups—initially with teachers, and then with headteachers. This work has resulted in several publications and many years of contributing to Education Leadership Training Programmes such as Teaching Leaders, Future Leaders, and the Principal's Qualifying Programme.

Contributors

Margaret Barr is Lead Associate (Scotland) for Growth Coaching International. Her career in schools included headteacher of a city secondary school, and mentor for new headteachers, and aspiring headteachers studying for the Scottish Qualification for Headship. She returned to university in 2012 to take an MSc in coaching psychology. Margaret now works with school leaders as a coach and facilitator of coaching training programmes. Voluntary roles include book review editor for *Coaching: An International Journal of Theory, Research and Practice*, and providing admin support for the coaching supervision leadership team of the Association for Coaching.

Judith Bell is a clinical psychologist and organizational consultant who joined the Tavistock Clinic in 1990. In her clinical practice she specialized in working with children and families and early in her career established clinical outreach services in schools. This sparked an interest in school leadership and organizational systems, which she went on to foster, and in 2006 she joined the Tavistock Consultancy Service, becoming its director in 2008. Judith now works as an organizational consultant and executive coach, with an approach informed by psychoanalytic and systemic thinking. Her clients range across sectors and include school and university leaders. She is a teacher and trainer of consultancy and coaching, having established and led the Tavistock Professional Doctorate Programme in Consulting to Organisations. She is a faculty member at Ashridge business school and a supervisor and coach at INSEAD.

Ben Bryant is Professor of Leadership and Organisation at IMD Business School in Switzerland. He has extensive experience in the facilitation of senior executive development programmes. He has designed, directed, and delivered programmes in Europe, the United States, Asia, and Australia for groups of senior executives from companies such as Oracle, Mars, British Telecom, Emirates Airlines, Standard Chartered Bank, SKF and RWE, Ericsson, GlaxoSmithKline, and Zurich Financial Services. He is also the co-recipient of the innovation in teaching award at London Business School. Prior to coming to IMD, he was a Fellow of the Centre for Management Development at London Business School where he was also Director of the flagship in-company development programme for senior executives, the Global Business Consortium.

Peter Earley holds the Chair of Education Leadership and Management and was Director of Academic Affairs in LCLL at UCL IOE. His central research interests are leadership, school improvement, professional development, inspection, self-evaluation, and school governance. Recent externally-funded projects include: leadership development of independent school heads (2016), effective headteacher performance management (2013); the changing landscape of educational leadership in England (2012), and the experiences of new headteachers (2011). His most recent books are: *Exploring the School Leadership Landscape: Changing Demands, Changing Realities* (2013), *Accelerated Leadership Development: Fast-tracking School Leaders* (2010, with Jeff Jones) and *Helping Staff Develop in Schools* (2010 with Sara Bubb). He was given the BELMAS Distinguished Service Award in 2015.

Toby Greany is Professor of Education at the University of Nottingham. He was previously Professor of Leadership and Innovation at the

UCL Institute of Education (2013–18), where he was also Director of the London Centre for Leadership in Learning and Vice-Dean: Enterprise. Toby's research is focused on understanding ways in which educational policy and practice interact and the roles of system governance, leadership agency, and evidence in this process. His Nuffield-funded research with Rob Higham into England's "self-improving school-led system" (*Hierarchy, Markets and Networks*, 2018) was described by *The Observer* newspaper as "a seminal analysis" (30 June 2018) and by *The Independent* as "a state-of-the-nation study" (1 July 2018). His most recent book— *School Leadership and Education System Reform* (2017)—was co-edited with Peter Earley. Previously, Toby worked for the National College for School Leadership (NCSL), the Design Council, and the Campaign for Learning. In 2005–2006 he was Special Adviser to the House of Commons Education and Skills Select Committee. He has taught in Brazil, China, and the United Kingdom.

Sarah Harrison is the Head of Learning Design and Accreditation at the Chartered College of Teaching, where she is responsible for the strategy and development of the range of professional development and accreditation opportunities offered by the Chartered College. This has included overseeing the design, setup, and launch of the Chartered Teacher programme. Previously, she worked at Ambition School Leadership as the Associate Director for Headship Programmes—responsible for the design and delivery of two national Headship Programmes, including the NPQH. Prior to this, she worked on curriculum design for middle leadership development programmes.

Clare Huffington is a freelance organizational consultant and executive coach and author of ten books, including co-editing *Working Below the Surface: The Emotional Life of Contemporary Organizations* (2004). She was, until 2007, the Director of Tavistock Consulting in London. She is a clinical psychologist and has worked as a teacher, educational psychologist, university lecturer, and family therapist before beginning to work with larger systems as an organizational consultant, as well as with a number of headteachers and senior leaders in education. She was President of the International Society for the Psychoanalytic Study of Organizations from 2009 to 2011.

Chris Munro is Managing Director (Australia/New Zealand) at Growth Coaching International. He has extensive experience in supporting and leading the development of teachers and school leaders, drawn from over 25 years in Government and Independent schools, and in Initial

Teacher Education at the University of Aberdeen. His current role sees him coaching school leaders and developing the coaching capacity of school communities across Australia and beyond. Chris holds a Master of Research degree from the University of Aberdeen and is an Accredited Coach at Senior Practitioner level with the European Mentoring and Coaching Council.

Barry Speirs is Head of Leadership Consultancy at RSAcademics, which offers specialist services for the search and selection, coaching, and development of school leaders and senior staff. He joined the company in 2014, after a long international career in Human Resources with leading multinational companies. His experience includes 14 years with Burmah Castrol and BP, where he held HR Director positions in the United Kingdom, the United States, and India, as well as a number of specialist regional roles in leadership development and employee relations for firms that include PricewaterhouseCoopers. Barry has a postgraduate qualification in HR and is a member of the Chartered Institute of Personnel & Development (CIPD). Barry now specializes in leadership training, development, and headship appraisals in schools. He is also the author of two research reports: "Leading An International School in China" and "The Art of International School Leadership".

Christian van Nieuwerburgh is Executive Director of Growth Coaching International, Professor of Coaching and Positive Psychology at the University of East London (UK) and Honorary Fellow at the Centre of Positive Psychology of the Melbourne Graduate School of Education at the University of Melbourne (Australia). Christian is recognised as a thought-leader in the field of coaching in education, and has published numerous articles, book chapters and books on the topic. He regularly delivers keynote addresses globally and undertakes research into the application of coaching and positive psychology in educational settings.

David Woods CBE has been a teacher and senior leader in schools, a teacher trainer in higher education, and a local authority adviser in two local authorities. He was the Chief Education Adviser for the City of Birmingham before joining the Department for Education in England as a Senior Education Adviser working closely with Ministers to develop educational policy and subsequently becoming Head of the Department's Advisory Service. He joined the London Challenge programme from the beginning as the Lead Adviser and then became the Chief Adviser for London Schools and the London Challenge. He has the unique distinction of having being the Chief Education Adviser for England's two biggest cities, Birmingham and London. He has written and spoken extensively on educational leadership, on school improvement, and on related education matters. Currently he is an Education Consultant working with schools, local authorities, Multi- Academy Trusts, and Teaching Schools, as well as being a Visiting Professor at Warwick University and at the Institute of Education, University College, London. He was Chair of the London Leadership Strategy (2012–2018) and Chair of the Birmingham School Improvement Advisory Board, as well as being a member of the National Education Commission for Wales.

Biddy Youell is a Child and Adolescent Psychotherapist at the Tavistock and Portman NHS Foundation Trust. A former teacher, she has retained an interest in the application of psychoanalytic ideas to non-clinical settings, particularly in the field of education. Her clinical specialism is work with children who have been traumatized, abused, or neglected. She has published widely, teaches on a number of Tavistock courses, and is committed to finding ways to support the wider children's workforce.

Serving school leaders

Yvonne Baron began the journey to establish a new Jewish primary school in Mill Hill, with five other proposers in 2010. After a period of co-leadership and planning, Yvonne was appointed head of Etz Chaim Jewish Primary School in September 2013 and has continued to lead the school as it has grown to eight classes, 41 staff, 126 families, and 211 children. Yvonne has a very hands-on approach and enjoys the diversity of the role. The opportunity to start new school has enabled Yvonne to do things differently and embrace the elements of twenty-first-century learning. She has developed "continuous provision" across the school, within an integrated day. Last academic year, Etz Chaim continued to be judged as "Good" by Ofsted and was judged as "Outstanding" by Pikuach (the inspection of Jewish Studies). The school reached a significant milestone as its first cohort of Etz Chaim graduated last summer.

Denise Buckley began her career in Ireland. She then moved to London to study towards a PGCE. She rose quickly through the ranks and became a headteacher within five years. Denise has worked in various types of schools and areas in Kent and has held two headships. She is currently head of a Catholic school in Kent.

Ellen Clarke is in her first year as deputy head at Park View School, a diverse comprehensive school in Tottenham, London, following several years working in other roles at the school. She was part of the Teach First 2006 cohort and has also worked as a management consultant for PriceWaterhouse Coopers. Outside school, her passions are books, theatre, and cooking.

Jerry Collins is the north London regional director for Ark Schools. He was founding Principal of Pimlico Academy, which, in its first two years, improved from "Requires Improvement" to "Outstanding." Jerry was also Founding Principal at Ark John Keats, an all-through school in Enfield, which was also graded "Outstanding" during Jerry's time as principal.

Sarah Creasey is in her second year as head of Parliament Hill School, a culturally and socially diverse school in north London. An English specialist with 24 years' experience of working in inner city comprehensive schools, she has specialized in raising the achievement of students from disadvantaged backgrounds, whole-school literacy, and principled curriculum development. She has worked as a facilitator with middle leaders through the Teaching Leaders programme and is interested in professional learning for leaders. Having worked in two state girls' schools, she is committed to the development of outstanding provision for girls.

Sally Deverill is a highly regarded British Horse Society Accredited Professional Coach (Level 3) and qualified Montessori teacher. She has a BSc (Hons) in Equine Science from the Royal Agricultural University and 45 years riding experience, including eventing, hunting and polo. She has been teaching and coaching for 40 years and is currently training recreational riders, Pony Club under-10s, and young professionals gaining equestrian industry qualifications, as well as rehabilitating and producing riding horses from abandoned/neglected horses.

Trevor North is a primary school headteacher and leadership consultant for an educational charity. He began his career working with challenging and vulnerable pupils in a residential setting for children in care. This passion for inclusion kick-started his career in education with a dedication for including all leaners, despite their challenges. Seeing what could be achieved through collaborative problem solving, his ethic of excellence has led to significant success in a range of challenging and demanding circumstances in primary education. His work has ensured that schools in challenging circumstances have improved their performance and raised standards across several settings. Beyond school leadership in the United Kingdom, he currently provides coaching for headteachers and leaders in significantly deprived areas of Northern India and consultancy on the curriculum content for change management and leadership training.

Sarah Pringle is in her fifth year as principal of Seahaven Academy, East Sussex. She studied Modern Languages at York and Strasbourg universities and completed a PGCE at the University of Nottingham. She started her teaching career in North Yorkshire, followed by two schools in Kent and then 15 years in a variety of senior roles in and around West Sussex, working predominantly in schools in challenging circumstances. Having been part of a team that led a new academy to outstanding, Sarah moved on to another school in the same group as principal. She swiftly led the school to its first ever "good" Ofsted judgement, accompanied by continuous improvement in results, oversubscription, transformation of the school's reputation in the local area, and a planned expansion to accommodate larger student numbers. Sarah is now enjoying working with other heads as part of school–led improvement system and as a mentor.

Andrew Webster is in his fifth year of headship at Park View Secondary School in Tottenham, North London. He originally studied as a classical flautist and jazz saxophonist at Leeds College of Music and then trained and worked as a music teacher and head of music at Lister Community School in Newham. In 2008 he was accepted onto the flagship Future Leaders programme, which led to his appointment as associate assistant head at Forest Gate Community School, Newham, followed by five years as deputy head at Elizabeth Garrett Anderson School, an outstanding girls' school in Islington.

Kate Williams is an experienced leader who has led Longhill High School in Brighton from "Requires improvement" to "Good" in two years. Kate trained as a mathematics teacher and has held pastoral and academic leadership posts before gaining her first senior leadership role in 2009. All of Kate's leadership experience is immersed in raising standards in challenging circumstances. This is what drives her. She has an iron will and a sheer determination to make a positive impact on young people's lives. She is a believer in hard work, respect, and compassion. Kate and her school are outward-facing and proud to be a truly comprehensive school serving all of a rich and diverse local community.

Introduction

Sustaining depth and meaning in school leadership: Keeping your head

Andrea Berkeley & Emil Jackson

This is a book about the emotional and psychological experience of school leadership. It aims to explore what being a school leader means and feels like—in particular, the felt experience of life as a headteacher. It describes both the pressures and the rewards of the role, together with some of the ways that headteachers and other school leaders have found to sustain and develop themselves in what has become an increasingly complex, challenging, and highly accountable role.

The book is rooted in our belief that school leaders are likely to be at their best when they are able to be themselves and find their own unique way of taking up and inhabiting their leadership role in relation to others. In practice, this is a lifelong challenge that is much easier said than done. After all, as most school leaders know, any given day is liable to assault them with relentless pressures—both internal and external—all of which conspire together to propel them out of more reflective states of mind into more reactive and impulsive ones. This book therefore aims to offer a range of chapters, approaches, concepts, and perspectives that will, we hope, collectively support school leaders to maintain an emotional equilibrium while navigating the multi-layered tightrope of intrapsychic, interpersonal, and organizational dynamics inherent in school life.

The paradigms that underpin our thinking and the conceptual framework of this book are primarily psychoanalytic and systemic. These include an appreciation of unconscious processes and the powerful ways they can manifest within individuals, teams, and schools as organizational systems. While we both have an active interest in and respect for other approaches, these are the conceptual frameworks that have—in our experience—proved most influential, supportive, and effective in helping school leaders to make deeper sense and meaning out of their experience.

At the same time, we do not think that any one paradigm can be all-encompassing. Rather, we believe that a wider range of different approaches, concepts, and leadership styles may all be appropriate and valid for different leaders and schools—at different points in time, in different circumstances, cultures, and countries. In view of this, we have invited contributions and chapters that describe and illustrate a broad selection of lenses and approaches, all of which have proved effective, supportive, and developmental to leaders across a range of settings, both in education and in business. In doing so, we hope to offer readers a more comprehensive understanding, and, by extension, choice, about what might be most suitable for themselves and/or the organizations in which they work.

Our hope is that this book will be a relevant, accessible, supportive, and developmental contribution for all those involved in or with leadership in education. These include headteachers, principals, middle and senior leaders in education, school governors, multi-academy trusts, executive coaches, consultants, advisers, inspectors, and training providers working in education. By inviting contributions from a diverse range of perspectives within the fields of education, business, psychology, and psychotherapy, we hope to explore school leadership—and the development of school leaders—through a fresh lens.

The concept and focus of the book

The concept and focus of this book arose from our longstanding engagement and interest in the support and development of school leaders, together with our own professional relationship and dialogue over more than 20 years. We are indebted to colleagues from our different fields who have helped us conceptualize our thinking from direct experience and who have generously contributed to our book.

Andrea Berkeley's interest began with her first leadership role as head of Sixth Form at Hampstead School in North London, when she realized that a good degree, sound pedagogy, and successful teaching alone were not sufficient to lead and support 200 diverse and often troubled teenagers and their tutors through an education phase that would significantly affect the rest of their lives. Seeking support for her new role, she enrolled on the Tavistock Clinic's "Emotional Factors in Teaching and Learning" course, which gave her a fresh perspective on working with adolescents, sustaining her in a role that eventually led to promotion to deputy headship. Here she first encountered the concepts and theoretical frameworks—described in chapters 3 and 4 of this book—that, together with conventional vocational programmes of study, were to prove an enduring influence on her own leadership understanding and development.

At that time, in the mid-1980s, there were no standard, nationally accredited qualifications for school leadership, so she took an Open University Diploma in Education Management to prepare for this more senior role. Fortunate to work for an inspirational and forward-thinking headteacher, the late Dame Tamsyn Imison, she was also introduced to theories about leadership and management from fields and disciplines outside education and was given opportunities both to train in leadership coaching at the Industrial Society (now the Work Foundation) and to develop as a leader by learning experientially through the "group relations" approaches of the "Understanding Behaviour in Systems" programme at the former Grubb Institute.

These influential learning experiences were later to sustain Berkeley through 13 challenging years as head of a large secondary school in the London Borough of Brent, Preston Manor. Her early years, leading staff through a period of essential organizational change in order to raise the attainment and aspirations of students—in Ofsted terms, from "serious weaknesses" to "outstanding"—were tough. They coincided with a period of unprecedented changes to national education policy in the early 1990s, including the introduction of public examination league tables and a national framework for school inspections. The socially disadvantaged environment and the varying needs of students was challenge enough in itself. Far more difficult to manage was the hostility, as well as resistance to change, from staff. Along the way, she had benefitted from personal and professional support, which provided a containing and reflective space within which to process her emotions and maintain her own equilibrium.

Improvements at the school coincided with the inception of the National College for School Leadership in 2000 and an innovative suite of development programmes for school leaders. An invitation to train as a headteacher coach for London Challenge at UCL Institute of Education followed. She began to receive invitations to speak at conferences and to contribute to Department for Education working groups and seminars. She confesses that until then she had been so focused and absorbed in day-to-day challenges—feeling beleaguered at times—that it felt like change had happened by accident or luck. Crucially, it was the coaching training with London Challenge and the Institute of Education that reignited her theoretical interest in leadership and culture change, leading her to reflect on what strategies had made a difference—and kept her sane. Around that time, the working relationship between Emil Jackson and Berkeley, which led to this book, began.

Jackson initially completed an undergraduate degree in Management Sciences after which he completed his training as a child and adolescent psychotherapist at the Tavistock Clinic in 1999. With a passion for work with adolescents and a special interest in the application of psychoanalytic approaches in community-based settings, Jackson was delighted to be appointed by the Brent Centre for Young People—a psychoanalytically oriented mental health service for adolescents. The funding for Jackson's post was secured by Maxim de Sauma, the clinical director of the Brent Centre for Adolescence, following a successful grant application to the John Lyon Trust to develop the Centre's outreach work in schools. Following his discussions with Berkeley, Dr de Sauma thought Preston Manor would be a receptive school and so agreed to set up a joint pilot outreach project. One of Jackson's key responsibilities was to lead this project.

It was agreed that the best use of such a scarce resource was to dedicate some of Jackson's time each week to support teachers in their work with students, in addition to his direct work with young people. Along with individual consultations to help teachers think about students causing concern, Jackson suggested piloting "work discussion groups" for staff, in the belief that, over time, these would enable a greater number of students to be thought about by a greater number of staff. Two pilot work discussion groups were offered to 16 staff who expressed interest, including teachers, teaching assistants, and the Special Education Needs and Disability Co-ordinator (SENDCO). Although Jackson's time was externally funded, the project required matched funding from the school, in terms of staff time.

The vast majority of teachers were energized by being helped to understand what might be going on for certain students; to make sense of how and why some students and class groups would get under their skin and leave them feeling almost instantaneously undermined, criticized, angry, or impotent. They were also very relieved to be helped to make sense of some of the pain, guilt, and shame they sometimes experienced with more needy, vulnerable and disaffected students.

One year later, funding was found to set up a third group for heads of year, given their key pastoral responsibilities. These groups were designed to support the heads of year not only in their direct work with students, but also in their line management of teams of class tutors. It quickly became clear that the issues they encountered in leading others were fundamentally rooted in the need to understand and contain the emotional and psychological challenges inherent in their roles.

By 2002, Jackson had also started working in the Adolescent Department of the Tavistock Clinic while continuing to work part-time at the Brent Centre for Young People. With the backing of both organizations, he was able to build on the Preston Manor experience and lead the development and management of a number of similar projects in other local secondary schools in Brent, Westminster, and Barnet, mostly funded by the schools themselves. Several of these original outreach projects are still going strong, 20 years later.

Throughout this period, Jackson and Berkeley established a continuous professional dialogue, developing a mutual interest in the dynamics and leadership of schools. Early in 2003, Berkeley discussed with Jackson a collaborative project she was heading up with seven other Brent secondary schools, following a successful bid for three years of government funding. There were different strands to this project, one of which related to leadership development. Given the established success of the work discussion groups, they shared a belief that this model might be transferable as a unique way to provide professional support to senior leaders involved in the collaborative. This was not something that either they or the other headteachers involved had ever heard about before. But their observations, together with feedback from the pastoral leaders about the impact of the groups on their leadership roles, indicated that it might be of interest and value to set up a group for senior leaders, to help them to understand and contain the emotional and psychological pressures of their leadership roles. Given the scale of the project, Tavistock Consulting, formerly the Tavistock Consultancy Service (TCS), led then by Clare Huffington, was commissioned to provide individual executive coaching for the heads involved, alongside work discussion groups and day conferences on aspects of leadership and the management of change—a substantial investment. It took some persuasion to convince the other heads to try these innovations, but, as Berkeley held the purse strings of the project and was not asking them to contribute any resources other than time, they agreed to give it a go.

Berkeley and Jackson's mutual interest in leadership development was gaining momentum. Jackson sought the support of TCS colleagues in adapting his existing psychotherapy and consultancy experience to more of a coaching role with headteachers and, in particular, to focusing on the leadership dimensions to their role. At the same time, he was gaining further experience in consulting, coaching, and supervising coaches in an increasingly diverse range of public and corporate settings. Contemplating retirement from headship at the end of this three-year period, Berkeley completed the TCS executive coaching programme and became a tutor on the National Professional Qualification for Head-teachers (NPQH) at UCL Institute of Education and a lead facilitator on the Leadership Programme for Serving Headteachers (LPSH) at the National College for School Leadership (NCSL).

Following retirement, Berkeley was invited to assist with the design and delivery of Future Leaders, an accelerated training programme for headteachers, and Teaching Leaders, a leadership programme for high-potential middle leaders (now merged and part of the Ambition Institute, a graduate school for teachers and school leaders). Berkeley also invited Jackson to set up and co-facilitate adapted versions of work discussion groups with participant groups on Teaching Leaders. Over a five-year period, these groups also continued to receive overwhelmingly positive feedback.

The evolution and subsequent development of this early consulta-tion work proved to be a catalyst for an evolution in both Jackson's and Berkeley's professional interests and careers in ways that could not have been anticipated. Over the past 16 years, they have both worked as executive coaches and consultants with hundreds of aspiring and serving headteachers and dozens of senior leadership teams,. They feel privileged to be still working with talented, principled, and courageous colleagues, gaining further insights into school leadership in these most challenging of times.

Overview of chapter sequence and content

The following is an overview of the book's chapters, which can be read either in sequence or as separate chapters, each dealing with a different and overlapping aspects of leadership.

In keeping with our overall theme and approach, *Part I* explores the personal experience of leading schools, provides an overview and analysis of current and historical trends in school leadership, and offers some theoretical frameworks for making sense of these. *Part II* explores psychodynamic approaches to supporting and develop-ing school leaders and senior leadership teams. It includes executive coaching, work with leadership pairs and groups, and experiential learning. It also explores the impact that trends in executive education continue to have on the training and development of leaders. *Part III* explores trends and approaches to school leadership development more generally, including the impact of personality preferences; influences from the business world and other sectors; the growth of mentoring and coaching as a leadership intervention; the design and evaluation of leadership development programmes; and a case study on whole-system development.

We give the last word, in *Part IV*, to ten serving headteachers and deputies and their first-hand accounts of leadership journeys.

Part I. Context and concepts for contemporary school leadership

Chapter 1 delves deep into some of the complexities, ambiguities, and widely felt emotional pressures of education leadership. Reflections are based on Andrea Berkeley's first-hand experience of headship, combined with 12 years' coaching and consultancy with hundreds of school leaders and several chief executives of multi-academy trusts and education charities. Although the chapter focuses mainly on the unique leadership role of the headteacher or school principal, many observations also apply to the distributed leadership roles of other senior staff in today's schools. The chapter concludes with some thoughts on what seems to help school leaders manage the inevitable psychological pressures so that they may continue to find fulfilment in their roles.

The three chapters that follow contextualize the personal and anecdotal exploration of the opening chapter with an overview and analysis of the research on school leadership, together with the key theoretical frameworks that inform and underpin the book as a whole.

In chapter 2, *Peter Earley* and *Toby Greany* provide an overview of current theories and trends within school leadership and the history behind them, drawing upon a range of recent research, including their own. They argue that, although there is no widely accepted definition or agreement about what good leadership looks like in a school, different approaches have been dominant at different times. They describe the current policy context within which school leaders have to operate in an increasingly complex political environment, with high accountability and expectations and subject to unprecedented public scrutiny. They comment in particular on the challenges and opportunities posed by national education policy agendas that promote both competition and collaboration, aspire to close achievement gaps between children from privileged and disadvantaged backgrounds, and encourage "system leadership" across a growing number of alliances, federations, and Multi-Academy Trusts, replacing the traditional local education authorities. They argue that school leaders today require higher degrees of self-awareness, emotional intelligence, and political literacy than ever before, needing both intellectual breadth and agility to deal with complexity and to tolerate ambivalence. They conclude that the provision of appropriate and effective support and opportunities to develop as senior leaders is therefore crucial.

Against the backdrop of Earley and Greany's research-based analysis of the current context and climate for school leadership, chapters 3 (by Biddy Youell) and 4 (by Judith Bell) provide the core theoretical and conceptual frameworks that underpin and inform the premise of this book. They explore the internal dynamics of schools as social institutions and some of the conscious and unconscious emotional factors that influence learning, teaching, and leadership. Both authors' exploration of psychoanalytic and systems psychodynamic concepts are illustrated with examples from their experiences of working in and consulting to leaders in the field.

In chapter 3, *Biddy Youell* offers a psychoanalytic framework for understanding some of the emotional pressures and unconscious dynamics inherent within the headteacher's role and that of other leaders within the school setting. The underlying assumption is that school effectiveness is directly related to the way the school is led and how the headteacher and leadership team harness the resources of staff and students and manage the many competing demands they face. The chapter explores some of the intra- and interpersonal dynamics that play out in school settings, suggesting that leaders are better able to lead when they can recognize and understand their own emotional experience and that of their staff and students.

Developing this theme further, in chapter 4, *Judith Bell* focuses on group and organizational dynamics and how they impact those who lead and work in educational settings. Bell further considers how such dynamics might best be understood, acknowledged, and worked with to develop leadership effectiveness. In her exposition, Bell describes the application and integration of three frameworks of thinking and research that overlap both conceptually and historically: (1) systems thinking, which helps us to consider an organization within its different contexts, as well as to make sense of the interplay between the parts and the whole; (2) psychodynamic thinking (described in more detail in chapter 3), which helps leaders to make sense of the significance of unconscious dynamics in school life, and how these can manifest in the form of emotions, anxieties, conflicts, and blind spots. Finally, (3) Bell illustrates how a deeper awareness and understanding of group dynamics—in particular, how anxiety can drive groups off their primary task— enhances the ability to create engaged, high-performing teams.

Part II. School leadership development: psychodynamic approaches

Chapter 5 opens this section with a description of some significant ways in which school leaders—headteachers in particular—can be supported through the provision of one-to-one coaching sessions. *Emil Jackson* and *Andrea Berkeley* argue that while school leaders frequently feel overwhelmed by the range and *quantity* of their responsibilities, it is *the quality of the emotional and psychological demands* of their role which invariably takes the heaviest toll. By describing some commonly encountered scenarios, the chapter aims to illustrate the importance of offering leaders thinking time and space away from the front line of school life. Jackson and Berkeley further hope to illustrate the potential for coaching to enable school leaders to develop the emotional literacy and resilience to withstand, understand, and make effective use of the emotional and psychological dynamics that continually reverberate in schools. Finally, they consider some of the costs to school leaders—and education more generally—when adequate reflective space, such as is offered through coaching, is not made available.

Traditionally—and perhaps especially—in schools, the leadership of an organization can be seen as singular. Most people's conception of leadership is grounded in an idea of the individual leader or, as in the case of schools, the headteacher. Nevertheless, however lonely headteachers may often feel, they do not in fact lead alone. In chapter 6, *Clare Huffington* considers any headteacher's most important relationship with the school's chair of the governing body or board of trustees. The working relationship between these two key leaders is crucial to a school's well-being and progress. It is surprising, therefore, that so little appears to have been written about it in the education leadership literature. Huffington's chapter begins with some thinking about changing ideas on organizational leadership that open up new possibilities for shared and collaborative models of leadership. For instance, it is not uncommon these days for heads to work with an "executive" or "associate" headteacher, roles that can be ambiguous in relation to boundaries, authority, role, and task. Similarly, although the chair of governor's role is strategic and the head's managerial or operational, this sharing of responsibility is never as simple as that. Based on experience of coaching a leadership pair of head and chair of governors of a large comprehensive school over three years, Huffington's chapter aims to contribute some thinking about this working relationship. Beginning as a pilot, it continued as a regular arrangement and served as a creative think tank, container of anxiety and occasional crisis management, as well as a place for reflection and mutual feedback.

Continuing this theme, in chapter 7 *Emil Jackson* and *Andrea Berkeley* describe their experience of piloting "work discussion groups"—sometimes known as "work study groups"—with a group of eight headteachers who had formed a collaborative partnership, funded by an early 2000s government initiative, a forerunner of today's Teaching School Alliances. Despite their responsibilities to the children, staff, families, and communities they serve, it remains rare for headteachers to feel looked after in their own work. Even when they have an excellent relationship with their chair of governors, senior leadership team, or local authority, it is not uncommon for headteachers to feel profoundly alone with their most challenging dilemmas and decisions. Facilitated by Jackson—and later Berkeley—with an external consultant, these "work discussion groups" offered a regular, safe, confidential forum in which school leaders were able to consult to each other about issues, dilemmas, or challenges preoccupying them. To the best of our knowledge, work discussion groups for headteachers is not something that has been written about elsewhere.

Chapter 8 concludes the section by exploring the innovative approaches of "experiential learning" and the writing of personal narratives as a means of enabling school leaders to reflect upon their experiences and enhance their leadership development, and effectiveness. Drawing on his extensive experience of senior leadership development in the corporate world, *Ben Bryant* suggests that headteachers and school principals have much in common with chief executive officers (CEOs) and senior executives in the corporate world because of the responsibilities of their roles and the expectations of certainty and clarity that are placed on them. He argues that, although educators have understood the importance of experiential learning more than other sectors—applying it increasingly to many areas of the school curriculum—rarely do they apply experiential learning approaches to their own leadership development. Senior executives tend to miss opportunities to learn because they become defensive and stuck in their role. He argues that although opportunities for learning in senior executive roles in both corporate and academic settings are ubiquitous, the *opportunity to learn* from that experience is often not taken up. If it is, it frequently takes the form of shallow clichés and unhelpful generalizations about what makes a successful leader. Drawing on case studies of executive learning by three senior executives, he demonstrates how it is possible for senior leaders to sustain their learning through in-depth exploration and making sense of their experiences. His research shows that executives can enable and sustain their learning through a combination of personal narrative writing and dialogue. The narratives in particular are a vehicle to help executives get in touch with the more visceral (rather than intellectual) experience of leadership while the dialogues are helpful for deeper sense-making.

Part III. School leadership development: trends and approaches

The chapters in Part III look, from different perspectives, at the growth and trends in leadership training and development programmes. In each case, their effectiveness is considered in relation to preparing professionals for more senior roles and for helping educational establishments with talent management and succession planning, as well as the primary aim of school improvement.

Based originally on the ideas of Carl Jung, the psychometric tool Myers–Briggs Type Indicator (MBTI) is now one of the most widely used tools worldwide to understand and assess personality preferences. Opening this section, in chapter 9, *Emil Jackson* describes how MBTI can be used as one approach to build leadership effectiveness and optimize team relationships in school settings. He outlines some of the central ideas about MBTI personality preferences and draws on his application of MBTI in school settings to illustrate how it can help school leaders to identify, understand, and more respectfully appreciate how and why different personality preferences might complement and conflict with each other. He further illustrates how vital insights gained through an understanding of MBTI can provide school leaders and their teams with a common language to openly discuss and accommodate different personalities and behaviours, facilitate effective collaboration, and reduce the risk of unhelpful and potentially toxic misunderstandings.

In chapter 10, *Barry Speirs* and *Andrea Berkeley* explore the ways in which government and education training providers have looked to the business world for ideas, models, and processes for developing leaders and measuring their impact. They describe leadership development processes that have proved successful in the business world and evaluate their applicability to the education sector. They write from differing perspectives, based not only on contrasting past experience in the business and educational worlds, but also on more recent experience, working successfully in each other's fields. Their analysis takes into account the advent of National Professional Qualifications (NPQs) for middle and senior leaders, aspiring and serving headteachers, and executive headteachers and Multi-Academy Trust (MATs) CEOs.

Mentoring or coaching as a supportive and developmental activity has been widely accepted by the education profession, although opportunities to engage with an external executive coach in the depth and manner described in chapters 5 and 6 are usually only available to headteachers, executive heads, or CEOs. Often the reason for this is lack of resources or a preference for professional mentoring, performance, or instructional coaching. However, there is a growing trend for encouraging school leaders to adopt a coaching style of leadership, as a means of developing staff and distributing leadership. In chapter 11, *Chris Munro, Margaret Barr*, and *Christian van Nieuwerburgh* explore the concept of coaching cultures and its implementation. Drawing on a different range of psychological theories and approaches that have also proved to be effective, they describe some of the other ways that coaching can be introduced more widely into schools. Their work is illustrated via reflections from practitioners in Australia and the United Kingdom. They argue that the creation of a whole-school coaching culture led by heads and senior leaders results in changes in attitudes and habits across many aspects of school life, creating more positive and supportive organizational climates for learning and personal growth.

In response to the trends and approaches outlined in Part III, the last two chapters explore the provision of school leadership programmes at scale across the education system. Chapter 12 looks specifically at provision that aims to promote transformational professional development and school improvement. Drawing on her experience of designing and delivering programmes for serving and aspiring headteachers, including the NPQH, *Sarah Harrison* explores some leadership development design principles aimed at providing a balance of challenge and support and positive long-term impact. This chapter may be of interest to providers of school leadership development, including local authorities, MATs, Teaching School Alliances (TSAs), and Research Schools, education charities, or commercial organizations. Offering a framework for how a provider might effectively design a programme, together with how programme design can go awry, some aspects of this chapter also offer a transferable resource to those seeking to design and develop CPD on a smaller scale, such as within an individual school.

Chapter 13 looks at an example of leadership development for school improvement across a whole city's education system. *David Woods* surveys the impact of The London Challenge, which managed, between 2003 and 2011, to turn London around from the lowest-performing region in the country to the highest. Although the transformation of London's schools cannot be attributed to any single element or methodology, Woods describes and evaluates some of the strategies that led to its success, some of which echo those described in other chapters above. In particular, he describes how the initiative fostered and nurtured a collective sense of responsibility for the whole system among London's headteachers, and how it also encouraged networking and the sharing of good practice—that is, collaboration rather than competition—and set up an impressive range of leadership development programmes and training in coaching, peer review, and peer support.

Finally, in chapter 14 we give the last word to ten school leaders from different contexts. They describe—often movingly—the central emotional and psychological challenges of their leadership experience. The purpose of the chapter is to offer some insights about the *normal* range of experience of life as a school leader. They reflect on their thoughts and feelings, ideals and values, and their learning and development. Where relevant, they draw on the ways in which coaching and other approaches to leadership development described in this book have helped and supported them. Although there are many common recurring themes, each voice reflects an individual and personal experience.

PART I

CONTEXT AND CONCEPTS FOR CONTEMPORARY SCHOOL LEADERSHIP

Keeping your head: the unspoken realities of headship

Andrea Berkeley

"If you can keep your head when all about you
Are losing theirs and blaming it on you ..."
"If" Rudyard Kipling (1910)

T he ability to "keep one's head" under any circumstance may not be an official prerequisite for school leadership, although resilience is a demonstrable competence for achieving the National Professional Qualification for headteachers (NPQH). However, Kipling's words resonate strongly with school leaders and are often quoted by them. Leading and managing a school is a complex task that involves ensuring a safe and stimulating environment so that learning and teaching can take place. This requires the ability to maintain emotional equilibrium and a reassuring authority in the face of the competing and changing demands of a wide range of stakeholders—students, parents, staff, governors, central government, local authorities or academy trusts, employers, and tax payers.

Literally keeping "one's head" is also a major concern for governing bodies needing to recruit and retain headteachers at a time of teacher shortage, particularly in areas of social disadvantage. Headteachers themselves, and those involved in their training, support, and development, are interested in how they remain focused, resilient, and mentally healthy—how they "keep their heads" in an increasingly complex and constantly changing educational landscape.

This chapter describes some of the complexities, ambiguities, and emotional pressures of educational leadership. Although the chapter makes most frequent and explicit reference to the role of headteacher, its implicit intention is to include the distributed leadership roles of other senior staff and middle leaders, such as heads of subject departments and pastoral leaders. Observations and reflections are based on 14 years' first-hand experience of headship, combined with 14 years' experience working as a consultant and coach with school leaders and chief executives of multi-academy trusts and education charities. The chapter concludes with some observations on what seems to help school leaders manage the inevitable emotional and psychological pressures and find fulfilment in their roles.

The narratives heard from headteachers and other senior leaders—collectively, on leadership development programmes like the National Professional Qualification for headteachers (NPQH) or individually, in longer term coaching conversations—resonate strongly with my own experience of headship. Phases, size, and characters of their schools vary: from one-form-entry primary schools to all-through academies with 2,000-plus students; single-sex and co-educational, grammar schools and comprehensives, faith schools and Free Schools. Their social contexts differ: from rural to inner city, from run-down coastal towns in Kent and Northumberland to the heart of the post-industrial north and the Black Country; from Halifax to Hastings, from Liverpool to Brighton. Their student intakes are varied and subject to change: some are socially and ethnically mixed, while others cater for a predominant group or a shifting population. Some have brand-new buildings designed by high-profile architects, and some make do with rundown Victorian buildings and huddles of terrapin huts. Although effective school leadership needs to be sensitive to context, the narratives of leaders in very different neighbourhoods cohere into one compelling, consistent narrative. Regardless of context, school leaders are invariably passionate about learning and teaching and have a strong sense of moral purpose. They relish their power to make a difference to the lives of young people but often feel powerless in the face of external pressures, particularly socio-economic and political ones. Given the burden of their responsibilities and their range and complexity, it is perhaps inevitable that their expectations of themselves and their hopes and wishes for young people sometimes conflict with the pressures of the role. Many of even the most effective and devoted headteachers who love their work describe feeling lonely and full of self-doubt while having to maintain a strong, confident public persona.

Sources of pressure

There seem to be three main sources of pressure: *external "on the boundary"*, from government agencies, parents and governors, the wider community, and social trends; *organizational*, from certain interpersonal relationships and group dynamics within the school as an institution; and *internal*, arising from the school leader's own psychological make-up and inner world interacting with the pressures of the role.

External pressures: on the boundary

Continuous change, increased accountability, and scrutiny

In common with top leaders in other fields, headteachers have to balance external pressures against the day-to-day management of the school, both subject to unpredictability and change. In that sense, they occupy a boundary role. At one and the same time, they are accountable to both central government and a local authority or academy trust, and to both parents and boards of governors or trustees. Ultimately accountable for the school's outcomes, they are responsible for the attainment and welfare of students as well as the performance, development and welfare of staff. Ambiguities are inherent in such a boundary role. "They must always be looking both inwards and outwards, a difficult position which carries the risk of being criticised by people both inside and outside the system for neglecting their interests" (Obholzer, 1994, p. 45).

External pressures will vary and change according to a school's socio-economic context, physical environment, and wider social trends. For example, rising poverty, unemployment, and crime will impact on a school's capacity to support children from socially disadvantaged homes and to protect them from a potentially harmful environment, so that they can thrive and achieve at school. In such contexts, school leaders are often managing multiple child protection cases, permanent exclusions, and criminal activity among students outside the school, including drug and alcohol abuse, as well as trying to form supportive relationships with hard-to-reach or hostile parents. Demographic changes in an area may result in schools struggling to provide adequately for an increased number of children without English as a first language or a shifting population of refugee children. In middle-class areas school leaders may feel the pressure of more demanding and less deferential parents, with a consumerist approach to what they expect from schools.

Significant changes to the way the education system has been organized and managed in England in recent years have added further pressure and complexity to the boundary roles of school leaders. The education landscape has become more diverse, blurring boundaries around schools and adding new types of schools, such as specialist academies and Free Schools, federations, and alliances of schools. Multi-Academy Trusts (MATs) have by and large replaced local authorities, which have traditionally managed schools. These MATs vary in size and are sponsored by a diverse range of private enterprises, universities, and educational trusts. Diversity among schools has created more competition in the system, while at the same time there is more uniformity in the way schools are judged and assessed by the National Office for Standards in Education, Children's Services and Skills (Ofsted). Independent schools are also under increasing pressure and scrutiny, struggling with fee affordability and political hostility in turbulent economic times. Both sectors are experiencing unprecedented reductions in funding and are having to provide more with fewer resources.

The source of external pressure most frequently cited by school leaders is increased public accountability and scrutiny, as a result of systemic changes in the way schools are managed and their performance measured. Continuous changes to public examinations and more rigorous inspection regimes have added to the already onerous burden of complying with changing regulations—around governance, safeguarding, and data protection, for instance. Although schools today have more freedom than previously—to choose and organize their curriculum, decide how to spend their budgets, and pay their staff in response to local need, for instance—they are at the same time held to account by nationally determined targets and performance indicators, with attainment and progress bars being raised year on year. Ofsted inspections are now conducted at a day's notice. As one headteacher put it, "Just when I feel that the school is doing well, the government changes the goalposts, so that we feel that we are failing again. At the beginning of each week I wait for the notification call from Ofsted. If I haven't heard by 1 pm on Wednesday, I know that I can relax a bit, until it starts all over again the following week."

Every headteacher welcomes improvements to systemic arrangements for the safeguarding of children and young people from abuse and neglect, and their specific responsibilities and accountabilities in this respect. However, many fear that the legal and reputational consequences of failing to protect children has made their roles so risk-averse that they may be denying their students many activities that enrich schooling. When addressing child protection issues, headteachers often need to make decisions while taking into account a complex matrix of external and internal relationships around the child in question: parents or foster carers, teachers or other staff, social services and the police, to name but a few. Similarly, headteachers often find themselves under pressure when deciding whether or not to permanently exclude a child from school. For example, a headteacher may be reluctant to exclude, given the complex needs of a student and family circumstances, but may feel that the "right" decision is the one that takes into account the benefit for the whole student and staff body. Nevertheless, there may still be external pressure from parents, lawyers and pressure groups and internal pressure from staff and unions, despite having made a decision to exclude—or not exclude—with integrity and compassion. A governing body or an independent appeal panel may also overturn the headteacher's decision, resulting in additional pressure from staff who are unhappy with a student being reinstated. For many headteachers, especially those leading schools in socially disadvantaged areas, both these statutory responsibilities can be disproportionately time-consuming and bureaucratically burdensome, given their many other duties.

Collaboration and competition

New types of schools, together with public examination league tables, have brought new and unexpected external pressures, creating a climate of competition among professionals whose culture has been traditionally cooperative and collaborative. In addition to concerns about their school's position in the examination and test leagues tables, headteachers may be surprised to find themselves competing for students and limited resources with emerging academy trusts and Free Schools. Although the DfE's stated intention was to offer more choice to parents and to provide additional school places in areas where there is a shortfall, some headteachers are openly hostile towards new types of schools for ideological reasons. They claim that new types of schools are covertly selecting students by introducing complicated admissions criteria and effectively undermining comprehensive education. Others fear that academies and Free Schools exclude students too readily and put a great deal of energy into trying to prevent the admission of students who have been excluded from other schools. The validity of these claims is difficult to verify—and some may be apocryphal—but it is fair to say that a newly built academy with state-of-the-art facilities can have a devastating effect on neighbouring schools, attracting more students and indirectly reducing the funding of other schools.

Ironically, as competition between schools grows, there is pressure to collaborate from the Department for Education (DfE), which encourages and—most importantly—funds a *"self-improving system"*, where schools support each other in improving standards of provision and attainment.

Naturally school leaders welcome opportunities for professional development and learning from each other. When asked to evaluate training programmes, such as NPQH, they invariably rate the opportunity to network with other heads and deputies most highly. Elsewhere in this book, we have illustrated how work discussion groups can facilitate leadership learning and mutual support among senior leaders. Similarly, headteachers and their teams have responded positively to schemes such as National Leaders of Education (NLE), where headteachers of successful schools assist others of raising standards and head up Teaching School Alliances (TSAs), responsible for initial teacher training, in partnership with universities, and continuing professional development at all levels. However, the impact and reach of TSAs and NLEs has been mixed (NCTL, 2016). Alliances work well and relationships are amicable if they are formed on an equal footing, but, like other systemic attempts at inter-school collaboration, the DfE's intention has been met with scepticism by some headteachers, suspecting cost-cutting motives. As one cynic observed, the rise of public sector partnerships can be attributed to "the suppression of mutual loathing in pursuit of government money" (Parker & Gallagher, 2007, p. 15).

It is also not easy to embrace collegiality if you are the headteacher of a school in "special measures", assigned an "interim governing body" and an "executive or consultant head" to oversee improvements. Feelings of resentment, hostility, and often shame need to be suppressed in order to make relationships with supporting professionals work and may also sometimes result in unproductive mutual dependency. Several headteachers I worked with found difficulty in taking up their own authority when consultancy support ceased as the school came out of "special measures." In another situation, the consultant had gained so much personal satisfaction from his helping role that he was loath to leave at the end of his contract. In turn, the headteacher he had supported feared offending him by showing that he no longer needed support.

Parents and carers

Probably the most important and ambivalent boundary relationship for school leaders is that with parents and carers. Schools may rise or decline in popularity and local demographics may change, so headteachers need to recruit students proactively, attracting parents and raising the profile of their schools. One of the most important dates in the school calendar is the annual open evening, a highlight of which is the headteacher's address to prospective parents. The impact and influence of the headteacher's words cannot be underestimated, as I have experienced from both sides of the school gates—as a former headteacher, carefully and nervously crafting my speech and, as a mother and grandmother, eagerly and anxiously interpreting every nuance of the headteacher's words. What aspects of school life are highlighted? What are the headteacher's values and beliefs? Will my child fit in?

Headteachers recognize that parental choice, support, and engagement is crucial to their school's survival and success and acknowledge that all parents, even the most wanting or vulnerable, want the best for their children. However, cultivating and maintaining good home–school relationships requires consistent effort, empathy, and high-level communication skills. Ideally, parents want to feel very much part of the school community, especially during the early years and primary phases of schooling, and headteachers want parents to actively support their child's education. In practice, meeting the expectations of a diverse community of parents is almost impossible. Parents may feel excluded or objectified by school staff, especially during adolescence, when a natural distancing between children and parents occurs. And school leaders, when under pressure, may sometimes experience parents as interfering and demanding, over-anxious and protective, hard to engage and unsupportive of school aims or rules, while acknowledging that the majority are supportive, concerned, helpful, and available.

Despite increased security measures, schools have become more accessible and welcoming to parents. A large majority of headteachers make an effort to be physically present at the schools gates, recognizing the benefits of parental contact, listening to concerns and observations, suggestions, complaints—and compliments—and responding to them promptly and sensitively. However, in today's less deferential and consumer-led world, the imperative for headteachers to be visible and available can aid school effectiveness and parental satisfaction but can also be another source of pressure. Without warning, they can be confronted with questions or complaints they are not ready to answer or with personal criticism. For instance, one newly appointed headteacher was stopped at the school gate while politely greeting people in the morning, to be told by a parent, "I just wanted to let you know that I think the school has really gone down since you took over." Investigating parental complaints repeatedly tests headteachers' values, judgement, and ability to manage their emotions. If their investigation finds in favour of parents, they can be accused of unfairness and lack of support by their staff. If they conclude that a complaint is unjustified, parents may accuse them of defensiveness and collusion with teachers and, at worst, subject them to verbal or even physical intimidation.

It is widely recognized that leaders in all fields are subject to unconscious phantasies and projections about what they represent as an authority. This is particularly evident in the way parents—and also staff—relate to headteachers. As everyone has attended school—with the exception of a home-schooled minority—they carry within them a mental construct of what was probably their first authority figure. Their concepts of authority may be benign and dependable or threatening and punishing, depending on their own experience of schooling. This may account for conflicts between parents and teachers often seeming so emotionally charged and at times hostile. Headteachers recognize that they need to maintain calm composure and objectivity in order to exercise authority fairly and justly, in the best interests of young people and their parents and teachers.

The balance of parental bouquets and brickbats and their effects often depends on the school's context. In socially disadvantaged areas schools often provide an oasis of calm and order for children from dislocated or chaotic homes and may be the only stable and dependable part of their lives. One headteacher of an inner city primary school described how often she finds herself listening to and supporting unhappy or distraught parents, adding, "Some days I feel like I am shoring up a human tide of misery." Others despair of "hard-to-reach" parents who collude with their children breaking school rules or describe encounters with parents that quickly and without reason or warning escalate into confrontation, which requires sophisticated skills of negotiation and diplomacy. Another found himself so often drawn into mediating disputes between parents in the playground that on some days he said he felt "like the compere of 'The Jeremy Kyle Show'." Parents from certain social or ethnic backgrounds will have had such negative experiences of schooling themselves that they will avoid contact or make assumptions about how they are being judged by school authorities, often without foundation. One headteacher blogged anonymously (Primary School Headteacher's Blog, 2012) about how, on a very ordinary day, she was in reception when she heard a parent arguing with the school receptionist about her child's confiscated mobile phone: "She saw me and launched into a vitriolic attack. As Heads we symbolise the establishment, and any resentment people may have towards authority can be directed towards us personally. When something like that happens, it is very difficult to remain unaffected. I was a picture of calm while in the situation, but afterwards I was left holding all her fury. I am generally a resilient person, but it is very difficult not to take things personally when they are hurled at you with real ferocity."

In large secondary schools, headteachers more often find themselves as the ultimate authority when the way that a complaint or a concern has been addressed by delegated staff has failed to satisfy parents. In more affluent areas, school leaders experience parents as much more demanding and critical and less likely to accept the school's authority. There is often more pressure from parents to be heard by the head-teacher personally, which can be very time-consuming. As another headteacher put it jokingly, "I tend to get to see the mad, bad and the sad—rather than the majority of parents who are happy with their children's education."

The local community

No school is an island. All schools serve the communities in which they are located as a public amenity, providing facilities for adult education, childcare, sport, weddings, and religious meetings, for instance. Part of a school leader's role today is to ensure that the school and its facilities are well run but also to engage with the local community more generally. It can be surprising how much school leaders are expected to participate in local activities and concerns beyond the core business of education. Headteachers have a public role on the boundary between the school and its community, which it both represents and reflects. These can range from forming productive partnerships with local businesses to respond-ing to local residents' complaints about students' antisocial behaviour, litter-dropping, or parking to giving statements to the local press about public examination results.

Social media: new boundaries, new pressures

Just as safeguarding legislation and security measures have made cita-dels of our schools in a physical sense, social media has expanded and blurred boundaries around schools, changing the public role and exter-nal pressures of headteachers. The advent of the internet has widened opportunities for learning and teaching, but its misuse can threaten children's safety and well-being as well as damage a school's reputa-tion. Internet sites such as Twitter and Facebook are easy platforms for parents and students to air their opinions when in disagreement with school rules or policies—over uniform or codes of behaviour, for exam-ple. They are also openly and speedily accessible to local and national press, only too eager to search for stories, particularly at the start of the academic year when news is slow. With scant training in media manage-ment and public relations, headteachers sometimes find themselves and their schools subject to trial by Twitter, Facebook, Google, and online local press, the complaints forum of choice for Generation X parents. Although new media can be a positive way of raising a school's public profile, headteachers need to find additional resources to monitor and police social media use, not only to protect students and staff, but sometimes also to manage a school's reputation. Similarly, schools have found emailing and texting a useful way of communicating directly with parents, but many headteachers describe "the tyranny of email" when, for example, parents send emails with complaints or queries late at night, demanding replies the following morning.

Organizational pressures: inside the boundary

Leading and managing people

Headteachers and other school leaders are often selected because of their educational values and vision and their expertise in pedagogy, curricula, and pastoral care, not necessarily for their skills in leading and managing people. Leadership of course is not simply about getting people to do things. It is about getting them to want to do things. One definition of leadership is "to create the conditions for people to thrive, individually and collectively, and achieve significant goals" (Pendleton & Furnham, 2012). For school leaders, this means creating the right conditions for teachers and support staff to thrive—looking after the staff so that they can look after the students. Educational leadership is only one aspect of what is required to lead schools as organizations (Handy & Aitken, 1986).

How school management has changed

The organizational role of school leaders has changed significantly since the introduction of Local Management of Schools (LMS) in the Education Reform Act (1988). To put it simply, it seems that school leaders have been exhorted to be managers of schools as organizations in the 1980s, visionary leaders of people in the 1990s, and transformers of school cultures and standards in the 2000s. As a result of LMS, which started the process of change in the late 1980s, some headteachers today are more like chief executives of small- to medium-sized businesses, responsible for devolved budgets, financial planning, site management, and human resources, as well as their traditional responsibilities as leaders of students and staff. Most significantly, along with their governing bodies, they are accountable for the school's academic outcomes and finances. One of the organizational pressures on school leaders is balancing the management and leadership aspects of their roles. "Too much management and a school may run smoothly on the spot. Too much leadership and it may be running all over the place and never smoothly"

(Southworth, 2009). Creating a vision and direction for staff to follow, then motivating, monitoring and developing them while simultaneously directing the tasks, systems, processes, and resource management to deliver that vision, is demanding work. To a certain extent, that is the accepted lot of top leaders in other fields. However, the way in which headteachers in particular are perceived as leaders and managers is not always a true reflection of their day-to-day reality. Traditionally, they have been viewed by parents as leaders of children and young people and by teachers as academic leaders—*"first among equals"*. Paradoxically, headteachers are still likely to be identified by parents and the general public as pedagogical and pastoral leaders, whereas they are now more likely to be viewed as managers of resources and leaders of people by staff within the school. Although it is widely accepted that the tasks and responsibilities of running of a school are too many, varied, and complex for any one person to manage, the mental construct of an all-knowing, all-things-to-all people leader, with both executive and symbolic functions, is still very strong in the minds of many. "I was an experienced deputy with NPQH when I was appointed, but nothing quite prepared me for what others expect of me. Everybody wants my approval and expects me to know everything. I'm afraid of being found out!" It is therefore very common for newly appointed headteachers to experience *"imposter syndrome."* In consequence, many new headteachers may find delegation difficult and are prone to working excessively long hours. However, one of the important tasks of leadership is to address the dependency culture that can prevail in institutions such as schools, often unconsciously. As a result of the almost *"parental authority"* that can be projected into their roles, even experienced headteachers sometimes have to work hard at distributing leadership and empowering others to take up their own authority.

On the whole, headteachers manage the institutional resourcing, organization, and safeguarding of hundreds to thousands of students and their teachers confidently and effectively. In practice, the complexity of their organizational tasks and their attendant pressures are underestimated, as are the number and the range of daily interpersonal interactions required to complete them. Many find that they lack financial or business management expertise at the start of headship, and some continue to feel insecure in this aspect of their accountability role. Financial management is one of the areas for development most frequently cited by trainee headteachers on NPQH programmes. Even established headteachers can feel overwhelmed by the pressures of being accountable for the school's financial management, without adequate support from a business manager or governor with specific expertise.

Leading people in a climate of high accountability

The requirement to hold staff to account for academic outcomes is a constant source of pressure on school leaders, especially in the wake of frequent changes to the ways in which the performance of schools is judged and measured. In practice, this means assessing the performance of teachers and other staff and managing underperformance and, in extreme cases, disciplining and dismissing staff. Performance management is still relatively new to schools—although it is common in other fields. It often challenges the collegial culture of teaching and continues to be an anathema to teaching unions.

There is no doubt that changes to the way that schools are managed, along with targeted training for school leaders—and the dreaded Ofsted inspections—have raised educational standards. They have inevitably also increased organizational as well as external pressures on school leaders and changed the way they relate to their colleagues. Most recently, headteachers are urged to refocus their priorities on leading the school's primary task of teaching and learning—which might seem rather obvious. Research suggests that leadership is second only to classroom instruction in its influence on student learning, as senior leaders improve student learning indirectly, through their influence on staff motivation and working conditions. Furthermore, research found that almost all successful leaders draw on the same repertoire of practices, and a small handful of personal traits explains a high proportion of variation, such as being open-minded, flexible, persistent, and optimistic (Day et al., 2010) They are consistent, skilful at strategic planning, and able to distribute leadership effectively, and they make staff development a priority. This research reflects similar findings in the United States, Canada, and Australia (Day & Sammons, 2013). The difference between outstanding and inadequate leadership is stark: Barber, Chijioke, and Mourshed (2010) found, from Ofsted data, that for every 100 schools with good leadership and management, 93 will have good standards of student achievement, but for every 100 schools that do not, only one will have good achievement.

Many agree that the leadership of learning and teaching should be the core business of headteachers. Others, like Becky Allen of the UCL Institute of Education question the manner in which headteachers are now held to account directly for the outcomes of teaching and learning.

> In the past, when inspectors paid a visit, it was to learn about a school. Now they check the headteacher knows their school, which means they must look at planning, monitoring and other evidence teachers

submit to their leadership team. When schools were given several months' notice of an Ofsted visit, they could gather this evidence ahead of an inspection. But with the notice period now as little as 24 hours, this kind of evidence can no longer be manufactured when needed. While this is a good thing, it does mean inspection-compliant paperwork must be ready at all times, which puts pressure on teachers and school leaders. [Allen, 2017, p. 9]

This requires headteachers of a secondary school, for instance, to have up-to-date knowledge of the teaching standards of all staff and consequently being held to account for the examination results of around 100 teachers. So, the external pressure of national initiatives, inspection regimes, and increased accountability is transferred via headteachers, down to middle leaders, teachers, and even to students themselves. One headteacher described what she called the domino effect of layers of accountability in the academy trust responsible for her school:

The attainment bar is raised continuously. I know that my staff and I can't work any harder but I am constantly torn between finding new ways of motivating them or defending them to my bosses. The trouble is that in a MAT I have a feeling that I am being held to account for the sake of someone else's performance management targets. My boss is pushing me because she is pushed by her line-manager, who is being leaned on by his CEO, who in turn is being set more ambitious targets by the DfE.

Cultivating followership

I once surprised a fellow coach working in a different sector by saying that it is rare for a headteacher to bring concerns about a student, the curriculum, or technical aspects of management to a coaching conversation, although moral dilemmas around permanently excluding students and distress over a teenage suicide are often a cause of anxiety.

Training and development for aspiring school leaders appropriately encourages moral purpose and the articulation of vision as the main means of inspiring and motivating staff to improve educational outcomes. Their mantra might be said to be: "Articulate moral purpose and high expectations; promulgate 'growth mindset', make transparent use of performance data to drive up standards; have a plan and stick to it." Training on the nuts and bolts of school management—human resources and financial processes, data and project management, etc.—has also improved and become more accessible. However, the issues and pressures that most concern school leaders—brought to coaching or work discussion groups, for example—involve relationships with other adults and people management generally. As one headteacher put it after a coaching session:

> We only scratched the surface of my personnel issues last session, and I have several others I would like to talk to you about next time. In the meantime, could you recommend a book I could read about dealing with difficult/complex people, from the angle of empathizing rather than just having difficult conversations? I have two other colleagues that I just can't seem to make any progress with. One is super-sensitive and the other has such a thick skin nothing sinks in!

Almost without exception, new headteachers have the moral authority, combined with the higher-order conceptual thinking and communication skills required to present their strategic vision for the school to staff. They will have ideas for improving the educational experience for young people and will need to release and develop the school's human capital to realize that vision. What they will not yet be aware of is how differently every individual listening to their first address to staff or school assembly is receiving and internalizing their vision: Do I agree with their philosophy? Are they as good as the last head? How do I fit in with this vision? Will I be able to teach my way? Will there be change? If so, will it suit me? Will they like me? Is my job secure? Similarly, I recall very well the cavalcade of staff arriving at my office door, wanting to meet me personally in my first weeks of headship. Looking back, I can remember how first impressions were subsequently confirmed or not and how understanding the motives and drives of other adults and the subtle art of influence and developing followership takes time to learn and is never perfect, given the infinite variety of human beings. "Leadership would be easy to achieve and manage if it weren't for the uncomfortable reality that without followership, there could be no leadership … [requiring] followership to be an active process of participation" (Obholzer, 2004, p. 33).

Patrick Lencioni has observed, "As is true in many mission-driven organizations, there is a real temptation in schools for leaders to want to be all things to all people. Of course, with limited resources and high stakes, the cost of not being strategic is great" (Lencioni, 2012, p. 116). Even in small schools, headteachers can find themselves exhausted by the competing needs and demands of different individuals and groups and need to carefully guard their personal boundaries in order to concentrate on leading strategically. For many school leaders, pressures stem not from reluctance to gratify staff, confront problems, or avoid conflict, but from innumerable daily interactions, varying in gravity, requiring different levels of attention and communication, often on a minute-by-minute basis: from chairing a safeguarding investigation to reprimanding a child seen dropping litter; from negotiating the catering contract to comforting a recently bereaved teacher; from giving one-off verbal feedback to a teacher on a lesson to months of consultation on a staffing restructure; from taking assembly to briefing the caretaker on a school event; from reassuring a worried parent to speaking with the local press or MP. As one experienced headteacher put it, "Sweating the big stuff *as well as* the small stuff all day long is why the job is so exhausting." Another described it as "being in the thick *and* the thin of things". More "difficult interactions" may include competency, disciplinary or exclusions hearing panels, consultations with union representatives, demanding or aggressive parents, governors, or local residents complaining about students and external agencies, such as social services. Paradoxically, some of the same headteachers report feeling energized by the variety, pace, and unpredictability of interactions. Some even enjoy the political cut and thrust of difficult negotiations, such as staffing restructure, adding that the role is never boring.

Most school leaders are engaged in a continuous process of leading culture change at any stage of their tenure, intentionally or not—making their mark as a new leader, in response to inspection judgements, new policies or legislation, staff turnover, or wider social trends. This requires not only a great deal of energy and commitment, but also emotional and political literacy. The more they understand human motivation and behaviour—their own and that of others, as individuals and in groups—the more they are able to tolerate the tensions that inevitably exist among staff with different ambitions and vested interests.

Sharing and distributing leadership

Today's schools are too complex to lead and manage without an effective senior leadership team with devolved responsibilities and accountabilities to support the headteacher and an effective working relationship with the chair of governors or board of trustees.

Sharing leadership with governors

A strong chair of governors, able to form a good working relationship with the headteacher, based on trust and a sound understanding of their different functions, can make a considerable difference to a headteacher's confidence and capacity. This crucial relationship—explored in more depth elsewhere in this book—can be a vital source of support to what is essentially a lonely role on the boundary between multiple stakeholders and competing concerns. It is an ambiguous relationship, as headteachers are employed and performance-managed by governors but also inform and advise them. Many chairs of governors are not only knowledgeable and helpful, but also mindful of the headteacher's well-being in a demanding job and will make supportive suggestions, such as working from home one morning a week or supporting the provision of external coaching. However, like other volunteer groups representative of local democracy, governors can also be another source of pressure, especially if dominated by individuals with affiliations to political parties or trade unions, parents, or others seeking a power base—when they have instigated the setting up of a Free School, for instance. Confusions can arise around the differentiation of operational and leadership roles and, at worst, can be a source of constant challenge, conflict, and stress. In the past, it was rare for headteachers to be dismissed, but since the advent of academy trusts and a stronger steer from central government to improve standards across all schools, the headteacher role has been likened by some to football managers. It is not unheard of for experienced professionals with previously unblemished careers to be dismissed for not reaching attainment targets within 18 months. On the other hand, the responsibilities and accountabilities of governing bodies have increased in inverse proportion to the scarcity of suitable candidates for headship, putting added pressure on governors and school resources.

Distributing leadership to senior and middle leader teams

In today's complex and often very large schools, headteachers have deputies and teams of senior leaders to assist them. Research into school leadership continues to suggest that there is a correlation between the increased distribution of leadership roles and responsibilities and the improvement of student outcomes (Day et al., 2010). However, it is not always easy to turn a group of high-performing professionals into a team, nor for some headteachers to let go some of their authority. It is quite common for new headteachers in particular to find delegation difficult and team leadership stressful, especially if they have inherited a team. As Huffington, James, & Armstrong (2004, p. 71) put it, distributed leadership "presents challenges to one's individual competence, professional, technical, and managerial; to one's readiness to make and act on judgements and handle the risks consequent on uncertainty, while accepting accountability for decision and action". Even when given the opportunity to recruit new and talented senior leaders, headteachers can find themselves with a group of high-performing individuals who work in silos or in competition with each other. As a result, building a well-functioning team in order to delegate responsibilities efficiently can be another source of pressure on headteachers and a concern that often arises in coaching conversations.

Effective team-building requires a conscious effort to understand each individual's strengths and blind spots and the group dynamics at play at any one time. This lays down the foundation for generating a high degree of trust, which allows other positive aspects of teamwork and relationships to function—such as conflict resolution and collective accountability (Lencioni, 2005). Many headteachers find that employing the services of an external consultant to facilitate team-building can be helpful, as it frees them up to observe and interact with team members. It is noticeable that the headteachers who seek to understand themselves and others are most able to distribute leadership that will realistically deliver an aspirational vision, without exhausting human capital. Through fostering trust and mutual understanding and investing in the understanding and development of their senior teams, they are able to bear the emotional cost of distributing leadership.

Boundaries within: the internal world of school leaders

Personal histories

On occasions when there is an opportunity for headteachers to share their personal histories, I am struck by how many have experienced difficult childhoods or educational setbacks, like failing the 11+ or having to retake A levels. They often attribute their career choice to such early childhood problems and speak passionately about social justice, equality, and inclusion, viewing headship as a means of making a better society. Conversely, some school leaders speak of happy childhoods and privileged education, leading to a desire to share success with future generations. Education charities specializing in school improvement are characteristically staffed by individuals wanting to give something back from their privileged backgrounds. Similarly, John West-Burnham's research (West-Burnham, 2002) into the characteristics of effective headteachers found strong correlation with religious faith or spirituality.

In the canon of leadership literature there are many useful models to help headteachers find their own leadership style. These range from Daniel Goleman's repertoire of coercive, authoritative, affiliative, democratic, pace-setting, and coaching leadership styles (Goleman, 2000), to McKinsey's 7S framework (Peters & Waterman, 1984), to a more recent analysis of five types of headteacher featured in the *Harvard Business Review* (Hill, Mellon, Laker, & Goddard, 2016). However, as Biddy Youell writes in chapter 3 of this book, "We are all subject to the influence of internalized experiences that are not readily available to our rational minds. In schools, the agenda in the external world is inevitably influenced by the internal worlds and unconscious agendas of all the people involved" (p. 60). So it is not surprising if headteachers perceive the demands of the external educational agenda and their particular school contexts through the lens of their internal worlds. As their drives and motives are so often closely connected to the ways in which they have internalized their own childhood and adolescent experiences, they will inevitably also "keep their heads" under pressure and approach leadership and team working in uniquely personal ways.

Taking up authority and managing power

The way headteachers manage their authority and power will often reflect their past experience of authority figures. They may want to emulate them or lead very differently. As one newly appointed headteacher said, "I learned so much about leadership from my previous head—how not to do it!" Some newly appointed senior leaders struggle with taking up authority in what is traditionally a collegial profession. Even those with previous leadership experience are often surprised to be treated with seemingly random degrees of warmth or hostility by different staff members. Their success now stands or falls on collective achievement, and an emergent leader needs a different set of skills and a capacity to gain job satisfaction from enabling others to succeed and grow. They may feel the need to relearn ways of operating and motivating themselves, suppressing their personal achievement drives in the service of others. They gradually become aware of, and are surprised by, the power invested in their role by others, actual and illusory. Taking up authority might even undermine the very achievements that led to their headship—being a highly competent and well-loved deputy, for instance—which may then be experienced as a loss. And if they have been promoted internally, relationships with peers will shift, alliances will form or break, and they may feel isolated or compromised by former peers who would like "special treatment."

In order to lead effectively, headteachers need to know their own minds and be sufficiently emotionally robust to tolerate disapproval, anger, and even hatred from staff when difficult decisions are taken and unwelcome boundaries are set. This may come easily to some heads but be a source of considerable stress for others. For instance, newly appointed headteacher John brought to his coaching session concerns about Marion, a member of his senior leadership team who had previously been his line-manager in another school and who was considerably older and more experienced. He felt uncomfortable with Marion's frequent complaints and disclosures about other members of the team and perplexed by her irritation when he did not act upon her advice.

Individual responses to the pressures of leadership

Some school leaders embrace today's emphasis on accountability and autonomy as an opportunity to make their own decisions and to improve teacher performance. They can tolerate the ambiguity of a system that encourages independence at the same time as exerting more central control and scrutiny. Others feel crushed by continuous change and what they perceive as forced autonomy, regretting the loss of dependence on local authorities for support and influence. They feel that their autonomy is illusory, resenting what they perceive as micro-management by Multi-Academy Trusts, reporting directly to the DfE, and intense local competition generated by school performance league tables. They report "burn-out", loss of control and confidence in their own abilities, no matter how hard they work and how impressive their achievements.

For some, the shadow side of the personal idealism and altruism they brought to the role is that "good" is never good enough when Ofsted categorizes their school "good" rather than "outstanding". When unpredictable events beyond their control preoccupy their days disproportionately, such as a serious assault on a student, a suicide, or an (unfounded) accusation of racism, some feel personally vulnerable and prey to self-blame and doubt. Shortly after the 2017 Birmingham terrorist attack, for instance, one headteacher of a multicultural school described complex feelings of wanting to protect her students, while at the same time fearing that violence could erupt at any time, from both outside and within the school gates.

Containing anxieties

By virtue of their vocational roles, school leaders naturally provide psychological and emotional containment for the anxieties of students, so that they can mature and learn, and for teachers, so that they can complete their primary tasks of teaching and nurturing. They also find themselves indirectly or unconsciously—and sometimes consciously—containing the anxieties of parents, employers, politicians, and even wider society. Increasingly, schools have become repositories for anxieties about social problems, whether it be childhood obesity, teenage terrorism, knife crime, or drug abuse. Part solutions to such societal ills often result in schools being tasked with responsibility for preventive measures—for example, improving targeted health education. Although headteachers would not deny their duty of care in this respect, such initiatives often result in another layer of curricular compliance to add to an already daunting list of regulations. For some, this may require containing the anxieties of their staff about extra workload and bureaucracy, insufficient training, resources, and time and fear of being blamed if they fail to identify a student at risk—for instance, of self-harming or cyber-bullying or being involved in extremist activity.

Continuous changes in social policy and statutory responsibilities can be experienced by some as a persecution, giving them sleepless nights about whether they have made the right decision—for example, about a child protection case. Ironically, there may be resistance even when teachers themselves have lobbied for policy change or statutory guidance, for example in tackling rising mental health problems among young people. Those headteachers who recognize and are able to manage this containing function of leadership often speak of "sitting on" a policy document until they are able to "domesticate it" before implementation, in order to minimize the pressure on staff. One headteacher described his role as a "toxins filter", protecting his staff from continuous and disruptive change, adding "That's why I value my coaching sessions, as they give me a chance to offload and to put pressures back into perspective."

Self-actualization and gratification—in the service of others

To a lesser and greater extent, all professionals are involved in what Maslow (1959) called self-actualization in their choice of work, although most headteachers see themselves as working in the service of others, driven by altruism and moral purpose. However, the drive to fulfil oneself personally and professionally and the drive to serve others and make a difference to students' lives can create internal conflict. In the course of coaching headteachers in particular, I am often puzzled by their apparent acceptance of excessive workload, long hours, and tolerance of unrealistic demands for attention by staff and others. And, of course, with hindsight, I also recognize my former self in headteacher role! I recognize the internal conflicts manifest in some headteachers' inability to delegate effectively or let go of principles or plans in the interests of pragmatism or school politics; the dangers of dogmatism and feelings of omnipotence when making unpopular decisions or in remaining wedded to an idea or policy even in the face of strong opposition. Often inner conflict arises from decisions or moral dilemmas that need to be taken or resolved alone, and in confidence—child protection cases, staff disciplinary or restructuring issues, permanent exclusions. This is where a confidential coaching relationship can be very helpful as, in some instances, it may not be possible to share with a chair of governors since he or she may need to remain impartial for a forthcoming hearing.

Some headteachers, particularly those who have chosen to work in challenging contexts, thrive on conflict resolution, experiencing an adrenaline rush from the risks they take in the course of their work and the "near-misses" they have in averting crises, violence, and crime. They enjoy the cut and thrust of winning tussles with whichever adversary is in the ascendance at any time—unions, local authorities, or external agencies, for instance. Underlying the banter at headteacher gatherings, there is sometimes a competitiveness about who is most under pressure—something again I recognize from personal experience! HMCI (Her Majesty's Chief Inspector) Amanda Spielman likened this to a Monty Python comedy sketch where people compete with claims to have had the toughest childhood and warned against underperforming schools getting caught in a culture of "disadvantage one-upmanship" (Coughlan, 2017).

Perhaps the most surprising inner conflict that some headteachers experience arises from the guilt that is often generated by taking pleasure in the personal successes of their roles. A study of aspiring school leaders under age 40 (Edge, Descours, & Frayman, 2016) found that many headteachers were unintentionally discouraging the next generation from wanting to take up headship. They were unconsciously put off applying for headships by their perception of the daunting responsibilities and risks they associated with the role and by the poor examples of overwork they witnessed—despite the headteachers professing to love their jobs. The study suggested that the headteachers felt guilty about enjoying the role and the agency and power it affords because they were only too aware of the stress and strain on themselves and their staff. They felt that they had to work even harder and longer hours than anyone else in order to justify the power they enjoyed. This is a strikingly complicated finding, encapsulating the ambivalence in headship and suggesting why so many headteachers describe headship as being both "the best job in the world *and* the worst job in the world".

Internal strain of constantly being on show

Schools as organizations are characterized by frenetic energy, and, unless headteachers are highly disciplined in managing their personal boundaries and protecting mental space to think strategically, they may feel exhausted by hundreds of interactions, ranging minute by minute from the brief and trivial to the substantial and critical. Headteachers are expected to be "visible"—model behaviour, pick up litter, attend every school event, be always available to staff, and, in primary settings, to children and parents. If they are not, accusations abound: "He's never here" or "She's always in her office." It is well known that a leader's mood can affect those around them. Equally, the strain of being constantly on show and permanently available can have an adverse effect on managing time and work life balance. Apologizing for lateness to family or colleagues, headteachers are often heard to say, "I just couldn't get out of school on time, because so many people keep stopping me to ask me different things." How to manage corridor conversations and confrontations more constructively frequently features in coaching conversations.

Reflective, responsive, and sustainable leadership

Daniel Goleman's work on emotional intelligence strongly influenced national leadership programmes for aspiring and new headteachers in the 1990s. In the 2000s, headteachers were encouraged to build on their moral authority by developing resilience, mental toughness, and "positive mind-set" (Dweck, 2012) in response to the inevitable emotional pressures they were facing. This shift in approach may well reflect tougher times and a change in political climate requiring a different style of leadership. As Viv Grant famously wrote of the experience of headship in an era of high accountability, "The emotional toll was intolerable. And I felt alone. It is difficult to show any vulnerability when, as a result of the 'accountability' culture, your every word is interpreted and translated into the language of either 'capable' or 'incapable'" (Grant, 2015).

National programmes for the training and development of school leaders have greatly improved, particularly in technical, vocational, and strategic aspects. However, delivery is variable, and it is rarely acknowledged that headship is a complex and often lonely role that requires reflective leaders who understand schools as organizations and who can examine their emotional responses to their work and relationships with others. "What is needed is emotional support and a space for headteachers to reflect on how well they are doing the job and what they could do better. Social workers have supervision to help them process their toughest cases and corporate executives have space for lessons learned in between projects. School leaders need something similar" (Grant, 2015). Having a reflective, non-judgemental space in which to freely express and explore these feelings with a coach, or in a facilitated group, can help leaders contain and diminish anxieties and be in touch with the "organization in the mind" (Armstrong, 2005). It can normalize the inevitability of success and failure, winning or losing in equal measure, in situations where outcomes are a matter of external judgement in a regulatory framework, rather than moral certainty.

Prevailing leadership—and leadership that prevails

This chapter has explored some of the complexities and emotional pressures of school leadership. However, it should not be forgotten that most school leaders manage and negotiate them successfully and find their roles profoundly fulfilling. Headteachers who love their profession far outnumber those who "have had enough" and want to resign. The rewards are many, and most headteachers—including myself—feel a deep sense of loss upon retirement: a loss of community and collegial camaraderie, being part of something bigger than oneself—but also of self-identity. As I hope this chapter has illustrated, school leaders do require an unusually high level of "psychological presence" as well as visibility and availability, being all things to all stakeholders. The experience of being fully present is also, states Khan (1992), the experience of being vulnerable, taking risks, and feeling anxiety. That may well be so, but being a school leader also offers the possibility of being wholly one's authentic self in role—a rare privilege in working life.

I hope that this chapter sets the scene for the chapters that follow, providing academic and theoretical perspectives and practical examples of supportive development activities that school leaders have found helped them not only to survive but also to thrive. I would like to end with some observations on insights gained from school leaders who continue to thrive, often in very challenging circumstances. They are the ones who value, motivate, and empower others and can articulate how they achieve that. They know how to select good people, train them, nurture and trust them. They are primarily ambitious for others and let them take the credit, and in doing so, of course, they command loyalty and respect. They are modest and self-effacing, more collaborative than charismatic, and tend to say "we" not "I", illustrating the eponymous Chinese proverb, "When the leader's job has been done well, the people say they did it themselves."

None of them claim to be the finished article, and many admit to self-doubt and fear of failure in today's climate of high-stakes accountability. They try to remain optimistic and positive, to be resilient and adaptive, and, perhaps surprisingly, don't jump through every accountability hoop thrown at them. They keep their students and staff at the front of their minds in every decision and change that they make. They don't bend or compromise their ideals but are flexible, creative, and, more importantly, reflective and balanced in their approach. They ask for feedback from their teams, are able to accommodate a variety of views, and are not afraid to admit mistakes and change direction. They provide clear direction while trusting staff and distributing leadership with confidence across the school. They consult widely but are not afraid of making decisions, even hard ones, on their own. They value both teams and individuals—and show that they do. They apply pressure and support in equal measure, firmly hold others to account, but also show staff they are valued and appreciated. They reward staff justly and fairly but do not condone underperformance. They are reflective and careful in their judgements and decisions but are not afraid to take risks, nor to acknowledge their humanity and fallibility.

They are both practical and academic—emotionally, politically, and spiritually intelligent. More significantly, they know how to read the runes and scan the political horizon, read the barometer of parental satisfaction, sense the morale of the staff—and can sniff a ruck brewing among students at a three-mile radius, in minutes. They are intellectually curious, with an infectious love of learning—and they can hack it in the classroom as outstanding teachers. The most effective are not afraid to be observed teaching by trainee teachers and given feedback. They are inspirational, with a clear vision and sense of direction informed by a heart-felt set of personal values, which they communicate clearly to others. With this kind of leadership, energy can be released to return to the primacy of teaching and the joy of learning in schools.

More significantly, none of them would claim to be all of the above all of the time. They continually seek to understand themselves and others. They keep their heads in the process—and governing bodies get to keep their headteachers.

CHAPTER TWO

The context and challenges of contemporary school leadership

Peter Earley & Toby Greany

Interest in leadership is not new and has attracted the thoughts of many writers over the centuries. However, despite this considerable historical interest, there is no widely accepted definition or agreement about what good leadership looks like, in a school or in any other organization. For some, it's a little like beauty, being in the eye of the beholder. Indeed, "leadership" has been subject to fads and fashions: different approaches and conceptions have been dominant at different times. We know that leaders adopt a wide variety of approaches, that no one leadership style is effective in all contexts, and that very few "great" leaders have maintained their success over long periods of time.

Leaders today work in a "VUCA" environment—volatile, uncertain, complex, and ambiguous—and so need to apply strategic thinking and judgment to situations. Pillans (2015, p. 14) uses this acronym when referring to business leaders, but the same is increasingly true of those working in the public sector. As such, all leaders require intellectual breadth and agility to deal with complexity, resolve paradoxes, and make informed decisions. Leaders need self-awareness, interpersonal skills, and high degrees of resilience. The provision of effective support and opportunities to develop as senior leaders is therefore crucial. However, leaders in the public sector, including education, must operate in an increasingly complex political environment, with high accountability and expectations, and subject to unprecedented public scrutiny. It has been suggested, therefore, that the requirements for effective leadership extend beyond those required in a purely business environment (Benington & Hartley, 2009). Leadership in this environment "requires adaptive systems, practices and leadership that can respond to complex, cross-cutting challenges with no clear consensus about causes or solutions and whole-systems thinking between different sectors, services and organizational levels. Adaptive leadership requires emotional intelligence, self-awareness, political awareness, negotiation skills and the ability to mobilise action and promote collaboration" (Greany et al., 2014, p. 30).

In this chapter we give consideration to the current policy context frequently encountered by educational leaders who work in publicly funded or independent schools. We draw upon a range of recent research, including our own, for both sectors, to provide an overview of current theories and trends within school leadership and the history behind them. Our focus is also on recent and current priorities and pre-occupations for school leaders: we comment in particular on the challenges and opportunities posed by national education policy agendas that promote both competition and collaboration and aspire to close achievement gaps between children from privileged and disadvantaged backgrounds. Finally, we consider the emerging and future needs of school leaders with particular reference to "system leadership" and the growing number of alliances, collaborations, and Multi-Academy Trusts now operating in the new landscape of the English education system.

Leaders and leadership

In a field where there are numerous definitions of leadership and the significance of leaders for organizational success continues to be debated (e.g., Croft, 2016; Scheerens, 2012), it is perhaps helpful if we commence by presenting our own position as "leadership researchers". To begin, there is no shortage of research studies and reports which state that school leadership is a crucial factor in school effectiveness and the key to success and improvement. In education, empirical studies linking student outcomes to leadership, especially principal leadership, date back to at least the mid-2000s when Marzano and colleagues in the United States undertook a meta-analysis of 69 studies, involving over 14,000 teachers and 1.4 million pupils, and concluded that replacing an "average" principal with an outstanding principal in an "average" school could increase student achievement by over 20 percentile points (Marzano, Waters, & McNulty, 2005). More recently, Day and Sammons (2013, p. 3) note that "international examples of original research provide consistent evidence that demonstrates the impact of leadership on school organisation, culture and teachers' work". Such research, they state, offers empirical evidence that the quality of leadership can be a crucial factor in explaining variation in student outcomes between schools. However, Seashore Louis, a leading writer who has been involved in many impact studies over the years (e.g., see Leithwood & Seashore Louis, 2012; Louis, Leithwood, Wahlstrom, & Anderson, 2010), remarks that:

> Although leaders affect a variety of educational outcomes, their impact on students is largely indirect and is relatively small compared to other factors. While formal leaders interact with pupils in many circumstances, the impact of schooling on students occurs largely through more sustained relationships that occur in classrooms and peer groups. [Seashore Louis, 2015, p. 1]

Croft too strikes a cautionary note when he refers to the "tendency to over-state the importance of leadership as a standalone factor in improving attainment, to the neglect of understanding of how it interacts with other key school factors" (Croft, 2016, p. 3). He further notes that leadership's influence on outcomes is "mediated by a number of school-related factors that are more proximal to the student level, if not also influenced by ongoing and interactive contextual factors" (p. 6).

Student outcomes are largely shaped by out-of-school factors, like the family, the community, and socio-economic status or social class (Gorard, 2010; Smythe & Wrigley, 2013). Nevertheless, schools can and do make a difference, and the more effective tend to be well led and managed. What leaders do and say, and how they demonstrate leadership does affect pupil learning outcomes, albeit mediated through others. A major British study into the impact of school leadership found that school leaders "improve teaching and learning and thus pupil outcomes indirectly and most powerfully through their influence on staff motivation, commitment, teaching practices and through developing teachers' capacities for leadership" (Day et al., 2009, p. 2). They also refer to the importance of school culture and trust and suggest that school leadership influences student outcomes more than any other factors, bar socio-economic background and quality of teaching. However, as Osborne-Lampkin, Folsom, and Herrington's (2015) systematic review of the empirical studies published between 2001 and 2012 on the relationships between principal characteristics and student achievement in the United States suggests, it is not a simple matter to research, and correlation does not imply causality. In summary, while it is challenging to quantify the exact effect size or the precise combination of factors that lead to impact, the research evidence does largely reinforce the argument that "leadership matters".

Leadership matters in schools because of the impact it can have on teachers and teaching. Teaching, especially the quality of the teacher and the teaching and learning environment, is seen as the most significant "within-school" factor to impact on student outcomes. For example, Hattie (2015, p. 2) concludes that the greatest influence on student progression is "having highly expert, inspired and passionate teachers and school leaders working together to maximize the effect of their teaching on all students in their care". Leadership—and headteacher leadership in particular—can be a primary driver for improvement, influencing the teaching and learning environment and the organization of the school, which, in turn, indirectly impacts on student outcomes.

Leaders therefore play a major role in developing teachers and other staff. Significantly, though, it is "leadership", rather than just the "leader" that is key. This helps us move away from the outdated and contested notion of the individual "heroic leader" or "superhead". Individual leaders are, of course, important, but it is notions of leadership capacity that are crucial to on-going and sustained organizational success. Headteachers "parachuted in" to "turn around failing schools" may or may not succeed, but long-term success will only be likely if the leadership of that school is distributed, dispersed, and developed—and if continual capacity-building ensues. For some, including the authors, developing people, realizing potential, and empowering others is the hallmark of effective leadership.

As already noted, the importance of leadership has long been recognized, but there is still no clear, agreed definition of what it is. Definitions are both arbitrary and subjective, but the central concept is usually "influence" rather than authority—both are dimensions of power, with the latter usually associated with a formally held and recognized position (Yukl, 2002). Northouse (2009, p. 3), in synthesizing the research, offers a definition of leadership as "a process whereby an individual influences a group of individuals to achieve a common goal". There are many others, for example:

> A set of actions, including language actions (words), whether taken directly or by empowering others to act which fulfils visions, and produces results, outcomes, and consequences that otherwise would not have occurred. [Scheer & Jensen, 2007, p. 3]

> Leaders determine or clarify goals for a group of individuals and bring together the energies of members of that group to accomplish those goals. [Keohane, 2010, p. 23]

> Leadership ... is not simply about getting people to do things. It is about getting them to *want* to do things ... if one can inspire people to want to travel in a given direction then they will continue to act even in the absence of the leader. [Haslam, Reicher, & Platow, 2010, pp. xix–xx]

School leaders articulate the definition of the organization's moral purpose. . . . The values that underpin this moral purpose are linked to the
vision, considering where we want to be and what sort of organization
we want to be in the future. [Davies & Davies, 2005, p. 16]

Although they all have their strength, our own preference is for the last
definition, as this suggests movement towards a different and preferred
state—that is, "change"—and leadership does normally imply some
aspect of proactivity and improvement. Also, the notion of "influence"
is neutral, whereas leadership is usually linked with "values'": school
leaders' actions are clearly grounded in personal and professional
values.

We also concur with recent thinking that sees leadership operating
at all levels of an organization, with leaders working to create an environment in which everyone can grow and talent is developed. We see a
leader as someone who creates an environment in which everyone can
flourish. As remarked by a successful head, "It was like watering some
seeds. The potential was there, they just needed light and water to get
them to the next stage of flowering" (Myatt, 2016). Leaders therefore
promote and encourage leadership—they see leadership as something
that can be found and nurtured at all levels of an organization, including, in schools, at student level. So whereas traditionally leadership has
been related to a position within an organization, many organizations
now expect employees at all levels to demonstrate leadership. One
example of this came from a recent study of ours (Greany et al., 2014),
which looked at leadership in non-educational organizations: what
we found was that private, public, and voluntary sector organizations
were all keen to encourage their staff to look outwards, for example
through volunteering activity or via social media. In this way the
whole staff, not just the senior leaders, could act as "boundary spanners"—helping to identify emerging trends in the wider world and to
consider how the organization might respond. Without this broader
perspective on leadership, organizations are, in our view, less likely
to be successful.

Understanding leadership

Northouse (2009), in a comprehensive review of the leadership literature,
notes the wide variety of theoretical perspectives and points to the fundamental differences between trait, behaviourist, political, and humanistic
approaches to theories of leadership. He points to the emerging view that
leadership is a process that can be observed in the behaviours of leaders
and the need for leaders and followers to be understood in relation to
one another and as a collective whole. Pendleton and Furnham (2012)

identify and summarize four mega-trends in the development of leadership theory and thinking: classical leadership (from antiquity to the 1970s); transactional leadership (from mid-1970s to mid-1980s); visionary leadership (mid-1980s to 2000); and organic leadership (beyond 2000). They look at the predominant leadership styles and key approaches of leaders in each of these stages as well as the power relationships between leaders and followers, the latter ranging from domination, negotiation, and inspiration to co-creation. Organic leadership, their latest mega-trend, has a leadership model that is based on "buy-in" and mutual sense-making, authentic, and distributed leadership and co-creation.

With reference to the education sector, Earley and Weindling (2004) offer a number of typologies and categorize leadership theory chronologically under five headings: trait or "great man" theories (1920s), style theory (from the 1930s), contingency or situational theory (1960s and 1970s), power and influence theory (throughout history but popular in the 1990s), and personal trait theory (2000s). The latter, dominant since the 2000s, sees effective leadership as superior individual performance centred on notions such as emotional and contextual intelligence. In education, it is probably true to say that the dominant conceptions of leadership are seen as transformational, learning-centred, and distributed. These and other common notions and theories of leadership—managerial, moral and authentic, system, contingent, and teacher leadership—are discussed by Bush and Glover (2014).

Research conducted in the commercial sector (Pillans, 2015, p. 16), identified three key trends driving how organizations view leadership and how future leaders are developed. They are:

» Leadership is increasingly seen as a *process*. For example, Heifetz (1994, 2002) defines leadership as the process of mobilizing people to face difficult challenges. Leadership is enacted through a network of people rather than residing in one all-powerful individual or a rigid hierarchy.

» Shared or distributed leadership is on the rise. Leadership is seen to be a central requirement of all organizational members, regardless of whether or not they are responsible for managing others.

» There is a growing desire for "authentic leaders" who are trustworthy, genuine, and consistent. A key focus for leadership development is seen as helping individuals understand their own purpose, values, and character and what that means for their leadership style.

Although the research was conducted outside the public sector, there are clear parallels with education and how school leaders have been trained and developed, some aspects of which we explore next.

Recent developments

The role of school leaders, especially headteachers or principals, has changed considerably over recent decades, in particular with regard to the levels and patterns of accountability, the nature of their responsibilities, and the extent of institutional autonomy (Schleicher, 2012). An interest in leadership has grown globally as there has been a growing recognition of its impact on the performance of educational systems. School leadership has changed over time to meet the ever-growing and changing demands of policy-makers and other stakeholders (Earley, 2013), yet the constant factor over this period has been the need for schools continuously to raise standards and improve the quality of teaching and learning. This period has been described by Cranston (2013, p. 131) as "an era of standards-based agendas, enhanced centralized accountability systems where improved student learning, narrowly defined, becomes the mantra for school leaders, who themselves are subject to enhanced accountabilities". The key to improving educational standards is increasingly seen in the growth of human capital—in particular, increasing the quality, knowledge, and skills of teachers and leaders in schools.

In England and elsewhere, policy makers have continued the trend towards decentralization and institutional autonomy, devolving decision-making power and resources to schools in the belief that this will improve quality and increase innovation. In order to incentivize these outcomes, they have put in place accountability systems that combine quasi-market pressures (such as parental choice of school coupled with funding following the learner) with central regulation and control.

However, a challenge found in all devolved education systems has been how to design and implement performance management and accountability systems that provide clarity for schools, parents, and government funders on what success "looks like". Also, is there a clear assessment of whether or not schools are offering a quality service (Ehren, Perryman, & Shackleton, 2014) without descending into an unhealthy "performativity" regime led by toxic leaders (Craig, 2017). As we have noted elsewhere:

> Overly tight accountability systems can flatten the very freedom and autonomy that governments want to encourage; schools can narrow learning by teaching to the test; they can look up to second guess what they think the inspectorate wants to see (rather than at the evidence base); and they can game the system through "cream-skimming" or by massaging their exam performance through various subtle tricks. [Greany & Earley, 2017, p. 2]

In view of these challenges, leaders in schools need to guard against the implicit pressure that such high-stakes accountability systems can exert on them to narrow the curriculum and adopt instrumental improvement approaches that do not build sustainable human capacity. We return to this challenge in the following sections.

Leadership training and development

In England the Education Reform Act of 1988 and the introduction of decentralization and school-based management have meant that the skills and capabilities required of school leaders have had to change. Simkins (2012) offers an insightful and detailed account of these changes and maps three distinct eras of school leadership development in England: "the era of administration'; "the era of management'; and "the era of leadership".

The era of Administration lasted from 1944 to the mid-1980s, when teachers had high degrees of autonomy, and the work of school administrators, as "lead professionals", was commonly underpinned by values derived from professional practice, situated within a bureaucratic framework of rules and procedures. Simkins argues that during this time, a "patchwork quilt" of local authority leadership development provision drew closely on social science theory.

The second era, that of Management, from the mid-1980s to 1997, was characterized by growing government worries about how schools were performing. Simkins notes that administrators were reconstituted in policy as "managers" who were responsible for how well their schools performed against centrally defined criteria. Leadership training and development began to be shaped by generic occupational standards and competencies, often informed by commercial-sector business management theory (Earley, 1993).

The third contemporary era, that of Leadership, began in 1997, Simkins argues, as New Labour articulated a "modernization" agenda. Simkins argues that this was built on the managerial framework of school accountability and autonomy but added "leadership" as a "stronger agentic thrust to instituting change and improving performance in the public sector" (Simkins, 2012, p. 625). In November 2000, the National College for School Leadership (NCSL) was created with the aim of offering support and providing both greater policy influence over, and great coherence with, leadership development provision. A five-stage career framework for leadership development was published: as emergent leadership, established school leadership, entry to headship, advanced leadership, and consultant leadership. A range of development programmes was developed for each stage, including: Leading from the Middle; Leadership Pathways; the National Professional Qualification for Headship (NPQH); and the Leadership Programme for Serving Headteachers (for further details see Bubb & Earley, 2007).

Since Simkins' publication in 2012, we might wish to refer to a fourth era of school leadership as the era of "system leadership" and the growth of executive leadership and academization. Some of the key developments in this fourth era include the development of Teaching Schools and their alliances and Multi-Academy Trusts (MATs), overseeing groups of schools—and, since 2016, government-appointed Regional Schools Commissioners to administer and regulate the new schooling landscape. We argue elsewhere (Greany & Earley, 2017) that this focus on school-to-school collaboration and networks, orchestrated through "system leadership", can be seen as a policy response to the weaknesses inherent in quasi-market systems—where competition between schools prevents the spread of knowledge and expertise.

Successful school leadership

Before we turn to recent developments and the priorities and preoccupations facing English school leaders, it is worth stepping back to ask what we know from research into successful school leadership across different contexts and over time.

We refer here to "successful"—as opposed to "high-performing"— leaders quite deliberately, because we want to distinguish them from a small but worrying group of "toxic" leaders (Craig, 2017). Toxic leaders are those who drive their schools to achieve high academic test scores at the expense of staff well-being, a collaborative culture, and a broad and balanced curriculum. Successful leaders also want to secure the highest possible standards of progress and attainment for all children, but whereas the "toxic" leader may be doing this because they are fearful of the consequences of failure or because they want the personal, ego-boosting credit that comes with success, the "successful" leader is working within an ethical and intellectual framework that grounds their actions in a deeper moral purpose (Day et al., 2010). They are focused on helping every child, whatever their background, to enjoy learning and to reach their potential, because this is the best chance that a child will have for a fulfilling and productive life (Matthews, Rea, Hill, & Gu, 2014). They draw on data and evidence in assessing the school's performance and in tackling areas for improvement. They are transformational and learning-centred in their approach, able to shape a compelling vision and to enact it through a focus on constantly improving practice backed by strong organizational management (Day et al., 2009). They are "good" with people and believe in helping staff to develop and grow, including through distributing leadership and high-quality professional learning. They provide challenge as well as support. They are fascinated by the content and process of learning and the ways in which it can be enhanced, for staff and pupils (Robinson, 2011). They are sensitive to the school's context and the wider context within which it operates. They adapt their leadership to reflect that context while also working to alter it—for example, by collaborating with other schools and parents. They are committed to the success of all, so think and act as "system leaders". They remain resilient, curious, outward-looking, optimistic, collaborative, and committed to social justice, but they are also pragmatists: prepared to challenge policy where required, but to subvert it when necessary.

Of course, this description of the skills and attributes for "successful" leaders risks making them sound like super-heroes, a notion that has been consistently discredited. As Ancona, Malone, Orlikowski, and Senge (2008) have argued, all leaders are imperfect and incomplete, so it is distributed leadership and teamwork that makes a difference (Harris & Spillane, 2008). This includes teacher autonomy and leadership, since staff need to feel supported and trusted if they are to develop efficacy (Micklewright et al., 2014). The role of senior leaders in such contexts is, above all, to shape the environment so that everyone can and does blossom.

Current priorities and preoccupations

Returning to the current English education landscape, over several decades and regardless of political party in power, the national policy agenda has been to raise academic standards. Key reforms since 2010 have included: a more demanding accountability model for schools; a new National Curriculum and framework for national tests and exams; significant changes to how teachers are recruited, trained, performance-managed, and rewarded; a move towards a national funding system; and structural changes, especially the growth of academies and Multi-Academy Trusts. Such policy reforms are designed with the aim of creating continuous improvement and innovation that will raise standards but also close the achievement gap between children from privileged and disadvantaged backgrounds.

Securing equity as well as excellence has been a strong theme in successive governments' reforms agenda. The link between poverty and educational outcomes has a long history in educational research (Smythe

& Wrigley, 2013), and although socio-economic differences matter significantly, schools still make a difference to how well a student achieves. The evidence on whether schools can overcome children's background characteristics is summarized in the reframing of Bernstein's famous 1970 article by Gorard (2010): "Education *Can* Compensate for Society— A Bit." The quality of teachers and teaching—followed by the quality of leadership—is critical in making this "bit" of difference, particularly for disadvantaged children (Barber & Mourshed, 2007; Sutton Trust, 2011).

The differences between the performance of poor children and that of their better-off counterparts is concerning. Some schools have managed to close this attainment gap entirely, while in others the difference between the two is unacceptably high. "Closing the gap" has been a key policy agenda and a preoccupation for school leaders, particularly since the introduction of the Pupil Premium (see below). Similarly, the notion of the self-improving school system (DfE, 2010) and associated developments, such as Teaching Schools and academization, have been priorities for school leaders alongside other more prosaic matters, such as curriculum and assessment changes, preparation for Ofsted inspections, and managing budgets (Earley et al., 2012).

The Pupil Premium

The attainment gap between students has been described as England's long trail of underachievement. OECD data show that other countries do not have such a gap, and in an attempt to remove or at least reduce this gap, an educational initiative, the Pupil Premium (PP), was introduced in England in 2011. This gave schools additional resources (£955 for secondary pupils and £1,345 for primary school pupils in 2020) to help narrow the attainment gap between children entitled to free school meals (FSM), which is a proxy for economic disadvantage, and the rest of the school student population. A condition of the additional funding for children with FSM entitlement was that schools were obliged to evaluate the impact of their use of the fund. Schools must report annually to parents and provide evidence of impact when the school is inspected. This policy initiative has led to school leaders looking closely at a range of improvement and intervention strategies and their impact and effectiveness, especially on poor pupils.

The introduction of the Pupil Premium resource to fund interventions has occurred at the same time as a renewed interest in England in the idea of teaching becoming an evidence-informed profession. The notion of practitioner inquiry and research engagement has been exemplified with the introduction of further initiatives within schools to close the performance gap and to raise standards more generally. Schools are being encouraged and funded to promote intervention strategies and to evaluate their impact.

School leaders have a range of intervention strategies they can deploy to assist them in making decisions about the deployment of PP funds. The Teaching and Learning Toolkit—a summary of educational research, explaining which intervention strategies work and, just as important, which do not—was developed with support from the Education Endowment Foundation (EEF). The Toolkit is an accessible summary of educational research findings covering over 35 topics and summarizing research from over 10,000 studies. The Toolkit is a live resource that is regularly updated as new findings are published (http://educationendowmentfoundation.org.uk/toolkit).

Although it has its critics (Wrigley, 2016), the toolkit aims to give school leaders the information they need to make informed decisions about intervention strategies that might work in their context to narrow the attainment gap. Evidence that the PP fund is proving effective is still emerging, although FSM children did improve faster than their non-FSM peers in the 2014 Key Stage Two results (Lupton & Thomson, 2015).

Towards a self-improving system

The importance of research and inquiry, which the Pupil Premium has helped to encourage, links closely with the notion of a self-improving system where the responsibility for school improvement is seen as resting with schools themselves. Schools and teachers are understood to learn best from one another with Teaching Schools and their alliance partners leading the way (DfE, 2010). Government plans to raise standards and improve the quality of teachers and school leadership through school-to-school support and peer-to-peer learning is referred to as a "self-improving system"—or what the Secretary of State described as a decentralised culture of self-improvement in schools (DfE, 2010). A national network of Teaching Schools—of which there were over 800 by 2017—is modelled on teaching hospitals and gives outstanding schools (as judged by external inspection) the role of leading professional development and contributing to the raising of standards through school-to-school support.

One of the priorities of Teaching Schools has been the development of practitioner inquiry and encouraging an evidence-informed culture. Research-engaged schools or research learning communities develop criticality in relation to accessing research and data, they know how to collect and generate data and relevant evidence to support decision-making for school improvement (Maxwell & Greany, 2015). School leaders develop an ethos or culture that brings about critical reflection and inquiry to secure continuous improvement. Their schools strive to be learning organizations (OECD, 2016), building in time for collective inquiry, reviewing evidence, evaluating impact of interventions, and continually striving for betterment (Stoll, 2015). The need for schools to evaluate the impact of the PP, the introduction of the EEF and the wider movement promoting an evidence-based approach to school-based decision-making (e.g., Goldacre, 2013) have all contributed to this change of culture (Brown, 2015). An important part of the changing educational landscape in England and a challenge for school leaders is a clearer understanding of research approaches and the use of data and inquiry to drive school improvement (Earley & Bubb, 2014).

The future needs of school leaders

In this section we wish to address a key issue in England's future leadership development landscape: the move towards a self-improving school system, which includes a greater role for Multi-Academy Trusts, school-to-school support, and system leaders.

The rationale for school-to-school support is that credible, serving leaders and teachers are more effective in "turning around" struggling schools than external consultants or local authority staff. School-to-school support is being encouraged through "system leaders" who exercise leadership beyond their own schools, sharing their expertise and their school's practice with other less effective schools through school improvement partnerships and collaboratives. Even where formal school-to-school support is not required, it is clear that schools need to look outwards and work proactively in collaborative structures that can provide support and challenge as local authorities disappear. For this reason, many schools are forming or joining Multi-Academy Trusts.

It is often noted that leading a collaborative is not the same as leading a single school: in the former, no single leader will hold formal, positional power, so the challenge is to exert influence and steer towards a shared goal without succumbing to inertia. In many cases this influence relies on being able to persuade colleagues to sign up to a long-term vision based on shared values that genuinely reflects the needs of all pupils in a locality. This relies in part on being seen as trusted and credible along with highly developed facilitation skills and a commitment to co-designing solutions with peers, rather than imposition. All this requires acute sensitivity to different perspectives and tact, coupled with a pragmatic drive to find workable solutions. System leaders working in these collaborative structures are often effective at modelling the kinds of practices and behaviours that they want their colleagues to develop, for example towards knowledge sharing.

Peter Matthews had a formal role assessing and evaluating many of the first National Leaders of Education (NLEs). He set out a summary of the qualities and practices that he observed, including: "strong and principled moral purpose", "thoughtful and systematic", "earn trust ... through consulting, valuing, and developing the people with whom they work, and having belief in them", "build confidence, capability, and self-esteem in the people with whom they work, as well as institutional capacity through growing other leaders", "inordinately high expectations, great optimism", "decisive and prepared to take unpalatable decisions", and "find innovative and often unorthodox solutions" (Higham, Hopkins, & Matthews, 2009, pp. 116–117). This list suggests that the early pioneers of system leadership were driven, charismatic, even maverick individuals, undaunted by the challenges of taking on underperforming schools, often in the most deprived socio-economic circumstances. Subsequent evaluations of the early academy chains (Hill, Dunford, Parish, Rea, & Sandals, 2012), Teaching Schools (Gu et al., 2015), and wider partnerships (Chapman, 2013) have produced similar lists.

Of course, one person's inspirational leader is another person's empire builder, and system leaders have consistently faced the charge that they are first and foremost interested in their own power and prestige. Yet system leadership is not all about single heroic individuals. The most successful models are clearly about teams working together across multiple levels of the traditional school hierarchy. What successful system leaders appear to be able to do is create the conditions for this collaboration to happen, in particular through their ability to read and respond to different contexts and to engender trust and reciprocity within and between schools (Higham, Hopkins, & Matthews, 2009; Robinson, 2012).

Turning to the specific practices that system leaders undertake: at one level, their work can be very hands-on, dealing with immediate crises in failing schools and finding ways to apply learning on school improvement from one context to another (Robinson, 2012). Equally, though, it is becoming increasingly clear that some system leaders are moving beyond the day-to-day leadership of learning in a single school. Senior leaders in larger MATs—which are technically companies and charities and might have annual turnovers of £200m or more—are increasingly seen as Chief Executives: strategic leaders who must understand all aspects of business development, organizational design, and risk management (Hill et al., 2012). It is too early to say whether certain MAT leadership approaches—or even whether certain MATs—are consistently more effective in this than others, or how MAT leadership might evolve once the founding generation of heads move on and the sector begins to mature to reach a steady state. What seems clear, though, is that the MAT CEOs will require a sophisticated understanding of issues such as organizational design and strategic thinking at levels that traditional headteachers have not acquired. There is, therefore, a need to consider how the new CEOs can be helped to access and adapt learning and research from the business and voluntary sectors as quickly and successfully as possible.

Conclusion

As schools have gained more autonomy, so the role of school leaders, especially headteachers and, more recently, chief executive officers, has become more important. Policies relating to decentralization and school autonomy have given considerable powers to school leaders who, as we have noted elsewhere:

> sit at the fulcrum of high-autonomy-high-accountability systems and are expected to resolve the policy paradoxes of both competition and co-operation … they should: exercise their autonomy to innovate in response to parental needs, whilst at the same time meeting centrally prescribed targets and requirements; improve literacy and numeracy scores every year, whilst maintaining a broad and balanced curriculum; close attainment gaps, while pushing the brightest and the best; and collaborate with their peers to develop skills and capacity, while competing to ensure that (their schools) move up the local hierarchy. [Greany & Earley, 2017, p. 4]

How, then, can leaders lead in autonomous and accountable systems in ways that recognize and resolve, or at least mitigate, the tensions that they face?

It is important that the job of school leaders, especially headship, is seen as do-able. As Drucker (2011) has said:

> No institution can possibly survive if it needs geniuses or supermen to manage it. It must be organised in such a way as to be able to get along under a leadership composed of average human beings.

Are school leaders today expected to have too many skills, making the task seem impossible for "ordinary mortals"? Do the expectations of headteachers exceed what any one individual alone can reasonably achieve (Earley, 2013)? Hence the importance of distributing leadership and effective teamwork in schools. It is also important that "success-ful" leadership is not seen as finite, and that leadership agency can be shaped and grown. School leadership, especially headship, has often been seen as "a work of passion", and most of those working in educa-tion do so with a "moral purpose". The challenges are many: the need to raise standards, rising expectations from government, inspectors, parents and students, a highly diverse school population, a chang-ing curriculum, assessment, etc.—and although they may change, they will not disappear. School leaders will continue to operate in a VUCA environment—volatile, uncertain, complex, and ambiguous—and so will need considerable support and on-going development if our schools are to provide the kind of education needed to live and work in the twenty-first century.

CHAPTER THREE

Emotional factors in leading teaching and learning

Biddy Youell

A well-functioning school is a place where creativity can flourish. The extent to which this is possible is directly related to the way the school is led and how the headteacher and leadership team harness the resources of staff and students and manage the many competing demands they face. This chapter offers a psychoanalytic framework for exploring some of the emotional pressures and unconscious dynamics that are inherent within the headteacher's role and that of other leaders within the school setting. The underlying assumption is that a leader is better able to lead when he can recognize and understand his own emotional experience and that of his staff and students. This chapter focuses on intra- and interpersonal dynamics, while chapter 4 (by Judith Bell) explores group and institutional factors.

Monday morning. Girls secondary school. 1968

It was Mrs G's first day in her new post as headteacher of a traditional girls' secondary school. As was the custom, I (one of the head girls) collected her from her study to accompany her to assembly. Used to walking a pace or two behind the previous head, I was surprised to be told to walk alongside. "Why are you back there? You're making me nervous." Mrs G looked flushed and uncomfortable. I was even more shocked when the new headmistress ripped her academic gown off her shoulders and cast it aside onto the floor. Within a moment, she seemed to think better of this and asked me to help her put it back on. As we struggled to get it into position, she grumbled, "ridiculous garments." She paused at the door of the assembly hall, took a deep breath and entered as the school community rose to its feet. There was an expectant silence as she climbed the steps to reach the platform and then turned to face the audience and said a confident "Good Morning." When I sat down in my place alongside my peers and picked up my hymn sheet, I realised my hands were trembling.

There are many ways of thinking about this brief vignette, but there can be no doubt that the first assembly was an emotionally charged challenge for this new headteacher. It was also a significant moment for the Head Girl, who was full of curiosity about this new leader. The Head was unable to contain her own anxiety. She tried to suggest that it was the Head Girl who was making her nervous, but it seems clear that it was she who was projecting anxiety. Indeed, the girl found that she was trembling as she sat in her place in the hall. The Head seemed unsure as to whether she wanted or needed the external authority symbol of the academic gown. She wanted to cast it aside, but on this first occasion she felt she needed it, or perhaps feared that the staff and girls would get too big a shock if she appeared without it. It is not clear whether she was actually able to think any of this through at the time. It seems much more likely that her unconscious anxiety tripped her up and led her to act out her confusion, pulling herself together just in time. A few weeks later she stopped wearing the gown, and everyone assumed that she was, by then, feeling less anxious, more secure in her authority and better able to follow her own beliefs.

The headteacher's job description

A quick survey of some of the current advertisements for headteacher posts reveals a staggering range of expectations. Many job descriptions have very specific elements related to the particular challenges facing a school, such as its position in the league tables, changes being brought about by government directives or by the transfer of school management from local authority to private or third-sector organizations. Generic summaries state simply that headteachers are *leaders* of their schools, responsible for creating the right conditions for children and staff to achieve their best. It sounds remarkably straightforward but takes no account of the myriad interpersonal relationships involved, or the complexities of the pressures that come from a political context of continual change.

The school context

Whatever the setting, leadership roles place demands on the leader's innate capacities, experience, and emotional resilience. As the chapters in this book will go on to explore, there are a number of personal qualities that leaders need in order to lead in a way that allows them to exercise their authority and inspire cooperative and creative "followership" (Obholzer, 1994). Managing their own and other's emotional states is part of what all leaders have to do, even though there are those who insist that in a well-regulated organization, reason prevails and emotions should be kept under control. Others, including the author of this chapter, see it differently. Emotions should be recognized, but they need a context in which they can be linked to thinking and reason. It is the aim of this chapter to set out the reasons why this is a particular challenge in school leadership and why awareness of unconscious factors might prove invaluable.

Schools are complex communities. There are tens, hundreds, or even thousands of people of different generations coming together for a large proportion of the day, five days a week, approximately 38 weeks a year. There are students, teachers, administrators, caretakers, cleaners, and all kinds of support staff and volunteers. Just outside the school, but looking in with varying degrees of investment and responsibility, are the parents, the governors, and the commissioning body … whether it be a local authority or a private company. Ofsted inspectors, politicians, and the media are never far away. In a manufacturing or service company, success is measured by what is produced and sold. Output is measured, income set against expenditure, and as long as the products or services are of sufficient quality and workers are reasonably content with their lot, the company is seen as functioning well. With schools, successful outcomes are more difficult to measure. Exam results are one yardstick, but academic success does not take into account the complexities of the relationship between potential and achievement. It does not allow for the subtleties of the demographic and certainly does not serve as a measure of "wellbeing", "good citizenship" or "happiness."

The unconscious

Psychoanalytic theory and its applications are based on the assumption that there is something called "the unconscious", a part of the mind that is below the surface. Elements of it emerge from time to time, often catching us out when we least expect it. According to Freud (1901), the unconscious mind is the primary driver of human behaviour. Since Freud, many theorists have contributed to the development of a more dynamic, flexible model of the mind, but the underlying theory remains the same. We are all subject to the influence of internalized experiences that are not readily available to our rational minds. In schools, the agenda in the external world is inevitably influenced by the internal worlds and unconscious agendas of all the people involved.

Anxiety, containment, and learning

Psychoanalytic theory holds that learning inevitably involves a measure of anxiety. Put simply, in order to learn something, we have to be prepared to accept that we do not already know it and that somebody else does. Not knowing (a fact or a skill) is an uncomfortable state that has to be tolerated if learning is to take place. Kleinian theory of development is based on a belief that anxiety is a necessary spur to learning. Without a measure of anxiety, we would not take the risks involved and would remain in a passive, undeveloped state.

It is worth noting that while psychoanalysis is sometimes criticized as a science that looks at everything that can go wrong in childhood, Klein (1931) was the first to write about something she called "the epistemophilic instinct": the innate human desire to find out about the world. She was of the firm belief that in ordinary "good-enough" (Winnicott, 1949) circumstances, young children are actively curious about other people and about their own experience; they want to learn.

Bion (1962) developed a theory of learning along lines similar to Mrs Klein's earlier work. He privileges "learning from experience" above "learning about", and he roots this in his observations of the early relationship between a mother (primary carer) and her baby. He coined the phrase "container–contained" to describe the way in which a mother unconsciously takes in and makes sense of the baby's experience as she focuses her mind on what he is communicating through his cries, his expressions, his physical movements, and so on. The baby is assailed by sensations that he is not equipped to process cognitively. His mother's focus on him and capacity to understand something of his experience and to tolerate his distress is described by Bion as a capacity to "contain" anxiety.

In the pre-verbal phase of life, the infant who has sufficient experience of a mother who is dependable and usually effective in relieving anxiety, discomfort, and distress will come to believe that the world is a welcoming place, full of interesting people and possibilities. Failures in the container–contained relationship in early childhood can come about for all kinds of reasons. Some babies are easier to comfort than others, and real-life events can put pressures on parents that render them incapable of relaxed, focused, flexible parenting in spite of their best intentions. Bion (1962) extends his theory to a version of maternal containment that leaves the baby with a double dose of anxiety. Not only is he not helped with his own distress, but he has to absorb his mother's frustration and possibly her unconscious resentment and hostility. Sadly, we also know that some parents repeat their own neglectful and abusive experiences in parenting their children. It is easy to recognize the long-term effects of this kind of maltreatment on the capacity to make relationships and to learn.

The school as container of anxiety

When a child goes to school, the school institution and its staff take over some aspects of the parental role. Children look to the adults for the containment they need in order to function positively in what is a new and challenging environment. To offer containment requires the adults, whatever their role, to be open to the feeling states of the children and young people without being overwhelmed by them. It requires a capacity to observe, reflect, and respond in a thoughtful way. It requires a degree of self-knowledge to be able to differentiate between what is being communicated by the child and what is one's own feeling. It also depends on there being someone who can, in turn, offer a degree of containment to the container. In families, an anxious or over-deployed mother may turn to a partner or to her own parents to support her in her maternal role. In schools, a teacher may turn to a colleague, a senior leader, or indeed to the headteacher. Gianna Williams (personal communication) introduced the idea of a Russian Doll model of containment, with layer upon layer holding the system together (whether family or institution). The headteacher could be seen as the biggest doll, the outer layer of containment for all the other dolls. The children, teachers, and support staff all need to know that somebody has them and their needs in mind. Of course, the head also needs to feel that somebody is able to understand the pressures and support him in his role, whether this be members of his leadership team, the chair of governors, a professional mentor, or people in his private life.

Many examples come to mind of times in a school when containing structures can break down under stress. In the face of SATS, public examinations, or Ofsted inspections, it is not uncommon for anxiety to spill out and for individuals at all levels to feel that nobody can manage the pressure. Students encounter staff who are preoccupied and on edge. The needier children and young people are likely to feel emotionally unsafe, and the more disaffected students may take the opportunity to act out. Staff who feel unsure of themselves are likely to communicate their uncertainty to the leadership team (see section on Projection below), and so it goes on. It is not just the students in schools who need to perform to the best of their ability. Teachers and headteachers are vulnerable to seeing their reputations or even their careers ruined by failures in this kind of process.

There are, of course, less extreme examples of times when layers of containment prove inadequate. It may be that a single, struggling student can set a process going which gathers momentum and leads to a headteacher having to answer to his governing body. When a teacher is having a hard time with a class and does not feel that his concerns are being listened to, he may put pressure on his head of year to do something about one child who seems to be a ringleader. The head of year may, in turn, put pressure on the headteacher to exclude the child. If nobody is able to stop and reflect on the wider issues, it is unlikely that the relationship between the teacher and the class will be improved by the removal of one student.

Stages of development and times of transition

School life spans a number of developmental stages; from early childhood to late adolescence or early adulthood. Each age group has a particular set of developmental tasks to achieve. Infant schools are alive with the emotions involved for parents and children of that first compulsory separation. Even if the child has been in day-care or nursery, "starting big school" has a particular meaning. "Learning" gradually takes over from "playing", and teachers begin to feature as authority figures with expectations about behaviour and about achievement. Rivalry between children begins to be about who is perceived to be the best, the cleverest, the most attractive, the most popular, or the teacher's favourite. Very young children (under 5 years) are generally passionate in their responses, with tears and tantrums accompanying setbacks of all kinds. Latency-aged children (approximately 5–11 years) are perhaps less volatile, but emotions are never very far from the surface. At puberty and in adolescence there is often a return to something akin to "tears and tantrums". Passionate feelings accompany surges in hormones, and secondary schools find themselves dealing with a heady cocktail of emotional states, both conscious and unconscious.

There is a parallel here between the stages of development that children pass through and the career development of teachers and school leaders. All teachers have been through the school system themselves, but the first time a Newly Qualified Teacher (NQT) steps across the threshold of the classroom, he is likely to experience a surge of anxiety, awareness of newness and feelings of vulnerability. These feelings are different from, but reminiscent of, the feelings of the five-year-old starting school. A teacher's career also involves a series of transitions: from NQT to fully qualified teacher, Head of Department, Head of Year, etc. Each promotion involves a new set of demands and challenges, culminating for some in taking up headship. My example at the beginning of this chapter highlights the headteacher's first appearance in front of the school community, but there is also the first Governor's meeting, the first Ofsted, the first permanent exclusion, parent complaint, forced redundancy, etc.

School institutions are divided up to reflect the key developmental stages of childhood and adolescence, but it is an inexact science. All school communities will include some individuals who are out of step with their peers and who are, nevertheless, required to progress at the same rate. The discrepancies may be due to different rates of physical development or may be the result of life experiences. A psychoanalytic framework for thinking about development would hold that much depends on the way early separations and transitions have been managed within families. If early anxiety about separation has been contained in the sense described above, the likelihood is that the child will manage, and even relish, that first entry into nursery or school. If early separations have been traumatic or the child has experienced traumatic loss (e.g. family bereavement, being taken into care, loss of country or language, etc.) every change and transition, even those small changes that take place within the school day (a change of teacher or classroom), may unconsciously stir up unwelcome memories and acute anxiety.

We are all susceptible to a degree of anxiety when we face any transition, involving, as it does, some degree of loss and uncertainty. Schools have become much more sensitive to the major transitions. A great deal of thought is given to the way in which children take their first step into nursery or infant school. At later transition points, there are usually plans in place to prepare children in advance. Children visit their new class, meet their new teacher, and at secondary transfer spend time in their new school before the summer break. It is generally accepted that they need to know in advance if a teacher is leaving and be given opportunities to say good bye.

It may be less commonly accepted that times of change and transition are also unsettling and emotionally challenging for staff—some of whom will try hard to avoid the emotional impact. It is still the case, for example, that teachers often leave it to the last moment to tell their class about some impending change. This is rationalized as a way of avoiding upset and anger but actually serves to deprive everybody of adequate time and space to process the emotional experience. I am reminded of a teacher who left a head-of-year post after six years in the school. He did not feel he had done a good job and certainly did not think any-one would miss him. He did not exactly keep his decision a secret but somehow managed not to tell many of the students he taught. On the last day of term, when the headteacher made a formal speech of thanks to the departing teacher, a ripple of shock passed through the assembly hall. He was very surprised some days later to receive a letter from a small group of students saying how sorry they were to lose him and apologizing for their behaviour. They were convinced the teacher had left so abruptly because of them. This example sticks in the mind because it shows so clearly a significant discrepancy between the teacher's per-ception of his importance to the school and the student's disproportion-ate sense of responsibility for his departure. More time to discuss and process this together would have been likely to leave everybody feel-ing more appreciative of each other, even if having to be in touch with some sadness and regret. It would also be likely to reduce the risk that unprocessed feelings—such as anger and guilt—would be unhelpfully exported into the students' relationship with their subsequent teacher. This dynamic is something that is easy to recognize with supply teach-ers who are often in receipt of all sorts of mixed feelings (often anger and resentment), which are displaced from the "real" and "loved" teacher who is absent. The strength of such feelings can easily hijack a lesson altogether. But these same dynamics and difficulties are just as significant at other levels within the school—for instance, when there is a change of leadership, especially if the outgoing and incoming leaders and their teams have not allowed adequate space to consider what this change means for them.

Envy, rivalry, and competition

A degree of envy and rivalry is inevitable wherever human beings come together within organizations, but particularly so in an education system that promotes competition. Individual children may be told to challenge themselves and not to be concerned about what others are achieving, but that is a meaningless exhortation when comparison is inevitable and so much depends on "success" and "failure." Fear of not matching up to the standards we demand of ourselves, or which others demand of us, is a universal fear against which we develop all kinds of defences. In classrooms, this is often what is behind disruptive behaviour: the clowning around, the picking of a fight. Refusal to work at something or the insistence that the task is "boring" usually masks a fear that the task is beyond the child's or class group's capabilities. Fear of failure in the face of examinations or inspections can "paralyse" both individuals and institutions, even when the evidence would point to the likelihood of success. High achievers sometimes articulate a fear that the better they do in tests, the more they fear that there will be a sudden collapse, and their cleverness will be found to be fraudulent. Repeated failure has a devastating effect on individuals and on institutions.

A child's capacity to manage their envy of more successful peers and engage in competitive activity (whether in terms of academic success, sports, popularity, etc.) will again depend to a large extent on the foundations laid down in the early relationships within the family. Melanie Klein (1931) suggested that overcoming or tolerating envy is one of the tasks of early childhood. She suggested that some babies are characterologically more envious than others and need more help in coming to terms with reality. Accepting that the mother (or primary caregiver) is not the sole possession of the baby is the first step. Later comes awareness of other relationships and of the position of the child outside the parental couple. This is the essence of what is described as the oedipal configuration: the realization that one has to share the mother's attention with others, notably the father/partner or another significant figure. The child's first experience of rivalry is usually felt in relation to one or other parent or sibling. Again, it is easy to identify the children and young people who have not fully accepted this reality and who seek exclusive relationships, finding threes difficult to manage or being unable to share.

Envy and rivalry among staff is as inevitable as it is among the students. Even if it is covert and largely unconscious, it can be extremely powerful. The scope for projection and splitting (see below) is considerable, as individuals vie for position and groups get together to influence the headteacher's opinions. If a headteacher is not alert to the dangers inherent in splitting, he may not recognize the signs when gang-like behaviour or bullying is taking root in his staff group or among the children. There is a real danger of a headteacher believing the "propaganda" being spread by one particular group and unwittingly going along with scapegoating an individual or another group. This is particularly common at times of institutional stress, such as in the face of an inspection, when one teacher or class can so easily become identified as the weak link, with an accompanying fantasy that if they were performing better or were got rid of, everything would go well. If the headteacher is not alert to the inevitable presence of envy and rivalry, he may also fail to spot the ways in which his own authority is questioned. These rivalrous feelings often feel embarrassingly infantile and are therefore difficult to own up to.

Projection and splitting

With acknowledgement of the existence of an unconscious mind comes the question of how this influences thoughts and events in the external world. Projection is the term given to the unconscious transmission of feelings from one person to another. It is a word in common usage to describe the way in which somebody rids themselves of unwanted feelings, which are absorbed by a receptive other. In the example of the "attuned" mother, she is able to take in and process the emotional experience on behalf of her baby, who cannot yet speak or process thoughts. In all relationships, if the projected emotion is not manageable and cannot be made available to thinking, it may lodge in the other person and may result in them acting out (reacting unconsciously).

I have quoted an example elsewhere (Youell, 2006) of a school community on a Monday morning where uncontained anxiety is projected from group to group without anyone being able to stop and reflect. In this example, a deputy head is taking a call from County Hall (then the commissioning body) and arrives late to the staff briefing, red in the face and agitated. He complains that the Head is off sick again and starts to berate the staff for their shortcomings: the state of the staffroom, the poor showing at a parents' evening, and so on. They absorb the tirade without comment, but when they leave the staffroom, they immediately start to shout at groups of older adolescent boys about minor infringements of uniform rules. It seems inevitable that these boys will move on down the corridors to pass on the abuse to younger students.

We may all be able to think of individuals who somehow leave us feeling something that we do not recognize as our own or we know we did not feel before the encounter. A colleague, for example, who leaves us feeling unaccountably depressed or agitated, anxious, angry, or belittled after a brief conversation has successfully projected their state of mind into us. It is then possible, or even likely, that he will go away feeling relieved, while we feel burdened by what we have taken in. It is the countertransference that enables us to notice when an encounter has resulted in a sudden change in our state of mind.

Splitting is another word in common usage. It usually describes the way in which people try to divide one person from another in a destructive way. An example might be an adolescent who manages to disrupt what might be the constructive communication between his parent and his teacher by inaccurate reporting of the one to the other. As a psychoanalytic concept, it is seen more as an internal, unconscious process through which people protect and defend themselves against experiencing unwelcome feelings and avoid grappling with unwelcome internal conflicts. As such, it can be a necessary and protective manoeuvre. For example, a child or staff member who is struggling with a troubling personal issue needs to be able to split this off in order to get on with his or her task in the school. Everyone will be familiar with the way students can idealize one teacher and denigrate another. There may be identifiable, external-world reasons for this, but it may also be that it is a reflection of projected emotions. The child who does not want to own his own limitations may project all his "stupidity" or "shame" into another. In the same way—but more easily overlooked—a child may project all the "cleverness" into another student or into the teacher and leave himself feeling stupid. The same dynamic can hold sway in the staffroom, with one teacher or group of teachers projecting competence or incompetence into their colleagues. At a more systemic level, excessive projection of competence into the senior leadership team and headteacher can contribute to something akin to a dependency culture.[1]

Transference

Transference is a core concept in psychoanalytic clinical work. However, the transference is not something that happens only between patient and clinician. It is active wherever there is a relationship in which one person fulfils a role in relation to the other, particularly if one is in some kind of position of authority or responsibility: doctor and patient, priest and parishioner, teacher and student, and, of course, the entire school community and the headteacher. The transference describes the way in which we bring aspects of ourselves and patterns of past experience to bear on current relationships, so that we come to expect particular kinds of response. Teachers are entirely familiar with the experience of a student anticipating a particular response long before it happens. An example might be a student who accuses the teacher of "picking on" him when he has not yet said or done anything. Often this has more to do with the internal state of the child, and possibly with his real-life experiences with his actual parents, than it does with the behaviour of the teacher.

For children in school, the headteacher is the highest authority: a relatively distant figure to whom they assume everyone in the school is accountable. Depending on the nature of the school, the headteacher will be either more or less familiar to the students. They will know a certain amount about him, based on their actual experience, but they will also bring a host of unconscious expectations to bear on their view of him. Theirs is likely to be a parental or grandparental transference. A selection of adjectives used to describe the same individual head might range from fair, kind, wise, and clever to strict, mean, rigid, or unfair, depending on the expectations of the individual children.

Similarly, the transference relationship a teacher may have to a more senior colleague or to the headteacher may colour the way interactions proceed. A teacher may expect kindly "maternal" protection from the Head or may, at the other extreme, expect to be criticized or even punished. In the moment, the Head may, in unconscious phantasy, be experienced as if they were any one of a variety of previous authority figures.

Parents also bring their pre-existing assumptions to bear on their interactions with teachers and headteachers. Their own internalized experiences at school and their feelings about their children's strengths and weaknesses will inform the way they approach the Head. They may or may not be conscious of their anxiety, and it may lead them to behave in a way that is unnecessarily defensive, aggressive, or apologetic. The headteacher or other school leader may then find themselves dealing with a range of transference phenomena in a single meeting.

Countertransference and observation

If it is accepted that unconscious dynamics are active beneath the surface of a school institution, it becomes important to identify ways in which they can be brought into consciousness and made available for thought and reflection. In clinical practice, the capacity to be open to unconscious communication is termed "countertransference". Psychoanalytically informed observation, whether in a clinical session, a school, or any other setting, requires the observer to be open to the emotional states of others. It requires an awareness of the many ways in which defences against anxiety manifest themselves in human behaviour. It requires that attention is given not only to what is seen and heard, but what is conveyed through projection. The observer examines his own emotional responses and makes a quick judgement as to what belongs to him and what has been communicated from the other. This may sound like a super-human set of skills, but it is actually relatively simple. If we approach interactions with an open and attentive mind and interpose a moment of reflection before reacting, we can often make sense of what is being communicated and adjust our responses accordingly.

The usefulness or otherwise of applied psychoanalytic thinking really depends on the development of observational skills and awareness of one's countertransference responses in the way described above. It is really a matter of being open, attentive, and willing to ask oneself a simple series of questions. What is happening? How do I feel? Is my emotional response entirely my own, or might it be a communication from this child or colleague? If so, what might it tell me about them? How should I respond? What would be most helpful ... for the child, the colleague, for me, and for the institution?

I will conclude this section with an example from a primary school, which may serve to illustrate some of the points made in the forgoing paragraphs. This was a school with a good reputation in the local community. The teachers seemed to enjoy their work; they worked hard and were committed to doing their best for the children, many of whom came from disadvantaged families. When the Head reached retirement age, her staff were sad but confident that the deputy who would take over was "of the same mould". There was *no question* that Ms X would be the next headteacher. The outgoing Head was just one who assumed it would be so and more or less said so to anybody who asked. To everyone's shock and dismay, the governors decided otherwise, and they appointed an outsider: an ambitious young woman who had impressed at interview. The staff governor on the interview panel felt that her opinions had been ignored, and she told her colleagues what an uncomfortable experience it had been. Ms X was angry; she left the school for a headship elsewhere, and the staff were left distressed by what they experienced as a double loss. More than one teacher referred to it as the break-up of a well-functioning family. There were a lot of unanswered questions. Had the governors felt that things had become too "cosy?" Had there been complaints from parents that nobody had known about? Was the deputy thought to be too left-wing, too permissive, too concerned with pastoral care, and not concerned enough with academic achievement? Among the children, various stories took hold as to why Ms X had left. Some children were sad, while others preferred to imagine some kind of scandalous behaviour ... an affair with the caretaker, perhaps!

The new headteacher was indeed very different but the way the change had been managed meant that she was given a frosty welcome. Everything she did in the first term was greeted with sighs of disapproval, and the more her colleagues disapproved, the more strident she became and the more determined she seemed to be to turn everything upside down. A number of teachers left, and parents began to question whether they had chosen the best school for their children.

One can see the way in which splitting and projection took hold in this school as it faced, or failed to face, the loss of a much-loved leader in the retiring headteacher. The governors seemed to feel the need to impose their authority, rather like a parent being determined to show his children who is in charge. They were not prepared to listen to any complaints or answer any questions. The staff were not able to process their loss and embarked on a campaign of splitting: idealization of the old and denigration of the new. Absorbing all the projections of disappointment and hostility, the new headteacher seemed unable to think about the situation she had come into and heavy-handedly imposed her will on her new colleagues. It was not a happy place for the adults, but, worse, it was not functioning as a container for the emotional experience of the children. Not surprisingly, academic standards began to fall and behaviour to deteriorate.

The internal world of the school leader

It would be misleading to paint a picture of the headteacher as the passive recipient of all these unconscious communications and emotional pressures. He equally brings all aspects of his internal world to bear on his role and is an active participant in the dynamics that unfold between him, his staff, governors, the children, their parents, and the external stakeholders. He will have a leadership style or set of beliefs that reflect, to some extent, relationships in *his* internal world. He is not immune from acting out his unconscious feelings and may project unwanted aspects of himself and his experience into his staff, the children, the parents, the governors, etc. I am reminded of a Head who started the first staff meeting of the Autumn Term with, "Isn't it just dreadful to be back? How are we going to bear it?" This headteacher could not contain his own depression and made it very difficult for his staff to remain buoyant in the face of relentless gloom. They felt the headteacher to be vulnerable and could neither support him nor challenge his authority. What was not clear was whether this headteacher had always been this kind of leader, subject to his own despairing internal world, or whether he was worn down by years of "authority-sapping" dynamics within the school and between the school and the outside world.

A different version of a headteacher being dominated by forces from his internal world would be the one who feels apologetic about exercising authority or issuing any directives. His internal world is undermining him, leaving him doubtful about his own worth. This might be the "democratic" headteacher who consults on everything, needing to feel that there is absolute consensus on all decisions. At the other end of the scale is the autocratic headteacher who consults on nothing, and issues instructions at a distance and/or via email from behind his office door. His belief, informed by his harsh inner world, is that you need to rule with a rod of iron if you are to maintain order. The message conveyed is that he knows what he is doing and he just needs everyone to get on with what they have to do. This situation may be sustainable for some time, especially if the headteacher has the approval of the governors, but is likely, in the end, to be challenged by disaffected staff and students who will gather strength (and avoid other rivalries) from having a common enemy.

How can the headteacher or school leader protect his sense of his competence from powerful projections of anxiety? I have mentioned above the exhaustion that can result from feeling that one is not known for who one actually is and the ensuing loneliness that can then be so central to the headteacher's experience. This points to the need for a headteacher to feel supported by close colleagues who know and respect him. It is hard for headteachers to find the right distance between themselves, teaching staff, support staff, and the children. A lot will depend on personal style, but the importance of "learning from experience" and remaining open to making adjustments to practice cannot be over-stated.

Gender

I have referred to the headteacher as "he" throughout this chapter. Much of what has been described is not at all gender-specific. However, aspects of the transference may need to be thought about slightly differently when referring to female headteachers. In primary schools, women heads are often experienced as "motherly" by children, teachers, and, indeed, by parents. This is likely to be mixture of transference assumption and reality. A male headteacher in a primary school perhaps has to work harder to convey a nurturing side of himself in his role. In secondary schools, women sometimes attract accusations of being unfeminine in their ambition to be leaders of such a large workforce, and there may be undercurrents of resentment in groups of female staff if all the senior managers are men and they feel they do all the "women's work". Gender stereotypes are powerful, and boys and girls at various ages and stages of development will have particular gender-related responses to accepting the authority of one or other gender, as will their parents and staff. These things are difficult to talk or write about and quickly stir up anxiety about not being properly aware of the equalities' agenda. However, they are powerful dynamics, and headteachers need to attend to them if they are to recognize projections of envy or hostility when they arise.

Conclusion

Much of this chapter has focused on examples of when things go wrong with a headteacher's leadership role. I want to conclude by making a positive case for headteachers being supported to understand unconscious communication as a protective aid to their management and enjoyment of their work. As has been spelled out in the forgoing pages, a dose of anxiety is an unavoidable—even healthy—element in any learning or teaching activity. However, understanding the concepts of containment, projection, transference, and countertransference, and being willing to recognize that envy and rivalry are part of the human condition, can be liberating. It all helps to make some sense of the seemingly random, irrational feelings and behaviours that can so quickly become obstacles to the primary tasks of teaching, learning and leading.

Note

1 For further description, see chapter 4, by Judith Bell.

CHAPTER FOUR

Individual, group and organizational dynamics: a theoretical overview

Judith Bell

T his chapter offers an overview of some of the key psychodynamic, group, and systemic concepts relevant to leadership in
education. It describes group and organizational dynamics that
impact those who lead and work in schools and colleges and considers how such dynamics might best be understood, acknowledged, and
worked with so that the tasks of leadership and management can be
achieved more effectively. Examples are given from the author's experience of coaching leaders in the field.

Leaders in education have a complex set of responsibilities in their
roles: keeping children safe; ensuring learning takes place to an agreed,
acceptable standard—usually monitored closely; imparting a set of values and developing behaviour according to an accepted moral code (that
may or may not be explicit). There is the responsibility for nurturing and
developing the next generation, ensuring that disadvantage is addressed
and that outcomes are fair for all.

When we try to understand what is going on with a child who is not
coping well in the classroom or who is not reaching their potential, it
is as important to consider what he or she may be thinking and feeling
as it is to look at what is going on for them in their lives at home and
at school—as well as how they are being taught. Similarly, in trying to
understand how schools perform and how the people in them can be
helped to function as best they can, we need to look at what people bring
to their roles, how they relate to others, and how they think and feel

about their work, as much as what is happening in the context in which they are working. Context in this case may mean both the immediate local milieu of the school community and the wider backdrop, which will, of course, include political and social agendas that may exert a powerful influence on how those in leadership positions take up their roles and address their tasks.

A systems psychodynamic approach refers to the application and integration of three frameworks of thinking and research that overlap both conceptually and historically and together offer an heuristic model with which we can understand organizations and the behaviour of those who work within them.

First, systems thinking and ideas allow us to locate the organization in its different contexts and to understand the interplay between the parts and the whole.

The second of these frameworks—psychodynamic thinking (described in more detail by Biddy Youell in chapter 3)—enables us to understand the significance of the unconscious on behaviour, creativity, learning, and development. It helps us to gain awareness of emotions, anxieties, conflicts, and our own blind spots and those of others and allows us to be more fully present at work and to manage effectively the complexity of working relationships.

Third, a deeper awareness and understanding of group dynamics helps us to make sense of what is really going on in groups at work and is key to creating engaged, high-performing teams.

Systems thinking

Like a biological organism, an organizational system requires a dynamic interaction with its environment to survive. For example, schools cannot survive in isolation; they require an active relationship with the world outside their boundary. They must respond to the needs of their environment, provide places for the requisite number of children, and be in touch with the locality to provide continuity and context. They take direction from government via established management and governance pathways, and they must account for their performance to local and national bodies. They also take direction from parents to varying degrees. They may have an additional commercial management or a relationship with a charitable foundation. Add into this mix relationships with other schools and colleges in the area, health and children's services, connections to local faith-based organizations, and the complexity is evident.

Conceptualizing an organization as a system in this way draws attention to its boundary and the regulatory processes that maintain that boundary. Within the boundary the task of the organization takes place—in schools, students are educated, socialized, cared for, etc. Resources are needed for this task—teachers, materials, buildings, etc. Standards need to be set and monitored. The boundary is crucial; what goes in must be appropriate and in the right balance in order to ensure that what comes out is what is needed. "Management" in any organizational context involves actively managing this boundary on behalf of the system—that is, making decisions on behalf of the organization as to what goes in and what comes out. It will be clear that within every system is a series of sub-systems each with their own managed boundaries and their own sub-sub-systems and there is an interdependency between the parts of the whole. If parts of an organizational system become detached from the whole, then its overall efficacy becomes compromised (see Campbell, Draper, & Huffington, 1991; Roberts, 1994).

Socio-technical systems

All organizational systems rely on human behaviour and are therefore influenced by how the individuals within them think and feel. In human service systems where "inputs" and "outcomes" are about people, human behaviour is obviously the greatest determinant of how well such systems function. When individuals are acting rationally, with conscious thought and creativity in play, organizations will function at their best.

The application of systems thinking to organizational life was developed Miller and Rice in the 1960s (Miller & Rice, 1967). Their work demonstrates that an organization adapts to the limitations imposed by a) "the technological system"—what it has at its disposal to address the task with which it is concerned (equipment, buildings, materials etc.) and b) the social system—the emotions and behaviour of the people. These two systems are closely linked and in successful organizations there is a good fit between them—a "socio-technical system". How social systems influence the success or failure of organizations has been studied in depth and is described in more detail later in this chapter.

Psychodynamic thinking

Central to psychodynamic thinking, as described in chapter 3, is the concept of the internal world, which refers to our inner thoughts and feelings, derived from relationships and experiences from the beginning of our awareness. How we think about, feel, and react towards other people whom we encounter in our external world has to do not just with how they behave towards us (though of course this is important) but also what they may mean to us in terms of the individual internalized model of relationships that we carry and have constructed over time. The internal world is largely unconscious—its content or impact may not be within our awareness. It may trip us up or take us by surprise or lead us to follow blindly a less rational path. We may become driven by hidden feelings and impulses that distort the way we might experience and perceive a particular situation or person—and we may not be aware that this is the case.

EXAMPLE

> Martin: a headteacher who had a great deal of trouble delegating to one of his two assistant heads, but not to the other. The two assistants, one male, one female, were equally competent and had complementary skill sets, yet Martin found it very hard to trust one of them, Andrew, an older man, and was not allowing him to take up fully his assistant head role. Andrew, unsurprisingly, was pushing back, and the two would often clash. There did not seem to be any issues to do with Andrew's competence but the two were locked in a tense and unproductive relationship. In Martin's coaching he came to understand that an early experience of being badly let down by paternal figures in his life had led him to a position where he found it very difficult to trust that men could deliver.

The key here is to think about what personal meaning and resonance tricky work situations may represent and trigger for us.

Our internal world is central to our personality development[1] and therefore to how we relate to others, how we manage our feelings, how we make decisions, and, more generally, how we live in the world. It may influence our chosen profession, how we want to advance our career, and how we approach our work. This may result in a pull towards particular professions for certain personality types (expressed by the caricature of introverted accountants or extraverted actors), and it may lead to professional groups having more similarities than differences, which needs to be thought about and managed. In chapter 9, Emil Jackson describes how an understanding of personality preferences and personality types, through the lens of the Myers–Briggs Type Indicator (MBTI), can help school leaders to better understand how people work together and how, as leaders, they may create a context in which staff are able to perform at their best. At a deeper level, one's personality may also contribute to us selecting and following a particular professional path as a way of resolving dilemmas that originated earlier in life. For example, Tucker's work (Tucker, 2010), which investigated how primary school headteachers experience and manage stress, revealed a common thread: a number of the heads he interviewed described a personal experience of failure in educational terms. This experience was unique to them and ranged from failing the 11+ exams to not getting accepted by an Oxbridge college. What was important was not the nature of the failure itself, but the meaning it held for the individual who then, through their career choice, Tucker postulated, found a means to compensate for this "failure".

Defences against anxiety

We commonly refer to "defensive behaviour" when describing how people respond in situations of uncertainty, stress, or anxiety. In the work environment, defences are a means of managing difficult emotions so as to ensure that we are not overwhelmed by them. Some individuals are more able than others to bear difficult feelings and to manage their personal response to stressors, thereby ensuring that they don't "take things out" on others or enact their emotional states, for example by aggressive or spoiling behaviour.

Some defensive behaviour is adaptive and, indeed, essential to organizational life. This would include *altruism, tolerance*, and *forgiveness*—different means of adopting a consciously constructive attitude to others, along with some use of *humour* to cope with painful topics. Some less adaptive defences that avoid difficult emotions are very common and can be managed, although they might be irksome to be around—for example, in the context of a teacher struggling to meet a deadline, feelings of anger about being burdened by the task may be displaced away from a headteacher and directed instead towards a colleague. Alternatively, feelings may perhaps be intellectualized in order to create distance from the emotional elements of the situation. Stronger defences may be maladaptive and create tension, difficult feelings, and distraction from the task in hand. Examples include *passive aggression;* the *"acting out"* of feelings without conscious awareness of the emotion driving the behaviour; or *splitting* off of feelings from one's own awareness and *projecting* them into others. Those into whom feelings are projected may identify with what is being projected and behave as though they "owned" the feeling—for instance, when being made to feel stupid or ashamed. In this way colleagues can get caught in a tangle of feelings that is difficult to work though. To get a sense of this kind of projective process, consider a staff member who, lacking confidence and perhaps low in self-esteem, may unconsciously relate to colleagues in a way that invites them to behave in an uncharacteristically dismissing or critical manner towards them. Sometimes recipients of the projected feelings may themselves have a tendency towards taking on that position and may behave in ways that seem familiar. Concepts and insights such as these are often intuitively used by teachers and senior leaders in relation to understanding and managing similar dynamics with students, though these are not necessarily transferred to the adults with whom they work.

Unconscious processes at work

As well as thinking about what individuals bring to work, we also need to consider the unconscious emotional processes that play out in organizational life which may prevent teams and organizations from functioning effectively. Some elements of organizational behaviour might be symbolic or representative of hidden emotions and meaning. For example, the preoccupation of a staff group with the inefficiencies of an administration system may represent a feeling of not being listened to or communicated with by management. Anxieties at work create internal disturbance. If this cannot be articulated and thought about, it may be expressed unconsciously in ways that make it very hard to stay on task.

EXAMPLE

In a large inner-city comprehensive school the leadership team, teachers, and support staff were finding it very difficult to work together. There was conflict in the senior management team such that the senior members barely spoke to one another. There were also accusations of bullying, and two of the most senior teachers were on long-term sick leave. Unsurprisingly, standards and results had fallen, leading to a rating of "requires improvement" at the last Ofsted inspection. Whilst several different factors contributed to this difficult situation, of particular significance was the fact that the school had merged with another school, and the two staff groups had not integrated well. The number of students had increased without matching resources, levels of staff sickness and absence were high, and students' behaviour was extremely challenging. The everyday anxiety of managing a large group of young people had escalated through a felt inability to keep children (and staff) safe. Considering the potential for such changes to impact emotionally on those involved, very little space was given to processing this. Staff meetings were held to discuss the practical arrangements but proved ineffective as staff used them to vent their anger without any opportunity to attend to the underlying emotional aspects of the change through reflecting together and learning from experience. The leadership team and teaching staff were therefore increasingly overwhelmed by toxic emotions, without adequate support to process them.

Social systems as defences against anxiety

Particular work contexts result in the prevalence of particular types of anxiety. In education settings, concern is for the safety, development, and outcomes of children and young people. Safety is a complex issue: children need to be educated in a safe environment and, at times, to be protected from adults in their world and from each other. Staff, too, require protection, sometimes from their students, their parents, and from the impact and demands of the role. The felt anxiety concerning the safety of children is intense and can be overwhelming. As a result, one should not underestimate the extent to which it can be defended against by turning a blind eye, as in the following vignette:

EXAMPLE

Anna, a primary school teacher in her fourth year of teaching, began a new role as a Year 5 teacher in an inner-city school. In this new school, she found her students' behaviour in the classroom very challenging. She was shocked by the extent of the deprivation she perceived and the physically aggressive behaviour of the children towards each other and towards her. She asked for additional resources. The head was unable or unwilling to make available additional staff, despite Anna's strongly expressed feeling that neither the children nor Anna herself were safe in the classroom. Although initially sympathetic, the head conveyed a view that Anna should be able to cope without extra support. Anna then began to feel that she was inadequate and not up to the task of being a teacher. She resigned and left the school abruptly. The following month a supply teacher was assaulted and badly injured by a student in the class.

In this example, while the teacher may indeed have been inexperienced and in need of setting some firm boundaries, we might also consider the extent to which the headteacher may have been struggling to manage the impossible tension of having a young teacher in need of support in her role without the resources to provide for this. Her "just get on with it" message might therefore have been an understandable defence against this reality and, in particular, her sense of her own inadequacy and impotence. Defences protect individuals from the experience of anxiety and intense feelings, and in organizations they may also get played out collectively. Turning a blind eye is one means by which those in positions of responsibility may protect themselves from overwhelming anxiety. When this happens on a collective basis (as in the Mid Staffordshire NHS Trust—the subject of the Francis report; Francis, 2013) the effects can be devastating. This is a concern and risk for all managers and organizations, particularly in the absence of adequate opportunities to think and reflect.

The impact of anxiety on how people work was illustrated in an important study investigating reasons for the high dropout rate of nurses in a London hospital (Menzies, 1959). She showed how nursing practice was unconsciously organized around avoiding the distressing and unbearable feelings aroused by the nature of the nursing task. For example, at the time of the study, the significance of the nurse–patient relationship was purposefully minimized by routine practices that restricted opportunities for any meaningful engagement with patients. Through this, nurses were "protected" from the intimacy of the nursing task and the suffering of patients. Avoiding these feelings may have provided temporary relief, but ultimately it undermined the emotional dimension to the work, resulting in the young nurses deriving little satisfaction from their role and diminishing the quality of patient care. Menzies Lyth (1988) points to the importance of understanding the nature of the anxiety associated with the task of an organization and identifies the centrality of organizational defences in how tasks are managed, in order to protect individuals from the anxiety of the task.

How to recognize the unconscious at work and what to do about it

There are times when we all can find ourselves behaving in ways that are governed primarily by the unconscious, irrational parts of our minds rather than by a reality-based, thinking mind. How can we recognize this, and what can we do about it? (See Table 4.1.)

The primary task

Miller and Rice's work described above drew attention to the significance of role and task in the survival of an organization. The primary task of an organization is what it needs to achieve in order to thrive—attained by means of a set of roles and responsibilities. Lawrence and Robinson (1975), described in Miller (1993), showed that this primary task can be elaborated into three component parts: the normative task (the formally defined task: "*what we believe we do*"), the existential task (the meaning or interpretation which the members attribute to their roles: "*what we say we do*") and the phenomenal task (the task that can be inferred from people's behaviour and of which they may not be consciously aware: "*what we actually do*"). To illustrate this idea, we can think of a college that has as its explicit purpose (normative task) to provide vocational programmes of high quality to students aged 18 or over. Its existential task may be

Table 4.1.   **Recognizing and responding to 'the unconscious at work'**[2]

What to look out for	*What to consider*
» Finding yourself without the authority that would be expected from your role. » Unexpectedly finding yourself saying or doing something inappropriate or exaggerated. » Unexpectedly finding yourself feeling angry or distressed. » You, or those around you, exhibit an inappropriate dependence, e.g. a failure to take responsibility, tribalism or victim behaviour. » Unrealistic optimism or pessimism. » A culture of blaming others, whinging or complaining. » Over-emotional responses that distract from the task in hand.	When such experiences feature in your working life, it is always worthwhile to stop and take time to reflect on what might be going on at a deeper level. The chances are you are experiencing the impact of unconscious feelings—your own or others'—that are too difficult to keep in conscious awareness and manage openly. Thinking things through with a trusted colleague or manager is a good starting point, but sometimes it can feel easier to turn to an external person such as a coach or mentor. You might reflect on what prompted your feelings or behaviour: is that a usual response for you, or did it come out of the blue? Did it remind you of other situations, perhaps in the past or in a non-work setting? Try to identify what particular meaning the issue has for you. It can also be valuable to think about others. Could you be experiencing feelings that have been projected into you? If you are feeling helpless, sad, incompetent, might these be the projections from colleagues who are finding those feelings unbearable and communicating them by making you feel them? If so, what support might they need from you? Do you tend to be the one who picks up on certain feelings? What is going on for you in the wider context? Are you trying to manage impossible tasks without being able to admit that they are impossible?

to address youth unemployment and make courses available to disadvantaged young people by enthusiastic teaching staff making links with the local community. As a phenomenal primary task, however, it may be that the enthusiastic staff, by going out to the community, are serving a different purpose—one of keeping despair and depression at bay by working together on challenging threats for survival at the expense of direct teaching. In other words, the phenomenal primary task may involve activity that is inadvertently inhibiting or undermining the formal task. The survival and growth of an enterprise requires the three levels of the primary tasks to be in alignment.

Organization in the mind

David Armstrong has written about the significance of emotions in organizations and organizational life. He states: "Every organisation is an emotional place … because it is a human invention, serving human purposes and depends on human beings to function" (Armstrong, 2004, p. 91). People, as we know, are emotional beings and bring with them the range of human feeling: love, hate, fear, anger, pride, shame, guilt, envy, gratitude, and so on. That emotions shape our experience of organizational life and influence its course is indubitable and has passed into widespread awareness with the development of the idea of "emotional intelligence" (Goleman, 1996). There is now a consensus that leaders need to be aware of how emotions influence, or indeed disturb, the way in which their organization functions. Armstrong, however, takes this further with a shift of focus and considers that emotion in organizations can tell us about the organization itself, not simply how it is working. Emotions, considered in this way, can pinpoint the psychic reality with which an organization is engaged. This shift of focus is from a consideration of the emotional life *in* the organization to that of the emotional life *of* the organization. Armstrong developed this through the idea of "organization-in-the-mind", which was first noted by Turquet (1974). Organization-in-the-mind refers to the psychological construct of the organization that has been "taken on board, is registered with, or has otherwise taken root in an individual in an organisation" (Armstrong, 2005, p. 5). It refers to the psychological meaning of the organization (and its people) to the individual. It is related to the primary task of the organization: for example, the organization-in-the-mind of a hospital is likely to be linked to an emotional experience that includes anxiety associated with vulnerability and fear of death, while that of an investment bank may include fear, greed, and excitement connected to gambling for high stakes. It is, however, a personal construct that also takes account of the meaning that individuals may derive from their work experience. In an education setting the organization-in-the-mind of an individual teacher or leader would include a sense of the meaning that education has for them. So, a headteacher whose personal history has included a sense of failure will relate in a differently to their role at an emotional level from a headteacher who has experienced success throughout life. What is important is that this internalized perspective may not be within conscious awareness, yet may influence how the head or senior leader takes up their role and behaves towards their colleagues. Opportunities to think about themselves in role in coaching, work discussion groups, or consultation can help school leaders to understand their own organization-in-the-mind and how this may be influencing the way in which they work.

Authority and power

For school leaders, having authority in one's role is essential to being able to act effectively and with influence. Often lines of authority are not clear or individuals who are authorized to take up a position find themselves stymied or constrained. This may be particularly so in the new context of executive headships and Multi-Academy Trusts. From where does authority originate and what are its parameters? According to Obholzer (1994), authority refers to "the right to make an ultimate decision", which may, of course, be binding on other people. When individuals are appointed to a leadership role, they are given authority to take up that role by the body that authorized their appointment, which will typically sit in a position of governance and will retain the right to remove the individual from their post if their conduct or progress is deemed unsatisfactory. If the appointment was the result of a fair and open process, then authority is enhanced. In other words, authority comes *by virtue of being chosen for the role*. Obholzer terms this "authority from above".

Authority from above is necessary but not sufficient on its own. It will not be possible to work effectively if the leadership is not endorsed and supported by those over whom the leader has authority: "authority from below". This refers to followership—cooperation, acceptance, and willingness to sanction the leader in role. In simple terms, accepting a role in a school implies acceptance of the given authority structure. It is a condition of employment, and it will generally be outlined in a job description and it will be stated to whom a staff member will report. Of course, there are degrees of followership and acceptance, and there may be ambivalence about—and resistance to—the leadership, which may be enacted consciously and unconsciously through varying degrees of cooperation. The leader has to manage this effectively. How they do so will depend on how well they are able to draw upon their own "internal authority".

How well a leader is able to access their own authority and what sort of authority they bring is, in large measure, to do with their own internalized experiences of authority. Obholzer named this "authority from within" and describes it as the "authority-in-the-mind" of the leader. A leader who is authorized from above and has this sanctioned from below might still not be able to function as a leader if they don't have a sufficient degree of internal authorization. This internal authorization may have its origins in early relationships with authority figures, such as parents and teachers. It can, of course, vary in nature, which will determine the way in which the leader takes up authority and contributes to their leadership style, varying from a dictatorial attitude through to a *laissez-faire* approach.

It sometimes happens in situations of sudden change that individuals may find themselves in positions of authority without the requisite authority from above or below—for example, when acting up into a more senior role in the sudden absence of a leader. This can raise feelings of anxiety and rivalry and so care should be given to establishing clarity, agreement, and sanction for the role, when temporary positions are being negotiated.

EXAMPLE

Nina was a popular head of courses for 16–18-year olds in a Further Education (FE) college. She described herself as "burned out and overwhelmed by the task". She often worked late into the night and found it hard to draw a line between her work life and her home life. She described herself as having a "single-parent" approach to her role. In her coaching sessions, she had an opportunity to explore her own experiences of authority. Nina characterised her parents' attitude as "stand on your own feet, don't expect help, if you're going to get anywhere, it will be by your own hard work". This had stayed with her as an internal feeling that she had to be self-reliant and that she shouldn't trust others to take on responsibilities. Difficulties arose when her college was required to merge with another provider, and teaching staff from a long-established college had to transfer to Nina's site. This change was contested, and there was protest locally. The transferred staff did not cooperate and withheld their "authority from below". Nina demonstrated a high degree of personal authority, which she managed well. However, her tendency was to rely on her personal authority and not to look for support "from above". Her senior manager viewed her as competent and tended to leave her to get on with the task; consequently, her relationship with "authority above" was under-developed. She occupied an isolated position and felt overburdened and without support.

While authority is an attribute of the organization and its roles, power is an attribute of the individual. Power refers to the "ability to act on others or on organizational structures" (Obholzer, 1994, p. 42) and may arise from external or internal sources. External sources of power are what the individual has control over—for example, pay, progression, privileges, etc., as well as political and social influence. Internal power derives from one's skills, knowledge, experience, and personal attributes, which influence the degree of personal authority an individual may bring to their role. There is a third source of power, and that is projected power—where followers may unconsciously "give up" their own power and project this into the leader, amplifying the power differential and risking a culture of dependency.

As Obholzer points out, the way in which leadership roles are described may indicate the relative contribution of power and authority and influences how potent a leader can be in role. For example, "director" or "manager" suggests a balance of the two, while "dictator" suggests power without authority, and "coordinator" suggests authority without power. "Locum" or "supply" would seem to indicate that the authority in the role is limited. This matters, because it influences how people behave towards the individual in role and the degree to which authority is conferred.

Group dynamics

Within the field of education, working in groups with students and with colleagues is a feature of everyday life. Group work can be positive and creative when contributions from all participants result in the whole being greater than the sum of the parts. Groups can also be difficult places that can feel irrational, frustrating, and anxiety-provoking. Many people will have had the experience of being in a group and being either overwhelmed or somehow constrained, not able to say what they had intended or coming out with something unexpected. We may not acknowledge this (nor even be aware of it), but we are inclined to act defensively as a way of managing that anxiety.

There are certain features of a group that contribute this:

» *Inclusion/exclusion*: one can feel both inside and a part of the group and at other times an outsider and apart from the group. Associated with inclusion is the idea of an "in-group", perhaps a clique that holds certain privileges and can arouse feelings of envy. Associated with exclusion is the idea of an "outsider" and rejection from the group. Individuals may feel more comfortable with one position or the other. A common example of group exclusion in schools can be seen in the way that assistant heads might perceive and experience the relationship between the head and their deputies as an inner sanctum from which they are excluded.

» *A group's capacity to embrace or manage difference and conflict.* Can members occupy different positions or hold contrary or contested points of view? In some groups, difference is not well tolerated. For example, in a school with a strong culture of tradition and conformity, dress, behaviour, background, and attitudes are important to established members of staff. Deviating from this group norm may result in an increased risk of exclusion ("he/she is not one of us"). By this process a gang state of mind and corresponding behaviour can develop (Canham, 2002). For creativity and innovation to flourish, differences need to be embraced and celebrated, yet the intensity of feelings that these differences can provoke often prevents this from happening.

» *Relationships in groups are complex.* Similar views held by different members of the group may be received differently depending on who is expressing them. This can be difficult for new members of a group who have not yet established their credibility, or those who feel less secure in their own position. Some leaders acquire a reputation for being unwilling to sanction ideas unless they are persuaded to feel that they are their own.

» *Development of trust.* Groups require us to be up close with other people, to make contact, and to expose something of ourselves, and our vulnerabilities. There are common worries about joining a group—will I have something valuable to contribute? How much should I reveal? Will my ideas be welcomed or rejected? In order for ideas to develop and creativity and innovation to flourish, the environment of the school needs to feel safe enough for teachers to take risks. Responsibility for this is often underrated and unacknowledged. Leaders can help develop trust by establishing reliable boundaries for the staff group, by paying attention to the roles people are given and/or by taking up and valuing contributions made by staff members, however different they may be. In this way competitiveness can be acknowledged and worked with constructively instead of becoming a derailing force.

Of course, we do not go into every new group situation with all of these thoughts uppermost in our minds, but such emotions are likely to be present in all groups. When we can't manage these feelings consciously and in real time, unconscious group dynamics will be more likely to dominate.

Basic assumption mentality

Wilfred Bion (1961) described two states of mind that groups can inhabit: "work group mentality" and "basic assumption mentality". Work group mentality is where the group is able to manage the task in hand and engage with reality unconstrained by defensive behaviour. We aspire to this, and frequently we achieve it. From time to time, however, particularly when there are unprocessed anxieties underlying a work situation that are being avoided, we function in what Bion called "basic assumption mentality".

Basic assumption mentality refers to a state of mind where a group is unconsciously preoccupied with difficult feelings, primarily as a means to evade underlying anxiety. Bion himself (1961) described three different types of basic assumptions, each of which is associated with different emotions and behaviours. He referred to these as "dependency", "pairing" and "fight–flight". To the three basic assumptions described by Bion, two more have since been added: basic assumption "oneness" (Turquet, 1975) and basic assumption "me-ness" (Lawrence, Bain, & Gould, 1996). A solid understanding of these basic assumptions is central to understanding why groups and teams at work fail to manage themselves effectively or to achieve their objectives.

Basic assumption dependency (baD)

In basic assumption dependency members rely on the leader of the group (who may or may not be the designated leader) to such an extent that they may act as if they have no ideas of their own, deny their capabilities, and fail to take initiatives. It is as though the group has lost the capacity to think and surrenders its own authority. Leaders will be familiar with "dependent" behaviour, which typically includes people asking for information they already have, unnecessarily looking to the leader for support, and avoiding responsibility for the task. Extreme dependency prevents development. Such groups do not manage their agendas or engage in decision-making. This behaviour spares members the experience of confronting their abilities or responsibilities when they are perhaps feeling disabled or without capacity. Rigid hierarchical structures can give rise to ba dependency and is a risk in organizations where a degree of dependency is normally present—as in education. (See Table 4.2.)

Basic assumption pairing (baP)

Basic assumption pairing mobilizes an unconscious wish to bring two people together, or perhaps for a group member (who may or may not be the leader) to join with an external individual to "save" the group. What is typical of this type of group dynamic is that the membership is preoccupied with the future and the hope that an ideal, almost messianic solution will arrive, thus avoiding attention on the present or the task

Table 4.2.   Recognizing and responding to basic assumption dependency

What to look out for	What to consider
Group members act as if they have no ideas of their own.	Encourage and invite all group members to take and offer ideas.
Members ask for information they already have.	Resist being seduced by the invitation to be the fount of all knowledge.
Members ask for guidance about how to do the task, denying their own capabilities.	Acknowledge the difficulties in taking responsibility but encourage people to rise to the challenge.
Difficult decisions are avoided or postponed.	Resist the pressure to do or answer for others when they have the capacity to do it for themselves.
There seems to be no initiative for action other than a reliance on the "leader of the group.	Acknowledge the difficulties in being a leader or being led. Suggest distributed leadership roles.

in hand. Typically, decisions are not made, and members are left with a sense of dissatisfaction and time wasted. There may be statements about new ideas or possibilities, but nothing actually happens. A staff team in baP might discuss planned curriculum changes but be unable to make decisions until some future date, after which an imagined crucial requirement is in place, such as new staff appointed, new equipment available, but without the application to make such things happen. (See Table 4.3.)

Table 4.3.   Recognizing and responding to basic assumption pairing

What to look out for	What to consider
Group members express the hope that someone (or something) will help them "get going" on the task.	Seek to involve all group members in discussing ideas.
There are lots of statements about new approaches or ideas being possible, but nothing happens.	Acknowledge that too much talk about what "could" happen might be a signal that what is happening is not being discussed.
Trainers/leaders are given unrealistic powers or knowledge.	Suggest individuals might lead on specific aspects of the task.
Decisions are not taken, agendas not completed.	Ask group members how their ideas could be acted upon.
The group is passively observing two people conducting an apparently lively discussion.	Ask how others may be involved in this topic/task.

Basic assumption fight–flight (baF)

Fight–flight mentality emerges as an unconscious attempt by a group and its members to avoid engaging with a difficult task or situation. In fight mode the group may be characterized by hostility or aggression, and there may be talk of challenge and confrontation. In flight mode members may cancel meetings or arrive late, engage in irrelevant conversation, and generally avoid addressing the task in hand. For example, a senior leadership group tasked with implementing budget cuts may become sidetracked by the felt injustice of this and preoccupied with how to protest. This behaviour serves to unify the group, protecting it from the pain of engaging with the task and the apprehension that the implementation of the cuts will result in division and conflict between them. (See Table 4.4.)

Basic assumption oneness (baO)

In a basic assumption oneness type of group **(Turquet, 1975)**, members behave in an undifferentiated fashion. Agreement is high, and individual differences of perspective cannot be tolerated, resulting in an impression of unanimity. This is akin to the concept of group-think (Janis, 1972). As a case study to illustrate this idea, Janis used the decision-making by the US administration that lead to the invasion of the Bay of Pigs in 1961. The Kennedy government had accepted uncritically the CIA proposals for invasion, and while some members of the team had initially raised

Table 4.4.   Recognizing and responding to basic assumption fight–flight

What to look out for	What to consider
Group members blame external factors (managers, lack of time, no money) for all that feels wrong/uncomfortable. Group members talk of confronting others Group members talk of giving up Groups become distracted by peripheral tasks to avoid more contentious or anxiety-provoking issues	Acknowledge that by focusing on external factors the group is avoiding some of the angry and fearful feelings within the group. Remind members that the task is "in here" not "out there". Encourage the group to express and value different points of view. Suggest constructive roles related to the task, and find strategies to provide focus on the task in hand. Explore what might be being avoided and why, and how it might be addressed more safely.

Table 4.5.   Recognizing and responding to basic assumption oneness

What to look out for	*What to consider*
There is no expressed disagreement, even though individually there may be dissent.	Acknowledge that difference may be difficult to work with but is important to understand and value.
The group has difficulty in identifying exactly what the consensus is.	Work to create an environment in which differences can be tolerated and the fear of difference can be understood. Individually ask for opinions.

objections, they then censored themselves in order to preserve a consensus. Clearly the stakes were very high, and the anxiety about being an "outlier" had to be minimized by becoming part of the group. Similarly, in staff group settings, this behaviour is not uncommon and seems to represent a fear of differences. BaO suggests that the group is avoiding any competition, conflict, or feelings of rivalry or envy that may be present. The discomfort of feeling outside the group—for example by having something unique to offer—disrupts the capacity for rational thought. (See Table 4.5.)

Basic assumption "me-ness" (baM)

In basic assumption "me-ness" **(Lawrence, Bain, & Gould, 1996)**, members of a group retain an individual perspective at the expense of any desire to understand or to take into account the position of others. There is resistance to participation in a collective enterprise, as if the act of joining with others may result in something that can't be managed. The prospect of belonging to the group is experienced as persecutory, so members retreat to their individual perspectives and silos to avoid the feelings that are aroused by coming together. At an unconscious level, this may be a fear of exposure, change, or development. Anyone who has tried to assemble a team to work on a challenging change or integration project, for example, is likely to have experienced a group that, in practical terms, is difficult to get together and seems emotionally resistant to collaborating as a team. (See Table 4.6.)

Sophisticated use of basic assumptions

It will be clear from the descriptions above that basic assumption behaviour in groups is fairly commonplace and is not indicative of a derailment. Groups can and do ordinarily move in and out of basic

Table 4.6. **Recognizing and responding to basic assumption me-ness**

What to look out for	What to consider
There is no consensus and members don't seem interested or inclined to pursue one.	Acknowledge that collaboration might be difficult but is essential for the effectiveness of the team as a whole.
There is a difficulty in staying on task, agendas may be ignored.	Individuals work in pairs or smaller groups with the task of understanding the perspective of the other.

assumption functioning all the time and recover sufficiently well to stay on task.

At times, basic assumption functioning can also be useful when mobilized in the service of the task. An army, for example, relies on a certain amount of fight–flight activity to keep its soldiers alert and ready to go into battle. In education, a healthy degree of basic assumption dependency can facilitate students to take up the role of learner. Bion called this the "sophisticated use of basic assumptions."

In being aware of these group processes, leaders can respond helpfully and steer the group, team, or class back towards more effective work group functioning.

Valency

Individuals in groups may display a propensity to be pulled into particular patterns of behaviour: for example, "the one who always puts a spanner in the works" … "the one who tries to keep the peace". Bion (1961) described this susceptibility to being pulled in to a particular way of behaving as "valency". It is a powerful determinant of how we take up familiar roles in groups.

Work group mentality

Bion intended the terms basic assumption and work groups to refer to states of mind that are in a dynamic relationship with each other. In work groups—in contrast to basic assumption functioning—reality is engaged with, and the group is able to focus effectively on its primary task, unconstrained by defensive behaviour. There is a capacity for conscious thought and unconscious working towards the task in the group, even in the presence of strong emotions.

It is clearly important to strengthen the capacity for groups and teams to become well-functioning work groups. This is more likely to be achieved when opportunities are created to attend to the emotional undertow that can disrupt rational thinking. Support for management teams and leadership groups might take the form of establishing some regular reflective space so as not to be hijacked by a basic assumption mentality.

Containing anxiety in organizations

Containment in a systems psychodynamic framework is an active concept. In the context of school leadership, it refers to the capacity on the part of the leader to grasp the emotional state of the group or organization and those within it and to work with this effectively. This means establishing conditions that facilitate a developing awareness in staff of the emotions at play and helping them to manage this in an environment that feels safe. This may be as "straightforward" as establishing reliable boundaries around staff meetings, building expectations of how people behave, and, importantly, creating opportunities for reflection and reflexivity. In making this distinction, I am referring to opportunities for helping staff to reflect on what they bring to their roles and how they are working, as well as opportunities to learn from the reflective process to explore new ways of working and taking up their role.

In order for schools to be able to harness the creativity of their staff, leaders need to provide a context in which there can be meaningful risk-taking and innovation. This requires the generation of a sense of emotional security in the staff group, in a similar way to the development of a confident sense of self that a child acquires from a secure attachment to a parent. This is a challenge in the context of today's education system that does not offer a great deal that is consistent and stable. Drawing on a systems psychodynamic perspective can help leaders in schools and colleges to understand the state of mind of their organization and the people in it. Making time to reflect on how people are working together from day to day can allow leaders to understand the anxieties at play. Leaders themselves need to be aware of their own "organization-in-the-mind" and, with this, their own emotional responses to their work and their staff. Coaching for individual leaders can greatly assist in this process by offering opportunities to reflect, take risks, work authentically, and hone their emotional intelligence for the benefit of the whole organization. Coaching for leadership teams can similarly offer a mirror to the team, enabling them to notice what might be going on below the surface and impeding their effective functioning. We know that high-performing teams are those that pay attention to how they are functioning as well as what they achieve.

Educational leadership in today's turbulent climate is a very challenging task. Leaders have to manage complexity, change, and uncertainty on behalf of their organizations and themselves. Those who are able to be attuned to the emotional data in the workplace and harness it as a source of strength and development will be most successful in enabling their staff and teams to work and be at their creative best.

Note

1 For a comprehensive account of the development of personality, see Margot Waddell's book *Inside Lives* (2002).
2 The phrase 'the unconscious at work' was coined by Jon Stokes, reflected in the title of the book edited by Obholzer and Roberts (1994).

PART II

SCHOOL LEADERSHIP DEVELOPMENT

Psychodynamic approaches

Executive coaching for the hidden realities of life as a school leader

Emil Jackson & Andrea Berkeley

All good teachers know that the quality of the teacher–student or teacher–class relationship lies at the heart of effective learning. The combination of an outstanding teacher together with an academically gifted group of students should guarantee outstanding progress and results. However, when class group dynamics or interpersonal relationships with the teacher are problematic, the learning potential of all concerned is quickly compromised. It is striking, therefore, that within initial teacher training and subsequent professional development, the emotional and relational factors in teaching and learning remain so neglected.[1]

These same principles hold true for leadership. Effective leadership is predicated on the effective management of relationships. One can establish a clear vision, rigorous policies, and precisely delegated areas of responsibility, but these will only come to fruition if the matrix of relationships which underpin the organization ensures that the whole becomes greater than the sum of its parts.

Effective leaders need little convincing about the profoundly psychological nature of the workplace when considering how best to optimize staff performance and morale. Nevertheless, even the most sophisticated of leaders still tend to underestimate the essential—but largely hidden—function they serve in containing and channelling the many disturbing and unconscious emotions alive in their organizations. These include anxieties, rivalries, insecurities, hurt, shame, hope, excitement, despair, and disappointment—all of which are inherent in organizational life but can wreak havoc in interpersonal and team dynamics when neglected. Being on the frontline of this maelstrom of emotions inevitably has an impact—whatever the context or organization.

In the current political and economic climate, there are few schools or school leaders who are not operating within an environment of relentlessly high pressure in which the "urgent" can easily triumph over the "important". It is increasingly common for school leaders to feel besieged by the relentless pace of school life and the endless demands on their time and energy. Under the umbrella of the headteacher's responsibilities, for example, lies the education and wellbeing of students, parental engagement, and the support and development of all staff. Further pressures in relation to recruitment and retention, budget cuts, and Ofsted demands to adhere to ever-changing frameworks can leave school leaders feeling increasingly pessimistic about the viability of their role.

However, while school leaders frequently feel overwhelmed by the *quantity* of work to be addressed, it is *the quality of the emotional and psychological demands* of their role—how they feel and how they are made to feel in their role—that invariably takes the heaviest toll. It is this—exacerbated by their felt sense of isolation—that can sometimes render it almost impossible for leaders to hold onto their own thoughts, remain in their own skin, and resist the urge to react impulsively. Even those leaders with the most firmly held set of values can be shocked at the speed at which they, too, can be driven to doubt their credibility and to behave in ways that directly contravene their personal code of conduct.

In view of the above, this chapter aims to describe some significant ways in which school leaders—in particular headteachers—can be supported through the provision of one-to-one coaching sessions. Through describing a range of commonly encountered scenarios, we hope to illustrate the importance of offering leaders protected thinking time, space, and support away from the front line of school life. We further hope to demonstrate the potential for coaching to enable school leaders to develop the emotional literacy and resilience to withstand, understand, and make effective use of the emotional and psychological dynamics that continually reverberate in schools. Finally, we consider the importance of coaching and other forms of leadership support as a *basic duty of care* rather than an individual indulgence—especially in the context of national concerns regarding headteacher wellbeing, recruitment and retention.

Approaches to coaching

There are a number of different models, approaches, and theoretical frameworks commonly adopted in relation to executive coaching (e.g. systems-psychodynamic coaching, cognitive behavioural coaching, GROW, etc.). This chapter does not aim to give an overview of these different approaches. Nor does it seek to compare the relative merits of each approach in relation to the others. Nevertheless, while we do not want to categorize our approach to coaching in a way that is too rigidly prescribed, it is important to clarify that our coaching mindset is underpinned by a combination of psychodynamic, systemic, and group dynamics thinking. Put simply, this means we take an active interest in what might be going on at the deepest levels, beneath the surface, within and between people, teams, organizations, and systems—both consciously and unconsciously. As well as paying close attention to what is said—and how it is said—we also take an interest in how issues that are brought to coaching might themselves manifest dynamically, in the here and now of the coaching relationship—between coach and school leader.[2]

The coaching work described in this chapter aims primarily to offer a reflective, developmental, and supportive space for school leaders to share, explore, and make sense of any issues, dilemmas, concerns, anxieties, or challenges preoccupying them in their leadership role. While strategies are frequently a by-product of effective coaching, these are not our *primary* objective, as they may be with more "solution-focused" mentoring. Rather, our belief is that the most effective solutions are more likely to emerge organically once the underlying roots of an issue—including our reactions to it—have been more fully understood.

Structure and frequency of coaching sessions

School leaders will naturally differ in relation to their development needs and how these needs would best be met. While some leaders may have an almost allergic reaction to the prospect of coaching, others may consider it a lifeline without which they would struggle to remain afloat, especially given the innately isolated nature of their role. In view of these differences, we do not believe it is helpful to prescribe what should be offered to whom. Rather, from our experience, we would want to recommend that a basic allowance for coaching sessions is secured for headteachers at approximately half-termly intervals (or 6–9 sessions per year of 1.5–2 hours each). If such an allowance for coaching can be agreed in principle, this could then be taken up on an ad hoc or more regular basis, as appropriate and as determined by individual head-teachers, with the support of their chair of governors (CoG).

Range of issues brought to coaching

A wide range of issues and dilemmas are regularly brought to coaching sessions by school leaders—from the most macro, systemic and strategic level to the most micro and operational level. Different leaders will naturally feel preoccupied by different issues—and even different aspects of the same issues—depending on their experience, personality, and the existing support available to them.

The centrality of relationships

Given that school life is underpinned by relationships that are inherently complex and multifaceted—operating at both conscious and unconscious levels—it is not surprising that the challenges encountered in relationships are a central preoccupation for school leaders. Some, for example, may have a flair for managing relationships with external stakeholders and for giving uplifting "state of the nation" speeches to their staff group but may feel awkward in more intimate one-to-one meetings. Others, in contrast, may be highly skilled in their management of individual staff members and in leading their senior team, but may lack confidence in their capacity to be directive or to lead the more strategic dimensions of their role.

Managing difficult conversations

However reflective or articulate the leader may be, most value the opportunity to be helped to think through the many permutations of difficult discussions that confront them on a daily basis. Typically, these involve discussions with an underperforming or aggrieved staff member, a complaining parent or parent group, or the chair of governors or governing body. Alternatively, they might involve a situation in which the school leader's authority or decision-making is being interrogated, for example by an exclusions' appeal panel.

School leaders know that discussions such as these need to be approached with appropriate consideration, caution, and respect, especially when personal sensitivities (including their own) can quickly result in a negative spiral of misunderstanding. As a result, they often appreciate help to clarify and put into words the thoughts, feelings, and fears that are being activated in themselves and in others, so as to manage the ensuing discussion as constructively and objectively as possible. Even in situations when potentially distressing messages do need to be given—and cannot be avoided—leaders can still feel tremendously relieved when they are helped to find potent ways to deliver these through their *heart* rather than through their *might*. In other words, when they are helped to give necessary feedback in a way that is underpinned by a more compassionate intent to support the other person—without either pulling their punches or reacting impulsively to push back or put down.

Help in assessing the roots of a problem

In the rush of school life, the pressure to "do" can corrode the ability to "be", and as a result people can quickly become detached from what is going on inside themselves and others. Leaders might, for example, arrive at a coaching session with some awareness that they are feeling agitated but unsure why or what it is about. They might be able to articulate that someone or something has "got under their skin", but they may be quite unaware of the extent to which this is impacting on them, draining their energy and disrupting their internal emotional equilibrium. Even the most considerate of leaders can become consumed by their own agenda in a way that renders them effectively deaf to the anxieties or preoccupations of others.

Given the multiple demands on school leaders on any given day, it is essential that they use their time and energy wisely. Too often, for example, leaders only discover retrospectively that they have spent a huge amount of time and resources addressing the "wrong" problem. To avoid this, leaders need an ability to release themselves from the grip of their subjective experience, to look beneath the surface manifestation of an issue and consider the wider context and dynamics at play. This includes space to consider what might be happening in the unconscious life of an organization.

Mary[3]

Mary, the experienced head of a relatively new Free School[4], brought to coaching her strained relationship with her chair of governors (CoG). The CoG was one of the founding parents of the school and had, historically, always been a great source of support. Recently however, the CoG had become more controlling and critical, including in the way he spoke to her at governors' meetings—something she found both confusing and hurtful. Mary had not yet found a way to talk to the CoG about this, partly out of fear that any attempt to broach the subject would exacerbate the tension and increase the risk of conflict. Mary added that, "Although it doesn't make sense rationally, sometimes the CoG's behaviour makes me feel like he wants me out!"

As we started to unpack and explore the situation, Mary conveyed how much the CoG had invested in the school. She told me that the CoG had been there from the school's inception—he had appointed Mary, and all three of his children attended the school. Emphatically, she added that the school was now full and had only recently been assessed by Ofsted as being "good with outstanding features". "Just when the CoG *should* be starting to relax, he is instead tightening the screws and making me feel I should be looking for another job!"

While first taking care to acknowledge the impact of these tensions on Mary, I also took an interest in what else might be going on in the organization—for instance by exploring the significance of the school being full for the first time, along with the outcome of the recent Ofsted inspection.[5] In response, Mary started to speak about the governing body—telling me that it has a high percentage of "founding parents" who have collectively invested hugely in the school. As she spoke, she conveyed a combination of deep appreciation together with some frustration. When I commented on this mixture of feelings, Mary agreed and told me how "The school has been our collective baby for the last six years ... we've been through a lot together". Reflecting on this, I acknowledged how hard it could be to trust anyone else with "your baby". I added that this made me wonder how anyone would ever be able to step down from their role on the governing body? Mary thought they would find this extremely difficult. "I can also identify with how they might feel", she said. "It is also hard for me to imagine anyone else doing the job after I have lived and breathed the school for so long". At the same time, Mary asserted her firm belief that "a critical part of my job is to ensure that the school can continue without me when the time is right".

As Mary described the situation, I became interested in the dynamics of the governing body. In particular, I became interested in whether the governing body might be struggling with underlying tensions resulting from the school's achievement and success rather than anything more ominous—tensions rooted in development, whether they be connected to growing pains or perhaps separation anxiety. When I articulated these thoughts, Mary responded with considerable passion—almost in an outburst—telling me that "the truth is ... I think the CoG has done his job—and done it really well—but the time has probably come for him to think about moving on now". She added, in a more conciliatory tone, that she thought "the CoG possibly even knows this himself".

Mary fell silent, seeming slightly stunned after she spoke—almost as if she needed time to digest the significance of what she was saying.

"I haven't said that to anyone before", she said. ". . . in fact, I didn't even know that's what I thought, until I said it out loud!" After a pause, Mary told me how "now I think about it—the tensions at the last governors' meetings intensified after one of the non-parent governors joked about how well things are going for the school, so maybe now is a good time for them to leave. His comment made people laugh at the time, but now I wonder whether it was more of a nervous laugh than a real laugh?"

By this stage in the coaching session, the focus of the Mary's attention had shifted significantly from how she (the head) was feeling to what might be going on for the CoG and the governing body more generally. The mood of our discussion had similarly shifted from one of confusion, agitation, and hurt to one of greater interest, concern, and sadness.

For the remainder of the coaching session Mary began to consider what a significant junction it would be for the whole school community when the CoG and other founding parents did decide to step down from their roles on the governing body. She realized that this had become a bit of an "elephant in the room" for the governing body. As she said this, Mary paused and looked subdued. I commented on this. Mary then continued: "... This discussion makes me feel a bit guilty ... it hadn't really occurred to me to think about what difficulties the CoG might be experiencing, or what support he might need from me as headteacher. We have worked really well together for over six years, but I wonder whether we are entering a new phase—not only in our relationship, but in the life of the school."

Although our discussion was far from finished, and while the hypotheses that had begun to be explored were yet to be tested, the head spoke of how the opportunity to explore and make some sense of what else might be going on, had "opened her eyes and left her feeling in a much more constructive state of mind". While she still did not know what, if anything, she needed to do, she realized that this was a much bigger issue than her relationship with the CoG, and that she should not misinterpret the situation as if the problem lay between them alone. She added that she found the idea of the school facing "problems of development" really helpful and thought that this might be something she could bring into governing body discussion, if and when appropriate.

Opportunities to consider personal and professional development

Few teachers start out with a pre-formed vision of being a future leader or headteacher. While some are naturally ambitious—gravitating towards roles with greater authority and responsibility—most start out as class teachers whose passion, personality, and skill gradually result in their progression up through the ranks towards more senior roles. Even in schools where "succession planning" is carefully considered, the focus tends to prioritize the current or future needs of the school over the career trajectories of the individual. The sense of care and duty that teachers themselves feel towards their students means that they may be all the more likely to further de-prioritize their own progression. For example, it would not be uncommon for a committed head of year to put off considering any new roles until they had "seen their students through to the end of Year 11'. As a result, it is often the sudden or unexpected departure of a senior leader that results in teachers having "opportunities" for leadership development and progression thrust upon them. And even then, some of the most talented teachers frequently assert that it had never consciously occurred to them that they were—or would be seen as—"*credible* leadership material".

In view of the above, school leaders highly value the opportunity afforded to them in coaching sessions to consider aspects of their own personal and professional development and longer-term thinking, within the wider context of school development, but outside a more formal appraisal structure.

Rebecca

In a first coaching session, arranged as part of a new senior team development programme, a deputy head, Rebecca, came in, sat down, and promptly burst into tears before she had even finished introducing herself. Rebecca was somewhat bewildered by her own response, quickly assuring me that she was "absolutely fine" and telling me that she had no idea that she was even feeling upset before she came into the room. Once she caught her breath and calmed, Rebecca began to tell me how she had recently been contacted by another school to encourage her to apply for their newly advertised headship. She continued to tell me how she had worked as senior deputy to her current headteacher for over six years. Rebecca conveyed her respect for and loyalty towards her head, together with her belief that they made an excellent team. She said she was not naturally ambitious and had never thought beyond working for him but acknowledged that the opportunity to apply for this role had been "screaming to be heard" since she first found out about it. Rebecca was almost apologetic in her need to justify why she thought this role might be an excellent "fit" for her, emphasizing that if she was ever going to apply for a headship "this would be it". She became tearful again as she returned to her attachment to her current head and the sadness and guilt she felt at the prospect of leaving the school. Rebecca said she supposed she always knew this day would come but "she hadn't ever wanted to think about it".

Rebecca's experience of unearthing this "unthought known" (Bollas, 1987) is not uncommon within coaching sessions, as leaders give themselves—often for the first time—opportunities to listen more carefully to what is going on inside themselves, with the help of an outside professional. However, even then, it is not uncommon for personal ambitions, desires, and anxieties to present themselves in only the most subtle, unconscious, or symbolic of ways—at least in the first instance. This can be seen in the following example.

John

John, a deputy head with whom I had a more established coaching relationship, began one session by reflecting on how many times we had discussed other people "moving on"—whether through promotion or as a result of performance management. He linked this back to the previous coaching session, in which we had explored how best to address concerns about one of his middle leaders. He told me how, as a result of our session, he had been able to have a more honest, robust, and constructive conversation with the middle leader. The following day the middle leader asked to meet with John. In their meeting, she expressed her appreciation for their discussion and said it had helped her make the "bold decision to resign and move on". Although John was sorry to lose the middle leader and was concerned about who would pick up her responsibilities, he believed the middle leader had made the right decision for her. She was "at risk of stagnating" and needed a change of role, which the school was not in a position to offer. He also hoped the gap might create new developmental opportunities for other staff.

John then went on to talk about a different member of the senior leadership team, who had also recently resigned to take up a post in another school after a prolonged period of discontent. John did not directly manage this person but said he had originally encouraged him to apply for the role, because he believed "he would be great *for the school*". In a more regretful tone, he added that he didn't think he had ever stopped to consider whether the role would be "right" for his colleague. "Retrospectively, I'm not sure I ever gave my colleague's needs much thought ... now he has spent eight years of his life in a job that wasn't great for him."

Within a coaching session, there are always different lenses through which material such as this can be considered. At a surface level,

John was updating me about our previous discussion and sharing his thoughts about some significant developments with colleagues. But, on a more unconscious level, I wondered whether John might be trying to make sense of something closer to home—through his two colleagues. Perhaps his thoughts about his middle leader's "good decision" to move on, and his guilt about his senior colleague's career trajectory, were pertinent in other ways? Perhaps it wasn't only *"other people"* moving on that he was telling me about.

I shared some of these thoughts with John and said that his preoccupation with the development of others made me wonder what thoughts he had about his own development. John responded to my comment with an expression of slightly frozen apprehension. I commented on his reaction, acknowledging how unsettling it might feel even to contemplate change. I then reminded him that coaching offered the opportunity to explore ideas and possibilities without any imperative to act on them. John sighed in relief, agreeing that he did need a "thinking space, which didn't require immediate action".

John then seemed to drift into his own thoughts. After a pause, he told me that he had never told anyone else … or perhaps he had never dared think about it himself … but sometimes he questioned whether teaching was the right profession for him. Conveying a combination of excitement and fear, he then began to tell me about his interest in property development, and how he sometimes played with the idea of leaving education and changing profession altogether. As if to reassure us both, he quickly emphasized that "he wasn't actually going to do this—*at least not now*—but he also didn't want to be too scared to think about it".[6]

As the session progressed and John's freedom to explore different possibilities increased, he spoke about how he realized that he had inadvertently imprisoned himself "in the box" and restricted his thinking. He connected this also to other important areas of his personal life and relationships, in which he often felt "too scared to take risks". Although John admitted that he felt somewhat unsettled by our discussion, he spoke of how helpful it was to begin to bring these different parts of himself together and not to treat them as if they were mutually exclusive.

Developing personal and professional authority in leadership roles

Sometimes it is the stories shared about a leader's personal life that offer the most precise insights into the challenges facing them in their working life—even though they might not yet be aware of this themselves. Often, these stories emerge as anecdotes near the start of a coaching session—almost in passing—leaving them at risk of being dismissed as part of "rapport building" as coach and leader establish contact. If, however, one respects a leader's unconscious knowledge of themselves—and works with an assumption that everything they share has potential relevance—it will naturally result in a different quality of interest in and attention to *all* that they bring to coaching. After all, it is invariably the defaults, dynamics, and triggers of our internal world that are most likely to accompany us and manifest wherever we go and to whomever we are relating.

David

David had been recently appointed to his first headship in a sixth form college that was now considered as "up and coming", though had struggled historically. He sought out coaching as he recognized he was struggling to establish himself with his senior team.

In the first three sessions, David spoke about the different challenges he was encountering at work. He focused, in particular, on tensions between himself and one of the college's long-standing and widely respected deputies, who had had to step down from his role as acting headteacher once David took up his post.

David arrived to the fourth coaching session apologizing that he might need to take a call from his builder. When I looked at him quizzically, he told me that he had just started building works, which had created tensions with his neighbours. David added that, although he didn't lack confidence, he hated conflict. He knew he needed to get better at addressing it, but his default response was always to avoid it.

David then acknowledged that the previous week he had managed it differently when "someone had blatantly jumped the queue and pushed in front of him at the cinema". At first, he was "going to acquiesce as he normally would have done because he didn't want to make a fuss, but then, unusually, he had let his irritation show and confronted the person directly". He chuckled as he described how he had managed to appear calm on the outside despite the anger and fear he felt on the inside. The headteacher said it was "just a silly example", but he was pleased, as he found it harder to be assertive in standing up for himself, despite being perfectly capable of doing so for others.

Initial updates such as these are not uncommon in coaching sessions but are too easily negated in terms of their significance, while one waits for the "real discussion" to begin. If, however, one adopts a more respectful interest in the unconscious and symbolic nature of communication, then this "chat" has the potential to offer a number of gateways into highly valuable and relevant coaching conversations. For example, might the tensions the head was experiencing with his neighbours also be a metaphor for the tensions he was experiencing as he began to "rebuild" a new senior leadership team? Similarly, might the head's experience at the cinema also be his way of communicating his need to develop greater confidence in advocating for himself, and to tolerate the anxiety that surges in him when he does so?

When I shared some of these possible connections, David responded with interest, telling me that "his default was to think of himself as being aggressive or dictatorial rather than assertive". He recognized that, as a result of this, he frequently overcompensated by accommodating others at his own expense (rather like being "pushed out of the queue"). He knew he needed to find his voice and authority with his team and that failing to do so would only be likely to fuel existing tensions, at both an interpersonal and team level.

Significantly, at this point David told me that he had "just remembered a weird dream I had last night". He said he never usually remembers his dreams, but last night he had dreamt he was attending a talk given by an ex-colleague of his—someone for whom he had great respect. David relayed how—in the dream—he had suddenly felt embarrassed when he arrived at the talk as he realized he was wearing a suit that didn't fit properly. It was much too small for him. He added that, "inside the conference hall, there were lots of people not listening to anything or anyone. It was chaotic".

There are always a number of ways one can approach and interpret the meaning of a dream, depending not only on the content of the dream but also on the context in which the dream is related. In this instance, it seemed no coincidence that David should suddenly remember such a dream just as we were exploring his tentative relationship to his own authority, in particular, with his Senior Leadership Team (SLT).

Without dwelling excessively on the dream itself, some brief exploration into his associations and its possible symbolism enabled David to express some deeper anxieties about his leadership. At one level, for example, David spoke of his fear that he would *"fall short* in relation to his predecessors—both the previous substantive head as well as the acting deputy". At another level, discussion about the dream also helped David to recognize tensions that might exist at a more unconscious and intra-psychic level—for instance between the part of him that has some belief in his capacity to take up his authority (represented in the dream by the colleague for whom he has respect) and another part of him, which continues to perceive and present himself in a somewhat diminished way—represented in the dream by his smaller-than-fitting suit. These perspectives resonated with David, who then made a connection between the chaos in the dream and the risk that a similarly chaotic atmosphere would develop in his SLT: "*if I don't pick up the reins of my leadership soon*".

For the remainder of the coaching session, David began to explore the range of discussions that might be helpful to have with his senior leadership team as a whole, as well as with some of the individuals in it. In particular, David reflected on how he needed to take a risk and have a more honest discussion with his deputy about the situation and how best they might work together.

David left this coaching session with a greater sense of clarity about the leadership task that lay ahead and a greater sense of confidence in his capacity to take this on. Metaphorically, he seemed somehow more substantial by the end of the session—as if he were now wearing a bigger and better fitting psychological suit.

In subsequent sessions, David's dream and its symbolism were revisited several times, acting as a catalyst for further insights. These included insights of a more systemic nature, when, for example, the David shared the difficulties he was encountering in raising the profile of the college despite their consistently improving results. As this was explored, David was able to recognize these difficulties both as a function of the way the college could be seen externally (by other colleges and prospective students) as well as the way it could be perceived internally (by his own staff). He likened this to being treated like a "small fish in a big pond".

Parameters of coaching

Although the focus of coaching is principally work-related—supporting the person in their leadership role in their organization—it is not uncommon for leaders to use some time and space in coaching to discuss issues of a more personal nature. There will naturally be a range of views about this among different leaders and organizations. Coaches, too, will have varying levels of comfort about their capacity to undertake work of a more personal nature, depending on their previous training and experience. Some, for example, will hold a firm conviction that coaching is "sponsored" (paid for) by the organization and coaching outcomes therefore need to be directly related to the leader's performance and related organizational goals. Others, including the authors of this chapter, take a broader view that incorporates the reality that—in order to be at their best—different leaders will need different types of support, at different points in their lives and careers. At times, for example, heads and other school leaders may be beset by challenges or crises in their personal lives which impact directly on their ability to conduct themselves effectively in their work and role, and for which they might need support.

While it is important not to confuse what belongs in leadership coaching as distinct from what belongs in psychotherapy or even occupational health, it is also unhelpful and unrealistic to think that there is no overlap between the personal and the professional and to draw too rigid a boundary line between what belongs where. In practice, for example, many leaders may be deterred from seeking professional help if it comes under the umbrella of "mental health". They might even find such a prospect terrifying in case it exacerbates their vulnerability or compromises their capacity to be effective in their role. Instead, at times like this, it is not uncommon for some leaders to feel that it is specifically their work role and identity that is helping to hold them together, reminding them of their competencies and resourcefulness and giving them hope about their sense of agency and potency, despite the adversity they are facing in their private lives. At times like this—notwithstanding the delicate consideration and judgement calls that need to be taken about what is or is not appropriate—supporting *the person at work* can enable leaders to manage themselves and their work role at a time when they might otherwise be at risk of collapse.

Containing anxiety and despair

Even without the trigger of a personal crisis, there are times when circumstances can conspire in such a way as to leave the most experienced leader feeling panicked, persecuted, and consumed with an impending sense of dread. A leader's felt sense of impotence is further exacerbated when they feel—or are made to feel—a disproportionate sense of personal responsibility for all consequences, even though the contributory factors and solutions may lie outside their control. The overwhelming nature of this burden may be inadvertently fuelled by the waves of emotion flooding in their direction from anxious parents, staff, and governors seeking the head's reassurance and containment. But sometimes the headteacher simply doesn't have the reassurance or containment to offer. Sometimes the reality is that the path ahead remains uncertain and void of any clear solution or guarantee.

At times like this, when a headteacher's world and school can feel like it is on the verge of fragmentation, coaching can offer an *essential space* for leaders to be helped to endure, manage, and contain their experience. But, even then, the contagious nature of anxiety and despair—like other highly charged emotions—may in turn be absorbed and internalized by others in close proximity—including the headteacher's coach. It may then be the headteacher's coach who, themselves, have first to do what they can to process, contain, and make sense of their own experience—albeit second-hand—as the necessary first step towards supporting the headteacher. In so doing, a cycle of containment may be established and the potential for an escalating and destabilizing cycle of projection and blame may be averted.

Sarah

Sarah, the experienced head of an Ofsted-rated "outstanding" single-entry primary school, arrived at her coaching session looking unusually panicked and dishevelled. Before sitting down, she had already launched into telling me what a bad state she was in; how her situation was "impossible", and how she didn't think her job was manageable. Without pausing, she went on to tell me how in the last week alone her only deputy suddenly had to go on leave due to a family crisis; her business manager had handed in his notice, having accepted a promotion in a Multi-Academy Trust; and her Year 6 teacher had been knocked off her bike and would be off work for at least a month. The head now had a growing list of anxious and angry Year 6 parents requesting meetings with her and demanding "answers" about who would now be teaching their children. On top of it all, the chair of governors had just left the country for a month-long sailing trip, and "Ofsted[7] could call anytime". Sarah told me that she had hardly slept for the past three nights. Tearing up as she spoke, she conveyed a sense of being close to breaking point.

As coach, it felt quite overwhelming just to hear what the head-teacher was saying and to receive her emotional state. At first, any attempts I made to acknowledge or think through the different crises she faced seemed only to agitate Sarah further. She immediately refuted anything I said, emphasizing the impossibility of her situation and the futility of my attempts to help her. At times, Sarah spoke to me with an almost angry edge to her tone, which, I noticed, started to produce feelings in me of helplessness and shame. It was as if I were now starting to feel responsible for my failure to solve her predicament. A sense of apprehension started to descend, as I felt increasingly out of my depth and doubtful about my efficacy; *Perhaps the head would be better off with a different coach who actually knew what he was doing?* The knot in my stomach tightened as I found it impossible to do or say anything useful. I glanced at my watch, inadvertently giving up on myself and our work, as I longed for the end of the session to release me from this experience.

At times like this, when we feel flooded and panicked by the situations we find ourselves in—whatever our role—our resilience and resourcefulness are further assaulted by the belief that "we *should not* be struggling" and that "other people would do better". As I tried to reflect on what was being communicated and how it was making me feel, I was struck by the significance of the impact the headteacher was having on me in relation to her own experience. I began to put words to some of my reflections—for example, commenting on the likelihood that anyone in such a situation would be feeling overwhelmed, full of self-doubt, and tempted by a belief that resignation would be the best next move. I was careful not to frame this as being the way that Sarah was feeling, but the way that *anyone*—whoever they were—might feel. Sarah managed a weary half-smile when I emphasized that this was, in fact, a rather "normal" response to an extremely stressful situation, adding that it would actually be rather strange for someone not to be worried about how on earth it was going to be resolved.

The process of putting some words to my experience helped me to restore my sense of agency. This enabled me to acknowledge the horrible reality that sometimes there were no immediate solutions while, at the same time, asserting that "*feeling* helpless" was not the same as "*being* helpless". After all, I warned, even when we can't make things better immediately, we can always make things worse! Sarah seemed interested in this, so I asked her how she might make things even worse for herself and the school—knowing herself as she does. The paradoxical nature of this question—engaging the head in considering how she might make an awful situation even worse—enabled Sarah to consider some of the areas over which she did still have some control. Sarah became more animated as she spoke about how grumpy and critical she had been with staff; how she was starting to react impulsively and unhelpfully with parents, and how she had been contemplating putting in a formal complaint about the lengthy and untimely absence of the CoG. Despite feeling slightly horrified by herself, Sarah began to speak with a renewed sense of motivation and some humour: "I definitely do not want to make matters worse!"

Towards the end of the coaching session, the atmosphere of utter despair eased slightly as we spoke about the importance of taking things one day at a time. At this point, inviting Sarah to focus in on her most immediate concern seemed to be helpful. It also enabled her to articulate her dread of having to face Year 6 parents whom—she had heard—had "started a WhatsApp group to complain about the school". In a defeated tone, she added that "... the worst thing about this is that I understand where they are coming from ... if I were a Year 6 parent, I would want to know what the school was doing; I would have lost confidence in the head; I would be feeling angry and anxious; I would be questioning whether it was time to jump ship and find another school."

The prospect of being confronted in person, and on line, by an irate parent gang is enough to haunt almost any school leader. However, having the opportunity to articulate her thoughts in this way gave us the opportunity to think more creatively about a range of possible approaches to such a meeting. For example, rather than either refusing to meet them or opening herself to a potentially destructive barrage of complaint, we considered how she might start the meeting less defensively—by proactively demonstrating her capacity to identify with the perspectives of parents and putting on the table, from the outset, all the questions, concerns, and criticisms she would have if she were in their shoes.

Sarah also found it helpful to imagine what she might say to parents if she trusted them enough to be honest with them and wasn't deterred by her vulnerability. She responded by telling me that: "the truth is … this is a real nightmare, and it isn't yet clear how things will be resolved, but I am totally confident that my staff will all do everything in their power to support our children and their learning while we work it out". Sarah spoke with instinctive conviction and authority. Feeling at least momentarily more hopeful, she then referred back to our earlier discussion about how people can always make matters worse. She said it made her think that as well as acknowledging the legitimate nature of the parents' concerns, she should also alert them to how easy it would be for them to make matters worse—for instance by behaving in a way that further aggravated the situation. In this vein, she could imagine encouraging parents to rise to the challenge of preserving as much stability and calm for their children as possible through this inevitably turbulent period.

As the coaching session drew to a close, Sarah spoke of feeling a bit like a "weight had been lifted off her shoulders". Even though she was still in the same situation, facing the same set of challenges, she didn't feel the same burden of shame, blame, and self-recrimination. And she felt less likely to make matters worse by acting impulsively. At the very least, she thought, she now had a few small but significant steps she could take to minimize further fallout while longer-term solutions continued to be explored.

Coaching for school leaders: a luxury or a duty of care?

School leaders and, in particular, headteachers of today are subject to ever-increasing responsibility, accountability, and scrutiny, which they have to navigate with decreasing resources, autonomy, and job security. At the end of the day, any problem can escalate in such a way as to become the headteacher's responsibility. Nevertheless, in spite of the insecure and overwhelming nature of their role, great leaders, like great teachers, remain committed to their vision and values and to doing all they can to create an atmosphere of psychological safety in their staff rooms and classrooms. They know that it is this that enables staff and students alike to remain ambitious about achieving their potential, despite the discomforts inherent in organizational life and learning.

Great school leaders know that their role can have a transformational impact—not only on the education of the students and staff with whom they work, but on their lives and futures. But for all the resources they invest in securing everyone else's development and wellbeing, they are notably prone to neglecting their own. Rather than viewing regular professional development, such as coaching for themselves, as a fundamental duty of care owed to them—as they might with any other member of staff—they are often inclined to think of it as a *luxury* or even an *indulgence*. This propensity can have devastating consequences, not only for the individual school leader but for everyone around them—in and outside school life.

So, who supports the headteacher?

In theory, headteachers should be supported primarily by their CoG, together with the governing body and local authority officers, as well as by their senior leadership team. In practice, however, it does not always work like this—especially if tensions between the head and CoG start to undermine trust in what *should* be a more benign and constructively critical relationship.[8] When this happens, headteachers can find themselves feeling all the more isolated—having to manage extremely difficult situations, dynamics, and emotions with precious little support. As a result, it is no surprise that the wellbeing, recruitment, and retention of headteachers is now becoming a national concern.

Whether a school is in the midst of a period of change, anxiety, and stress—or whether it is seeking to build on its success during a period of relative calm and consolidation—it is essential for school leaders to secure adequate space and support to digest and process all that they are having to contain at an intra-psychic, interpersonal, and systemic level. Coaching with a suitably qualified and experienced practitioner offers such a space—a space in which leaders can be helped to stand, understand, and make effective use of the complex and multifaceted dynamics and pressures of school life. Particularly in the case of headteachers—given the hidden emotional and psychological weight and isolation of their role—it is this space, or its absence, that has the potential to tip the future trajectory towards sustainability and development rather than fragmentation and breakdown—not only for the headteacher, but for the whole school community.

Coaching is not a panacea. In fact, the flooding and reactive nature of a school leader's experience can, at times, result in a slight frustration with coaching's more gradual process of exploration and sense making. But if this initial tension can be tolerated and thought about dynamically, leaders usually end up with a much more convincing sense of command over their thoughts, feelings, and actions, together with greater confidence about their insights and capacities. It is this combination that then helps to restore in leaders—and in those around them—an atmosphere of calm, containment, and clarity, along with greater resolve about what really matters and how best to proceed.

Notes

1 In secondary Post-Graduate Certificate in Education (PGCE), for example, it is not uncommon for there to be no input whatsoever on child and adolescent development or the management of relationships.

2 Further information about psychodynamic and systemic concepts and approaches can be found in chapters 3 and 4, written by Biddy Youell and Judith Bell, respectively.

3 All names and identifying details have been changed to preserve confidentiality.

4 Free schools are funded by central government but not run by the local council. They have more control over how they organize themselves and can be set up by groups like parents, charities, businesses, faith groups, and universities. They can set their own pay and conditions, change the length of school days and term dates, and do not have to follow the national curriculum. But they cannot select students by academic ability.

5 Although we have written in the language of "we" for much of this chapter, the coaching illustrations are drawn from actual experiences and therefore are written from the perspective of the individual coach, using "I".

6 This discussion and John's associated anxieties may also have expressed another layer of significance in relation to the coaching. For example, it may also have unconsciously expressed his interest in—and fear of—moving on from the coaching relationship towards something more separate and independent. This was not explored at the time but would also be an important avenue to consider.

7 Ofsted is the Office for Standards in Education, Children's Services and Skills. Ofsted inspect and regulate services that care for children and young people, and services providing education and skills for learners of all ages.

8 Rather concerningly, the view of some headteachers is that the current guidance on the performance review of heads and accountability of governors is more likely to encourage CoGs to keep their distance from headteachers and to challenge more than support.

CHAPTER SIX

Leadership and governance: leadership pairs coaching

Clare Huffington

Many of us will know of examples of conflict between a headteacher and chair of governors of a school where fever pitch has been reached and an impasse has developed over a decision affecting the school, often about something seemingly unimportant, such as school uniform. It affects everyone in the school community and can often be difficult to resolve because there are no ready support mechanisms or a toolkit to hand to address the issues. When the relationship is working well, however, the joint creativity between the headteacher and chair of governors can stimulate huge energy and forward movement in school life, to the benefit of all.

The working relationship between these two key leaders of the school is so important to its well-being and progress, it is surprising that so little appears to have been written about it in the education leadership literature. This chapter aims to contribute some thinking about this area of school life. It concerns an experience of coaching a leadership pair of a headteacher and chair of governors of a large comprehensive school over three years meeting once a term throughout that time. To preserve client confidentiality, this case is actually a composite of several experiences of coaching leadership pairs both in the public and private sectors, including education. Beginning as a pilot it continued as a regular arrangement and served as a creative think tank, container of anxiety, and occasional crisis management as well as a place for reflection and mutual feedback. It functioned as a complement and support to other leadership structures both within and outside the school.

The chapter begins with some thinking about changing ideas on organizational leadership which open up new possibilities for the development of shared and collaborative models of school leadership.

Models of school leadership; moving from positional to relational leadership

Traditionally, and perhaps especially in schools, the leadership of an organization can be seen as singular. Most people's conception of leadership is grounded in an idea of the individual leader or as in this case, the headteacher. However, there are paradoxes for leaders to hold in mind. People want strong leaders with vision—but they also want to shape the organization themselves; they need leaders to make unpleasant but necessary change happen—but they want to collaborate in new change initiatives; they want individuals to look up to and identify with, yet do not want charismatic dictators; they want people who come in from the "outside" with a magic wand, but they want people who understand the insider view and how the organization works in practice.

Today's leaders need to be able to work with these dynamic tensions of leadership. Change in how leadership needs to work, increasingly acknowledged since the turn of the century, gives rise to complex emotions associated with authority and responsibility. The idea of leadership at all levels, or distributed leadership, is seen as a requirement in organizations with flatter hierarchies, horizontal networks, and strategic alliances with suppliers and even competitors. Decisions need to be taken away from the centre of the organization at the point of contact between the organization and its environment. However, the difficulty in implementing distributed leadership emerges in the tensions associated with the central leader giving away power and other leaders taking it up. As well as delegating authority downwards, accountability also flows upwards. So there are new anxieties distributed across the organization as well as leadership (Armstrong, 2004). With less clarity about who is in charge of what and how people can successfully navigate these more charged relationships, difficulties and splits can arise.

Fletcher (2004) uses the term "post heroic leader" to explore the complex dynamics of organization leadership and challenges the idea that leadership is done by *a* leader. Instead she proposes that:

> ... post heroic leadership re-envisions the *who* and *where* of leadership by focusing on the need to distribute the tasks and responsibilities of leadership up, down, and across the hierarchy. It re-envisions the *what* of leadership by articulating leadership as a social process that

occurs in and through human interactions and it articulates the *how* of leadership by focusing on the more mutual, less hierarchical leadership practices and skills needed to engage collaborative, collective learning. It is generally recognized that this shift—from individual to collective, from control to learning, from "self" to "self-in-relation", and from power over to power with—is a paradigm shift in what it means to be a [positional] leader. [Fletcher, 2004, p. 650]

The possibility of a leader or even a senior group of leaders providing a single vision and goals and being able to enact leadership across the organization because they are authentic, charismatic, or transformational is an insufficient leadership idea when organizations increasingly need to unite multiple interest groups, diverse cultures, and staff working across vast geographic and virtual space and when organizations are challenged by fast-moving economic and political events. Instead:

Organisational leadership capacity is enhanced when the executive team is able to enact leadership effectively as a unit; when interdependent groups can identify an emerging organisational problem and pull together to deal with it; when leaders and group members in various parts of the organisation readily connect with each other about interdependent work, shared challenges or shared expertise and when individuals and groups engage in dialogue with one another rather than act in isolation. [Van Velsor & McCauley, 2004, p. 19]

This shift in leadership conceptualization is a shift from an entity-based paradigm, in which leadership is equated to the inputs leaders make into a system because of their personal capabilities and attributes, to a relational view of leadership, in which leadership exists in the spaces between leader and follower and in the organizational and political dynamics arising from power and authority relations. A relational view of leadership is an alternative paradigm and views leadership as socially constructed by those in leadership relationships, understood through an analysis of how relating is experienced, and as dynamic between leader and followers (and others) (see, for example, Cunliffe & Eriksen, 2011; Drath et al., 2008; Fitzsimons, Turnbull James, & Denyer, 2011; Ladkin, 2010; Uhl-Bien, 2006; Western, 2008).

Leadership pairs

The relationships formed between the senior leaders of an organization are particularly important, especially senior leadership pairs. For example, chief executive and chair of the board, or headteacher and chair of governors in the school context, is a particularly important and complex partnership, which, to be at its most effective, needs to work on an honest, open and democratic basis while acknowledging the dynamic issues embedded within the partnership. The chair appoints the chief executive/headteacher, is responsible for performance review and remuneration, and can also fire him or her. This leaves most heads feeling uneasy about the relationship, even if they get on very well and their values are aligned. At the same time, the chief executive needs the freedom to run the organization without too much interference from the chair (Nadler & Spencer, 1998). This, together with the often confused and confusing tensions between the strategic and operational roles of the two parties, creates a potentially explosive mixture of dependency, authority, and power issues to contend with in managing the business of the organization and leading it into the future with a vision. I would suggest these elements are present to varying degrees in all relationships in organizations but are in particularly concentrated form in senior leadership pairs.

It no longer seems sustainable or effective to keep these pairs apart as a way of managing the tensions between them: for example, for the headteacher to lead the Senior Leadership Team and for the chair of governors to lead the Board in a parallel but potentially split or uncollaborative fashion. There are numerous examples of business failures resulting from lack of communication and collaboration at the top of businesses, for example the big banks in the United Kingdom that ended up in public ownership due to spectacular leadership failures at the top level. Indeed, new governance arrangements for banks and other organizations are designed to avoid such splits happening in the future. In order to share and distribute leadership tasks and to create the conditions for working collaboratively across silos and multi-interest groups in the wider organization, executive and other senior teams need to be able to work collaboratively. Indeed, by their management of the potential divisions, competitive dynamics, political agenda, power plays, anxieties, and splits inherent in teamworking, the organization as a whole might find it possible, not only to go beyond the disasters caused by the lack of working together, but to enact collaborative working more effectively.

What creative possibilities might emerge from an effective working partnership between the headteacher and chair of governors of a school if they were prepared to "give it a go"? What work might they do together in areas where they both already make a contribution but where this could be better coordinated—for example, long-term strategic planning, development of future members of the governing body, or representing the school in the community: How might they work better at areas where there are frequent tensions: What new projects might they develop together? And how might a coach, as a third party, assist in creating a context or containment for exploring some of these issues? These questions were central to the thinking behind the leadership pair coaching described in this chapter.

School context

The author was already working as a coach to the headteacher (HT) who had been in post for one year following his predecessor, a powerful figure who had led the school for some years previously. It felt to the HT that he was stepping into very big shoes and that it was a real challenge to develop his own vision and establish his authority with the Senior Leadership Team (SLT) and to bring about the change and transformation needed to be a really effective school. He believed he had been appointed by the chair of governors (COG) to bring about these changes but was finding it hard to get started. He lacked confidence, was uncertain of how he was viewed by key stakeholders in his success, and often felt stressed and lonely. He was not sure what kind of a leader he needed to be to achieve all he expected of himself and all he thought others expected of him. We discussed his relationship with the COG, something about which he also felt uncertain. Out of this discussion emerged the idea of a three-way meeting with the COG to test out some of the HT's ideas, doubts, and fears about how to lead the school, in particular to see how far the HT and COG, the most senior leaders in the school, were aligned in their thinking. The HT wanted to find out what kind of change and transformation the COG now wanted to see and to what extent he could and would support the HT to bring it about. The HT approached the COG with the idea of a meeting with the author as a third-party present as a coach and facilitator and found him very willing to take part.

The first meeting: objectives and ground rules

Before the first meeting, the coach met the HT to work on a draft agenda for the meeting and to clarify its purpose. This was as follows;

1. Vision for the school, especially changes needed.

2. Reflections on the shared working relationship between HT and COG; areas of strength and areas for development.

3. Questions and conclusions, especially including creative thoughts about the school's current and future direction.

It felt important to have a large reflective space to operate in at that first meeting, which might also have been the last. This is because the coach felt it needed not to have too many constraints to discussion and not be too business-like so as to create a different working context for the pair from the outset. The meeting took place in the coach's office, a neutral space, which required both the HT and the COG to travel a distance to get there, offering the additional benefit of reflection time on the journey to and from the meeting, whether or not they travelled together. The coach was careful to point out to the HT that she would not be acting as his coach in that meeting but as facilitator or coach to the relationship between the HT and the COG. She also told him that she would preserve the confidentiality of their one-to-one working relationship while working with the pair. The aim would be to encourage communication and to support and challenge both parties in the interests of the leadership of the school as a whole. This would be a pilot in which to explore and test out a method of improving collaboration at the top of the school.

At that first meeting, it was important to start by outlining some ground rules, first about the coach's role in the same way as described above, and second, about the confidentiality of the meeting. Nothing would be reported outside to others—for example members of the SLT or governing body or to anyone else—without prior agreement between all three people involved. Third, the need for honesty and the benefits of risk-taking were emphasized.

As the meeting began, the coach noted the relative tentativeness between the HT and the COG. While they were used to discussing business items in formal meetings, they were not used to thinking about themselves in role as part of a system or as a leadership pair within a system. Some of the questions posed by the coach were familiar, but rarely discussed in practice, for example;

How do you decide on the future vision for the school?

Who are the major stakeholders in your view?

What do you feel are the priorities of the major stakeholders in the school's future?

How do you divide up the leadership tasks for the school? Engaging more actively with questions such as these clearly introduced a different, more systemic way of thinking about themselves and their role in relation to the school—and not a wholly comfortable one, as clear answers were not forthcoming and they had to struggle with them.

It was clear that the HT and COG were relating well as professionals and were personally cordial but that in neither the professional nor the personal context was there the depth to facilitate better shared leadership. They were also uncertain how to share feedback about strengths and areas for development in their working relationship. After all, while the value of such conversations might seem self-evident, in practice they are frequently avoided—even by the most senior of leaders—due to the emotional discomfort they incur. Nevertheless—supported by the encouragement and structure provided by the coach along with the help to make such discussions feel constructive and emotionally safe—the HT and COG were soon able to develop their capacity to dialogue with greater honesty, clarity, and trust.

The meeting started to feel it was working when the HT opened up about how vulnerable he felt about certain things, for example that perhaps there was a view that the existing deputy head should have been given the role of HT, not he, as an outsider. The COG was able to reassure him on this point and also give him feedback on the qualities he had that made him more suitable for the job than the existing deputy or the previous headteacher. In turn, the COG was able to talk about his concerns about some members of the non-teaching staff to whom both he and the HT related. This allowed both of them to enter more creatively into the final part of the meeting, which was deliberately less structured in that they were invited by the coach to talk about any conclusions, thoughts, or feelings they were taking away, including ideas, whims, or dreams that had come to mind. This resulted in a generative flow that may have had no "home" before: a really ambitious idea about a new school building that the HT had in mind; a need for a plan about succession for the whole of the SLT; and how to give sabbaticals to long-serving members of staff.

Both parties said they had found the meeting extremely useful, challenging but also a relief, emphasizing that they wanted to continue this joint venture together.

Regular meetings

It was from this start that regular meetings followed, using the pattern of the first meeting as a template. The meetings were scheduled to take place once a term for two hours, preceded by a planning slot for the coach with the HT to catch up on recent school events and likely agenda items for the leadership pair coaching. The COG was also invited to send agenda items beforehand.

The topics and themes we covered in our meetings are described below.

1. Use of authority and power

This area was potentially the most contentious in the relationship between the HT and COG. While they are both leaders, there is a hierarchy between them. They also have different areas of authority and responsibility, never fully spelt out and in constant flux, despite guidelines from the DfE (2015a) headteachers' professional associations and the National Governance Association. As such, it was not surprising that discussions about the role of HT and COG within and outside the school system continued and were, in fact, a running item throughout the work.

There were many examples of splits and tensions that arose. On one occasion, the HT arrived looking very irritated, and it emerged that he was cross with the COG for what he perceived as interference with his role. A parent had contacted the COG about bullying in one particular school year, and the COG had begun an enquiry into this by talking to other parents and children and suggesting that another member of the governing body should visit the school and investigate—all without discussion with the HT. In this case, it had not occurred to the COG that he was overstepping a boundary as he felt he was, and should be, the court of appeal for complaints or issues about the school. From the HT's point of view, he should have been consulted on what the school knew and was already doing about bullying, and that the COG had created a split—or "us and them"—between school and parents, which was unhelpful. In the leadership pair coaching session, it was possible to encourage them to talk first about the particular situation and then about the general issue of bullying. This not only included a reviewing of the relevant policies but a valuable and potentially delicate discussion about how concerns could be better explored, including how and when the COG should and should not intervene directly in what the HT saw as internal school matters.

In a reverse situation, the HT talked to the local press about a new building project, including its cost, without the knowledge of the COG. The COG was telephoned by the local authority, accusing him of being indiscreet, and he was furious, as he felt he should have been consulted about any external contacts the school made with the press or local authority, and that they were not being "joined up". As this happened at roughly the same time as the reverse example above, it seemed like a case of "tit for tat" in that the HT and COG were both playing in grey areas of authority and responsibility. Again, this needed careful discussion with both particular and general learning points emerging.

As part of offering some structure to help focus and facilitate their discussions, the coach, at one stage, shared a worksheet (Worksheet 6.1) developed for a business organization when she was working with a CEO

Worksheet 6.1.   Roles of the chairman and CEO

	Chair	CEO
I: Board responsibilities		
• Providing leadership to the Board.		
• Engaging the Board in assessing and improving its performance and in making key decisions		
II: Strategic responsibilities		
• Sets corporate strategic direction (vision and strategy)		
• Communicates and builds commitment to corporate strategic direction with internal and external constituents		
• Establishes organizational structure and operating systems to ensure achievement of strategic objectives.		
• Serves as principal external representative		
III: Policy-related responsibilities		
• Translates corporate vision and strategy into organizational policies, directives and procedures.		
• Ensures implementation of policies, directives, procedures.		
IV: Operational/performance management responsibilities		
• Sets corporate performance targets		
• Manages operations of the organization in ways consistent with strategic goals and performance targets.		
• Ensures there are clear risk management procedures.		
• Manages resources across lines of business and resolves conflict between business units and staff functions.		
• Manages financial information and compliance activities		
• Manages the attraction, retention and development of a high-performance workforce.		
• Ensures the right leadership team is in place.		
• Develops succession planning processes for leadership positions.		

Note. Based on material from "Executive Teams" by Nadler and Spencer (1998, pp. 77–80).

and Chair as a leadership pair. It had been a useful focus to help them to clarify their areas of respective responsibility and accountability. They were each given a copy to fill in before a leadership pair coaching meeting, and then their responses were shared and discussed, with conclusions reached. The important learning was that, while there were some clear boundaries between their roles, most areas were negotiable based on circumstances, so it was absolutely crucial for them to have a very good working relationship so they could discuss and negotiate how best to use themselves in their roles in the grey areas so as to secure the most effective outcomes.

For each responsibility, assign one of the following options in each column; Unique, Shared, Primary, or Secondary. While this list of responsibilities may not be a perfect fit with your organization, working on your respective roles will provide a starting point for a meeting to discuss the most effective way for you both individually and collectively to use your skills, knowledge, and experience in the leadership and management of the organization.

While this was developed as a model of leadership and governance for a leadership pair in a business setting, it provided a useful focus for discussion for the HT and COG in thinking about areas in which they both had responsibility. In particular, this helped to ensure they discussed how best to deploy themselves in role and how to avoid the risk of role ambiguity, overlap, and potential conflict. It also underlined the areas each needed to manage separately. While they did not develop a formal matching table to the one above, it did help them to clarify how they could use their formal and informal authority and power together and separately to get the job done most effectively. For example, in the case of a serious accident in which a student sustained a life-threatening blow to the head in a rugby match and in which there was a question about whether the school was to blame in any way, leading to an escalating crisis, the HT and COG pulled together and discussed how to manage the parties involved—who would deal with each and in what way, while following the school procedures for handling such a situation.

2. Giving mutual feedback

It was clear from the beginning of the work with the HT and COG that they were not accustomed to reviewing their working relationship. Their usual formal meetings were business-focused or else consisted of the COG conducting a performance review with the HT based on his objectives, thus emphasizing the hierarchical nature of their relationship. The coach sought to develop the collaborative aspect of their leadership roles and encouraged them to give one another feedback about how they were working together. Although this began rather tentatively in the first meeting, giving feedback to one another became a regular feature of each meeting. Having a simple structure for this was important—for example, each could ask *"Is there anything I should start, stop or continue doing?"*

More informally, this could evolve into something more fluid and future-focused, for example, *"How do you think I should handle the meeting with parents about changes in admission policy?"*

We were following the ideas behind a 2 × 2 matrix that the coach shared with the HT and COG (Worksheet 6.2). The aim was to develop an intimate *professional* relationship for the benefit of the shared leadership of the school, rather than a distant or intimate *personal* relationship or the *distant* professional relationship that they felt they had experienced up to this point. As part of deepening their understanding of themselves and their impact on others, they each undertook an individual Myers–Briggs Type Indicator assessment (Briggs Myers, McCaulley, Quenk, & Hammer, 1998) with the coach, with individual and shared debriefing.[1] They both said they found this extremely helpful, and this became a shared reference point for future feedback discussions. For example, the HT learned that, because the COG was very clear "Introvert" while he was an "Extrovert", he tended not to share his thinking about a topic ahead of it being discussed in a governors' meeting. He learned to ensure he discussed contentious topics with the COG before meetings, so he understood any important issues that might otherwise arise in the meeting and be a surprise to him. The COG also learned that his thinking could be enhanced by sharing it with others before coming up with conclusions that then might be difficult for him to shift. The meetings with the coach formed the beginnings of termly "think tanks" that the HT and COG held off-site to develop their thinking together about the school and future plans.

3. Looking after each other

It was important for the HT and COG to be able to look after each other, especially as the school was going through a stressful period

Worksheet 6.2.   Relationship distance and intimacy

	Personal	*Professional*
Distant		
Intimate		X

for a variety of reasons, including concerns over student achievement, parental complaints, and financial worries. As the top leaders in the school, they held the overview of the whole system between them, with all the responsibility this entailed. At different times both the HT and COG experienced high levels of stress. The tendency could then be for each of them to retreat into more defensive and accusatory states of mind, focusing on the failures of the other. At these times, joint meetings could get cancelled—often due to the "pressure of work" for example. However, with the help of a third party, the coach, they were able to share their feelings and continue talking together, which helped to contain some strong emotions and put things into a different perspective. They were also able to share tasks to lighten the load when one or other of them was feeling overwhelmed, clearly a relief to them both. For example, on one occasion there was a discussion about the meaning and cause of the rise in parental complaints, not only in terms of the individual students involved but also at a systemic level. Looking at complaints as a symptom of anxiety, for example, the HT and COG discussed what the reasons for an increase in anxiety in the system as a whole might be, along with how this might be addressed. As a small example of one of the possible hypotheses discussed was at a time when a large group of new inexperienced teachers had arrived in the school, and training sessions were organized for all staff in dealing with parents with complaints. This appeared effective both in managing staff anxiety about the actual complaints as well as in reducing the number of complaints overall.

4. Talent management and succession planning

A frequent theme was recruitment, retention, and development of both teaching and non-teaching staff. In common with many schools, older and experienced staff were retiring, leaving large gaps needing to be filled by younger staff, who needed support and development to catch up fast. The COG and governors could access potential mentors for these people, especially for non-teaching staff (e.g. finance director) from their business connections. It was also possible for the HT to get support and authorization for teaching staff to get extra training and individual coaching to help them grow into senior roles with the backing of the COG.

The HT and COG worked together on quite a sophisticated succession plan for the most senior roles in the school, including for themselves in due course, so as to ensure both care and continuity were preserved. It included the idea of sabbaticals for senior teachers to allow more junior leaders to take on acting roles in their absence, so as to test them out with support to increase their chances of promotion into senior role opportunities when they arose.

5. Creativity and innovation

Possibly the most important aspect of the meetings was the sense of space for reflection and growth: so it was not just about containment of anxiety but also containment for development and exploration or "pro-tainment" (Huffington, 2004). Protainment refers to a different kind of containment on the part of the leader, helping others to work through frustration or acting as a shield from overwhelming anxiety; it is containment that can communicate the pleasures of self-discovery of the world and encouragement for exploration and curiosity. This is a kind of *joie de vivre* and links to what Lacan (1977) has called "jouissance" and Hirschhorn (2003) has called "flow". Leadership today probably needs to be as much about encouraging autonomy and creativity in others as about merely containing anxiety.

The HT and COG often discussed or tuned in to the mood of the school as a way of starting the meetings, and this often proved to be very productive, as straight away it created a "feeling into" mindset rather than a "thinking solutions" mindset. They were connecting with the emotional life of the school as a way into their planned leadership response, which they would work on towards the end of meetings (Armstrong, 2005). For example, at the start of one meeting, the HT and COG wanted to discuss exam results but were asked by the coach to first tune in to the mood of the school at the time. They began talking about conflicts and complaints from the non-teaching staff of the school. This led them into reflections on the relationship between those on the "front line" of the school dealing with parents, often the administrative staff, and how the demands of the parents had become more pressing over the last few months, and the possible reasons for this. This took them into quite different territory for the rest of the meeting, which was, in the end, connected to exam results but in an indirect way that led to different conclusions and actions than they might at first have imagined.

In this school in common with all others, everyone was busy all the time, doing the business of teaching and learning and the leadership and management associated, with little or no time for reflection and review. It was rarely possible to ask how the school as a whole was doing, what could be done better, or even what wild thoughts do we have about the future? It was, however, possible for the HT and COG to have these kinds of thoughts with the help of a third party, the coach, even though space within the leadership pair coaching had to be fought for: the coach always had to ensure that the latest crisis did not dominate the coaching and that at least 30 minutes was allowed for free-floating thinking. A possible outcome of the fact that this reflective space was in place was that they noticed that reflective spaces began to pop up in other places in the school! Spaces were set up for teachers and/or students in which there was no fixed agenda but an opportunity to reflect on a particular theme—for example, teachers new to the school were given a discussion forum to raise any issues, questions, concerns, or ideas about their experience in the school to date.

Other leadership pairs

As well as the leadership pair coaching with the HT and COG, the HT also invited the coach to facilitate other leadership pair meetings for himself with key members of his SLT, for example a new deputy head and an outgoing experienced head of department, respectively. These were when he wanted a better systemic view for himself and the person concerned about their role in relation to his, and vice versa, as well as mutual feedback and a reflective space. These meetings were experienced by the HT as useful and as effective as the ones with the COG, although not organized on a regular or continuous basis.

Reflections and outcomes

This three-year leadership pair coaching with the HT and COG of a school was an interesting and effective intervention that proved to be transferable within the school and could be repeated elsewhere. The outcomes reported by the clients and by the coach were:

1. A deeper collaborative working relationship between the headteacher and the chair of governors, in both their formal and their informal working relationships; plus, a more planned and nuanced use of their individual and shared leadership strengths and areas for development.
2. A more reflective leadership approach developed by the top leadership pair but observable in the school as a whole—both for problem solving (e.g. parental complaints) and creative development (e.g. reflective spaces offered to staff and pupils).
3. Specific outputs such as succession planning for the SLT, mentorship programme for teaching and non-teaching staff, sabbaticals used for staff development.

At the same time as acknowledging the positive outcomes of collaboration between leadership pairs, it is no substitute for collaboration across the system and was not in this case used as a way to avoid or override this, as could have happened. For example, some leaders create a "circle of pairs" between themselves and each other member of a leadership team (Armstrong, 2004). This is when dyadic relationships are used as a defence against working with the complex team dynamics required for more collective leadership. Was it too cosy and exclusive a relationship, and did it exclude or preclude other pair or team relationships that should or could have happened? The coach was mindful that the work should not be focused on the HT and COG as a couple but as a pair of leaders of a system and to constantly help them make sense of their relatedness both to one another and to the whole system with its subsystems. This was not always easy, especially as they were not equal partners in all their functions and responsibilities. The HT was pre-eminent in educational matters and the COG on appointments to the Board and appointing the HT, for example. As well as having different roles in relation to the system, they also thought differently on a range of issues, not only because of their roles, but also because of their personalities, backgrounds, and experiences, and this brought richness as well as challenges at times. So it was important to be able to hold all these distinctions in mind and think them through carefully.

Is it a possible criticism that the leadership pairs coaching undertaken here got in the way of wider collaboration across teams in the school? This was discussed by the coach with the HT, and as a result termly SLT development off-site meetings were organized and facilitated by a different external team coach, not the author. It seemed important that the SLT could have their own facilitator who could be perceived by the team as neutral and not overly influenced by the headteacher's views. The COG also organized development events for the governing body. As a test of wider collaboration in the school, it would perhaps have been a good idea to survey the staff and governing body as a whole about their engagement in the school system before and after the intervention, asking them to rate leadership and collaboration between staff at all levels. Staff engagement surveys are commonly used in the private sector as a way for the leadership of a company to gain feedback about staff morale, communication, and collaboration, so they can make changes accordingly. This might have been usefully used in this school partly as a test of the leadership pairs coaching intervention.

Conclusion

In recent years, school leadership has become considerably more challenging. The landscape in and around schools has become increasingly pressured in terms of constant changes, with diminished time for consolidation. There are ramped-up expectations of performance and achievement at the same time as cost-cutting and failure to replace inadequate buildings and facilities. Pressures such as these can represent a threat to good school governance in that they are liable to result in tensions and splits between those in charge of the school—that is, the headteacher and chair of governors—just when their close collaboration is all the more important. At times like this, the leadership pairs coaching for the headteacher and chair of governors was felt to be essential for protecting the integrity of the school leadership as well as for containing anxiety and promoting the creativity, exploration, and experiment that is so crucial for teaching, learning, and development in adults as well as in children.

Note

1   For further information about the use of Myers–Briggs (MBTI) in education, see chapter 9, by Emil Jackson.

CHAPTER SEVEN

On the leading edge of learning: work discussion groups for headteachers

Emil Jackson & Andrea Berkeley

Overview

Despite the significance of their responsibilities to the children, staff, families, and communities they serve, it remains rare for headteachers to feel looked after in their own role and work. Even when they have an excellent relationship with their chair of governors and senior leadership team, it is not uncommon for headteachers to feel profoundly alone with their most challenging dilemmas and decisions. In view of this 'felt sense' of isolation, this chapter describes a pioneering project of collaboration between eight headteachers. In particular, it explores the unique potential for "work discussion groups" to offer headteachers an innovative opportunity for peer support, learning, development, consultation, constructive challenge and camaraderie.

To the best of our knowledge, work discussion groups for headteachers is not something that has been written about elsewhere.

Introduction

Everyone remembers a good teacher, and every parent and teacher recognizes the crucial role the headteacher plays. Indeed, there now exists a solid body of research indicating that school leadership is second only to the quality of classroom teaching in determining school effectiveness and academic success (Leithwood, Day, Sammons,

Haris, & Hopkins, 2006). The role of the headteacher—increasing in complexity, responsibility, and accountability—has been under intense scrutiny for many years in wave after wave of reform, with education at the top of successive governments' agendas. Headteachers now control multi-million budgets and are responsible for the hiring and firing of hundreds of staff as well as for ensuring that curriculum and academic standards are fit for purpose in the twenty-first century. Many headteachers may also be responsible for more than one school, and now all are expected to support, partner and/or collaborate with other schools in what the Department for Education calls a "self-improving system".

There is ample evidence that educational standards really have risen in the past two decades, as a result of continued investment and central government directives. However, whatever the government, a paradox remains: although educational standards continue to rise overall, the performance gap between the highest- and lowest-performing secondary schools and the richest or poorest children remains constant (ONS, 2006a; Sutton Trust, 2009). National and local policy attempts at closing this gap have often been persecutory ones—naming and shaming, special measures, increasingly challenging performance indicators, and unremitting inspections. Others have been more supportive (if also directive), with interventions in inverse proportion to success. These have included National Strategies in literacy, numeracy, and behaviour management and interventions that promote development in the 1990s—for example, designating schools with specialisms, encouraging them to share best practice and giving them responsibility for training and supporting other schools in challenging circumstances. In the past decade, processes for what is called "system leadership"—the notion of schools working collaboratively, with more experienced and effective headteachers becoming "consultant leaders" for other schools—have been formalized. Greatly influenced by the thinking of Leadbeater (2008) and Fullan (2007), the DfE has introduced National and Local Leaders in Education (NLEs and LLEs), who are trained to support other headteachers and schools, and leadership development programmes for executive headteachers who run more than one school. Overall, training for aspiring headteachers and senior and middle leaders has improved greatly in recent years with a suite of National Professional Qualifications (NPQs) for all levels of school leadership. However, these national qualifications are not mandatory.

Despite new "collaborative" structures in the education system, school leadership is increasingly demanding and can often feel lonely. The authority invested in headteachers is daunting, though in reality less powerful than it might seem. Headteachers not only work for a larger system, they sit on the boundary between multiple accountabilities—parents and governors, local authorities and academy trusts among them—while also containing and maintaining coherence within the school. And if they are to succeed, they face the challenge of looking after the people who look after the children. Traditionally there has been scant provision for the continuing professional development of experienced headteachers beyond their early years of headship, and this has diminished further since the demise of the National College for School Leadership.

Local gatherings of headteachers are usually for practical or political purposes. The core business of education—learning and teaching—is rarely mentioned at these meetings. Attendance tends to be irregular, in line with vested interests—except when allocation of funds is being discussed, and then it is 100%—and participation varies. Sharing of concerns or good practice is more likely to take place in the lower echelons of schooling structures. At national conferences the atmosphere may be more relaxed and egalitarian, with opportunity for intellectual discourse and consideration of values and aspirations. At a local level, however, the tension between competition and collaboration can impede useful discussion.

The work discussion group model

Before describing the work discussion groups for headteachers and school leaders in more depth it is first necessary to outline the work discussion model, its development within educational settings and the context within which the headteachers' groups were established.

Overview

In essence, work discussion groups (WDG) provide regular opportunities for workers to join with other colleagues—facilitated by an external professional—to share, explore and make greater sense of aspects of their experiences and interactions at work.

Typically, WDGs are offered as a core module within a broader professional training qualification or as an adapted bespoke resource within an organizational setting, such as a school or residential care home. In both contexts, WDGs are traditionally offered to people working directly with clients, though they have the potential to be adapted for people working at all levels, in any field of work.

WDGs are usually—though not exclusively—facilitated by psychoanalytically trained professionals who have a depth of clinical and theoretical understanding about interpersonal, intra-psychic, and systemic concepts and the myriad ways that unconscious dynamics are played out within organizational settings.

History and evolution

Work discussion groups have evolved to become one of the most central and highly valued models of training and supervision that have been developed at the Tavistock Clinic over the past 60 years.

The evolution of the work discussion methodology is a result of contributions from a number of original thinkers in the post-war period. These include: Elliot Jacques, Isabel Menzies Lyth, A. K. Rice, Eric Miller, Pierre Turquet, and Wilfred Bion. As far back as 1957, Michael Balint (1957) wrote about his weekly case conferences for doctors (mostly general practitioners). These "Balint Groups", as they became known, offered regular opportunities to doctors to focus on difficulties in the doctor–patient relationship that were disturbing the doctor's professional capacity and decision making.

The first work discussion seminars labelled as such were pioneered by child psychotherapist and psychoanalyst Martha Harris. The main task of the group was (and still is) to facilitate an extension in the worker's frame of reference and understanding, so that interventions could take better account of the emotional factors at work in relationships. The work discussion group therefore addresses possible unconscious meanings of client behaviour and communication (including non-verbal communication) and the emotional responses of both client and worker. Through this, a deeper appreciation of the emotional factors that impact on working with and caring for troubled and troubling client groups can be achieved. Where appropriate, the work discussion group might also address group processes and institutional factors influencing the setting.

The WDG does not primarily focus on the teaching of any particular technique or strategy for how best to intervene. Rather, WDG members are encouraged to consider and discuss appropriate ways of dealing with situations and dilemmas described *only after* their possible meanings had been explored in some depth (Rustin & Bradley, 2008: pp. 4–7).[1]

The development of work discussion in educational settings

The Tavistock Clinic has a long history of developing innovative school-based projects and training courses for teachers and other professionals working within education (Harris, 1968; Jackson, 1970; Salzberger-Wittenberg, Henry, & Osborne, 1983). The potential benefits of exporting the Tavistock model of work discussion to other settings have been described by Klauber (1999), Canham (2000), and Rustin and Bradley (2008). Jackson has focused more specifically on the development of work discussion groups within educational settings (Jackson, 2002, 2005, 2008b, 2014).

Work discussion groups for teachers and other staff

The conception of a work discussion group for headteachers originally evolved out of a well-established and successful mental health project run by the Brent Centre for Young People (BCYP) with a local secondary school, Preston Manor School (PMS). The two authors were, at the time, the school-based child and adolescent psychotherapist and headteacher for the respective organizations.

The core components of this initial outreach project included a range of work with students and staff, but it was the work discussion groups for staff which had, by far, the most significant and far-reaching impact. These groups were open to any staff working with students and were attended by teachers, teaching assistants, learning support assistants, school receptionists, and other school-based professionals. Separate groups were also set up for heads of year, responsible for the pastoral well-being of the students in their year group.

Common themes emerging in group discussions often focused on difficulties arising in the teacher–student relationship, for instance in relation to attachments, separations, anxiety, hostility, and challenging class group dynamics. Teachers especially welcomed the opportunity to think about emotional factors that were impacting on teaching and learning along with more specific concerns, such as the management of risk.

The success of this project, and, in particular, of the work discussion groups at Preston Manor, resulted in the establishment of a number of other similar projects across a range of primary and secondary schools—some of which have now been running for almost 20 years.

Evaluation of teacher groups

Over many years, across many schools, the vast majority of teachers have evaluated work discussion groups as being some of the most effective training they have ever received.[2]

Significantly, in Preston Manor School, where a culture of work discussion groups had permeated the organization, it was shown that, over a three-year period, the 22 staff attending the three parallel work discussion groups had a significantly lower rate of absence than the staff group as a whole (Jackson, 2005; 2008a; Warman & Jackson, 2007).

Furthermore, as a direct result of this work, a DfES/DoH report identified work discussion groups with teachers as a "Model of Good Practice" (DfES/DoH, 2006).

Work discussion groups for headteachers

The inter-school work discussion groups for headteachers described in this chapter were one of a number of development activities run in a collaborative of eight schools in the London Borough of Brent, forming what was called a "Leading Edge Partnership"—an initiative funded by the Innovations Unit of the Department for Education in the early days of "System Leadership" thinking, from 2003 to 2006.

Schools bidding for "Leading Edge" status had to demonstrate a proven track record in innovation and collaboration. Three hundred schools across the United Kingdom were invited to form local partnerships and helped to finance collaborative and innovative activities to improve standards and pilot system leadership and collaboration. Leading Edge schools were also expected to take part in the dissemination of innovative work.

As headteacher of the designated "Leading Edge School" in the local area, Berkeley invited a number of schools to form a partnership. Although she had to work hard at overcoming the initial mistrust of her colleagues, they all welcomed the funds and freedom to try out some new ideas. The partnership comprised six large secondary schools (including one faith school) and two Pupil Referral Units (PRUs) for students excluded from mainstream education. At the time, three schools were in "challenging circumstances",[3] three were very successful by national standards, and four had new leadership.

The partnership identified areas for development and examples of best practice, resulting in a plan with three strands: teaching and learning, social inclusion, and leadership development. Almost all headteachers identified leadership development needs for their senior and middle leaders but not, interestingly, for themselves. Jackson and Berkeley then proposed the innovation of introducing two inter-school work discussion groups—one for headteachers and another for deputy headteachers—suggesting that the effectiveness of this method with teachers might be a transferable tool for developing the leadership and management skills of headteachers and senior leaders.

The possibility of "starting from the top" with work discussion groups was readily adopted by other headteachers. Jackson[4] agreed to facilitate the groups jointly with a colleague from the Tavistock Consultancy Service (TCS[5]). This work ran in parallel to other development work, including individual executive coaching, conducted by external training providers and the schools themselves.

Work discussion groups at work—structural considerations and applications

Most of us will naturally be more interested in the *process* of running work discussion groups—how they work, what preoccupations head-teachers share, how reflective capacity develops within the group and what impact this has on leadership. However, for the model of work discussion to be successfully adapted, it is first essential to consider some structural and contextual factors.

Timing and duration

One concrete, though critical, factor to consider is the timing of the group: when meetings will take place; the duration of meetings, and the expected life span of the group. Senior leaders, for example, would not be able to attend weekly meetings, as might teachers or support staff. A more viable structure would involve longer, but less frequent meetings, for instance two-hour meetings, at monthly or half-termly intervals.

In order to give a group a chance to establish itself and to allow senior leaders adequate opportunity to discuss their own work, an initial period of a year could be considered. This time limit reduces the likelihood that senior leaders will feel over-committed while still allowing for the group to be extended at the end of the initial period.

Location

Given that a headteachers' work discussion group is a collaborative, cross-school venture, the location of group meetings may be significant to participants. For example, some resentment may be encountered by those travelling much longer journeys. Equally, a headteacher "hosting" the group in their own school might feel a sense of responsibility that could interfere with their freedom to participate as an "ordinary" member.

When possible and financially viable, it is helpful to consider a neutral venue for WDG meetings. This can feel more freeing for participants and reduces the likelihood of unwelcome disruptions.

Group size

To function most effectively, work discussion groups ideally accommodate five to eight members. If the group is larger, participants have less space to formulate their thoughts or contribute to discussions and can become marginalized. Although participants receive more individualized attention when the group is smaller, it can place excessive pressure on them to present their own work, leaving little time to reflect on the insights or experiences of their colleagues.

Open vs. closed groups

For group cohesion and trust to develop, it is preferable for group membership to remain stable, once established. However, within a senior leaders' WDG, as within any work-based group, it is important to be mindful about the potential for feelings of inclusion and exclusion to be aroused, along with other unhelpful divisions. For example, members within the wider forum of local headteachers may feel marginalized by what is perceived to be the intimate and trusted inner circle of the WDG.

One way to mitigate against membership being too rigidly "closed" would be to incorporate a review of the group and its membership towards the end of an agreed period, for instance after the first year. At this point, it may be less disruptive for members to join or withdraw from the group.

Ground rules

Although headteachers and other senior leaders are likely to have substantial experience in the management of expectations, boundaries, and codes of conduct within their staff and student groups, it is essential to discuss what ground rules are necessary to preserve trust and cohesion within their own WDG. It is also important for there to be shared discussion and understanding about the aims and objectives of the group and what members hope to get out of it. Similarly, the facilitators' role needs to be clarified, as do the parameters of the group work. It is useful, for example, to remind the group that although emerging insights may subsequently result in decisions being taken, the WDG is not itself tasked to be a decision-making meeting. Finally, while some interplay between personal and professional preoccupations is both expected and valuable, the work-related focus for the group is to be preserved and distinguished from something more akin to a psychotherapy group.[6]

Confidentiality

The importance of maintaining the highest level of discretion and confidentiality is paramount when discussing individuals, teams, or relationships—all the more so, given the subjective nature of the narratives shared. This is especially the case within a headteachers' group in which delicate and volatile situations might be discussed—some of which could toxify, should sensitive information be "leaked" or misrepresented outside the group.

Working method

Over the past 20 years, Jackson has explored several ways of running work discussion groups in educational settings. His preferred method for running groups is similar to the original Balint groups and involves the facilitator helping the presenter to "unpack" their issue in sufficient detail so that they can be thought about productively by the group. One of the additional by-products of this approach is that it allows the facilitator to help group members to develop their capacity to listen and question with the intent to understand rather than simply to reply (Covey, 2004). This is especially important in the early phase of a group, when there is often a natural tendency to assert one's competence and interject rather impulsively with one's own solutions. While this is generally well intentioned, it can leave presenters feeling rather bombarded and unheard—especially if their colleagues have not yet understood which aspects of the issue are even preoccupying them.

An agreed order of presentations can be helpful, because it ensures an equitable distribution of time and gives presenters space to organize their thoughts in advance. However, given the turbulent nature of school life, it is important to allow for the possibility that participants might arrive with something urgent requiring their immediate attention. The group might, therefore, start with a brief "check in", so that a decision about how to make best use of the time can be agreed. Allowing for a check-in also provides an opportunity for participants to feed back about issues discussed in previous meetings.

What constitutes a "presentation" to a work discussion group?

The word "presentation" can connote something that involves Power-Point, handouts, and best practice delivered with polished finesse. This is the antithesis of what is meant by a "presentation" within a WDG. "Presentation" in this context simply refers to the principle that some-one (the "presenter") will bring an issue, concern, or preoccupation (the "presentation") to share and explore with the group.

Hopes and expectations of headteachers

As part of the initial phase of work, headteachers were invited to consider what preoccupied them most in their work role and, linked to this, what they hoped to get from attending the work discussion group. Responses included: improving skills in delegation; handling difficult discussions; team-building; addressing problematic staff cultures (e.g.

of dependency and grievance); conflict management and resolution. Recently appointed headteachers were also particularly interested in building confidence and emotional resilience in order to maintain a work–life balance.

Format of meetings

It was agreed that meetings would take place monthly for two hours, with two headteachers taking turns to present a current issue or preoccupation. It was further agreed that urgent issues could be given priority when appropriate.

The groups were co-facilitated by Jackson and Hoyle (a colleague from TCS)—a partnership that integrated "on the ground" experience with children, adolescents, and teachers, together with consultancy work of a more organizational nature.

Learning and anxiety

At the outset, most headteachers joining the work discussion group were already substantial leaders in their own right. Certainly, all had considerable experience of developing and managing individuals, teams, and schools. The consultants therefore needed to be mindful about the existing knowledge and skills in the group, as well as the likelihood that, despite this, headteachers might nevertheless feel apprehensive about putting *themselves* into an unfamiliar learning environment. This was especially the case given that the opportunity for reflective discussion and collaborative learning with peers was a completely unique and unprecedented venture for them. It was also in striking contrast to the more familiar experience of headteacher forum meetings within the local education authority at the time, where attendance was variable, the atmosphere tended to be cold and rivalrous, and the focus of discussion was usually on business, policies, and money.

The presence of such anxieties was poignantly illustrated in the informal, but significant, "preamble" discussion between headteachers as the group gathered for our introductory meeting.

For example, as we sat waiting for the last few people to arrive, one headteacher started speaking, in somewhat embarrassed tones, about how "I missed parts of the initial teacher training … perhaps I can go back and do it now!"

A few minutes later another headteacher commented, "Do you know all the nooks and crannies in your school? I don't. Whenever I look round the school I'm always finding more places I never knew existed."

"Really? When I walk down the corridors my staff worry that I am coming to check up on them and that I am going to kick them out of their classroom into a smaller room!" her colleague replied.

At the start of the following meeting there was similar "passing" discussion about the mixed feelings evoked by the increased police presence and the introduction of security cameras in schools. The group agreed unanimously with one headteacher who commented on how "it makes us all feel like we are being watched".

At a conscious level, the headteachers were keen to commence our work and hoped it would offer a safe and supportive opportunity to catch up on developmental building blocks that had either been missed or short-circuited in the past. At the same time, although the "casual" conversation described above was not referred to directly, it did register in the minds of the consultants as a symbolic representation of the anxieties that *are ordinarily and inevitably generated in any new learning venture*: a fear of not knowing, a fear of being downsized and a fear of being exposed, criticized, or publicly shamed.

Despite these anxieties however, headteachers quickly engaged with the task of the work discussion group and soon began to share their experiences with the consultants and each other.

WDG example 1: managing the boundary between personal and professional

Presentation

One headteacher wanted to think about an issue concerning one of her deputy headteachers, John.[7] She described John as the "bedrock of her school" but told us how she had to call him and another deputy headteacher (Sarah) into a meeting to "tell John off" and sort out difficulties between them. The problem was that John had been underperforming and not fulfilling his responsibilities for some time. The headteacher relayed how, in the middle of the meeting, John suddenly broke down in tears. The headteacher described how she had been taken aback and "went cold"—not knowing what to do or how to handle it. John then proceeded to "pour out his personal problems", explaining how he was the primary carer for his elderly father and his disabled wife—all of which consumed his energy, leaving him no time for himself or anything else (including his leadership role in the school). After sharing some further details, the headteacher ended by saying that she didn't know how to manage John or the impact his difficulties were having on other members of the SLT who were having to bear the brunt of his workload.

Initial response from the group

The headteacher's description of the situation generated some strong reactions. Several headteachers immediately jumped in to offer advice and "solutions". Comments were made about "involving occupational health", "taking him through capability", and how "individuals need to deal with their personal problems outside the workplace". The headteacher was also challenged by another group member, who thought her attempts to "rescue the deputy" were inappropriate. "After all", the other head asserted, "the deputy is being paid to do a job, and he must do it!"

At this point in the discussion, one of the consultants alerted the group to the way they were also now jumping in (understandably) to "rescue" their colleague with advice about how she could stop rescuing her deputy! We also encouraged the group to slow down and think about what else we needed to know to get a fuller picture of the situation before jumping into solutions. The atmosphere and tension then seemed to calm.

Group discussion and reflection

Gradually group members began to invite the headteacher presenting the issue to give further contextual information: How had this situation come about? How long had it been going on? How were other members of the SLT experiencing it and reacting to the deputy?

The headteacher outlined her concerns about the growing tension between her two deputies—emphasizing how Sarah had been complaining about John's failings (as she saw them), and how these were now preventing her from being effective.

In the work discussion group, the consultants invited the group to think about what impact this was having. Group members got interested in the contrast between the headteacher's and Sarah's reaction to John. While, for example, Sarah had felt critical and blaming of John—preoccupied largely with how John compromised her effectiveness—the headteacher felt guilty for having confronted him at all—not least "failing to support" someone when all he was doing was supporting others! In fact, the headteacher felt that if she were John, she wouldn't have been able to cope with the emotional pressure and would have wanted to focus instead on how to protect him from any additional work pressures.

When encouraged to think further about the possible significance of these two *apparently* conflicting reactions, the group began to consider the possibility that both were important parts of the whole picture. Perhaps, for example, John oscillated between feeling detached and resentful towards his family for hindering his life (like Sarah felt) and terribly guilty for feeling like this and inclined then to over-compensate by relieving them of any responsibilities (like the headteacher felt).

The headteacher acknowledged that, like John, she had gone into her "default position" by trying to reduce John's responsibilities and shifting these to others. She felt she could not expect more of John, and that this would "reduce his stress".

In the group discussion, headteachers became interested in how aspects of John's relationships with his family were being repeated in the workplace in his relationships with the headteacher and other colleagues. Even within the group discussion itself, some sort of parallel process was activated as group members were initially divided between more frustrated/firm and more guilty/compassionate responses to the situation.

Once adequate consideration had been given to the specific issue that was presented, group members began to make broader links with their own work contexts. Several members shared their own uncertainty about how best to support others in their work role and when it is, or is not, helpful to set firm boundaries. In particular, the group were helped to grapple with the difference between support that is necessary and enabling, as distinct from support more akin to a rescuing. Through exploring this, the group also became interested in how they might unwittingly contribute to a problem being fudged rather than addressed—thereby running the risk of conveying the message that the problem was indeed overwhelming and better avoided altogether (like John felt about his situation).

Although the headteacher who presented the issue was initially concerned that her colleagues would be critical of her leadership style, she commented on how the discussion had restored a sense of perspective and clarity to her thinking. She also commented on how her frame of reference had shifted from, "I can't bear to see him suffer; what other role can I give him? How can I *prevent* the situation from breaking down?". Instead she was now wondering, "how can I help him face his suffering *and* manage his role so as to give him the best chance of moving forward from this? How can I address the reality of the situation to ensure that supporting him does not come at the expense of everyone else?" Other headteachers also felt invigorated by the depth and supportive feel of the discussion, much of which resonated closely with preoccupations they shared in relation to their own staff.

Isolation and loneliness in role

Within the headteachers' group, members came with a wide range of experience, from the lead headteacher and one other, who were very well-established leaders, to others who were only just entering their first year of headship. There was an equally wide continuum between headteachers in relation to confidence in themselves as leaders and their sense of internal license to take up their roles and authority.

Irrespective of experience, most headteachers commented on the loneliness inherent in their role, with no colleague to trust in the way they were now talking to each other in the work discussion group. This was movingly apparent when one headteacher became tearful after admitting to feeling "ganged up on" by her leadership team in a way that left her feeling "inadequate, impotent, and humiliated", with her authority compromised. Although this disclosure to the group felt potentially exposing and compromising, the headteacher was extremely appreciative of the way her colleagues rallied around, helping to clarify her thinking and articulate her insecurities in a way that left her feeling more robust, secure, and supported by the end of the meeting.

As the depth of group discussion, cohesion, and trust developed, headteachers were increasingly willing to share, and be helped to think through, many diverse and complex situations they encountered in their role. These included: the management of challenging staff and team dynamics; disciplinary procedures and staff dismissals; relationships with students, parents, governors and the local community; and situations involving mental health concerns of both parents and staff. One central, recurring theme related to the myriad difficulties experienced by headteachers in taking up their authority and leadership role, delegating to others, and addressing passivity or dependency in their staff.

WDG example 2: managing dependency, delegation, anxieties, and development

In one meeting, a headteacher raised a problem relating to staff discipline and motivation. He described having to deal with a lot of hopelessness and apathy in staff who walked around the school "sighing, crying, and behaving in a generally miserable way". He felt irritated at their passivity and was "tired of being drawn into the role of being the nasty one". On one occasion, he was horrified to find himself telling a teacher, "I don't think you have the capacity to change."

In discussion, once some necessary space had been allowed for group members to let off steam and complain about the lack of ambition in their staff, heads were encouraged to think about the possible causes of staff passivity. One headteacher commented on how "incorrect assumptions are sometimes made about people's wish to develop". This led to a discussion about "growing pains" and how passivity might belie anxieties connected not only to a fear of failure, but also to a *fear of success*. The group became interested in this and began to differentiate between a lack of ability and something that might manifest as complacency but might actually be rooted in anxiety about learning, development, and progression. The consultants also linked this to developmental difficulties sometimes experienced by children and adolescents who might retreat or sabotage themselves as they approach important developmental junctions, such as secondary transition, GCSEs, or the loss of familiar structures and relationships on leaving school.

In addition to reflecting on the possible causes of staff dependency, the consultants challenged headteachers to reflect on whether and how they might inadvertently be contributing to a given situation—for instance, if they themselves struggled to delegate effectively. This struck a chord: while some found it easy to delegate, others were less confident about whether, when, or how they would be able to relinquish control or bear the anxiety and hostility evoked when they faced their staff with additional demands. This was strikingly illustrated by one headteacher, who described a rather shocking situation in which the lack of resources in the Pupil Referral Unit (PRU), coupled with a challenged and challenging student group, meant that on one occasion she literally had to clean the toilets herself.

Within the group discussion, the headteacher of the PRU was helped to reflect thoughtfully on her own resistance to burdening her loyal and over-committed staff and the risk that this could potentially result in her own workload becoming unmanageable. Other headteachers identified with the "shit" one has to take when setting boundaries or facing staff with uncomfortable and unpleasant tasks (literally and metaphorically). This discussion also connected with broader systemic issues—such as the way in which PRUs could be perceived and used like "dumping grounds" for unwanted students deemed not to fit in with the "mainstream". The headteacher was also insightful about the way in which her smaller school, with its limited resources and reduced sense of status (vis-à-vis her mainstream colleagues) might contribute to her own professional identity as something of an outsider within her peer group.

Discussions such as these were significant not only for the headteacher's developing relationship with her staff and student groups, but also in relation to her peers, in whom she evoked greater compassion, recognition, and respect for the complexity of life and work in the PRU. This, in turn, led to an increased wish to support their colleague actively in other settings and, by extension, the work and status of the PRU.

By the end of the discussion, the thinking and insight of the headteacher and other group members, in relation to the original presentation, had developed substantially. They were able to consider in both conceptual and practical ways how one might respond more constructively to a staff member who seemed so negative, despondent, and stuck in their development. Different approaches were also "tested out": for example, rather than telling a staff member that they didn't have the capacity to change (which might feel crushing), headteachers were helped to reframe and explore their concerns that the staff member seemed to have given up on himself and his capacity to develop. In so doing, they could convey the fact that they might not share his belief, in a manner that aimed to enable the staff member to take charge of his own development within a more supportive and containing framework.

The place of "theory" within the work discussion group

Although work discussion groups are not viewed by either consultants or participants as "training" or "lessons", there are occasions when brief input about relevant theoretical concepts is welcomed and felt to provide a helpful structure to consolidate the experiential learning.

For example, given the intense, charged, and sometimes overwhelming nature of interpersonal relationships, it is no surprise that headteachers find it enlightening to be introduced to key psychoanalytic concepts such as splitting, projection, transference, and countertransference. In particular, the realization that the thoughts and feelings evoked in them by staff and students may not simply "belong" to them is often felt to be something of a revelation.[8]

In the group discussion described above, for instance, most headteachers recognized that they could be "drawn into" roles and behaviours that they didn't want. In relation to the teacher who was told he "didn't have the capacity to change", the group were helped to reflect on how the teacher might have *projected* his own feelings of inadequacy, shame, and self-criticism into the headteacher in a way that contributed to the headteacher behaving in an uncharacteristically dismissive way towards his colleague (*via projective identification*). Rather than simply acting on their feelings, headteachers were encouraged to treat their feelings and other *countertransference* experiences as valuable sources of information. This enabled them to make effective use of—rather than to feel inhibited by—the more uncomfortable aspects of their experience. Given the reality that teachers and headteachers often have to endure and contain a relentless bombardment of unconscious projections from students, parents, and each other, the protective potential of these insights should not be underestimated.

Given that school life takes place in class groups and staff teams, it is also helpful for headteachers to integrate their growing recognition of team dynamics with a more explicit understanding of concepts such as *valency* and *basic-assumption* functioning (Bion, 1961). This conceptual understanding could then be used with their own staff teams, for instance in re-channelling energies within a group veering towards *"dependency"* or in creating a more reflective and less polarized atmosphere within a group in the grip of *"fight–flight"* anxieties.[9]

Although concepts such as these are fundamental to all human relationships and therefore underpin any comprehensive psychodynamic training, they are rarely included in any teacher training or subsequent leadership development. In ironic contrast—in the authors' experience—it is relationship-based difficulties that most commonly cause otherwise effective and committed teachers and headteachers to become stressed or even to leave the profession altogether.

Outcomes and evaluation

Collaboration that results in and embeds genuine new learning is difficult to achieve. It often occurs as a by-product of some expediency—not infrequently the pursuit of government funding! However, in contrast to other meetings and activities running in parallel, the work discussion groups encouraged a different kind of dialogue as dilemmas and concerns were authentically shared, problems aired, and deeper understanding was collectively explored. By operating on different levels, the groups not only offered opportunities for individual headteachers to be helped with specific issues, but for all group members to extend their thinking and understanding about a range of issues. Furthermore, since the work discussion groups involved headteachers working together over time, the capacity for peer consultation between colleagues could develop not only within the group but outside it, enabling the work of the work discussion group to take on a life of its own.

Research literature in the field of education leadership abounds with references to emotional intelligence (Goleman, 1998) and the need to grow "emotionally resilient" leaders (Allen, 2009) as well as the "moral imperative of school leadership" (Fullan, 2003). As such, the emotional life of schools and school leaders does now "officially" have a place in the leadership literature and the training of headteachers. But, as with many other aspects of schooling and education, there is a tendency to reduce insight to a set of competencies that can be measured. The methodology of work discussion groups resists this and recognizes that "emotions, particularly anxiety, have a significant effect on the processes of organising and structuring of organizations and that individuals and institutions will seek to defend themselves against the very pain that difficult emotions bring" (James & Connolly, 2000).

What of outcomes? One of the most important outcomes of the work discussion groups was the unique opportunity it offered headteachers to think together in a *completely unprecedented* way—a moment in the month when they didn't have to respond to multiple demands, when they weren't required to make snap decisions or to contain others, a moment in the month when they did not feel so utterly alone in their role. Or—as one headteacher put it—*"The groups are the one sane moment in an otherwise mad month."*

Given that this process was not always comfortable, it was significant that over the three years that this group continued to meet, hardly any headteacher missed more than one session. Of course, the heads continued to meet in other contexts and for different purposes outside the group, but not with such exemplary attendance.

In open-group evaluation, headteachers said that they "valued the time and space to share issues, to support each other, and to unload". Several felt that "relationships across the borough had improved". Some reported that they had learned "different ways of taking up their authority by realizing that they didn't have to keep rescuing staff and could instead enable them to find their own solutions to their problems". They had gained a "better understanding of team dynamics" as well as of their own leadership style and its impact on others who were different. They felt that they had gained a "heightened awareness of conscious and unconscious processes" at play in their organizations, including a "clearer understanding about the impact of change". One head asserted that the work discussion groups "were one of the most significant professional and personal programmes that I have been involved with. I now enjoy my job more, and I'm energized. I feel that I am part of a high-performing team." Others commented on finding the sessions "stimulating and valuable", adding that they had resulted in group members collaborating in unanticipated ways, for instance by establishing action research into communications issues. Perhaps, most importantly, headteachers noted the way they had begun to hold each other—and the group—in mind. As a result, they were now much more likely to phone each other, to consult informally with each other about crises, and to share solutions and practical ideas.

But what about the kind of outcomes wanted by the DfE? Examination results of all but one of the schools improved during the three-year period, and of the six schools inspected by Ofsted, three were graded "good" and three "outstanding". Berkeley had a nervous moment when the HMI leading her school's inspection decided to test out whether being a Leading Edge school was a distraction diverting senior leaders from raising standards within their own school. The reverse was found to be the case.

After three years of working together in the work discussion group, consultants and headteachers alike were impressed by the way that some of the rather toxic and unhelpful rivalries, prejudices, and stereotypes between schools were gradually transformed into much more constructive competitiveness and collaboration. For instance, rather than simply wanting *to have* the "better" results and status of another school, headteachers grew interested in what it was that was working in other schools, what they might learn from their peers, and, by extension, what aspects of their own expertise they might have to offer their colleagues. Rather than treating their greatest worries and most significant achievements like heavily guarded secrets, the work discussion group became a place where these could be shared more openly by headteachers in the spirit of trust and collective development, for the good of the whole system.

Acknowledgements

The work described in this chapter was an innovative partnership of learning and trust. We would like to thank Terry Molloy and Christine Justic for their contributions to this chapter. We would also like to acknowledge the contributions of other members of the work discussion group: Gill Ball, Siobhan Crawley, Mike Hulme, Maggie Raffee, and Dame Ruth Robbins. Finally, we would like to acknowledge the significant contribution of Linda Hoyle, who was Jackson's co-consultant in the group.

Notes

1 More comprehensive information about the intellectual origins of work discussion can be found in *Work Discussion* by Rustin and Bradley, 2008.
2 For further information about the evaluation of work discussion groups for teachers, see Jackson, 2008a; Warman & Jackson, 2007.
3 Category as defined by the Department for Education (DfE), the central government department responsible for schooling, formerly known as Department for Children, Schools and Families (DCSF).
4 Jackson was, at this point, working as a child and adolescent psychotherapist in the Adolescent Department of the Tavistock Clinic.
5 Now re-named "Tavistock Consulting".
6 This is especially important to clarify when the facilitator is also a psychotherapist!
7 All names and identifying details have been changed to protect confidentiality.
8 For further description about psychoanalytic concepts, see chapter 3, by Biddy Youell.
9 For further description about systemic and group dynamic concepts, see chapter 4, by Judith Bell.

CHAPTER EIGHT

Learning leadership: lessons from the top

Ben Bryant

E ver since the work of Piaget and Dewey, educators have understood the importance of experiential learning more than other sectors. One hundred years after the theory of experiential learning was first articulated, this innovative approach to learning is finding greater application in many areas of the school curriculum as well as in the expanding sector of executive education.

But what about the managers of educational institutions, including school principals or headteachers? How might they benefit from applying experiential learning approaches to enhancing their own leadership effectiveness? Should they attend formal training, or could they learn more from reflecting on their own experiences?

In this chapter, I suggest that school principals have much in common with chief executive officers (CEOs) and senior executives in the corporate world. Because of the responsibilities of their roles and the expectations of certainty and clarity that are placed on them, senior executives tend to miss opportunities to learn because they become defensive and stuck in their role. These are what I call Executive Learning Disabilities, which are peculiar to senior executive roles. These should not be confused with the dispositional learning disabilities of children in the classroom. Rather, they are learning disabilities created within the specific role of a senior executive's authority. While formal training programmes may provide some valuable frameworks and concepts, leaders who focus on their experiences overcome the learning disabilities that emerge in senior positions and are more likely to learn and change. Through my research, I have discovered that executives can enable and sustain their learning through a combination of personal narrative writing and dialogue. The narratives in particular are a vehicle to help executives get in touch with the more visceral (rather than intellectual) experience of leadership, while the dialogues are helpful for deeper sense-making.

Drawing on case studies of executive learning by three senior executives, I posit that opportunities for learning in senior executive roles in both corporate and academic settings are ubiquitous, but the *opportunity to learn* from that experience is often not taken up. If it is, it frequently takes the form of shallow clichés and unhelpful generalizations about what makes a successful leader. I use the cases to explore the triggers for learning that are missed, often because of the learning disablers that come with executive roles. I also demonstrate how it is possible for senior leaders to sustain their learning through in-depth exploration and making sense of their experiences.

The conclusion for school principals and senior leaders is not surprising: our educational institutions will not change as much as they could unless leaders learn to identify their obstacles to learning and change themselves and unless experiential learning principles are applied to the experience of leadership.

Leadership development traditions and practices

For more than 50 years, management and leadership development has become an industry in its own right, and it is difficult to ignore the impact it has had on the training of leaders. While there are relevant post-graduate and Masters programmes, most management and leadership development is typically comprised of short programmes conducted from one day to ten weeks' duration.

Theories of leadership have also evolved over the past 50 years. There is now a plethora of theories that can inform any leadership development curriculum, such as leader member exchange (Graen & Uhl-Bien, 1995), charismatic leadership (Conger & Kanungo, 1987), authentic leadership (Avolio & Gardner, 2005), identity (Lord & Hall, 2005), and emotional intelligence (Goleman, Boyatzis, & McKee, 2013; Schutte et al., 1998). These theories have been summarized in several recent reviews of leadership development theory and practice (Day, Fleenor, Atwater, Sturm, & McKee, 2014; Dinh et al., 2014).

Concurrently, there has been a significant evolution in learning methods for leadership development, moving away from teaching leadership theory and case studies of "heroic leaders" to more contemporary methods that include feedback, self-awareness, self-reflection, personal coaching, and even therapy. Plato's well-known directive: "Know Thyself" has been declared "leadership's first commandment" (Collingwood, 2001; Petriglieri, Wood, & Petriglieri, 2011).

Self-awareness tools such as diagnostic surveys have become frequently used in leadership development practice. Numerous diagnostic tools, such as Hogan, LIFO, NEO, MBTI, Belbin, and Career Anchors, give insights into leadership behaviours, career derailers, personality, and preferences. Over time, they have evolved to focus on deeper and harder-to-measure drivers of human behaviour, such as emotions. Other recent research has also explored the identity and authenticity of leaders (Goffee & Jones, 2000) suggesting that perceiving, regulating, and managing emotions are integral to leaders' work.

Although these instruments usually rely on self-reported data, they have been complemented by 360° feedback surveys that awaken the leader's awareness of their impact. By making data anonymous, 360° surveys help leaders receive confidential and honest feedback from colleagues (e.g. direct reports, managers and peers) and, in so doing, overcome the dual problem of self-delusional tendencies of learners and the fear of retribution from those providing feedback.

The underlying assumption is that, confronted with data from the diagnostic tool, the learner will self-regulate towards a more desirable behaviour (Sims & Lorenzi, 1992). Thus, executives often leave the most reputable training institutions and programmes with greater self-awareness than ever before, excited and motivated to apply their learning and transform their organizations. There is some evidence that repeating 360° surveys after a period of time can show change in behaviour (Seifert & Yukl, 2010), but there are also suggestions that the change is difficult to sustain, because the learner either loses motivation or lacks the disposition to transfer and apply learning back to the workplace (Gurdjian, Halbeisen, & Lane, 2014).

Self-awareness has become a significant part of leadership development programmes, and the efficacy of such training has been extensively reviewed (Day et al., 2014). In short, learners tend to rate programmes highly at their conclusion, but the impact on their organization six or twelve months later is mixed, particularly if the programme provides no opportunity for follow-up. The reality of returning to work, old routines and roles quickly makes aspirations for change difficult to realize, leading to a demand for greater application of learning in leadership development activities.

To address this gap, executive coaching has emerged as a significant element of leadership development to help leaders identify and implement behaviour change (Luthans & Peterson, 2003) after receiving feedback. However, while the impact of coaching has been very beneficial, the reliance on a coach to assist with interpretation and development raises a number of interesting dilemmas for leaders who want to take responsibility for their own learning and to make it sustainable (Hooijberg & Lane, 2009).

Psychotherapy for executives is becoming more acceptable as the stigma of "visiting the shrink" subsides in society. Psychotherapy invites executives to develop awareness of deeper, less conscious (or often unconscious) issues and make sense of experiences in their context as they unfold. For example, Petriglieri, Wood, and Petriglieri (2011) reported on the leadership development outcomes of a one-year full-time MBA programme where students examined their experience as it occurred through 20 psychotherapy sessions. They also participated in experiential exercises and conducted behavioural experiments based on their own emotional exploration (p. 438). Their study not only reports deep changes in self and social awareness, it also broadens experiential leadership development to focus on contextual awareness, and deeper personal change.

A Piagetian renaissance

The work of McCall (2010) and his colleagues (McCall, Lombardo, & Morrison, 1989) led to what became widely known as the "the 70:20:10 model" for executive learning, asserting that experience accounts for 70% of executive learning, while coaches and mentors account for another 20% and training programmes account for only 10%. Although based on self-reported data from successful executives, few people have questioned McCall's principle, and it enjoys widespread acceptance in the sector, suggesting it has at least some face validity. As their responsibilities increase, most senior executives realize that theory and case studies lack relevance to their own context. Their own experience is not only unique, but also one of their richest sources of learning. But very little attention has been paid to *how* executives actually learn from experience and how they might extend or deepen their learning.

The origins of experiential learning go back to the work of Dewey (1938), who, in turn, influenced constructivist developmental psychologists Piaget (1955) and Vygotsky (1978). The biggest difference from other learning models is that the participant's own experience, rather than theory or case studies, is the starting point of learning, requiring participants to be open to all kinds of experiences as vehicles for learning. In leadership development, it involves making sense of complex situations, and more importantly, understanding how the individual leader impacted and was impacted upon in those situations.

Experiential learning has been a frequent intervention of leadership development programmes and often includes small-group decision-making simulations, outdoor exercises, and role-plays. In these scenarios, behaviour unfolds in a specified situation and timeframe and then becomes the basis of observation, reflection, and learning.

In the increasing search for novelty, leadership development programmes have expanded to include non-routine experiences, such as artistic experiences with music, theatre, and drama and discovery events, where managers visit unusual leadership situations such as humanitarian sites in Africa, slums in India, and high-tech innovation centres in China and California. The pedagogical assumption of these approaches is that confronting participants with provocative, surprising, and non-habitual experiences will trigger enhanced awareness of their own behaviour, thoughts, and emotions, allowing them to question their own mindset, assumptions, and routine behaviours to find alternative and more effective ways of leading. The criticism of these simulated learning experiences is that they do not reflect the participants' "reality". This criticism however, misses the point. They are not intended to reflect the learner's reality, but they can be an inspiration for change, rather than change itself.

In McCall's 1989 framework (McCall, Lombardo, & Morrison, 1989), learning from experience meant learning "on the job". Different techniques were developed for this, such as "action learning" and new assignments in different countries. Success and failure provide a critical feedback loop where intention, action, and outcome can be examined for potential learning. Through Kolb, action learning has become synonymous with *learning through reflection* (Kolb, 1984), having a significant impact on leadership development practice, through creating a systematic process for self-reflection in day-to-day work.

In the late 1980s and the 1990s, action learning became more widely practiced, due mainly to its success at General Electric, which ran action-learning programmes and teams to solve real and relevant problems (Tichy, 1989). The essence of this approach is that real problems can be solved in context while simultaneously generating or contributing to personal and organizational development.

One of the debates in the experiential learning literature is whether there is always a need for reflection in order to learn. Dewey expressed a strong point of view on this: "We do not learn from experience … we learn from reflecting on experience" (1933, p. 78). The need to reflect in order to learn has always been the principle of inductive learning—that is, deriving generalized principles from experiences. The need to separate the experience of learning from the experience itself has become an unquestioned principle of learning design. McCall (2010) argues that learning tends to take a back seat in action learning as participants tend to mostly focus on their primary task—leading. A natural response to this is to then create a space where the "task" is to focus on learning rather than solving work problems and achieving performance outcomes. This inevitably leads to learning becoming separate from the work experience.

However, this is not reflective of the Piagetian view of experiential learning, where play, curiosity, and intuition play a significant role in child development; so, if we insist that reflection is essential to create learning, we might be underestimating an executive's capacity to learn. Exposure to ambiguity and uncertainty in complex contexts requires not only recognition of patterns and cycles in those contexts, but also an understanding of the socio-emotional dynamics that will ensue. Containing and holding uncertainty and ambiguity for others while making choices where there is no clear right answer is a visceral emotional experience. Learning leadership involves attention to and mindfulness of that experience, making sense of complex situations while they are happening and understanding how they reacting and interacting in those situations. Learning from experience in this way involves overcoming defences, stepping out of comfortable routines, and displaying vulnerability and courage.

Thus, in an era of ever-increasing complexity, the need to separate the experience of learning from the experience of leadership is timely. Removing the task from the learning setting may help learners to explore more deeply, but in so doing, it loses the "here-and-now" aspect of learning while doing. If we assume that learning is an intellectualization of experience, we will want to learn in the cool light of day rather than while it's all happening. As we intellectualize our experience, we create a new rule of thumb, which we apply in new situations, but we also ignore or suppress the emotional and impulsive responses that will continue to drive our seemingly perfectly rationalized choices.

Techniques for learning while leading

A number of pedagogical methods have been developed to enable in-depth and in-the-moment learning from experience. For example, Work Discussion Groups, where the facilitator encourages learners to explore and make deeper sense of their day-to-day experiences, have been adapted for teachers and senior leaders in educational settings (Jackson, 2008b).[1]

> Discussions are, as one might expect, wide-ranging, stimulating, and challenging in style and content. Rather than pupil-related issues, they tend to address preoccupations such as line management relationships, difficulties in taking up—or being allowed to take up—authority, anxieties about delegation, relationships with other key stakeholders (e.g. governing body, local partners, etc.). [Jackson, 2008b, pp. 71–72]

A writing cure

"Learning narratives" can also help senior executives access deeper learning from their actual experiences. This tool has played a key role in my research into the enablers and disablers to executive learning.

Each narrative has three sections:

» *Description*: describe the events as a neutral observer without prejudice or interpretation. "What would an outsider, who knew nothing about the context or people, say?"

» *Exploration*: invites the narrator to articulate the thoughts and feelings that may have been hidden from view at the time. We suggest that these thoughts and feelings might "feel crazy and unreasonable" but that this is where great learning may occur. Quite often, the emotions can become re-triggered during this section.

» *Sense-making*: we invite people to entertain the idea that everyone is competent, and so how the behaviour observed and the emotions generated (even the crazy ones) can become "sensible"—that is, made plausible sense of. This is where psychodynamic and social psychological concepts are most helpful, because they normalize the experience and enable deeper processing and containment.

As part of my research, I invited senior executives to reflect on some of their experiences of learning before our initial meeting. They write a short narrative—typically about half a page—describing experiences that have surprised them, a success, a failure, or a major event. They offer explanations for each of the events and identify what they learned about themselves in the process.

I then introduce relevant psychodynamic concepts (e.g. common defence mechanisms, projection, splitting, transference, countertransference)[2] as well as frameworks from social psychology (sense-making, social identity). The written narrative then becomes an artefact for a fishbowl discussion with colleagues and/or a facilitator to explore and experience. It is important to recognize that the process of writing and discussing is where the learning takes place. The narrative is not a statement of learning, but a trigger for learning. As one executive said: "I don't know what I think and feel until I hear myself say or write it down."

The following three contrasting case studies help to illustrate different aspects of deeper executive learning[3] that can also be applied to school leaders.

Case study 1: Karl Mulhouse—learning from new contexts

This case study is an example of learning from new contexts, in which leaders must confront their assumptions.

Karl Mulhouse, a senior executive of a large German chemical manufacturer, was promoted and transferred to a CEO role in Ukraine in 2012. His immersion in a different leadership context, as well as the full responsibility for the financial performance of the local business, was a significant stepping stone in his career development. His company saw this challenging new role as an opportunity for Karl to experience complexity and interconnectivity in a different system. He knew that taking on this role meant he needed to question his assumptions every day. Even so, he got more than he bargained for.

Six months after his transfer to Ukraine, the country plunged into a deep political crisis. The president at the time reneged on promises to sign an agreement with the European Union, and Ukrainians across the country responded with massive street protests, resulting in the ouster of the current leader and the exposure of massive amounts of government corruption. The subsequent instability was escalated by Russia's annexation of Crimea and a military conflict in eastern Ukraine between Ukrainian military and pro-Russian forces. In managing the business amid this turbulence and uncertainty, Karl was confronted with decisions that challenged both his moral and his rational decision-making capacities.

During the crisis, Karl was torn between his desire to show loyalty to his staff and his responsibility for the financial performance of the business. He felt very isolated and moved to fulfil his staff's human needs for reassurance, financial resources, and safety while simultaneously facing demands for results from headquarters. He struggled to determine how much and when he should communicate with both staff and headquarters, and felt he needed to change his style from collaborative to more authoritarian when the crisis demanded quick decision making on his part. Throughout, he had to manage the anxiety levels of his staff, headquarters, and his own stress amid an information vacuum. After four years in the role, Karl was promoted to a regional manager role in Central America.

We asked him to reflect on his learnings and the development of his leadership skills during his work in Ukraine. Karl's initial response revealed three well-thought-through rules of thumb: "stay abreast of economic instability, ensure security of staff, and manage communications effectively."

Deeper learning

Karl's deeper learning narrative and dialogue confronted many unconscious behaviours and beliefs related to his style of leadership. He had a strong need to demonstrate confidence and conviction while also acknowledging his own doubts, uncertainties, and fears. He also recognized his fear of betrayal, having always been loyal to the company that had given him so many opportunities to rise beyond his own family's humble beginnings. A central insight for Karl was recognizing how his needs for security and attachment helped him to maintain relationships. He sought solace in his relationship with his wife, who helped to provide a secure base during times of high emotion and confusion. This allowed him to contain his feelings and not show too much vulnerability to his staff, who turned to him for reassurance and protection during this period of instability.

Finally, he explored his sense of identity and desire to work in emerging markets. Was his desire derived from his need to separate from tight bonds with a conservative family with humble roots, and the responsibilities it implied? Or did his choices also reflect his egalitarian values of supporting the underdog and helping others to improve their lives? These explorations gave Karl the confidence to move on to his next assignment with a clearer sense of identity and renewed sense of conviction in his values. He noted that this conviction now helps him make decisions more rapidly and that he is now prepared to accept greater uncertainty and higher risks of failure.

Case study 2: Georgina Brown—learning from new roles

This case study illustrates the process of learning from new roles. The most significant learning is not limited to discovering new practices, but rests in the confrontation of long-held beliefs.

Georgina Brown completed her Executive MBA when she was 42 years old. After completing her EMBA, she applied for a job as the CEO of a large hospital in the United Kingdom. The hospital employed approximately 1,000 staff. There were five final applicants for the position (from a pool of 15), and the panel unanimously agreed that Georgina was the best candidate. She was given a mandate to "do what she needed to do" by the hospital board. If the financial problems weren't solved, the hospital risked being closed by the National Health Service (NHS).

Georgina did not have a medical background: she had originally trained as a lawyer and accountant, but she had had a successful experience in restructuring a R&D unit within a large global pharmaceutical company. In her first months on the job she listened closely to the senior doctors and functional administrators on an individual basis, and after two months she began to discuss her ideas for change more frequently. In a presentation to the extended management team, she drew on her discussions, her own experience, and some of the frameworks she had learned in her Executive MBA programme. One of her first recommendations was that the hospital should overhaul its IT infrastructure. This met with some nods from about a third of the extended team.

About 30 minutes into her presentation, the senior paediatric consultant left the meeting abruptly to take an "urgent" phone call. After he left, three of four other doctors also excused themselves early, saying that they were "sorry" but they had patients to see. Of those that remained, some asked difficult questions, some said they did not understand her proposals to integrate departments, and others remained silent. After the meeting, the most senior orthopaedic surgeon, who was close to retirement, told Georgina privately that she had not yet understood the hospital, but that he was very glad that she had taken the job and told her to "keep going".

Georgina began to question her abilities. Perhaps she wasn't ready for this job. She approached the senior orthopaedic surgeon and sought his advice in confidence. Every time she proposed something, someone would say that it would not work or it could not be done, and Georgina would roll her eyes while looking at the senior orthopaedic surgeon. Sometimes people would tease her about her models and frameworks, saying things like, "Aren't you going to give us another one of your MBA matrix analyses Georgina?"

Georgina resigned from the hospital after nine months and took a six-month sabbatical, determined to learn from her experience. Her frustrations with the hospital were severe. She blamed many of the senior doctors, who did not really want change. She reflected that her initial learnings were: she should have (1) built a cohesive team sooner; (2) trusted her own judgements and decisions instead of seeking confirmation of her decisions; (3) have been better prepared for the politics of the hospital.

Deeper learning

Georgina's deeper learning narrative and dialogue took her into exploring why she began to self-doubt in this situation. She reflected on how she had been intimidated by doctors, and the authority of their role, and the possible origins of these feelings. She felt that she lacked the medical expertise necessary for the role, and, as a result, she could feel that the doctors did not respect her. She wondered why she had not made any bold decisions in the first six months and had hoped her more consensual approach would be as successful, as it had been in her previous role in the R&D organization. She also wondered whether and how the senior orthopaedic surgeon may have been using her in his own political battles with the other doctors—even if unconsciously. She found this insight difficult as she usually trusted older men more easily than her male peers.

Five months after resigning from the hospital, Georgina took on a CEO role at very large Geneva-based NGO in the health sector. One year into this role, she reported that she had taken stock of her sources of authority and the transference and countertransference dynamics with the senior orthopaedic surgeon that had become a part of her own sense of authorization and safety. She also learnt to embrace her naiveté—recognizing a lack of knowledge and expertise could lead to a different kind of confidence in asking questions. Her ability to lead large groups of people with conviction, authenticity, and integrity also shifted. She was now able to rediscover the harder edge of her authority in an unfamiliar environment and balance it with her more familiar empathic and vulnerable side.

Case study 3: François le Blanc—over-conviction disables learning

This case study describes how over-conviction can disable learning for leaders by reducing opportunities for dialogue and creating dependency in followers.

François le Blanc was the business development director for a large European food processor and manufacturer based in France, with ambitions to be CEO. It was clear to everyone that costs had to be cut as there was considerable over-capacity within the industry and many companies had failed to invest because of a long-term trend of low profitability.

In his current role, he reported directly to the CEO. In an external Board meeting, he put forward a proposal to acquire a competitor to increase their market share. François was well prepared. He had a plan to achieve immediate savings by closing the acquired production unit and transferring this volume to their existing processing plant. His financial analysis was detailed and perceived to be thorough, and his plan for implementing change seemed to be practical. He proposed a solid post-acquisition team and assembled a line-up of corporate finance experts, lawyers, and accountants, all of who came with good reputations.

The Board was initially sceptical. Growth by acquisition had not always been successful in the industry, but it did offer some advantages. François argued passionately for the acquisition, inviting board members to question their cautiousness. This would be different, and he was able to explain why.

The deal was approved, and François led the integration team, working long days and nights during the negotiations to ensure its success. Anyone who argued caution was challenged for being negative and closed to opportunities. As the acquisition date came closer, things started to go wrong for the company they were acquiring. The company had become less attractive. On the eve of closing the deal, François was questioned about some of these concerns, but he insisted that they should continue.

The deal went ahead, and the implementation plan was initiated, but some of the risks that had been raised earlier began to materialize. François began to experience stress on a scale that he had never felt before. He was barely sleeping and was never at home with his wife and children. Day after day problems arose that had to be solved immediately. Outwardly, he maintained a positive mindset, but privately, he started to consider impossible solutions and became more desperate. After a few months, the board conducted an emergency review and relieved François of his responsibilities. They decided to write off the investment and sell what remained of the assets.

François took a leave of absence for 12 months, believing his career was over. When trying to understand what went wrong, initially François believed that he could have made it work, *if only* he had not underestimated the need for better coordination between the two companies. He felt a lack of transparency from the acquired company had made his task impossible. He also felt they had been unlucky with some external market events that were beyond his control. He conceded that he should have listened to some of the doubters, but he argued that listening to them all the time would have resulted in getting nothing done.

After six months, François started to admit that his ambition had got the better of him. He acknowledged the huge personal commitment that had been made by the shareholders to ensure the deal took place. After a year, he began to fully blame himself feeling that he, and he alone, had been responsible for the disaster.

> I put down my failure at that time to a passionate confidence and belief in myself that literally bulldozed through objections. I took far too much on myself. I didn't seek opposite views or consider another path—I was fixed on the pre-decided original plan. I didn't listen to others or consider contingency planning. There was no sensitivity analysis. All of the issues that became the major elements of the fiasco were there on the day the deal was closed, but no final review was done to see if the original logic still existed—it did not.

Deeper learning

It took François four years to recover emotionally and mentally from this experience. With the assistance of therapy, he explored more deeply what he learned about himself.

> I paid a huge personal price for this disaster. I was diagnosed as having suffered from depression and anxiety and attended therapy for several years. Thankfully my wife and family stood by me for I was very low.

In his personal therapy, François explored his ambition, his need for recognition, and his need to prove himself. He also came to some important insights about his autonomy, distance and intimacy in his personal and professional relationships. He explored some of the repeated patterns that had evolved over many years.

> After four years I picked myself up and resumed my career within the same food business, becoming managing director two years later and driving the company to become the leading national food processor with a 15% market share.

François reports that he is a very different kind of leader today than he was before the acquisition. His intense and personal learnings have led him to become what he describes as "more grounded, less anxious, and more understanding of others". While he is still very demanding of others, he feels much more aware of the impact of his ambitions and of his need for achievement and recognition. He is also more conscious of his resistance to listening to the validity of different perspectives and is now using them to re-examine his own ambition and perspectives with a more open mind.

Discussion

Triggers for learning

These cases suggest that many experiences can be *triggers for learning*. As part of my research I analysed and coded over 500 narratives produced by senior executives and found that many of their daily experiences are opportunities to learn. School principals are no different in this regard. They do not necessarily need to attend training programmes in order to learn; they need the intention and desire to learn in order to look at everyday events as the basis for development. Thus, we invite school principals and other education leaders to pay attention to the following four potential triggers for learning:

Exposure to different contexts

In the personal development literature, it is well documented that exposure to different contexts is a highly effective trigger for learning. From class trips of increasing duration, to teenagers taking a gap year, to executives starting a new assignment in a different culture, anyone can use their experience in a different context to trigger growth. Different contexts do not need to be different cultures. On the surface, the aim might be to adapt and apply practices from one place to another, but many people report significant increase in self-awareness from cross-cultural assignments, although few are able to articulate what they have learned beyond "growing" or "maturing".

At a deeper level, exposure to different contexts confronts leaders with their assumptions and provides a chance to question and explore the sources of past successes and disappointments or failures. In other words, it is necessary to avoid becoming judgmental and to remain open as to how a new context can take us by surprise.

For school leaders, exposure to different contexts can mean visiting other schools or education systems or—to avoid this amounting to no more than a simple transfer of practice—other contexts, for example how the fashion industry creates new fashion or how prisons and prisoners learn, or do not learn, and why.

Taking up new roles

Learning in a new role, particularly a promotion, is not necessarily about simply discovering rules of thumb for success. Understanding the *context* of a new role and how the leader responds and takes up authority in that role is one of the most crucial sources of learning for any executive. The context of senior executive work is unique. While they will often try to derive simple clichés to encapsulate their learning, in reality their learning is subjective and situation-specific. This is seen in how they take up their authority and respond to the dynamic interplay between the context and their authority.

Establishing authority

In a school system is a school leader's most central leadership challenge, and the first six months in a new role are a critical period for laying the foundation. The dynamics in an educational context are unique in that learners and their parents might be seen as "clients", yet authority remains with teachers and principals. School leaders can attempt to take up authority by modelling approaches on previous influences and personal or professional role models. Identifying those influences can help educational leaders identify their tendencies and create the space for choice in the way they take up their authority in a new role.

Success and failure

In the age of the internet and relentless exposure to news and information, children still learn proactively about their world through their experiences. They are permitted, sometimes encouraged, to experiment, fail, and learn, and have fun doing so. Senior executives, on the other hand, are denied experiences such as experimentation and failure, because the stakes are too high, or because people expect them to have all the answers. Senior executives lose their interest in variance because the role demands predictability, reliability, and certainty. The impression that their leader knows the answers makes followers feel safe. However, this expectation inhibits a leader's freedom to explore and enquire. Most senior executives actively encourage variance reduction ("I don't like surprises"), while at the same time saying they want people to be innovative and creative.

When we ask senior executives to explore what they learned from their most significant failures, many respond with a narrative where the underlying learning has to do with the unpredictability or incompetence of *other* people, and not their own irrationalities. "I learned not to hire a person like that again". This defence against critical self-reflection is a lost opportunity for real learning.

A school principal's personal reflections on success and failure are potentially the birthplace of deep learning. In the absence of learning, past success as principal in a smaller school or as head of a department can constrain leadership choices, and past failures can lead to caution or *playing not to lose*.

A principal who avoids looking at opportunities for restructuring because of fear of failure or rejection may be seen as more successful than a principal who fails at restructuring through poor judgment or execution. As they become more senior, educators are less apt to take risks or innovate. The costs of failure may seem too high. It is important to consider: does past success encourage principals to experiment and learn from their actions, or to carefully replicate previous strategies and inadvertently limit their own learning? Exploring past success and failure in depth provides valuable lessons in how principals protect themselves rather than seek opportunities for greater effectiveness. It is important for leaders to realize that defensiveness brings about self-delusions that limit the choices leaders are consciously willing to consider. These limits can, in turn, block the effectiveness of the leader and his or her organization.

Learning disablers

This chapter has shown how narrative construction and dialogue can act as a tool to generate learning, both through the process of writing as well as in reflection and dialogue with a professional coach. In order to learn, like senior executives, school principals must overcome their own learning disablers—obstacles to learning directly related to their authority role. The *choice* to learn from their experiences is influenced in part by their motivation to learn and in part by their awareness of their own learning disablers. These learning disablers include:

Externalization of failure

Like senior executives, the role of school leader can be the object of personal and professional attacks from parents, governing boards, governments, media, and members of staff teams, including their leadership team. They are constantly expected to explain their performance and the outcomes of their organization. As they explain their decisions and performance, their explanations "externalize" their decisions and locate the incompetence outside themselves. Yet, in doing so, the problem rooted in their own thinking patterns still remains.

Inability to explore success

We naturally think that senior executives lose their tolerance for experimentation and variance because the role demands predictability, reliability, and certainty. Achieving a performance target is one form of meeting expectations. When predictability is achieved or the perfor-mance target is met, it is difficult to explore the deeper causes of suc-cess. There is a tendency to rationalize and simplify the success to a few key variables. If the performance target is exceeded, the emotional elation makes it even harder to truly understand the deeper causes of success, because there is a desire to rationalize the outcome—to link the outcome to an intentional decision or action by the senior executive that boosts his or her internal sense of competence, thus reducing feelings of being a fraud.

Unbalanced social distance

The role of the senior executive creates a social distance between them-selves and others, so they can lose touch with the reality of the organi-zation and miss vital clues about what is really going on around them. Social distance is created by fears of rejection and an acceptance of isolation in the role.

At the same time, senior executives can also be too close to some individuals in the organization. While offering valuable support, trusted relationships can become too comfortable to maximize learning. For example, the trusted person may become too supportive and not chal-lenging enough. Fuelled by a desire to rescue the leader from pain, they may simply become a trusted supporter, not a trusted challenger. Con-versely, trusted relationships can be taken for granted by the learner, and challenges can be ignored because they feel scripted or routine. Many senior executives also build trusting relationships with their HR (Human Resources) executive or chairperson as the source of important provoca-tions, as these roles provide a more complete view of the context. Still, these relationships may not be as open, deep, or provocative as external relationships because of the embedded authority differences. They can, however, provide an alternative view of the context and challenge the executive's interpretations of events and experience.

Fear of difficult conversations

Despite the extensive traditions of dialogue in many cultures and civili-zations, most senior executives do not know how to leverage the dynam-ics of team dialogue to create difficult conversations that lead to learning for themselves and their team. Most senior executives put diverse teams together in the belief that diversity will lead to debate, but in practice the level of Socratic dialogue, constructive challenge, and argument is often limited. Senior executives know how to create diversity, but not often how to leverage it. Diversity refers to team membership, but it does not necessarily refer to team process.

Divergence is a team process, and it can lead to conflict, disagreement, and difficult emotions. Our research suggests that most executive teams do not know how to debate and argue, nor how to be open to creating new solutions. We have found that anxiety and fear of divergent points of view illicit strong feelings—feelings that are created less by the substance of the debate and more by the history and team's experiences of role differentiation, authorization, envy, betrayal, competition, and coalitions that are usually sitting *under the table*, unspoken, but keenly felt. Even when a civilized and logical discussion is apparent *above the table*, the seemingly "rational" discussion is confused by emotional dynamics that are hidden or expressed through defences such as rationalization, intellectualization, representation and suppression. Team members then manage these dynamics by either containing their arguments or by digging in their heels with rationalizations that are stuck and repetitive, which only exacerbates the dynamic. Thus, executive dialogue often fails to create learning because the conversation above the table is a proxy for the conversation they are having with their feelings below the table.

Avoiding their own discomfort

Most senior executives can think of someone who antagonizes, frustrates or irritates them. Such frustrations can be dealt with by dismissing or firing that person, perhaps because they are "incompetent", "difficult", "hard work", or even a "pain in the neck". Sometimes the relationship is mutually fraught and they both know it, accepting that they just don't understand one another. Perhaps the antagonist cannot accept the authority of the senior executive, or the senior executive is threatened by the competitiveness of the antagonist. Such relationships can consume enormous amounts of energy and emotion, and the simplest response can be to bypass or marginalize them.

Antagonists are sources of dissonance. As senior executives already endure a lot of dissonance in their role, it is understandable that they seek to contain or resist the dissonance that antagonists can create, because they are time-consuming and energy-draining. However, by doing so, the senior executive is rejecting not only the discomfort, aggression, and feelings of incompetence that antagonists elicit but also their ideas and creativity. With the benefit of hindsight, senior executives might recognize that there was more value than they first acknowledged in the perspective of the antagonist and that they changed their actions or beliefs as a result of them. Nevertheless, admitting that the antagonist was right in the moment of dissonance will prove difficult.

Resistance to self-examination

When senior executives are invited to explore their life-shaking events, many are at first sceptical of such learning, wondering how personal events might help develop their leadership or anxious that they would be forced to face issues that they would prefer to leave unexamined.

Once there is a desire to learn, senior executives need to be aware that both the role and their temperament contribute to a failure to learn. It is not enough to say, "I learned that I should 'communicate more', 'delegate more' or 'involve and engage people in the change process'". Most senior executives and school principals are aware of such rules of thumb from books, theory, and their own experiences, and they rarely present new learning for such experienced people. However, by declaring their superficial learning, real and deep learning is avoided. Most senior executives have an unconscious desire to protect themselves from real and deep learning, and they may even believe that this is what makes them successful. However, if senior executives and school principals wish to learn, they need to open their experiences and behaviours to deeper exploration. And to do this, they need to secure enough psychological safety to be vulnerable, which does not come naturally to most executives in role.

Implications for school principals

School leaders are not so different from senior executives when it comes to learning. They share similar challenges in their roles, which demand conviction, certainty, and, to some extent, self-preservation. They have multiple responsibilities that make them the object of projections, splitting, transferences, and countertransferences, like any senior executive. As heads of learning institutions, one difference that might be argued is that they have a value set that is likely to be supportive of learning—and they are probably very supportive of learning for others. But does this protect against—or potentially exacerbate—the risk of self-delusion about their willingness and ability to learn about themselves and their leadership?

This chapter aims to provoke educational leaders to hold up the experiential learning mirror and ask themselves: What have I learned and what could I still learn from my experiences?

Notes

1 For further information about work discussion groups for headteachers, see Emil Jackson's and Andrea Berkeley's chapter 7 in this book.
2 For further description of psychodynamic concepts, see chapter 3 of this book, by Biddy Youell.
3 All three cases have been disguised and used with permission of the protagonists.

PART III

SCHOOL LEADERSHIP DEVELOPMENT

Trends and approaches

The impact of personality preferences on school leadership

Emil Jackson

E ach of us has our own unique personality make up which is an ever-evolving product of both nature and nurture. Notwithstanding our individuality, it is not uncommon for there to be repeated patterns in the way we gravitate towards and away from certain people, behaviours, characteristics and tasks. These patterns permeate many areas of our life and are often further exacerbated by the frenetic pace and emotionally charged nature of school life and leadership.

Why is it, for example, that some people or activities naturally leave us feeling engaged and energized while others so quickly get under our skin and leave us feeling drained and depleted? Why do some people find it impossible to relax before a task is complete, while others can't even start the task until the deadline is hanging over their head? Why does the relationship between some leaders and their staff operate so smoothly, while with others they become so easily misaligned? Is this simply a product of individual differences or are there any discernible patterns to the way this occurs?

This chapter explores important questions such as these through the lens of personality preferences as identified by the Myers–Briggs Type Indicator (MBTI). In particular, it describes how different personality preferences can complement and conflict with each other, both helpfully and problematically, within the context of school leadership. Drawing on a range of *everyday examples* involving interpersonal, intra-team, and inter-team dynamics, this chapter illustrates how an understanding of MBTI personality preferences can be used by school leaders as a non-judgemental tool to understand, respect, and support others, thereby optimizing working relationships. By extension, it also illustrates how the absence of such understanding, can easily result in unnecessary misunderstandings occurring, tensions and conflicts erupting, and leadership relationships being compromised.

A brief background to MBTI

The theory of personality preferences and psychological type was first conceptualized by the Swiss psychiatrist Carl Jung [1875–1961]. Based on his clinical work and observations, Jung believed that different patterns of behaviour evolved as a result of people's inborn tendencies (or *"preferences"*) to use their minds in different ways. In Jung's original theory of psychological type, he identified eight different patterns of mental activity. Although he considered these mental processes as being used by everyone, he believed that people have an innate preference for one of these functions over the others. He further believed that as a result of these preferences, individuals developed patterns of behaviour characteristic of their preferred function. Jung termed people's preferred mental process their *"dominant function"* (Briggs Myers, 2000, pp. 5–7).

Briggs and Myers later developed Jung's ideas with the aim of making the insights of *type theory* accessible, understandable, and useful in people's lives. Their research resulted in the identification of four dichotomies, each of which has two opposite preference poles. These four dichotomies encompass opposite ways of (1) using energy, (2) gathering information, (3) coming to conclusions, and (4) relating to the outside world. They believed that we have a natural *preference* for one or the other pole of each of the four dichotomies and that, collectively, these combine to create our personality type. In total, there are 16 possible combinations of preferences, and therefore 16 possible personality types (Quenk, 2000, p. 4). The application of this work has now been translated and adapted for use across many languages and nationalities across the globe. As a result, MBTI is the most widely used instrument for understanding "normal" personality preferences.

As with almost all psychometric tools, there is a wealth of evidence available that advocates both for and against the reliability and validity of MBTI. This chapter does not seek to review the literature base. Nor does it seek to make a systematic argument for MBTI, or against its critics. I do, however, hope to offer a description of the different MBTI preferences, together with my experience and observation about the significant ways that preferences tend to manifest between people and in teams in the context of educational settings and, specifically, leadership relationships.

My experience of using MBTI with school leaders

As a psychoanalytic psychotherapist, I am naturally interested in the way that our early experiences, attachments, and relationships are internalized over time, coloured inevitably by the nature of our unconscious and internal worlds. I was initially sceptical, therefore, about MBTI's focus on more limited areas of conscious mental functions when I first encountered MBTI in 2001 as part of a corporate consulting project.

My first experience of MBTI within educational settings was in 2004, when I co-facilitated a MBTI workshop for headteachers and senior leaders across eight secondary schools in London. Witnessing the way in which these school leaders engaged with, and made use of, their understanding of personality preferences persuaded me to complete the practitioner accreditation training. Since then, I have facilitated MBTI workshops for approximately 500 teachers and middle and senior leaders across all education phases. The examples and illustrations used in this chapter are drawn from this work.

While a psychoanalytic lens remains my conceptual anchor, and while I continue to view MBTI as *one* lens—not *the* lens—through which to understand personality preferences and differences, I am now convinced by its potential value when used appropriately and effectively.

MBTI uses and misuses: underlying principles and assumptions

In order to ensure that MBTI is used appropriately and effectively, some key principles and parameters need to be understood.

First and foremost, it is essential to appreciate that MBTI offers a framework for understanding peoples' personality preferences and the ways these can interact, complement, and conflict with each other. MBTI is not to be mistaken for an indicator of knowledge, skills, or ability. A simplistic example of this might be that the vast majority of us have a clear preference to write with our right or left hand. Our tendency to prioritize our use of our preferred hand comes naturally to us and requires relatively little thought or effort. We therefore tend to use it more and, as a result, tend to become more proficient in our use of it. In contrast, it usually takes much more energy and concentration for us to write with the same level of proficiency with our non-preferred hand.

What is important to note here is that having this natural preference does not, itself, give any indication of how well we write. Nor does it impede our ability to develop our use of our non-preferred hand were we to want or need to. It would just typically require a great deal more effort.

An understanding of personality preferences can be extremely helpful when trying to make sense of why certain people might typically be resistant to—or more likely to engage with—different tasks. However, having a preference does not mean you are good at that preference—or vice-versa. Because of this, the use of MBTI within any recruitment test or process is problematic and prone to mis-use. Rather, in work, as in life, we need to be able to use all preferences, whether or not they come naturally to us. In this respect, MBTI should not be used as an excuse to avoid anything!

While we all might have firmly held convictions and judgements about the way people "should" behave and the way that things "should" be done, MBTI offers a different approach to understanding difference. In MBTI, there are no "right" or "wrong" preferences. Rather, all personality preferences are valued equally, with different merits and consequences, depending on the context and circumstance.

An understanding of MBTI can be used to enable people to assess *their own* personality preferences. Although this chapter is not designed or intended to be a "self-assessment" tool, readers will inevitably recognize some of the preferences described in themselves. In relation to this, it should be noted that personality preferences are most accurately assessed when we are feeling relaxed and secure in ourselves—rather than when we are in "work mode" or feeling anxious, fatigued, or stressed. Furthermore, it should be noted that—tempting as it may be—judgements about MBTI preferences are *not* something to be imposed on anyone else. Not even by someone who is an experienced and accredited MBTI practitioner!

The Jungian-based theory underpinning MBTI asserts that our personality preferences are *inborn* (Jung, 1923). In other words, while recognizing that our life experiences may or may not have provided a context for our innate personality preferences to flourish, the theory asserts that our *natural* preferences remain consistent through our lives. At a personal level, I am neither convinced by nor opposed to this belief in our preferences being "inborn". I do, however, believe firmly in our ability to continuously develop our use of preferences as we evolve and mature in our minds and in our lives. In this respect, my interest in MBTI is located primarily in its ability—when used appropriately and effectively—to facilitate a climate of greater understanding, respect, and collaboration in our attitude to others, in our relationships in and outside work, in our teams, and in our organizations.

A note about the language of MBTI

It is important to note that MBTI has its own language and labels for preferences that should not be confused with the more colloquial use of the same words. The preferences of "Extraversion" and "Introversion", for example—in MBTI terms—are not about being gregarious or shy. Similarly, the preferences of "Judging" and "Perceiving" have nothing to do with being judgemental or perceptive.

It is also important to be aware that when discussing MBTI, the words *"type"* and *"preference"* are sometimes used somewhat interchangeably. Strictly speaking, however, *"preference"* is the term used to describe the four different pairs of opposite preferences (e.g. extraversion and introversion, sensing and intuition, thinking and feeling, judging and perceiving)—eight different preferences in total. *"Type"* is the term used to describe the cumulative combination of any person's preferences, of which there are 16 in total (e.g.; estj, infp, etc.). In colloquial shorthand, however, people might refer to someone as being a *"feeling type"* or a *"sensing type"* when describing someone who has identified themselves as having a "preference for feeling" or a "preference for sensing", for example.

The four pairs of personality preferences and their impact in school leadership

MBTI identifies and describes four different pairs of opposite preferences, which will be described in more detail below. These are:

1. **Extraversion (E) and Introversion (I)**, which relates to what and how we tend to be energized.
2. **Sensing (S) and Intuition (N)**, which relates to the type of information we prefer to give and receive.
3. **Thinking (T) and Feeling (F)**, which relates to the process by which we prefer to make decisions.
4. **Judging (J) and Perceiving (P)**, which relates to how we tend to organize ourselves in our lives.

Extraversion (E) and Introversion (I)

Overview

Extraversion and Introversion are words that are readily used and mis-used colloquially. In relation to MBTI preferences, they refer primarily to the different things that tend to energize us and drain us of energy. As a simple overview:

Extraverts (*E*) typically tend to be energized by activities and interests that are outward-facing, engaging actively with the external world. It is a bit like they are solar-powered—fuelled by energy that is sourced outside themselves.

While extraverts may spend plenty of time engaged in more introspective activities, they have a natural tendency to gravitate towards activities and interests located in the external world when they need to re-charge.

Introverts (*I*) tend to be energized by activities and interests that are more inward-facing, through engaging actively with their internal world. It is as though they are battery-powered—powered by energy that is sourced within themselves.

While introverts may spend plenty of time engaged in externally facing activities and interests, they have a natural tendency to gravitate towards more introspective activities and interests when they need to re-charge.

Needless to say, many activities hold equal interest and satisfaction to both extraverts and introverts alike. In this respect, it is not necessarily the activities that differ but, rather, the way in which introverts and extraverts tend to engage with these activities. For example, both may get great pleasure and energy from reading a good book. However, while an introvert might be perfectly content to digest and process his thoughts internally, an extravert would usually have a more natural desire to share his thoughts and reactions out loud with others as part of their digestive process.

Common characteristics

Extraverts and introverts typically tend to learn and approach new tasks in different ways. Extraverts tend to learn initially through action, by first trying something out or talking something through, after which they will be more likely to take time to think and reflect. Introverts, in contrast, tend to learn initially through observing, reflecting and rehearsing something within their minds, after which they might be more likely to take action and try something out.

While introversion and extraversion should not be confused with being shy or gregarious, introverts often tend to gravitate towards a depth of interests and relationships, while extraverts tend to gravitate towards a breadth of interests and relationships. By extension, while introverts can be outstanding class teachers and school leaders, too much time in larger group settings can leave them feeling quite drained. Equally, while extraverts can derive great satisfaction from more intense and insular involvement in specific interests and relationships, they often find themselves needing stimulation from a broad range of activities and relationships, especially when they are in need of recharging.

Different communication styles and their impact in team meetings

Extroverts and introverts tend to have different communication styles, which can create tensions if misunderstood, especially within group and team settings.

Extraverts usually prefer to talk things through *en route* to digesting or developing any new ideas. Often, they will find themselves completing their thoughts out loud, in an outwardly expressive way. As E.M. Forster said, "How do I know what I think until I see what I say?" At times, however, the extraverts' difficulty in holding incomplete thoughts in their head can result in them inadvertently talking over others in a way that can be experienced as lacking adequate consideration and being somewhat uncontained or even rude.

Introverts usually prefer to think things through, completing their thoughts inside their own minds before sharing them with anyone else. Because they don't need to share their thinking in order to complete it, they may not feel the same need to contribute to group discussion unless they are directly invited to do so. Even then, some may feel uncomfortable at being "put on the spot to reply in public". As a result, introverts are sometimes experienced as being somewhat reserved or even withholding. If their silence is misinterpreted over time, it can subsequently result in introverts becoming increasingly overlooked or even ignored.

Whereas a group of extraverts might engage in discussion through energetically talking at the same time, a group of introverts would be more likely to engage through listening to each other carefully, taking turns to talk if and when space emerges or when more directly invited to contribute.

Example: team meetings with an extraverted headteacher

An extraverted headteacher raised concerns about the effectiveness of her leadership team meetings in one of our coaching sessions. She was especially concerned that a culture of over dependency on her as head-teacher undermined the productivity of the team as a whole. To help her think about this, she asked me to observe a team meeting and feedback my impressions to her.

In the team meeting I attended, one of the most significant things I observed was the way in which the headteacher repeatedly interjected almost immediately, in response to any pause in discussion, or following anyone else's contribution. While her conscious intention was to keep the meeting flowing and to validate and support the contributions of her team, the nature and frequency of her responses created a hub-and-spoke effect that interfered with the team's ability to engage with and respond to each other. As a result, team discussions resembled a series of individual interactions between senior leader and headteacher, rather than a discussion that was located in the team as a whole. And some team members remained silent throughout.

The headteacher was open to my observations, which resonated with her. She was also able to use them to reflect with me on the dynamics of her team meetings and what might be going on—both at and beneath the surface. For example, the headteacher was aware of how frequently she ended up doing more work than necessary for her senior leaders and how often she found herself caught up in an intense debate with an individual while others seem to sit back and watch what was going on as if in the audience. In this respect, it was possible to think about how the dynamics of her SLT meetings resembled something akin to what Bion might consider to be a "dependency" or "pairing" group (Bion, 1961).[1] Similarly, we also thought about what the team as a whole might unconsciously be avoiding through channelling most dialogue towards and through the headteacher—for instance, their underlying competition and rivalry with each other.

The headteacher found these perspectives and insights helpful. This then led us to consider some practical ways that the headteacher might try to improve the dynamics of team meetings. The headteacher found it particularly helpful to think about the team dynamics through the lens of MBTI type preferences. Having already used MBTI with her team, she was aware that she was a *"very clear extravert"* and that several of her team were *"introverts"*. Her awareness of these differences enabled me to address the unintended impact of the head's natural tendency to think out loud in a way that was very direct, but not felt to be critical or judgemental. Doing so even enabled the head to laugh about her difficulty in, "keeping my mouth shut long enough to allow others to speak"!

Reflecting on the dynamics of team meetings through the lens of type preferences gave the headteacher a framework and structure for adapting her own participation in SLT meetings. For example, it galvanized her to *"listen in silence"* for longer and, when intervening, to focus her interventions on comments or questions that facilitated discussion and thinking *between team members* rather than between team members and herself. Furthermore, when she noticed herself or others occupying too much airtime, she was able to draw on the team's shared language of MBTI to encourage the "extraverts" to keep quiet so the "introverts" could contribute. She felt able to do this in a way that non-judgmentally addressed everyone in general and no one in particular.

While the headteacher continued to chair the meetings, she subsequently told me that these small but significant adaptations helped her to "effectively re-locate ownership of the agenda and engagement in meetings with the team as a whole".

Extraversion and introversion: tensions and adaptations

In the absence of an understanding of MBTI, it is not uncommon for introverts to experience their extraverted colleagues as being uncontained, domineering, verbose, and even rude, particularly within group settings. Equally, it is not uncommon for extraverts to experience their introverted colleagues as being uninterested or even withholding of their thoughts within group discussions—leaving extraverts unsure what introverts actually think or feel.

Adaptations for extraverts

Extraverts could consider helping their introverted colleagues by being more active in seeking their views and contributions and tolerating the frustration of listening to their replies without talking simultaneously. It is also important for extraverts to be aware of how they might be inadvertently experienced by others (e.g. as domineering and/or waffling), especially if they have a tendency to talk for some time before working out what they actually want to say!

It is also helpful for extraverts to be aware that introverts can feel put on the spot when asked to respond to an important issue or question without prior warning, especially in public. Typically, introverts appreciate being given some time, along with some written material, to formulate their thoughts and consider their responses before having to reply—for instance to a consultation document. Introverts would also be unlikely to appreciate someone initiating an impulsive conversation, for instance when passing them in the corridor or by turning up unannounced at their office, just because their door is open. This would be more likely to be experienced as an unwelcome intrusion that might put the introvert on the back foot and generate an unnecessarily closed or defensive response.

Adaptations for introverts

Although introverts may not experience an innate need to share their thoughts with others, they need to take seriously the way they might be mis-interpreted, together with the cost to overall team functioning when their potential contributions exist primarily in their own minds. Introverts, therefore, might need to push themselves to speak up more—and sooner—than they might ordinarily do, particularly in a pressurized and fast-paced team meeting when an invitation to speak might be unlikely to happen.

In a similar vein, it can be helpful for introverted school leaders to be aware of their natural tendency to overestimate how much of their thinking they have communicated externally (as against it taking place inside their minds). It is not uncommon, for example, for introverted headteachers to feel bemused and even frustrated about why other people seem unclear about what they want, when they themselves are so clear. Introverted leaders can also help their extraverted colleagues by allowing adequate time for brainstorming and shared discussion—something for which they might naturally have less of a need.

MBTI and the physical layout of an organization

The significance of these differences can also be felt in relation to the physical layout of any given organization. For instance, introverts might be more likely struggle to find the reflection time and space they need away from others when working in an open-plan environment or staff room. Equally, an extraverted school leader may struggle to be at their most creative and productive if they feel isolated, with insufficient stimulation and interaction for extended periods of time.

In view of these differences it is easy to imagine how introverted and extraverted preferences might also influence the likelihood of headteachers and other school leaders having an "open or closed door" approach to their leadership.

Sensing (S) and Intuition (N)

Overview

"*Sensing*" and "*Intuition*" are the terms that MBTI uses to describe the opposite ways we naturally prefer to give and receive information.

As a simple distinction, *Sensing types* (S) generally prefer to start with the detail and work towards the bigger picture. Sensing types are so called because they tend to absorb information via the five senses (hearing, taste, touch, smell and sight). In contrast, *Intuitive types* (N) tend to start with the bigger picture and only then take more interest in the detail. Intuitive types are so called because they tend to respond to detailed information with more of a "gut impression". Like all preference pairs, both Sensing and Intuition have their advantages and disadvantages, depending on the circumstances and how they are used.

Common characteristics

As a rule of thumb, *Sensing types* tend to seek and absorb information via one or more of the five senses. They generally prefer to start with the facts and details and want the information they are given to be accurate and precise. When approaching problems, Sensing types tend to seek specific solutions for which their starting point is usually history, research, and past experience. They typically take a practical approach to problem solving, remaining realistic in terms of what is or is not likely to be possible. Their approach often has a step-by-step structure to it, enabling them to build carefully towards any solutions or conclusions. Sensing types tend to be grounded in the present, focusing on "what is" rather than "what could be". Archetypally, Sensing type leaders tend to start with the operational and build towards the strategic.

Intuitive types generally start by wanting to know the bigger picture, vision, or strategy—the direction of travel and the overarching concepts that are relevant to any given situation. When faced with problems, Intuitive types tend to become energized by opportunities to be innovative in their approach to finding solutions. In other words, while they may take a close interest in what history and experience might indicate, they prefer to find their own creative way to address a problem or task. Intuitive types are more naturally energized by anticipating "what could be" and tend to feel restricted if they have limited room to think outside the box. Archetypally, Intuitive types tend to start with the strategic which then guides their decisions about what is needed operationally.

Both Sensing and Intuitive types can be very observant, but they tend to observe the same thing in quite different ways and through quite different lenses. For example, when asked to give feedback about an SLT or governing board meeting, a *Sensing* type leader might naturally give a detailed account of what "actually" happened; who attended, the agenda items, and what was discussed and agreed. In contrast, an *Intuitive* type might respond by sharing their overall impression of the meeting and relevant outcomes, perhaps including a comment about the atmosphere of the discussion. While perfectly good responses for those of the same type, such responses would be likely to frustrate the interests of the opposite type.

Sensing and intuition: tensions and adaptations

Whatever our preferences and prejudices, both Sensing and Intuition are always needed in the workplace, as in life. However, the "theory" that we need both types does not always insulate us from finding "the other type" difficult and frustrating at times. In the workplace, tensions typically occur in relationships when the leader is one type and the direct report is the opposite.

Example: Intuitive type headteacher with Sensing type deputy

A headteacher who is a clear Intuitive type would be likely to communicate their overarching vision and strategy to their senior leadership team along with some broad priorities. Typically, the Intuitive leader would be comfortable with some level of ambiguity and would not want to be excessively directive about how they wanted their objectives to be achieved. Instead, they would be likely to assume that others (like themselves) would want to find their own approach, with some choice and autonomy. While this leadership style might work well for other Intuitive types, it may prove problematic for someone with a clear preference for Sensing. Rather than experiencing the school leader as enabling of their autonomy and creativity, the Sensing type might feel at a loss about what is *actually* required of them; what this *actually* means for them; and, more specifically, what they *actually* have to do to deliver. Despite the Intuitive leader's best intentions, they might inadvertently be experienced by the Sensing type as being vague and woolly, resulting in the Sensing type becoming anxious, agitated, and potentially stressed.

In order to support Sensing types, it can be helpful for Intuitive type school leaders to break down their vision and objectives into more specific structured steps to give them the clarity and precision they need.

Example: Sensing type headteacher with Intuitive type deputy

If we take the same example through the opposite lens, similar tensions would be likely to occur. In giving instructions and direction for example, the Sensing type school leader would be likely to treat others as they might want to be treated themselves—by breaking down their requests into detailed step-by-step instructions, which they would want to have followed in quite a precise way. While another Sensing type might find such instructions clear, helpful, and a relief to receive, an Intuitive type might respond quite differently. If they are true to type, the Intuitive type might find themselves getting lost in, and overwhelmed by, all the detail—especially if they are not clear about the overriding objectives and vision. Furthermore, if the amount of detailed instruction was felt to be excessive, there would be an increased risk that the Intuitive type might experience the Sensing type headteacher as being a controlling micro-manager who "can't see the wood for the trees". Despite the Sensing type leader's best intentions, the Intuitive type's engagement might then be adversely impacted—both due to their perceived lack of direction together with their lack of autonomy in finding creative approaches that make sense to them.

To best support and engage the Intuitive type, it can be helpful for Sensing type school leaders to check that Intuitive types have adequate clarity about the overall direction, vision, and purpose of any given activity, together with some opportunity to find their own footprint in undertaking it.

The principles described here are equally transferable to relation-ships between other opposite pairings—for instance between a Sensing type chair of governors working with an Intuitive type headteacher and/or between an Intuitive type deputy and a Sensing type head of department.

MBTI and different responses to change

All schools and school leaders are likely to encounter significant change. The reality that we all have to manage change—individually and col-lectively—is simply a fact of life regardless of how we respond to the prospect of change. However, while we know *theoretically* that different people will have differing responses and needs during times of change, we tend not to interrogate more systematically what these differing responses and needs may be. An understanding of MBTI—in particular the combination of the first two preference pairs (E and I, S and N)—offers one very helpful lens that, when used thoughtfully alongside other more psychodynamic and systemic lenses, can enable schools and school leaders to more effectively navigate the impact and management of change.[2]

Example

One school with whom I have a longstanding relationship asked me to run a MBTI workshop for senior and middle leaders to help them prepare for a partnership with two sister schools, in a newly formed Multi-Academy Trust (MAT). While the headteacher was largely positive about the forthcoming changes, he was concerned about tensions that were start-ing to surface—in particular between the senior and middle leadership teams. He feared these tensions could escalate into something more toxic and destructive if left unmanaged and wanted to start addressing them by offering a safe and normalizing lens through which these could be explored.

Within the MBTI workshop, the group were helped to assess themselves individually as well as within the context of the wider team. As they did this, a striking split between them became apparent. Within the senior leadership team, everyone—including the headteacher—assessed themselves as being clear Intuitive types, with all but one having *Extraverted Intuitive* type preferences (EN). In contrast, within the middle leadership team, all six of the middle leaders assessed themselves as having *Introverted Sensing* type preferences (IS). In MBTI terms, these two groups are diametric opposites of each other—meaning that they not only have differing needs and responses during times of change, but their natural preferences may be an active trigger for stress in the opposite type.

The group as a whole found it both revelatory and helpful to be offered MBTI's accessible and normalizing framework for understanding their very different—but ordinary—response to changes.

When facing change, *Introverted Sensing types (IS)* tend to respond initially with anxiety and apprehension. Having a significant change sprung on them without warning could even trigger a reaction of panic and stress, at least in the short term. To help support and contain Introverted Sensing types, they typically appreciate having as much detail as possible about the plan, especially in relation to what is needed, by whom, and when. In managing expectations, it is also helpful to allow Introverted Sensing Types the time they need to digest and prepare for the changes, appreciating that they will be unlikely to share the extraverted intuitive's initial enthusiasm.

By contrast, *Extraverted Intuitive types (EN)* can feel quite energized by the prospect of change—sometimes all the more if it happens without much warning, as it offers them a license to innovate and to rise creatively to the challenge of what is needed. Rather than finding the prospect of change difficult, it is the absence of change and an excess of stability and conservatism that can be experienced by Extraverted Intuitive types as being stifling of their creative potential.

The discovery that the tensions between the senior and middle leaders were almost entirely aligned with their MBTI types came both as a surprise and a relief to almost everyone involved. An understanding of MBTI gave the teams a *common language* with which to think about their different reactions and the way these were triggering tensions between the two teams. It also helped them to normalize the judgements they admitted they were making about each other; judgements that, if left unaddressed, could easily toxify in a way that might be corrosive to their collective collaboration. As these tensions and judgements became increasingly possible to acknowledge safely, the middle and senior leadership teams could even begin to joke with each other—about each other—turning potential prejudices into more playful banter.

During the last part of the workshop it was then possible for the group to move forward in a much more collaborative way to think about how best to accommodate their respective hopes, fears, and needs, with a deeper level of trust that their differences were being respected by one another, even if they were not always welcome. This also enabled the group to think ahead about what further discussions might be needed with other colleagues, students, and parents—both in their school as well as in their partner schools, as they progressed towards becoming a MAT.

Thinking (T) and Feeling (F)

Overview

The preferences of "Thinking" and "Feeling" are all about the different processes by which we tend to make decisions. They are not about the end decisions we make—which may be the same, regardless of our type preference. Rather it is about the journey we take *en route* to making a decision; the criteria we apply and the way in which we prioritize what we take into consideration.

Put simply, when making decisions, *Thinking types* (T) tend to focus first on task, logic and outcomes, after which they take into account people and values. In contrast, *Feeling types* (F) tend to focus first on people and values, after which they focus on task, logic, and outcomes. In approaching decisions, particularly in relation to people, *Thinking types* prefer to step outside the situation in order to maintain a more objective and detached perspective. *Feeling types* tend to approach decision making by remaining more personally involved and connected more subjectively to the issue or person.

Common characteristics

When considering something, especially in relation to a decision, *Thinking types* tend to start by questioning and interrogating what they are presented with. Only if satisfied will they then move towards acceptance. In team meetings, Thinking types often gain a reputation for asking some of the more difficult and challenging questions that go against the flow of harmony. As a consequence of their focus on task and outcomes, Thinking types can sometimes be experienced as insensitive or abrasive, particularly if they are experienced as dismissing the validity of other people's feelings. When this happens, it can inadvertently compromise the engagement and productivity of others, in particular Feeling types.

Feeling types tend to approach decisions in a consensual way; doing what they can to keep all parties engaged while preserving harmony between people and teams. In their responses to others, Feeling types typically start from an initial position of acceptance and support. Sometimes it is only after they have accepted something that Feeling types realize they did not ask some of their more searching questions. In this respect, it is not uncommon for Feeling types to be apprehensive about challenging others, especially if they anticipate that their challenges will generate discomfort, anxiety, or hostility. While they are often experienced as caring and empathetic, Feeling types can also irritate others (in particular Thinking types) by giving what is considered to be excess attention to emotions and how people feel. This can be perceived by Thinking types as a weakness that runs the risk of hijacking rather than enhancing decision making.

Notably, both Thinking and Feeling types have a clear and strong concept of what is *"fair"*—they are just very different concepts. For Thinking types, being fair is typically based on treating people equally, through the consistent application of principles and criteria. For Feeling types, being fair is typically based on treating people as individuals with individual needs and circumstances that deserve more bespoke consideration.

Both these interpretations of what "being fair" means can cause tensions among team members—for example when a headteacher has to decide how to respond to an application for exceptional leave during term time.

Differing approaches to giving and receiving feedback

Giving and receiving feedback effectively is fundamental to teaching, learning, and on-going personal and professional development. Along with other core skills, the ability to tailor not only *what* one feeds back but *how* one feeds it back is absolutely essential to ensuring that feedback is experienced as developmental and motivating rather than discouraging and demoralizing. While this may seem like common sense, an appreciation and application of this "basic" knowledge is often neglected in line-management relationships as well as other aspects of school life, such as in classroom observations. This comes with a cost to all concerned.

Thinking types typically prefer feedback that focuses on task, competence, and outcomes. They tend to start with constructive criticism and then move (to varying degrees) to acknowledge what has been done well. Usually, Thinking types want recognition only *after* a task has been completed and if *results exceed expectations*. They are generally only interested in feedback from someone who is senior and/or who has established credibility in the field of the task. Thinking types are unlikely to appreciate being thanked for their efforts, especially if their efforts have not produced the desired results. For Thinking types this might be experienced as inauthentic and patronizing. Even when results have exceeded expectations, Thinking types are often apprehensive about giving positive feedback as they fear it may quickly result in complacency.

> I worked with one headteacher, for example, who told me how he could only bear to join his staff's celebrations for half an hour after they received their hard-earned "Outstanding" judgment from Ofsted. He told me how he feared that "excess celebrating would hijack motivation", so he felt compelled to retreat to his office to start thinking and planning ahead. The following day, however, he was met with some backlash from his staff, several of whom had interpreted his absence as "evidence" that, despite their hard work, they continued to fail in securing his approval or praise. Rather than inspiring their ambitions and motivation, some even reported that his response to their success threatened to undermine their pleasure, good will, and subsequent efforts.

Feeling types are equally concerned that task and outcomes are effectively addressed but typically seek feedback that focuses initially on personal impact and contribution. While Feeling types may be pleased to receive positive feedback from senior colleagues, they are equally pleased to receive feedback from other trusted individuals—whether they be peers, direct reports, students, or parents. Furthermore, unlike Thinking types, Feeling types tend to want some feedback, recognition, and appreciation for their efforts, *en route* to the completion of tasks. The absence of such feedback—for instance, by a Thinking type leader who is waiting for outcomes to be known before giving feedback—can result in resentment if it is interpreted as being withholding or implicitly critical.

Feeling types tend to give feedback in the same way as they like to receive it—by starting with positive appreciation and encouragement and then progressing (to varying degrees) towards more challenging and critical feedback. Sometimes Feeling type leaders find it uncomfortable to give more critical feedback, for instance in the management of underperformance, even when they know this is necessary. In situations like this, it can be helpful to remind Feeling type leaders that giving direct and robust feedback, from the heart, with the intention of supporting the other person, is part of their duty of care to the other person. Rather than being undermining or neglectful, they can be reminded that it is actually the absence of such feedback that is more likely to interfere with the development and progress of their staff.

In schools and school leadership—as in other relationships in all walks of life—an understanding about, and respect for, the differences between Thinking and Feeling type preferences can significantly enhance the quality of the feedback-learning-development process.

Differing approaches to providing help and support

While Thinking and Feeling types can both get energized by providing help and support to others, the focus and style of their support might differ widely. Blind spots in understanding the differences between these helping styles can result in unnecessary tension and conflict, despite one's best intentions.

When trying to help others, *Thinking types* naturally gravitate towards what needs to be "done" to "fix" the problem. They tend to support others by focusing primarily on the principles of the task and any actions needed to achieve the desired outcome. While this approach may work well for other Thinking types, it has the potential to backfire with Feeling types, especially if they are left feeling unheard or misunderstood. For Feeling types, the "fix" often comes through the appreciative acknowledgement of their experience and its impact on them as a person.

By extension, *Feeling types* naturally tend to help others by being supportive, understanding, and empathetic. However, despite their best intentions, this approach might be the very thing to agitate a Thinking type. Typically, for example, Thinking types prefer to be supported in a more practical and pragmatic way, by focusing on the task, desired outcomes, and what can be done to "solve" or "fix" the problem.

Example: Thinking type headteacher with Feeling type deputy

A headteacher spoke to me about his frustration with his deputy. The head valued his deputy highly but had become frustrated with her following an unpleasant incident with a parent who had become verbally abusive to her. The head told me he had already supported his deputy by talking through what happened, what now needed to happen, and how she might respond should a similar situation arise in the future. This support seemed to help initially, but the deputy had asked to meet the head again as she was struggling to let go of what happened. The head rolled his eyes as he relayed this, conveying frustration at what he considered to be her "relentless neediness".

Having explored the situation more fully, my impression, from the head-teacher, was that the deputy had actually been quite shaken by the experience. My natural response—led by my own Feeling type preference—was then to acknowledge the head's frustration while conveying my view that it would not be unreasonable for the deputy to be offered some further support, empathy, and guidance. The head rolled his eyes again. It didn't take much for me to realize that my approach hadn't been terribly effective or persuasive—regardless of whether or not I was right!

Reflecting on the head's response to me also reminded me that he was a clear "Thinking type". Using my knowledge of MBTI, I then adopted a different approach, by translating the same point into a more logical rationale, almost akin to a business case. In a more pragmatic tone of voice that did not convey the empathy I actually felt for the deputy—I then acknowledged that it was the head's choice as to whether the deputy was offered any further support. With that caveat, I alerted him to the risk that the absence of further support might result in the deputy feeling somewhat neglected and resentful of the headteacher—all of which might subsequently undermine their engagement and productivity. On the other hand, if the head were to give his deputy the time and care she needed, she might be more likely to feel understood and to bounce back more quickly to her naturally efficient and productive self.

With almost no hesitation, the head sat up and responded quite differently—telling me in a much more determined and resolved way, "You are right, I will make an appointment with her as soon as I'm back in school!"

The risk of conflict between thinking and feeling types

Without mutual understanding of their respective differences, there is greater risk of unnecessary tension and conflict being triggered between Thinking and Feeling types.

Even within an "ordinary" conversation, problems can quickly occur. A Thinking type might, for example, feel energized and stimulated when debating a matter of interest. Focusing on the *content* of what is said, they might passionately advocate for the logic and principles underpinning their perspective. However, rather than feeling energized by such a discussion, a Feeling type might, instead, experience this same discussion as a conflict—especially if they interpret the *manner and tone* of the Thinking type's passion as lacking respect or value for them at a personal level.

Such a situation could occur multiple times in any given day within the life of a leadership team. As a result, Thinking types might become increasingly frustrated by what they consider to be their Feeling type colleagues' over-sensitivity. Equally, Feeling types might become increasingly offended by what they consider to be their Thinking type colleague's brashness and insensitivity.

Greater understanding about, and respect for, these differences is likely to enable both Thinking and Feeling types to make constructive adaptations—not only to the way in which they engage in such discussions, but also to the way they interpret their experience of them—and the other person.

Judging (J) and Perceiving (P)

Overview

Judging and Perceiving type preferences relate to the different approaches that people take to organizing and structuring their life, work, and time.

Common characteristics

Judging types (J) have a natural preference for being orderly, structured, and decisive, and to make plans that they seek to progress until completion. Judging types tend to trust their plans and can become irritable or stressed if their plans are changed, especially at the last minute. Judging types don't usually like to be faced with uncertainty, and will often make back up plans to account for all eventualities. *Working out what is needed in advance* is key to helping Judging types feel calm and in control.

Judging types often like to make lists, which they enjoy ticking off. Sometimes, people whose judging type preference is more pronounced will even put something on their list that they have already done—just for the pleasure of then being able to tick it off!

When leading team meetings, Judging type school leaders can be very efficient in terms of time management as they progress through the agenda. They might, for example, allocate timings for each agenda item in advance, which they would adhere to in the meeting, regardless of how the discussion unfolds. However, at times, the speed with which they make decisions and close discussions can create tension with Perceiving types who prefer more space for less structured exploration and brain storming.

Perceiving types (P) prefer to approach life and work in a flexible and spontaneous way. They have a natural preference for keeping their options open for as long as possible, avoiding decisions that close down other possibilities before they feel absolutely ready to do so. Perceiving types don't mind making plans but can feel stifled if they are expected to keep to the plan. They tend to trust the process more than the plan so are open to their plans evolving organically *en route*.

Unlike Judging types who would typically feel stressed by any last-minute pressures or changes to the plan, Perceiving types might be actively energized by an unexpected curve ball, feeling that this is what often brings out the best in them. For Perceiving types, *working out what is needed along the way* is part of the pleasure of the journey. As a result of this, however, Perceiving types often need a clear deadline hanging over them in order to fully engage with a task. Without this, they might find it much harder to galvanize themselves fully.

When leading team meetings, Perceiving type school leaders like to allow ample space for discussion of agenda items without needing a definitive decision to close the discussion and move on. They might also see greater value than Judging types in allowing a discussion to veer off the agenda, so long as it seemed valuable and worthwhile. Although Perceiving types might plan the agenda timing in advance, they would not typically be governed by this in practice, even if it meant that some agenda items were ultimately not reached. The plan, in this respect, is treated simply as a guide rather than a bible. While this approach to meetings can feel engaging and energizing for other Perceiving types, it runs the risk of frustrating Judging types, who naturally seek a clearer structure, forward momentum, and closure. Judging types might also be left with a more innate sense of agitation if all agenda items were not reached (and ticked off the list!).

Tensions and adaptations

The natural differences between Judging and Perceiving types can also be a source of considerable tension and conflict in relationships, teams, and organizations.

Example 1

Take, for example, a "simple" meeting between two senior leaders—one who is a Judging type and the other a Perceiving type. The purpose of the meeting is to discuss and brainstorm how they might approach an important new task or project.

In advance of the meeting, the Judging type would be likely to have done some advance reading, reflecting, and planning to ensure that they arrive well prepared for the discussion. The Perceiving type, in contrast, may have done little in the way of pre-meeting preparation. For them, the meeting is the forum for preparation, so they might be more likely to arrive energized at the prospect of brainstorming together.

Although both Judging and Perceiving types will have arrived at the meeting with good intentions, their different approaches could easily result in considerable tension and frustration, together with a range of somewhat pejorative attributions about each other. For example, the Judging type might experience their Perceiving type colleague as being disorganized and even sloppy. Equally, the Perceiving type might experience their Judging type colleague as being rather controlling and restrictive, having done all the work already, and therefore leaving them little room to contribute in a more meaningful way.

When helped to understand their preferences and different ways of approaching the same tasks, people are much less likely to misinterpret the behaviour or to attribute negative judgments to each other. Instead, both might be more likely to accommodate the opposite preference with greater interest and respect. For example, the Judging type would be more likely to see the benefits of not doing all the thinking in advance and of factoring in some time for joint brainstorming together. Equally, the Perceiving type might be more likely to see the benefits of doing more advance planning and preparation than they would otherwise have done.

Subtle but important changes in understanding and perspective such as these are likely to result in more collaborative meetings and more productive outcomes for all concerned.

Example 2

The setting of and adherence to time deadlines is another common cause for tension between Judging and Perceiving types.

A Judging type headteacher might, for example, give their deputy a report to work on, letting them know it is in preparation for the governors' meeting in two weeks' time. While the Perceiving type might get started on the report straight away, their journey towards completion would be unlikely to be structured or linear. Instead, their energy and focus would be likely to meander at first, reaching a crescendo as the deadline approaches. For a Perceiving type, two weeks means two weeks, so the end of that time period would still be considered "on time". Meanwhile, the Judging type headteacher might have become increasingly agitated that their colleague has given them no time to digest the report in advance of the governors' meeting.

Tip for Judging types: In order to better engage Perceiving types with what has been delegated, they need to be given clear timelines that take into account their need for a deadline in order to galvanize their energies.

Tip for Perceiving types: In order to better support Judging types, Perceiving types need to be mindful of the way that Judging types can experience changes to a planned schedule, especially if they are last-minute.

Whole type dynamics—tensions following a bereavement

As indicated previously, different type preferences are not only significant in their own right but in the way they interact with each other cumulatively.

In the senior team of a large secondary school, tensions between two deputies started to escalate following the sudden death of one of the students as a result of a massive heart attack on the sports field. In the initial aftermath of the tragedy, the headteacher made a number of addresses to the whole school, staff, and parent groups. While continuing to support some individual staff and the student's family, he then tasked his two deputies with the role of following up on what was needed to contain the school community and to honour the student's memory, over subsequent weeks and months. Both deputies were devastated by what happened and were keen to support the school, but responded to their responsibilities in very different ways.

One deputy—an Extraverted Intuitive Feeling type (ENFP)—wanted to create opportunities for students and staff, in smaller and larger groups, to digest the emotional impact of what had happened. He thought it was important to give space for people to talk about their feelings and how they had been affected. The other deputy—an Introverted Sensing Thinking type (ISTJ)—wanted to get the school community active in raising money for a charity in memory of their colleague. His focus was on the logistics of the events around the fundraising and what was needed to ensure their success. While both approaches were important, valid, and underpinned by positive intent and compassion, the differences between the deputies threatened to drive a wedge between them, undermining their collective collaboration and efforts.

The ISTJ, for example, felt profoundly uncomfortable with the ENFP's focus on creating opportunities for outward expression of feeling and emotion. For someone who was naturally pragmatic, emotionally reserved and outcome-focused, this approach served as an active stressor, especially in the absence of any tangible outcomes. "How is this going to help us move on?", he questioned.

Equally, the ENFP found themselves becoming increasing agitated by the ISTJ's focus on practicalities. For someone who naturally expressed themselves outwardly and focused primarily on values and relationships rather than tasks, they experienced the ISTJ's pragmatism as being cut off emotionally and potentially obstructing the school's need to mourn. "How will we move on if there is no time for us to process this together?", he questioned.

At a time when the school was already struggling in the wake of this trauma, the deputies were at risk of being caught in an unnecessary conflict that threatened to escalate tensions, rather than contain the school's upset and trauma. It was only when they were both helped to make sense of each other's preferences and differences through the lens of MBTI—in a way that valued and validated both people and approaches—that their capacity to respect and collaborate with each other was restored.

MBTI and common reactions to stress

Much has been written about how different MBTI types might fall "*into the grip*" of thoughts, feelings, and behaviours that appear to be *out of character*—especially when we feel fatigued or stressed (e.g. Quenk, 1993; 2000). The details of this are beyond the scope of this chapter, though it is worth noting that when feeling unusually anxious, stressed, or fatigued, people often tend to behave like somewhat dysfunctional versions of their *opposite type preference*.

Extraverts, for example, often become uncharacteristically quiet and subdued and might be experienced as being somewhat sulky and withdrawn. *Introverts* might be uncharacteristically prone to more impulsive and unprocessed outbursts of anger or upset, which might be experienced as unusually rude or abrasive.

Similarly, when feeling stressed, a *Sensing* type might become overwhelmed by the bigger picture and feel that everything that has to be done, has to be done all at once. This can send them spiralling towards a sense of catastrophization and a belief that there is nothing that can be done to solve the problem—at least in the short term. Equally, an *Intuitive* type might lose their usual sense of perspective and instead become unusually preoccupied by relatively minor facts and details that—when they are feeling calm and secure—they would never normally worry about.

When assessing situations under "normal" circumstances, *Thinking* types tend to draw initially on logic and rational argument, rather than personal feelings and experiences. When stressed, however, Thinking types might become unusually sensitive, reacting more emotionally than the situation or trigger would usually suggest. Equally, *Feeling* types—who are usually led by their connection to personal values and empathy—might become uncharacteristically critical or apathetic, especially if they feel their values have been violated in some way.

Some basic understanding and recognition about how different types react under pressure and stress (including ourselves) can significantly increase our capacity to respond in the most effective and constructive way. It can also help to reduce the likelihood that we might react impulsively and unhelpfully, inadvertently making matters even worse than they already might be.

Conclusion

This chapter offers an introduction to MBTI's personality preferences and the way these can manifest helpfully and problematically within the context of school leadership. The nature and length of this chapter means that these descriptions can only be considered as the tip of the iceberg. There are many other layers of MBTI understanding worthy of exploring but that go beyond the scope of this chapter—for instance, in relation to how MBTI type preferences can impact individually and collectively on our responses to stress, change, different communication styles, and conflict.[3]

MBTI does not offer a panacea for understanding the complexity of personality differences. Nor should it be used as a vehicle to impose limiting or pejorative labels to people. This would be a major mis-use of MBTI. What is, however, extremely valuable about MBTI is its potential to help individuals, teams, and leaders to make much greater sense of the reality of different personality preferences—and their impact—through a normalizing, respectful, and non-judgemental lens. This does not mean that a deeper understanding of MBTI preferences suddenly transforms us into gurus of acceptance who transcend ever feeling irritable or provoked by others. Rather, I believe that a solid understanding of MBTI personality preferences helps us to *keep our head* and become more interested in and respectful towards others—and more appreciative of how and why we might react to them in the way that we do. Through this, MBTI has the potential to detoxify our experience of others and the way they impact on us—together with the judgements we so often rush to attribute to their behaviours. In other words, MBTI doesn't stop us finding X or Y difficult, but it can enable us to understand why we might find them difficult, so that we do not jump to premature judgements that they are "bad" or "wrong". Furthermore, an understanding of MBTI preferences offers us some vital insights and strategies, together with a common language to consider how we might constructively adapt the way we support and challenge each other so as to accommodate the needs and preferences of others. In school leadership, as in other walks of life, this can significantly reduce the risk of unhelpful and potentially toxic misunderstanding while increasing the likelihood of effective collaboration and teamwork.

Notes

1 For further information about Basic Assumptions, see chapter 4 in this book by Judith Bell.
2 This chapter largely focuses on describing and illustrating the way that different preferences manifest in everyday life and work. However, while each of these preferences should be understood in its own right, it is also important to appreciate that our preferences inevitably react with each other in ways that transcend the significance of the individual preference. In other words, the whole is greater than the sum of the parts. This example offers one such illustration of how type preferences can combine and interact with each other.
3 A range of publications that explore these areas more comprehensively is available from The Myers-Briggs Company.

CHAPTER TEN

Developing leaders: lessons from the business world

Barry Speirs & Andrea Berkeley

P eople have been writing about leadership for thousands of years. Among over 18,000 books on this topic currently for sale on Amazon is a collection of Marcus Aurelius' (Aurelius, 2015) essays on leadership from the second century! Leadership is a topic that interests many people, and no one has the definitive answer on how to lead. Leadership development—how to grow more of the right type of leaders—is therefore a hot topic in most organizations, including schools. As with many other aspects of education reform, government and national training providers have looked to the business world for ideas, models, and processes for developing leaders and for measuring their impact. In this chapter we describe leadership development processes that have proved successful in the business world and explore their application to the education sector. We write from differing perspectives, based on contrasting experience in the business and educational worlds.

Leadership development: key aims and assumptions

Perhaps the key issue for organizations today is that the demand for the type of effective leaders needed in an increasing complex world exceeds the supply. In a major study (Kerr & Toriello, 2012) almost two-thirds of senior executives identified leadership development as their number one concern. Deloitte, in their 2014 survey of over 2,500 leaders in 90+ countries, found the most urgent and important human resources issue to be the development of leaders (Deloitte, 2014). Other research (Gitsham, 2009) found that only 7% of senior managers were satisfied with their companies' leadership development policies, and the World Economic Forum identified lack of leadership as the third biggest global issue in 2015, with 86% of respondents agreeing that there was a leadership crisis.

Organizations investing in the development of leaders and succession planning in the business world are often trying to do three things:

» *Accelerate people's development*: to help people learn so that they can be promoted more quickly. Organizations may talk about their "leadership pipeline" or "bench strength" and the need to develop more leaders more quickly. At BP Azerbaijan, for example, the "need for speed" was particularly marked as the firm's licence to operate in the country was dependent on promoting local national staff to replace expatriate senior managers.

» *Broaden people's skills*: although playing to personal strengths is important, organizations want leaders to be good enough in a broad range of areas. While they may offer rewarding career paths to high-paid specialists, they see leadership positions as requiring more well-rounded individuals with a range of generic skills. Several organizations use "experience checklists": a mix of operational and strategic tasks, internal people management, and external customer responsibilities, where people need to prove proficiency across a range of areas before progressing to senior leadership.

» *Avoid careers derailing*: High-performing managers and leaders may have a problem: they sometimes do not get any critical feedback! Less than cordial relationships with peers, confidence verging on arrogance, or limited emotional control may be tolerated and can derail careers in more senior positions, if never challenged. So organizations often run development centres for "emerging leaders" where middle managers, perhaps for the first time, get detailed personal feedback on how they come across to others. Although difficult to swallow, such feedback can be an early warning system for ambitious individuals.

Organizations investing in leadership development know that the growth of leaders is a complex process, best viewed as a partnership between the individual and the organization. There are many tried and tested ways in which organizations can facilitate individuals' learning about leadership and make success more likely in a senior role. But leadership development is never something you can "do to" people.

Implications for schools and school systems

Traditionally, potential school leaders tended to work their way up a hierarchy through experience and age as "first among equals", by demonstrating excellence as a teacher, lecturer, or academic. The inspiring schoolteacher became head of department, the long serving deputy head stepped into the head's shoes upon retirement, some finding themselves ill-equipped to manage people and resources.

With the advent of National Professional Qualifications (NPQs) for middle and senior leaders and aspiring headteachers, a more strategic approach to the development of school leaders has been taken in the past 20 years, with similar aims to those above. In devising leadership development programmes, the National College for Teaching and Leadership (NCTL), trusts, and other providers have increasingly looked to business for models as well as partnering with traditional providers like universities and local authorities.

In the maintained sector, new charities and academy trusts have been formed in the past decade to target areas of social deprivation, where it is difficult to recruit middle and senior leaders. They are acutely aware of the need to accelerate leadership learning and broaden skills—often in partnership with or sponsored by business. For instance, the Teach First programme was introduced not only to recruit higher calibre graduates from Russell Group universities into teaching and to accelerate the acquisition of teaching skills, but also to grow a leadership pipeline within challenging schools. In addition, national programmes such as those offered by Ambition School Leadership and some of the larger academy trusts, such as United Learning, actively offer a suite of leadership programmes for identified "high potentials". To avoid careers derailing, the receiving and giving of feedback, humility, and moral purpose now tend to feature prominently in the leadership curriculum.

Leadership development: approaches and models

Some models or approaches are particularly influential in how organizations see leadership development. In this section we summarize what underpins some of the practices adopted before detailing what organizations do.

The 70:20:10 model

This model of leadership learning (Lombardo & Eichinger, 1996) suggests that typically people learn:

» 70% on-the-job (e.g. through challenging assignments);
» 20% through others (e.g. via observation, feedback, or coaching);
» 10% through formal training.

Not intended as a recipe or formula but, rather, a reflection of how people typically learn about leadership in practice, it stresses that development is "not all about training", providing a rationale for a more deliberate planned approach to "on-the-job" experience. It also recognizes the benefit of taking a blended approach to planning development experiences. Taking a simple example, an individual wanting to improve presentation skills might organize some presentation practice (70%), get feedback from observation (20%) as well as attending some training (10%). The mistake to avoid is just doing the training alone. In one organization there was a large spreadsheet with the name of each high potential middle manager, against which were three columns labelled:

» experience (70);
» support (20);
» training (10).

This would show the development actions planned for each individual for the next year.

Applications to schools and school systems

To a certain degree, the 70:20:10 model has historically been used informally or intuitively by enlightened headteachers and education authorities seeking to develop future leaders. Opportunities may be created for deputy heads to rotate responsibilities in schools, for instance, or to be seconded to other schools, not only to assist with a short-term project but also for their own development. Similarly, talented middle leaders might be temporarily seconded to the Senior Leadership Team (SLT) to undertake an action research project. Mentoring and coaching are also increasingly on offer. In terms of formal training, the 70:20:10 model underpins the design of NPQs, with varying degrees of implementation, depending on time and resources across schools. For example, trainee heads on NPQH complete a nine-day placement in an outstanding school, at the end of which they are required to make a presentation to the governing body on the efficiency of the school's use of resources.

Leadership Pipeline model

What you need to be good at evolves as you move up an organization. Technical skills are still an important prerequisite, but what distinguishes successful leaders is a different set of skills or attributes (see Figure 10.1).

A more detailed way of looking at this is the Leadership Pipeline model, based on critical career passages in a large business organization (Charan, Drotter, & Noel, 2001) (see Figure 10.2).

This influential model defines generic job levels in an organization and what individuals need to do differently to succeed on promotion. Organizations try to help people not to get "stuck in the bends" and invest in training, coaching, and support to help people both before and after such transitions.

The message is: when you get promoted, don't just work harder, work differently! This means changing the strategies that have made you successful to date. For some people this is harder than learning new skills, especially when promoted to a role that is similar but expanded in nature. For instance, in a fast-growing corporation a manager recruited to run the firm's restaurant business needed support when his 50 staff and two restaurants grew in five years into a multi-million dollar business of 30 restaurants with 1,000 staff.

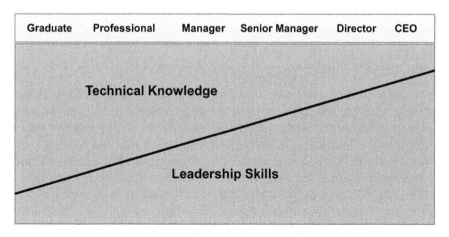

FIGURE 10.1   Getting ahead: what seems to matter?

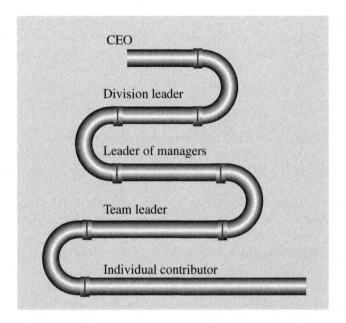

FIGURE 10.2   The leadership pipeline.

A particular development challenge for him was delegating and loosening his control of the operation.

The most challenging leadership transitions tend to be when managing people or teams for the first time or when adapting to new functions outside one's own experience, for instance as a division leader or CEO, when subordinates might have more technical knowledge.

Applications to schools and school systems

Attention to the Leadership Pipeline model is certainly evident in the design of NPQ programmes and in their selection and assessment criteria. However, newly promoted middle or senior leaders often find that the excellent classroom teaching skills that led to their promotion are no longer as important as managing other adults. This is often quite painful for high achievers, as they have to learn how to take satisfaction from the achievements of others in their teams, rather than from their own performance. The transition to headship also inevitably involves leading and managing more expert or differently skilled professionals than oneself, which can be especially challenging when managing underperformance. Similarly, both newly appointed middle and senior leaders may be confronted by the reality that the multifaceted demands of their role now mean they are not producing the same standard of lessons as they might have been before. The fact that they may not be as "naturally" talented in their leadership role with adults as they were in their teaching role with children can be particularly troubling.

Situational leadership and related ideas

The Situational Leadership Model (Hersey, 1986) suggests that to be most effective, a leader should adapt their approach to different people and situations. Examples of how organizations develop this flexible approach to leadership include:

» equipping leaders with additional people management skills: for example, equipping leaders with coaching skills, not to become coaches, but to use these less directive skills as a leadership style in certain situations with certain people;
» leadership training that raises individuals' self-awareness and understanding of different leadership styles, often through 360° feedback and peer discussions;
» recognition for skills such as cross-cultural competence and contextual intelligence, or at least a growing, even if sometimes begrudging, acceptance that you can't just transplant ideas and people across cultures;
» recognizing the high value of international, out-of-comfort-zone experiences as part of developing leaders;
» the importance of cultural fit when appointing senior leaders—perhaps seen as of equal or of even more importance than experience, especially after analysing why external senior appointments fail.

Applications to schools and school systems

The importance of developing Situational Leadership is widely accepted in educational circles. The work of Goleman (2000) on leadership styles and their impact on organizational climate, together with NCSL research (Day et al., 2010) on the importance of school context, are now firmly embedded in the design of most educational leadership development programmes. More generally—in our experience—the education sector is perhaps more attuned to understanding cultural plurality and promoting diversity than the business sector, by virtue of its core purpose of educating an increasingly diverse population. Governors in particular will be concerned to appoint headteachers with the right "fit" for their particular school context. Ironically, gaining international leadership experience has not traditionally been seen as an advantage. Those seeking to return to the United Kingdom are often considered to be "out of touch"—possibly due to continuous changes to education policy, testing, and assessment systems. More recently however, chains and franchises of British schools abroad have proliferated, and it is most likely that international experience will, in due course, be encouraged as a means to broaden leadership development.

Developing leaders in the corporate world: ways and means

The following tried and tested practices adopted by organizations can be adapted and applied to schools.

Staff development meetings

Regular senior leadership team meetings to review and enable individuals' development, often called "Talent Review" or "People Days", are a good way of making staff development and succession planning a priority, with the aim of growing leaders from within. A typical approach might be for each senior leader to take 10–15 minutes to lead a discussion about an individual in their team, typically focusing on people who are seen as of high potential, in need of a role transition or other intervention. The format could include:

» key strengths and achievements;
» development areas—top two or three;
» current, recent, or planned development activities;
» summarizing the individual's CV, career direction, and preferences.

A standard document such as a Personal Development Plan, often prepared by individuals themselves, may summarize this information, with other senior managers contributing feedback and ideas for development. This can ensure a wider perspective and some shared ownership of the organization's talent. Typically, the discussion results in actions that the senior leader can discuss with the individual. Sometimes individuals present their own career plans and development areas. In addition to greater involvement and transparency, this approach encourages ownership and has the advantage of ensuring follow-up.

Applications to schools and school systems

Successful schools have always made the continuing professional development of their staff a priority but perhaps not always in such a formal or systematic way. Small schools would find this approach impractical. However, in secondaries and the larger confederations of schools and Multi-Academy Trusts, more systematic and centralized approaches are emerging and, more generally, teachers and potential school leaders are expected to take greater ownership of their own professional development.

Identifying high-potential staff

The term "talent management" is used by most businesses to mean not only recruiting, developing, and retaining high-quality employees, but also the to identify early staff who are most likely to be successful in future higher level roles. They want to avoid a "one size fits all" approach to staff development, investing more time and resources in those with potential for promotion to senior roles. However, questions and concerns are often raised around the principle and practice of identifying high potential staff, including:

» Can you really assess "potential"?
» Does it create an elite entitled to automatic progression?
» How is high potential identified, and who decides on the process?
» Will it demotivate and increase the turnover of people not selected?
» How are individuals enabled to take ownership of their own career aspirations?
» Will processes reflect equal-opportunities policies and avoid unconscious bias in the definition of potential and assessment of performance, such as, for instance, defining leadership in traditional alpha male characteristics?

In response to these concerns, some organizations prefer to offer "development for all", recognizing that talent can be found in everyone. Others maintain that having a robust and fair process for prioritizing the development of those who show leadership potential is more cost-effective. Identifying high potentials is not about *whom* to develop but whom to develop as *leaders*. It may also be stressed that an accelerated route is not the only way to the top, as others may progress through lengthier and more rounded experience. For this reason, some organizations favour transparent processes with an element of self-selection, where anyone is allowed to express an interest. Others take a more covert approach to identification, depending on organizational culture.

High-potential staff are typically seen as 5–10% of any employee cohort, with nominations commonly made by relevant senior leaders, following an assessment centre or competitive interviews. These may be subject to peer challenge. Criteria for identifying high potential need to be defensible, visible, and evidence-based on actual achievements, avoiding labels and ensuring regular reviews so that people do not stay on the list without continuing to show promise. Common criteria include:

» sustained high performance, ideally demonstrated in contrasting jobs or environments, sometimes requiring minimum service length;

» evidence of learning from experience and of adaptability: many studies and commentators see this as the number one criterion (Connolly & Viswesvaran, 2002; Lombardo & Eichinger, 2003);

» evidence of self-development orientation, self-awareness, openness to feedback, courage, and a proven capacity to develop productive relationships;

» evidence of certain behavioural characteristics, such as drive, tenacity, resilience, and motivation to lead.

Applications to schools and school systems

Historically, identification of "high potentials" has been a contentious issue in the education world, particularly in the maintained sector, where equality of opportunity and a collegial way of working is highly valued. Although headteachers have always sought to develop potential, even if covertly, traditionally local education authorities (LAs) have been culturally opposed to the idea. In the past decade, however, there has been more interest in accelerated routes to senior leadership, both in national and local training and development programmes and among the academy trusts now replacing LAs. This is partly due to a strong desire by successive governments to "professionalize" the teaching profession, tackle underperformance, and raise educational standards—and for recruitment and retention purposes. A national "Fast Track" recruitment scheme, similar to that operated in the Civil Service, was introduced by the DfE in the 1990s. However, it did not find favour with most professionals, and, failing to recruit sufficient numbers of teachers, it was discontinued within a few years. Since then, however, selective programmes using assessment centres, like Teach First and Ambition School Leadership (in addition to NPQH)—which explicitly recruit "high potentials" against a set of criteria—have succeeded in expanding nationally. They appear to have avoided ideological conflict by positioning themselves as working only in schools in challenging contexts, with a mission to improve education outcomes for disadvantaged children, and their selection criteria include alignment with certain values and beliefs.

Broadening experiences

Key to leadership development is ensuring that staff learn and are challenged in different roles or environments. Some large organizations earmark specific jobs as "development positions", into which high-potential staff are placed for short tenures. These include "chief of staff" positions supporting senior leaders, head office strategy jobs, and general management of small, lower risk businesses within a group. Where possible in multinational firms, working outside your comfort zone with international experience is often seen as a prerequisite for senior leadership. More specifically, organizations may use a checklist to give individuals more rounded experience. The example in Figure 10.3 separates internal management and external client responsibilities and might be used to identify new experiences for enhancing an individual's CV.

Another simpler example is STEP:

> **S** trategic (working in planning, regional or, at least, less operational roles)
> **T** echnical (range of functional skills)
> **E** xposure (to new environments and more senior clients and colleagues)
> **P** eople (team management)

Management experiences
People
Leading change
International
Size / type of business
Cross-department projects
Exposure – to a range of senior leaders
Client areas of work
Key accounts
Business Development
Seniority of client contact
Industry, type, client services, innovation

FIGURE 10.3   Experiences checklist.

It is also common for leadership training courses to include an element of "real work", giving middle managers a new experience of more senior level work through participating in project teams, supported by a coach, that tackle real strategic work problems over several months. This helps individuals learn skills of project management and problem solving, to gain confidence in presenting to senior leaders and to how to work unsupervised.

Many commentators state that new, broadening, stretching experiences are the most effective way to develop leadership skills (McCauley, DeRue, Yost, & Taylor, 2014). While less tangible than investing in training, they may be ultimately more useful.

Applications to schools and school systems

With similar intent, it is increasingly common for schools to create short-term secondments to the senior leadership team to work on specific projects. As academy trusts extend their reach, they are better placed to offer wider opportunities like those described above, retaining quality staff and growing their own future leaders in the process. A positive consequence of Teaching School Alliances and the DfE's designation of some middle leaders in the maintained sector as "Specialist Leaders in Education" (SLEs) who support other schools, has been to broaden high potential teachers' experiences, in many cases leading to promotion. The support they provide may take the form of short-term exchanges or secondments. Another positive outcome of such collaboration between schools—in a "self-improving system", as the DfE describes it—has been closer co-operation between primary and secondary schools. This not only supports the transition for students but also the professional development of teachers in both phases.

The British Council supports and organizes short-term international study tours and exchanges for school leaders across the world. Similarly, British universities have a strong presence offering school leadership development internationally, notably University College London Institute of Education (UCL IOE). School leaders undoubtedly find these experiences energizing. They return with new ideas and a fresh perspective on their schools, having viewed their work through the lens of a different school system. One headteacher, for instance, goes overseas each year with a few staff to spend time in a specialist school where they all learn different approaches and techniques together. This is a highlight of the year for many of them and definitely improves team relationships and motivation to learn as well as extending their skills and knowledge. It will be interesting to see whether the recent proliferation of international schools in Europe and the Far and Middle

East will result in more substantial international leadership experience being viewed as career enhancing. Traditionally it has sometimes been viewed as a career *cul de sac*, with heads fearing that staff will be out of touch when they return to the United Kingdom.

Enlisting help of others: "the 20%"

Many organizations make learning from others a deliberate and planned process. This can take a number of forms, as outlined below.

Job shadowing

A simple, inexpensive, and effective way to see leadership in action. Typically, aspiring leaders spend two or three days following another leader. This works particularly well with a two- to three-day international visit where the two people travel together and the time is filled with an intensive programme of back to back meetings and social engagements.

Applications to schools and school systems

Job shadowing in school contexts is often difficult to organize because of the constraints of time and teaching timetables, but where it has been tried it is generally memorable and productive. It is encouraged on NPQH programmes and on initiatives that aim to link business and industry with education, with a view to broadening perspectives on leadership.

Peer support

Many organizations find ways to bring groups of peers together to exchange ideas, share knowledge, and help each other. At one organization there was a well-established practice of requesting a "peer review", a typical situation being where one part of the organization was introducing something new and wanted to check their plans. As a result of the process, people would often gain new ideas and perspectives, additional insights to manage an up-coming change, and reassurance that they were along the right lines. It was a lower stakes, less formal but often more detailed approach than seeking direction from within the hierarchy.

In another organization, a peer support group of 20 leaders met four times a year. They operated an "open space" approach with minimum structure in which people simply raised topics and those interested in that topic would break off and discuss it together. Importantly, there was no requirement to report back, so people could focus on the discussion in the moment rather than taking notes and planning for the plenary session. Over time the topics became more personal, with people wanting to discuss ideas relating to their own effectiveness and managing difficult working relationships.

Applications to schools and school systems

Peer support is particularly appealing to school leaders because the culture of the teaching profession is generally collegial. Several organizations provide support to schools, such as "Challenge Partners" (an offspring of "London Challenge"), who have made peer support and review a major feature of their school improvement strategy. They have found that when help and support are offered in an equal relationship with some reciprocity, they are more likely to be accepted. Similarly, the work discussion groups described in this book provided valuable mutual support and facilitated peer consultation in areas where they were introduced. Peer support was embedded as a concept into the development programmes for aspiring and serving headteachers designed by the Hay Group for the former National College for School Leaders in the 1990s (e.g., see Creissen, 2008). Although challenges of time and geography had to be overcome, generally participants welcomed this opportunity in the collegial ethos of that era. Since the 1990s the education landscape has changed considerably. Competition between schools has increased, and the former networks of headteachers and their deputies, coordinated by local authorities, have declined. More recently, however, new networks of peer support seem to be opening up, often initially to rally against some new government directive or on the back of some social-media-generated cause, like #metoo. The Heads' Roundtable and WomenEd are two such examples, as are the ambassador networks emanating from Teach First.

Coaching

Many organizations have invested heavily in coaching. As mentioned under the situational leadership model above, some businesses try to encourage leaders to adopt more of a coaching style of leadership and management in suitable situations. There are many ways of using coaching to develop leaders—setting up a coaching function within HR, training managers in coaching skills, writing coaching responsibilities into job objectives, assigning coaches, identifying "coaching moments", collecting feedback from subordinates, and rewarding coaches for success. Despite best efforts, there are at times barriers to coaching, not least that leaders are often terminally busy and may see coaching as too time-consuming.

Coaching seems to work best as a dedicated resource, through the provision of an external or internal coach assigned to an individual for a prescribed purpose and timescale (e.g. a job transition).

Applications to schools and school systems

Coaching is increasingly seen as a means to both develop and support headteachers, academy trust principals, and chief executives. For most headteachers, it is preferable to have a qualified external coach (often from business) rather than another local headteacher as a mentor, for reasons of confidentiality—and probably also to avoid competition—although many have both. Some—headteachers in particular—describe the experience as life-changing, and it is becoming common for governors to offer coaching as a means to support a headteacher's wellbeing and work–life balance.

Coaching has also been enthusiastically embraced as a strategy to develop senior and middle leaders in schools and is a common feature of school improvement and development programmes. This specific aspect of leadership development and support is explored in detail elsewhere in this book. It is important to stress, however, that coaching can be devalued or discredited if practised by educational professionals without recognized qualifications and supervision.

Mentoring

Where organizations distinguish between coaching and mentoring, mentoring usually involves the provision of support by more senior person outside the direct hierarchical reporting line, who has particular relevant subject or organizational knowledge.

Mentoring relationships may be hard to engineer. They may develop best over time, often informally, between two people who have some chemistry or common interests. A typical example might be keeping in touch with a respected ex-boss.

Mentors can help you navigate an organization, operate as a sounding board, and offer wise counsel. Organizations may try to set up mentoring programmes and match-make relationships, especially for new graduates or people early in their careers.

Applications to schools and school systems

Mentoring is well established in schools, both as an instructional intervention and to support leadership development. In particular, it has had a significant impact on the craft of teaching as all trainee and newly qualified teachers are now allocated a mentor. Mentor training, usually delivered by universities or TSAs, has improved greatly in recent years, and there is a growing trend for heads of subject departments and other lead practitioners to be trained in "instructional mentoring". All newly appointed headteachers are also usually assigned a mentor, provided by a local authority or academy trust. They will often be a local headteacher designated as a Local or National Leader in Education (LLE or NLE) or a consultant headteacher.

Exposure to senior leaders

Many organizations subscribe to the mantra that "leaders develop leaders", with senior people spending a significant part of their time on talent development and staff retention strategy, publicly stating that it is a key part of their job. This might take the form of informal interactions between senior leaders and high potential staff, as well as organized events. For example, a finance director visiting a business and lunching with the local finance department's high-potential middle managers, or scheduled career discussions with someone at a senior level.

Applications to schools and school systems

Exposure to senior leaders probably happens more naturally in the education world, given the egalitarian culture and the smaller scale of most schools. However, a more systemic approach is currently observable in the relatively new leadership posts of "associates" and "heads of school". By 2017, 62% of secondary schools and 22% of primary schools (DfE, 2017b) were run by an academy chain or had formed their own academy trust, appointing Executive Heads or Chief Executives to oversee the work of heads of school (formerly headteachers). There is also an increasing trend for associate headteachers or other senior leaders to work alongside more experienced colleagues to gain more experience. For many, this is a safe stepping stone into a high-accountability role, as well as a development opportunity.

Using leadership competencies for assessment and development

What are they and how are they used?

Competency models describe the knowledge, skills, and experiences that leaders should demonstrate. Some organizations invest millions into developing and using them to define organizational culture and to integrate them into all aspects of people management, including:

» Recruitment interviews and promotion criteria;
» Job descriptions and evaluations, person specifications;
» Performance reviews and other development feedback processes;
» Training course design;
» Assessment and development centres.

In terms of leadership development, use of competencies creates an agenda or language for people to identify the areas that they want to improve. This type of "gap analysis" is used for development planning, feedback, and coaching, and defines and perhaps extends the scope of what leadership means. In particular, this includes an interest in *how* things are done as well as short-term delivery against financial objectives, thereby recognizing the impact of behaviours such as teamwork and relationships on the longer-term health of the organization.

Different models in different organizations

It is often recognized that successful leadership is context-specific, aligned to the values and culture of a particular organization and environment. There are no universal blueprints or recipes for leadership skills, and many organizations like to have their own definition of successful leadership. The language and emphasis in such competency models reflect the organization's context and the culture to which they aspire. In one organization successful leadership may be described in terms of overcoming obstacles, in another communicating with empathy. At times, however, organizations may over-play their distinctiveness but describe very similar areas when asked to analyse what their leaders need to be good at.

Common leadership competences

» dealing with ambiguity and complexity, navigating conflicting aims;
» working out what needs to be done: planning, initiative, strategy etc.;
» conceptual and thinking skills;
» managing and influencing others, helping others succeed;
» making decisions: including where you don't have all the information;
» dealing with stress, building resilience;

» leading change;

» conflict resolution;

» managing yourself: different aspects personal effectiveness;

» understanding yourself: demonstrating authenticity and integrity.

A health warning!

Competency models can quickly grow in scope and complexity. For example, by defining:

» different competency sets for different levels in the organization e.g. graduate, middle and senior leader;

» different performance levels with descriptors within each competency e.g. a 4- or 5-point scale such as 1: awareness, 2: basic, 3: intermediate, 4: advanced, 5: expert;

» different components within each competency such as personal values, knowledge needed, actions demonstrated;

» evidence for a competency or how it applies in different contexts—such as internally and with customers;

» functional competencies—e.g. relating to jobs in the Finance Department, HR or Marketing, as well as the general, core, or leadership competencies.

Often competencies are restricted to seven to ten in number, which makes them more manageable but inevitably leads to overlap and less clarity. Perhaps the most comprehensive list of leadership competencies was developed by Lombardo and Eichinger (1996) with 67 discrete dimensions.

As may be obvious from the above list, competencies can become rather unmanageable, and there is a real danger of the tail wagging the dog! It is important that they remain a means to an end.

Applications to schools and school systems

Leadership competency frameworks are standard practice for assessment and selection on to education leadership development programmes, such as NPQs. Their use in recruitment, to headship for instance, is widespread. Some individual schools and academy trusts are also using competency frameworks, linked to whole-school improvement plans, to take a more strategic approach to performance management and the identification of development needs. One school, for instance, produces a multi-layered development map for all staff, indicating what activities are on offer for leaders and teachers at different levels. Like some business models, they can become unwieldy, often running to several pages and sometimes failing to reflect the increasing complexity of senior leadership roles.

Organizing additional feedback to diagnose development needs

Organizations often invest in additional tools and initiatives to provide more detailed, personal feedback that focuses on diagnosing non-technical, more personal leadership development needs. It is easy and safe for an aspiring leader to say they want to improve their financial management knowledge, for instance, but this is very unlikely to be the skill that holds them back.

In addition to annual appraisals, some common processes to elicit developmental feedback include:

» Upward feedback: where team members give feedback on their boss, e.g. anonymously via an online questionnaire.

» 360° feedback: As above, but extended to peers and boss. Many psychometric instruments have 360° versions that highlight differences between self-rating and the average ratings from other groups. Some have an online feedback system where, as part of preparation for the annual appraisal, anyone could give feedback to anyone else anonymously.

» Development centres: Where aspiring leaders undertake observed work simulations and are given detailed feedback.

» Personality profiles and other psychometric tests are often included as part of the above processes. These self-reports are typically collected through online questionnaires, producing a report that is verified and discussed with a trained facilitator. The report may show personality dimensions, motivations, skills, and preferences, giving people further insights and understanding to start a more detailed or structured conversation about themselves.

Part of what organizations are trying to do is help individuals get more clarity and precision on what they need to do or learn in order to progress in their career. A development goal, for example, expressed as "improve leadership" or "communication skills" could mean almost anything—or mean different things to different stakeholders. Organizations hope that through more detailed feedback—ideally discussed with

Getting clarity
on what you want
to get better at

"improve communication"

"Develop greater impact when
dealing with senior
colleagues and clients"

"Communicate in a
more succinct and
structured way"

Clarification – e.g. through additional
feedback and coaching discussions

Refined development need:
Communicate with more impact when dealing with senior colleagues and clients. Particular areas to
work on include:

• being more succinct and structured,
• checking that people understand and that they are getting the information in a way they want,
• explaining technical points in less detail and less technical language.

Figure 10.4   Diagnosing development needs.

someone else such as a coach or line-manager—aspiring leaders can
become clearer on what to work on.

This can be illustrated as shown in Figure 10.4.

Personal development planning

Personal Development Plans (PDPs) are a fairly standard aspect of
people development in organizations, a way of pulling together, at the
individual level, much of what we have described so far. They are often
separated from performance appraisals to encourage more open discussion where issues such as pay or performance rating are off the agenda.
They also emphasize that a PDP is owned by the individual. Typically,
an organization will follow a standard format such as the one in Figure
10.5, which includes a mini CV, ideas on career direction, as well as the
standard development needs and actions.

One particular focus of a PDP are the *development actions* that will
help people learn. Here it is important to refer back to the 70:20:10
model, committing not only to training courses but also to something
that is within individuals' control and not reliant upon additional
funding.

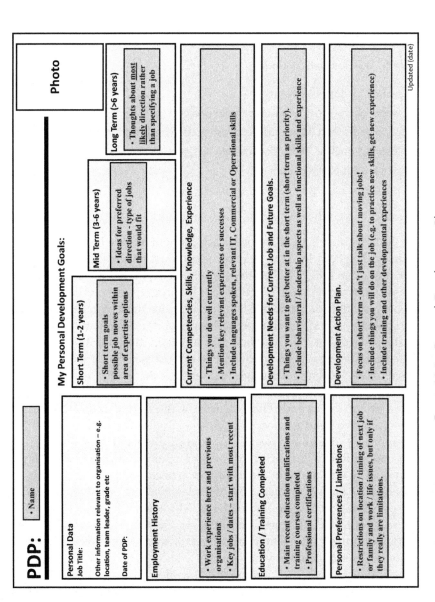

FIGURE 10.5   Personal Development Plan.

Many organizations have *development menus*: ideas for actions, including on-the-job experiences, that enlist others' help, as well as training and self-help resources. One such organization encourages each high-potential manager to undertake at least one of its "big 5" development actions each year:

"Big 5" development actions

- senior leader shadowing
- work on regional or international projects
- participate in a 12 month leadership training programme
- international or cross department assignment
- work on a Key Account

Applications to schools and school systems

Using 360° feedback to diagnose development needs is increasingly popular with school leaders. It features on most national development programmes like NPQs, linked to competency frameworks, and is often used as an assessment and selection tool by programme providers. Less commonly, schools or school systems may devise their own 360s to give ongoing feedback and development ideas to leaders. The Future Leaders Flagship programme, for instance, has a substantial handbook giving ideas for self-development, following 360° feedback. Some school leaders have taken feedback one stage further by seeking feedback through the use of student and parental surveys—although views sought may be more about the overall effectiveness of the school rather than the leadership of the headteacher.

Personal development plans are extensively used in schools and can be contentious if linked to appraisal or performance review. They vary in quality and may not always meet expectations, due to practical considerations. However, most school leaders welcome them if development opportunities are genuinely offered. More recently, governors who are mindful of their headteacher's wellbeing and work–life balance may offer the support of an executive coach or a short-term sabbatical as a result of performance review.

Psychometric tests and personality profiles are increasingly used in the recruitment of headteachers and other senior leaders, and the feedback can be used to offer support during the induction period of a new headteacher. They may also be used to help teams understand individual differences and ways of working together more effectively—as described in more detail in Part III of this book.

Leadership training courses

We have left this for last—deliberately—because while it is often the first thing people think of when it comes to developing leaders, there are so many other options that add more value. This section focuses on common features, concepts, and ideas found in the myriad internal and external leadership training programmes and opportunities.

Some key elements of leadership training

Context Helping leaders understand their organization—its market, performance, strategy, and how it sees leadership and career paths. Typical formats include talks, discussions and conferences with senior leaders and external expert input.

Understanding leadership Topics covered might include explorations of what leadership is, with analysis of successful people, research highlights, and a few key theories or models, including leadership styles and competencies and the difference between management and leadership.

Self-discovery and knowledge Using one of a vast range of instruments, psychometric tests, 360° feedback processes, reflective exercises, peer discussions, etc., to help people to understand themselves better. Insights and exercises might focus on personality, motivations, styles, analysis of time spent of different tasks, relationships, well-being, and even life goals. People gain insights into their strengths and areas to develop.

Work simulations People participate in observed, challenging work situations, often in teams, and get detailed feedback. Usually work tasks will be at a more senior level or out-of-comfort zone.

Peer networking and support Different levels of facilitation, process, or structure may be used, but the simple idea is to bring together people with similar interests to support and help each other. The hope is that groups or relationships formed would continue informally after the event.

Skills training An extensive list of topics may be included as part of a programme, or modules within it, to equip leaders with additional skills and to understand best practice. Examples include: difficult conversations, various aspects of personal effectiveness such as time management, resilience, presentation, and communication skills, planning, strategy, coaching, delegation, performance management, negotiating, interviewing, etc.

Topics Although some overlap with skills training, this category is more focused on key leadership challenges or current topics. Typical approaches would include expert input and case studies on change management, employee engagement, internal communications, strategy, ethics, stakeholder management, cultural awareness, talent management.

Broadening horizons Leadership training, especially on external courses, is often seen as a stimulus: a way of helping people understand more about the world outside their department or organization and providing food for thought, inspiration, new ideas, etc.

Blended learning In addition to attending a course, many training designs try to incorporate other training formats before, during, and after. For example, e-learning could be used to cover part of the knowledge content of the training, or delegates might work together in pre- or post research.

On-the-job work experience A very common format is to include work projects as part of the training programme, perhaps over several months. Here the focus is on the learning rather than the delivery of the work itself, with reflection and coaching built into the process. A typical approach would be to take on a new, more strategic initiative—perhaps introducing and managing a change in the organization. This format may also enable some connection with the trainee's line manager, who sponsors the work project and becomes more engaged with the training itself.

Connecting learning to the workplace A key challenge for training more generally is how to ensure that people use what they have learned by applying it back at work. There are numerous ideas and techniques to encourage, cajole, or audit this. Examples include: reporting back to senior management what you will do as a result of training; action planning at the end of a course and updating PDPs; follow-up conversations with faculty and your boss, or public commitments to colleagues; writing yourself a postcard in which you commit to specific actions that is then sent to you six months after the course. Another option is to require delegates to apply to join a course by making certain promises up front about how they will make best use of the training and what they are hoping to achieve.

Recognition   An often implicit aspect of training is recognition of an individual's value—a way to say thank you, well done or to give encouragement. This is particularly relevant when sending people on prestigious and expensive courses run, for example, by the major business schools.

Measuring impact   Linked to the point above is the constant concern in relation to return on investment. Some course designs start with this: for example, asking stakeholders of potential participants what they would like to see as a result of a new programme, then collecting feedback on these points before and after the course. At its most basic level, there are variations on collecting course feedback from attendees themselves: for example, understanding what people have learned and applied at various milestones after the course. Other options include tracking career or job success of attendees, or at least retention. However, at this higher level this can be difficult to quantify, given that there are so many other variables to consider in addition to the training.

The above may appear a bit like an uncritical smorgasbord of everything that could be included in leadership development training, so we would like to conclude with some personal observations on leadership development design principles—what we have found to be most effective and welcomed by leaders and stakeholders in our different worlds of business and education:

» training that is practical, realistic, and challenging, where participants enter a safe environment but are put under some pressure and stretched to do something they don't normally do;

» learning by doing that is magnified through built-in pauses for reflection, as it cannot be assumed that participants will naturally reflect on their own;

» opportunities to apply learning to their everyday roles and to reflect on their experiences;

» diagnosing individual development needs is time well spent; even if not taken further forward by planning development actions, individuals will be alert to opportunities and seek out relevant information;

» effective needs analysis may deliver a more relevant experience but is as much about engaging people as actually coming up with the agenda;

» not over-selling the need to measure impact and return on training investment. At best it is an assessment, a judgement, with some data captured and fed into the mix.

Conclusions

Throughout this chapter we have explored leadership development practices from the world of big business and their application to schools. While many of these ideas have been adopted or adapted by national education leadership providers, they are less established in schools generally.

There are reasons why many schools may increasingly take a more planned and deliberate approach to developing leaders:

» The establishment of school groups, such as academy trusts and international school chains, should lead to greater opportunities to grow leaders from within, with all the advantages that affords. A group of schools can, for example, more easily offer internal career paths and development opportunities and employ centralized HR specialists. It could attract and retain staff with a more sophisticated development offer, and establish a stronger culture and identity through promoting internally rather than recruiting leaders from outside. These cultural aspects are often a key consideration for academy trusts and for schools expanding abroad.

» There is an increasing recognition within schools, backed by case studies (Day et al., 2010) and Ofsted data (OfSTED, 2016), of the importance of leadership in raising standards and managing school improvement.

» Significant leadership shortages in schools (Wigdortz & Toop, 2016), for example, affecting one in four schools in England by 2022, which signals, among other things, that more needs to be done to help those with ambition and promise to reach leadership more quickly.

In the minds of many parents, staff, and pupils "the school *is* the headteacher", however unreasonable or unrealistic that might seem. How headteachers are seen to lead, their values, personal qualities, and interactions have a significant influence on how the whole school community feels about the school—and on staff retention and parental satisfaction. How often do people say this about other consumer choices, and what does this say about the importance of leadership development in schools? Developing leaders is certainly not a quick fix, and often what makes the difference is difficult to measure and slow to mature. At a time of high accountability and diminishing school budgets, finding more creative and personalized ways of growing school leaders and supporting their ongoing development seems more important than ever.

Existing and new national education leadership providers are only recently beginning to engage academy trusts and schools in talent management more strategically. Some have started to offer suites of programmes with clear career pathways from initial teacher training to executive headship. For individual schools, where the challenge is often time and money, one small step might be to introduce a Staff Development Meeting. It puts leadership development firmly on the agenda for every school and should work as a catalyst for other initiatives to follow. As Margaret Mead said, "Never doubt that a small group of thoughtful, committed, citizens can change the world. Indeed, it is the only thing that ever has."

CHAPTER ELEVEN

Creating coaching cultures in schools

Chris Munro, Margaret Barr, &
Christian van Nieuwerburgh

This chapter explores the concept of coaching cultures in schools. In their review of the literature on coaching cultures, Gormley and van Nieuwerburgh (2014) concluded that the development of such cultures promises to create more positive and supportive organizational climates for personal and organizational growth.

We place a particular focus on how and why headteachers and other senior leaders might promote this culture in their school and build the capacity of teachers as coaches. This will be illustrated by reflections from practitioners in Australia and the United Kingdom.

We argue that the realization of a whole-school coaching culture involves procedural and managerial changes in practice and, perhaps more significantly, changes in attitudes and habits across many aspects of school life, in order to enable a new and sustainable organizational "way of being" where students and educators flourish.

We first clarify the difference between coaching and mentoring and outline some of the psychological theories and approaches that underpin coaching in school environments. After defining a whole-school coaching culture for learning, we use the "Global Framework for Coaching and Mentoring in Education" (van Nieuwerburgh, Knight, & Campbell, 2019) to describe four educational contexts through which coaching can be introduced in order to build a coaching culture.

What is the difference between coaching and mentoring?

Coaching in education is defined by van Nieuwerburgh (2012, p. 17) as:

> ... a one-to-one conversation that focuses on the enhancement of learning and development through increasing self-awareness and a sense of personal responsibility, where the coach facilitates the self-directed learning of the coachee through questioning, active listening, and appropriate challenge in a supportive and encouraging climate.

A coach "facilitates the self-directed learning of the coachee" in a non-directive way. A mentor, on the other hand, tends to share knowledge and expertise with the mentee in a more directive way. While both interventions are helpful when used appropriately, this chapter focuses on coaching. We also refer to a "coaching approach", which Campbell (2016a) defines as "intentionally utilising the transferable elements of coaching in other conversations, wherever they might be appropriate and helpful". In a coaching approach, coaching skills and principles influence professional conversations that take place outside formal coaching sessions.

What psychological theories and approaches inform coaching?

School leaders need not necessarily have an in-depth understanding of the psychological theories that inform the practice of coaching. Nevertheless, it is helpful to appreciate some of the key theories and frameworks that underpin coaching and to consider the implications for culture change.

Adams (2016) identifies a range of useful psychological theories, principles, and frameworks that inform the application of coaching in schools. These are complementary to some of the psychodynamic and systemic approaches described elsewhere in this book. In brief, some of these are:

» *The person-centred approach*. This approach is based on the theory and philosophy of Rogers (1961). The coach is non-judgemental and holds that the coachee is the best expert of himself or herself. Thus, the coach's "way of being" facilitates the coachee's intrinsic motivation and sense of responsibility. This standpoint can be a challenge for leaders adopting coaching roles and approaches and will be explored more fully later. However, a coach who respects and values the contextual knowledge and expertise that the coachee brings to any situation is more likely to empower the coachee to take sustained action.

» *The solution-focused approach.* de Shazer's (1985) work on solution-focused therapy with families focused on the clients talking about their preferred future, without needing to analyse the problem. A coach using a solution-focused approach helps the coachee gain clarity about possible solutions and how to use their strengths and skills to achieve a solution. Where a school culture embraces a solution-focused approach, the focus is not on the problem but on supporting one another to find solutions.

» *Self-efficacy theory.* Self-efficacy is our belief in our own abilities. Bandura (1986) theorized that self-efficacy is the strongest predictor of our ability to set and achieve goals and persist when we meet setbacks. A coach can use a range of strategies to support a coachee to build their self-efficacy—for example, by using past successes to identify future possibilities. For teachers and leaders, external pressures, agendas, and responsibilities can erode this sense of self-efficacy. Coaching helps educators to find focus and identify achievable goals that matter to them.

» *Self-determination theory.* This is a theory of motivation. Ryan and Deci's (2000) theory is that in order to function and grow optimally, all of us have an innate psychological need to perceive that we have competence, autonomy, and relatedness with others. Coaching can help us to be more competent, to feel more autonomous, and to sense more relatedness, thus improving motivation and increasing empowerment. Again, this applies equally to school leaders and classroom teachers.

» *Positive psychology.* Seligman and Csikszentmihalyi (2000) founded positive psychology, the study of optimal human functioning that aims to discover and promote those factors that allow us to thrive. A coach can support the coachee to identify and use their strengths and positive emotions. This allows the coachee to take action in school that builds the wellbeing of themselves and others, enabling them to flourish. At the heart of the positive-psychology-based approach is the creation of a school community where the mental health and wellbeing of everyone is a priority. Leach and Green (2016, p. 169) provide an excellent overview of how to integrate coaching and positive psychology in education. They cite the growing research base that shows coaching to have benefits such as increased well-being, goal striving, resilience, and hope; alongside positive impacts on emotional intelligence, academic achievement, and attitudes to learning.

The above short examples are relevant not only to coaching itself, but also to the process of creating a coaching culture.

What is a whole-school coaching culture for learning?

Referring to organizations in general, Gormley and van Nieuwerburgh (2014, p. 99) proposed the following definition:

> A coaching culture exists within an organisation when it has embedded a coaching approach as part of its strategic plans in a transparent way. Coaching cultures should motivate individuals and facilitate cooperation, collaboration and connection within the organisation and with its external stakeholders.

When we apply Gormley and van Nieuwerburgh's definition to a school, the individuals and stakeholders are the leaders, teachers, students and all those involved within the school community. Building on the definitions above, we propose the following definition of a "whole-school coaching culture for learning":

> A whole-school coaching culture for learning exists when education leaders, teachers, support staff, students, parents, and other partners, intentionally use coaching and coaching approaches in a range of conversational contexts. For this to happen, coaching approaches should be widely understood and skilfully utilised across the school community. In such a culture, a coaching approach to conversations about learning will need to become part of an organisation's "way of being" with appropriate resourcing and explicit integration into the school's strategic plans.

We now expand on this definition, and shall return to it later.

The "Global Framework for Coaching and Mentoring in Education" (van Nieuwerburgh, Knight, & Campbell, 2019) sets out a helpful model of four contexts in which coaching and coaching approaches can be used in schools to build a coaching culture. Figure 11.1 presents each of these contexts within the landscape of the educational environment.

Educational leadership

One-to-one coaching can support aspiring, newly-appointed, and experienced educational leaders with their leadership development (Forde, McMahon, Gronn, & Martin, 2013; Goff, Goldring, Guthrie, & Bickman, 2014; James-Ward, 2013; Robertson, 2016). After learning how to coach, educational leaders can use a coaching approach to leadership interactions with colleagues (Adams, 2012; Barr & van Nieuwerburgh, 2015; Cantore & Hick, 2013). When such a coaching approach to leadership becomes the norm for leaders, they convey a coaching "way of being" (van Nieuwerburgh, 2014, p. 12). It might be said that coaching is not only the things that leaders do: it has evolved into the way that leaders are.

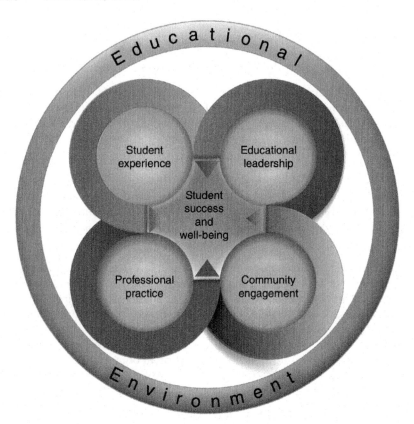

FIGURE 11.1   The Global Framework for Coaching and Mentoring in Education
[© Growth Coaching International; van Nieuwerburgh, Knight, & Campbell, 2019].

Professional practice

In its simplest form, coaching in the context of professional practice aims to improve teaching and learning, through coaching by external experts, senior leaders, or peers. Teachers see that coaching to develop their professional practice is a catalyst for their learning. Teachers may peer-coach one another (Hooker, 2014; Wong & Nicotera, 2003) with a focus on classroom practice, pastoral responsibilities, or other aspects of their work. In addition to—or instead of—a peer coach, they may have a designated coach: for example, an instructional coach (Knight, 2007) who has been internally or externally appointed. Using a dialogic approach (Knight, 2018), instructional coaches use their own knowledge and expertise about instruction (or teaching practice, as it is also known) to support the teacher as they seek to implement new practices.

Community engagement

Teachers can use coaching approaches when interacting with parents. Parents can be supported to develop their parenting skills through coaching from educational professionals or psychologists (Golawski, Bamford, & Gersch, 2013), or they can be trained in coaching skills, so that they can coach their own children (Graham, 2013).

Student experience

The interventions already mentioned are intended to lead to improved student success and wellbeing: therefore "Student success and wellbeing" is at the heart of the Global Framework. However, students can experience coaching with and by one another. Trained external coaches can work with students to improve academic performance and wellbeing (Passmore & Brown, 2009). Trained school staff can coach students in the same way, and trained students can coach each other. In the latter scenario, there are benefits for the student coach as well as the coachee—for example, with student coaches reporting improved attitudes to learning (van Nieuwerburgh & Tong, 2013, p. 20).

The Global Framework shows that the interventions take place within a broader educational environment. The environment will influence the implementation of the interventions and will, in turn, be affected by them.

Working towards a whole-school coaching culture for learning

It's a journey

Others have written about the steps, stages, or pathways towards establishing a coaching culture in organizations (Clutterbuck & Megginson, 2005; Creasy & Paterson, 2005; Hawkins, 2012; Passmore & Jastrzebska, 2011). While these are helpful, they inevitably run the risk of making the process appear somewhat linear. This viewpoint would miss the evolutionary, iterative, or cyclic nature of what happens within and between stages.

While we acknowledge the attraction of such delineated steps to success for school leaders, we also know that organizational change is rarely straightforward, and success at each stage of development depends on context. The following observations and recommendations are based on our own experiences and those of a range of schools at different stages of the journey towards establishing a coaching culture for learning.

Who and what initiates the journey?

It is likely that whoever initiates the journey will have identified with a compelling coaching experience themselves, or will have read or heard about successful coaching interventions. Robertson (2016, p. 17) draws on her work with school principals in Australia and New Zealand in describing how leaders who experience coaching "are generally no longer satisfied with less in-depth relationships with other colleagues and so are more likely to try to establish professional coaching relationships with them".

Campbell (2016b, pp. 131–132) suggests that the "essential role of conversation" in educational settings is a fundamental reason why coaching resonates so strongly with educators:

> Not only are the leadership and organisation of a school progressed through various conversations ... but conversations are also *central* to the work of that school. Learning and teaching occur through various forms of conversation (real and virtual) taking place in classrooms and playgrounds across the globe every day. Consequently, coaching resonates strongly with many educators. At its essence coaching is a conversation, and conversations are at the heart of learning, school life and work.

Quality coaching conversations go beyond routine procedural talk to get to the heart of the matter. They result in deep learning and sustained change fuelled by authentic connection and trusting relationships.

Schools provide a range of conversational contexts (Campbell, 2016b, p. 133) where coaching approaches can make a positive difference. Those with leadership influence in a school often identify problematic conversational contexts as the starting point for the introduction of coaching. They may start with something like "We want to change the nature of conversations around 'x' so that 'y' will improve, and we think that a coaching approach could help." As school leaders, it is not difficult to identify a wide range of scenarios like this that sit within each of the contexts mentioned earlier.

> "[We realised] that while we had established a culture of learning and teachers had many opportunities for professional learning, the missing piece was growth conversations for individual teachers."
> (Edna Sackson, Mount Scopus Memorial College, Melbourne, Australia)

> "We opted for coaching as we wanted to commit to staff a more sustained working relationship focused on developing classroom practice, growing their capacity to work with new ideas, and receive ongoing feedback. Also, it was to help align individual efforts with school priorities."
> (Jon Andrews, St Paul's School, Brisbane, Australia)

"The school had run a compulsory 'learning trios' programme for teachers. This involved peer observation and peer discussions. The feedback from teachers was that they enjoyed observing each other but were unclear about how to structure the subsequent discussions, which often became unfocused chats. It was clear to me that a coaching model would provide exactly the structure and solution focus that seemed to be missing. So I sought volunteers to integrate peer coaching into the programme of peer observation and collaborative professional enquiry."

(Robert Jones, North Berwick High School, North Berwick, Scotland)

In another scenario, the initiator may be driven by a more general philosophical view of teaching and of teacher learning. For example, they may be driven by the "moral imperative" argued by Wiliam (2014, p. 6):

We need to create environments in which teachers embrace the idea of continuous improvement … an acceptance that the impact of education on the lives of young people creates a moral imperative for even the best teachers to continue to improve.

"… the ultimate goal … was improved teaching practice and therefore improved student learning. Other long-term goals of coaching teachers on their practice were: a vibrant culture of professional learning, de-privatised classrooms, a shared language of practice, and teachers with increased reflective practice, and self-efficacy."

(Deborah Netolicky, Wesley College, Perth, Australia)

Although those proposing the introduction of coaching may not yet have a clear vision of what it will look like in practice across their school, they *will* know what is driving them to pursue it. This rationale for the introduction of coaching in a school context is key to the success of the initiative and an important area for leaders to examine. So, if coaching is seen to be the answer, what is the question?

"The wider culture shift in education has also sharpened my commitment to a whole-school coaching culture. The expectation that all teachers can be good or better has necessitated different types of conversations about teaching and learning—whether between the classroom teacher and student, the classroom teacher and their line manager, or between the Head and chair of governors."

(Michelle McLeod, Preston Manor School, London, England)

Robertson (2016) explains how coaching can help school leaders to uncover their "educational platform", which is based on the values and beliefs that underpin the decisions they make in their schools. Being coached, and the process of learning how to coach, can be a powerful form of leadership development that stimulates critical reflection on the learning relationships that they have across their educational community (Robertson, 2016, p. 45).

The implications of teachers' increased sense of self-efficacy as a result of being coached by senior leaders are very positive. By empowering teachers to take responsibility for their own learning and development and trusting them as their own contextual experts, school leaders flatten hierarchies and professionalize their staff by enabling them to exercise agency (Priestley, Biesta, & Robinson, 2015).

However, the notion of teachers identifying their own development priorities can be very challenging for some educational leaders. It may seem intuitive and appropriate to give strong direction on individual teacher goals. This is perfectly sensible at a whole-school level, since teachers do not operate as "freelancers" within the building, and it is fair to expect that their goals should align with whole-school priorities. However, when teachers are allowed authentic freedom within this "form" and are encouraged to determine their own goals and development needs, teacher development becomes more about mindful engagement and less about mindless compliance. As Wiliam asserts, "what we have learned is that when we start out by assuming the best of people, rather than the worst, then, in general, good things happen" (2016, p. 168).

Table 11.1 shows a range of common conversational contexts for coaching approaches and typical desired outcomes. School leaders can use it to reflect on which conversational context provides the starting point, and what will be different by employing coaching and/or coaching approaches in school.

The critical importance of authenticity

Coaching is about unlocking potential (Whitmore, 2009, p. 10). We believe that coaching in schools should be strengths-based and solution-focused. It should be a discourse of what is wanted and what is possible, rather than what is wrong and what has not worked; it should be a treasure hunt rather than a witch-hunt. At its best, coaching is an empowering and respectful conversational process designed to build individual and collective capacity and efficacy.

When educators consider their rationale for initiating coaching, it is worth reflecting on the above description. For example, what scenarios are

Table 11.1. Coaching approaches: common conversational contexts and desired outcomes

Conversational contexts	Desired outcomes
Professional practice	
» teacher professional learning » professional reflection » teacher goal setting and development planning » teacher collaboration » professional learning teams » curriculum/faculty/year-level teams » classroom observation and feedback » use of data » supporting beginning teachers	» more discerning choices of professional learning » more personalized professional learning » implementation of alternative teaching strategies » more focused use of evidence » recognition of strengths in practice » identification of strengths and capacity building » creating a safe space to talk about and develop practice, and thus de-privatizing classroom practice » increased awareness of classroom reality and increased self-efficacy and agency » observation and feedback is non-judgemental and serves the development goals of the teacher » more action-oriented team dialogue » differentiated support for beginning teachers
Educational leadership	
» Performance review and development processes » leadership skills » leadership functions » team operation » strategic planning » difficult/hard conversations » feedback conversations » managing mandated processes from governing authorities	» more positive and productive performance conversations » establishment of a culture of continuous improvement or enhancement » flattened hierarchies » leadership conversations are more developmental/growth orientated » more efficient and effective meetings » increased emotional intelligence » constructive feedback is sought, given and received more positively » increased collegiality and collaboration » externally imposed processes are implemented more sensitively and meaningfully

(continued)

Table 11.1.   Coaching approaches: common conversational contexts and desired outcomes *(continued)*

Conversational contexts	Desired outcomes
Student experience	
» academic progress	» increased academic attainment
» pastoral support and wellbeing	» wider range of achievement
» student goal setting and action planning	» increased student uptake of voluntary activities
» restorative practices	» reduction in instances of challenging behaviour
» behaviour management	
» student leadership development	» enhanced student wellbeing
» student voice	» building student capacity for peer leadership
» peer support and feedback	» students better able to articulate their learning
» positive education programmes	» improved attendance
	» reduction in exclusions from school
	» more agency-enabling conversations with students
	» conscious application of positive education strategies by students
	» students feel heard and supported as individuals
Community engagement	
» parents/carer communication	» parents report feeling better listened to, and more involved in their children's learning
» parent–teacher interviews	
» parents–student communication	» parents are more intentional in conversations with their children
» community leaders and groups	
» school governors/boards	» increased sense of partnership between parents and school
» liaison with external agencies	
	» parent–teacher communication is more dialogic
	» community leaders and groups engage more with school
	» improved relationships and better engagement with school governors and boards
	» more inclusive decision-making
	» schools and external agencies see one another as partners.

envisaged when viewing coaching as a possible intervention? How does the rationale for coaching sit with the philosophy of a coaching approach?

A school leader who is under pressure to improve student results may be tempted to view coaching as a response to teacher underperformance, or as a means of ensuring compliance. They may believe that coaching can be *administered* to teachers. While we recognize that the issues underlying these drivers may be very real, this deficit-based position is contrary to the philosophy of coaching.

To avoid doing more harm than good, we must ensure that coaching is not viewed as a manipulative strategy. Covert performance management thinly disguised as coaching risks undermining trust in the leadership of the school and in the true intent of coaching, the capacity for professional growth. Hargreaves and Skelton (2012) explore the issues of politics and school culture in relation to coaching and mentoring. They caution against the positives of coaching being diminished through "contrived collegiality" (Hargreaves, 1994), where a true teacher-driven collaborative learning opportunity has been hijacked by school administrators seeking to control and manage performance.

A related challenge for school leaders is the power imbalance inherent when formally coaching a direct report ("manager as coach"), as opposed to using a coaching approach in everyday work-related conversations. When leaders attempt to coach teachers who are accountable to them, they do so against a backdrop of perceptions based on previous relationships that could be described as the "corporate memory" of the school. These past experiences and impressions may be positive or negative and will determine the level of scepticism towards this new approach. Further, the coachee's perception of their relationship with the leader will influence how candid they feel they can be. Even if the coaching conversation is explicitly positioned outside any appraisal or performance review framework, positional seniority can stifle candour for fear of being judged or of some repercussion. Where this issue is not acknowledged, the teacher is much more likely to go through the motions and may expend considerable energy on "impression management"—telling the leader what they think they want to hear. While the leader cannot relinquish overall responsibility for the performance of their staff, they can set down a clear statement of intent about their role in the coaching conversation.

Leaders need to be sensitive to these issues when adopting coaching as a leadership strategy and allocating or matching coaches. In a study in Denmark, Spaten and Flensborg (2013) found that in order to succeed, the manager as coach should be aware of power relations, be sensitive and empathic in building the coaching relationship, and draw clear boundaries between their roles as leader and coach. In reality, this may be easier said than done.

> "Leaders are aware of the tension that exists when they take a coaching stance with someone whom they line-manage or are in a position of professional power over. We try to alleviate this by being clear and intentional about the role a leader is taking at any one time. Partly this is about prior explanation of the role and expectations of any process or conversation.
>
> If a leader needs to shift stance during a conversation, such as from coaching to consulting or evaluating, they will deliberately break rapport with the person to show that they are shifting stance, as well as being verbally explicit about this."
>
> (Deborah Netolicky, Wesley College, Perth, Australia)

The second issue is the leader's responsibility for inviting trust and building an authentic coaching relationship with the coachee. Coaching relationships are commonly described as "learning partnerships" or "helping relationships". Knight (2011) proposes seven "partnership principles" that should underpin teacher professional learning. Of these, the principles of choice—teachers should have a choice regarding what and how they learn—and reciprocity—we should expect to get as much as we give (p. 46)—are, perhaps, the most challenging for leaders as coaches. Leaders need to genuinely adopt a learner's mindset and an attitude of curiosity in order to enact these principles.

> "In the current educational culture of increased accountability and performativity, teachers are constantly the subject of critique and evaluation, establishing that coaching is not part of this evaluative aspect and impressing the development aspect of coaching is vital."
>
> (Alex Guedes, Thomas Carr College, Melbourne, Australia)

The rhetoric of coaching may sound authentic, but this must match the lived experience of the participants, if the potential benefits are to be fully realized. Leaders need to engage with the learning around coaching so that they can model practice authentically. Further, leaders need to go beyond simply endorsing or advocating coaching for others (by implication, lower down the organizational hierarchy) if they are seeking to move towards coaching as a way of being at an individual and organizational level.

> "Advice for anyone looking to develop coaching within a school: be honest with yourself as a leader. If what you really want is for teachers to start

doing some specific task or to adopt some specific strategy, then coaching is not the right tool. Coaching always gives the coachee control. Avoid compulsion. Forcing teachers to coach and be coached is a monstrous waste of time and energy."

(Robert Jones, North Berwick High School, North Berwick, Scotland)

Netolicky (2016) sums up the issues for us here:

"A belief in the capacity of teachers for reflection and growth implies that everyone is coachable, yet issues about the effects of hierarchical relationships on an individual's authenticity, openness, and vulnerability remain. When deciding who will coach teachers, schools should consider the ways in which trust, rapport, and emotion influence learning."

The influence of existing school culture

When we speak to schools about the initiators and drivers of coaching and how it has been introduced, they invariably refer to the conditions that existed in their school before coaching was introduced. These antecedent conditions are the norms, practices, and prevalent discourse that may enable or inhibit the rate of development and adoption of coaching.

The antecedent conditions for coaching will be different in every school and even in different contexts within a school. If educators are in tune with these conditions, they can be taken into account when considering the pace of change. Trust is a critical factor here. Just as individual coaching relationships depend on trust to be productive, so a coaching culture will thrive or wither on the levels of trust within the school's conversational contexts. As Covey puts it: "Nothing is as fast as the speed of trust" (2006, p. 3).

"I see exceptional coaches as well as some who have recently joined the challenge and there is a ramp-up in learning before they become as effective as they need to be to build relationships and trust."

(Alex Guedes, Thomas Carr College, Melbourne, Australia)

When thinking about the prevalent discourse in their school, leaders may reflect on the following questions:

» Do people use the language of trust, growth, ownership, empowerment, and learning? Or is their language about performativity, judgement, deficit, suspicion, and compliance?

» What norms or protocols are in place for different kinds of conversations or collaboration?

» How are stakeholders involved in decision-making processes?

» What other forms of collaborative learning, goal-setting, and development planning are in place?

» What processes are in place for gathering data, providing feedback, and discussing practice?

» What is the *lived experience* of these practices?

> "We intended to develop a non-threatening but cerebral culture of professional inquiry, conversation, and reflection, in order to develop professional culture, professional practice, and therefore student learning."
> (Deborah Netolicky, Wesley College, Perth, Australia)

> "Our coaches were all experienced teachers who had the respect and trust of wider staff, so this made it easier to get people to come on-board and model being coached for other staff."
> (Fiona Gontier, Haileybury College, Melbourne, Australia)

Advocacy and leadership

Earlier, we discussed the role of the initiator in proposing the introduction of coaching in a school. In our experience, the subsequent development of coaching practice across the school may not be led by the initiator and is often led by others. A common approach seems to be one of coaching initiated from the top but championed from the middle. This championing role tends to fall to an individual or small group of staff that act as advocates, as the practicalities of implementation are worked out and evolve. The role of advocate, or coaching leader, often falls to middle leaders who have professional learning or staff development roles, or to someone in a newly created role. There are several advantages to this approach. The coaching leaders are in a better position than a senior leader to give the project more of their attention and can maintain momentum. Further, those who already have a mandate to support teacher growth and learning are ideally placed to act as advocates for teacher development initiatives such as coaching and can be a conduit to the senior leadership of the school.

> "The Vice-Principal, an accredited coach, was very excited about introducing coaching at our school. His presentation to staff really focused on

the skills of the type of person that might be interested in being one of our coaches."

(Fiona Gontier, Haileybury College, Melbourne, Australia)

"This change was initiated and supported by Leadership, but it was guided by the staff. They were and are integral to this 'journey'. They are the 'keys'."

(Sophie Hunter, St Kevin's College, Melbourne, Australia)

Coaching skill development

At this point a school is beginning to build its coaching capacity through the training and immersion of these people who, ultimately, become the in-house experts in coaching. Timperley and Parr (2008) note that coaches are more effective when they have been trained, and Campbell (2016b, p. 140) reminds us of the importance of training in specific coaching skills:

> In defining coaching as a form of "conversation" it can be easy to trivialise and underplay the critical importance of effective coaching skill development training. Coaching *is* a specific kind of conversation, full of intention; subtle and not so subtle shifts in perspective; carefully nuanced language; and acutely refined listening, among other things.

This training element is a common feature in all of the stories that practitioners shared with us. Since this can be a significant resource investment, leaders need to carefully consider the range of training options available and how this will be utilized. The importance of high-quality training for coaches is identified as a key factor across a number of professional contexts (van Nieuwerburgh, 2016a).

Evolution and growth

When coaching in school begins, a conscious decision should be taken to allow it to evolve through a principle of "democratic voluntary involvement", as proposed by van Nieuwerburgh (2016b, p. 233). A common message from our conversations with schools is that teachers and leaders buy-in more readily when they can see and feel the beneficial outcomes of effective coaching conversations.

As more participants engage in coaching conversations and as coaching approaches begin to be utilized in interactions across the school community, so the benefits are felt by an ever-increasing number of people. By gathering and reviewing feedback data from those involved, schools can bolster the sense of democratic involvement in the evolution of these new ways of working and begin to build a common language, under-standing, and value of coaching. This is vitally important. To prevent the perception of coaching as yet another top-down initiative, time must be taken to establish shared understandings of coaching approaches and to promote the benefits of the approach.

School leaders have an opportunity to model the commitment to their own professional growth that they expect of their staff. In doing so they demonstrate that they have the courage to create opportunities for critical conversations (Robertson & Allan, 1999) for the benefit of themselves and their school community.

As those with most decision-making power in the school, leaders must be proactive not only in nurturing the continued growth of a coaching culture, but also in limiting potential inhibitors. For example, they can influence professional learning time, meeting agendas, timetables, and the structure of the school day, so that time is freed up to allow teachers to practise coaching skills and develop new habits. Staff can therefore benefit from the increased levels of awareness, increased clarity and improved self-efficacy that coaching conversations bring.

> "School leaders responsible for teaching and learning and CPD took the decision to move to collaborative professional learning, and this was the area that I led on. Core coaching skills provided the framework for the peer discussions and underpinned the challenge to improve class-room practice in order to enhance outcomes for pupils. Importantly, the sessions were facilitated by staff and designed to enable meaningful collaboration—principles that enhanced the coaching methods built into the whole school CPD programme."
>
> (Michelle McLeod, Preston Manor School, London, England)

Over time, as senior leaders and coaching champions continue to endorse, support, and participate in coaching, and as trust in the process increases, a tipping point is reached, where several things begin to happen:

1. More trained coaches are required because of increasing demand for internal coaching.
2. Trained coaches begin to think about the need for reflection to support their work—for example, coaching supervision (Clutterbuck, Whitaker, & Lucas, 2016) or peer reflective practice.
3. Additional forms of coaching are developed in response to need—peer coaching, technology coaching, career coaching, leadership coaching, etc.

4. Members of the school community (not necessarily the coaching leaders) begin to identify additional contexts where coaching could be of benefit.

The final point is significant, because it provides a strong indication that the school is beginning to own and expand the approach. Coaching is no longer simply an initiative.

> "Our coaching journey began with two trained coaches offering 1–1 coaching to teacher volunteers on any aspect of their practice. Now, three years on, we can see the embryonic signs of what might be described as a coaching culture: increasing uptake; reciprocal peer-coaching; eLearning coaching rather than tech "pushing'; leaders trained in coaching approaches; growth-based performance and development processes; and teachers consciously employing coaching skills with their students: in short, more coachable opportunities are being identified."
>
> (Chris Munro, St Kevin's College, Melbourne, Australia)

> "Having used coaching with teachers as part of their professional review and development, I was impressed at the level of ideas and actions generated from even one discussion. It occurred to me that if we want to meet our educational aspirations, then we must listen to the perspective of our learners and believe that they have answers. I plan to use a coaching model with our Pupil Council to help meet our school improvement plan targets. By allowing the pupils to set goals related to the targets and go through the coaching process to decide who, how, and when the actions will be taken, I hope that the learning experience for all will be improved and sustained."
>
> (Susan Bell, Bridge of Weir Primary School, Bridge of Weir, Scotland)

> "It seems to me that the more one is coached, the more of one's professional life one is willing to open up to examination through coaching."
>
> (Robert Jones, North Berwick High School, North Berwick, Scotland)

Embedding ways of working and moving towards an organizational way of being

Earlier in this chapter we proposed a definition of a "whole-school coaching culture for learning", which included coaching approaches to conversations about learning becoming embedded as a fundamental aspect of the organizational way of being. We have attempted to illustrate what we see as the key factors influencing the emergence of such a culture.

The precise timescale for the evolutionary period between initiation and the emergence of a coaching culture is practically impossible to define. As we have argued, this is due to the highly contextual nature of the journey. While formal coaching arrangements may be one part of a coaching culture for learning, the effects should be felt across the organization. The "way of being" can be experienced *within* one-to-one coaching conversations, but also between educators, by students, in leadership team meetings, and within the broader educational community.

So let us now consider what it might look like when a coaching culture starts to become our school culture. What are the indicators of *organizational alignment* and *normalization* of coaching interventions (van Nieuwerburgh, 2016b, p. 232)? Some suggestions:

» Coaching is no longer viewed as an initiative—it's just how we do things now.
» Common coaching language and principles are apparent in a wide range of conversational contexts.
» The intent of different forms of coaching, from formal coaching through to coaching-infused leadership approaches, is understood, and there is procedural clarity around these.
» Policies, strategic plans, and role descriptions reflect a common language and understanding of coaching approaches.
» Sustainable resourcing is in place to support internal coaching.
» Coaching and coaching approaches are apparent across all four contexts.

> "One thing I am looking more for now is the change in language. More solution-focused. Where staff would once want problems solved, the culture has shifted to doing, learning, and reflecting."
> (Sophie Hunter, St Kevin's College, Melbourne, Australia)

> "Don't dismiss the time issue. It is all too easy as a leader to become frustrated when teachers tell you they don't have time to engage in coaching, but if you want teachers to coach each other, you have to make time for it to happen in your plans."
> (Robert Jones, North Berwick High School, North Berwick, Scotland)

Conclusion

The desire of school leaders to establish coaching cultures in schools is indicative of the compelling argument that coaching and coaching-infused approaches to conversations can have a positive impact on all members of the school community. Coaching develops a school leader's capacity to become a true "leader of learning", focusing on the quality of education in their school and their own leadership development with greater agency and political empowerment (Robertson, 2016, p. 60).

In some ways, the evolution of a coaching culture can be seen to be a natural development over time, based on the experiences of those who have benefited from coaching interactions and training, and then become advocates for these approaches. Further, as reflective educators, teachers, and leaders who have experienced the positive effects of coaching on their own practice are more likely to identify opportunities to apply the approaches in other contexts.

We began this chapter with the observation by van Nieuwerburgh (2014) that the development of coaching cultures promises to create more positive and supportive organizational climates for personal and organizational flourishing. By consciously changing the nature of the interaction in the myriad conversational contexts across a school community, we can create an environment that is more conducive to personal growth and development and where students and educators can flourish. The lived experience of a coaching culture is fundamentally one of better quality conversations that lead to an improved learning environment for everyone in the school community.

Acknowledgements

The authors would like to acknowledge the following schools and individuals who generously shared their coaching implementation stories with us. Bridge of Weir Primary School, Renfrewshire: Susan Bell, Head Teacher; Haileybury College, Melbourne: Fiona Gontier, Coordinator–Coaching, Craig Glass, Senior Vice Principal; Mount Scopus Memorial College, Melbourne: Edna Sackson, Teaching and Learning Leader PYP, Jocelyn Blumgart, Teaching and Learning Coach; North Berwick High School, East Lothian: Robert Jones, Deputy Head Teacher; Preston Manor School, London: Michelle McLeod, Leading Practitioner and Associate, Senior Leadership Team; St Kevin's College, Melbourne: Sophie Hunter, Teaching and Learning Coach, Chris Munro, Dean of Professional Practice; St Paul's School, Brisbane: Jon Andrews, Head of Professional Learning; Thomas Carr College, Melbourne: Alex Guedes, Head of Learning; Wesley College, Perth: Dr Deborah Netolicky, Co-ordinator of Coaching Cycles for Teacher Growth.

CHAPTER TWELVE

Designing, managing, and evaluating school leadership programmes

Sarah Harrison

E ffective leadership transcends the individual "leader", building a team of high-performing professionals with the required skills and attributes to ensure the organization's long-term success. Instead of success being reliant on an individual, "True leadership is about making other people better as a result of your presence— and making sure your impact endures in your absence" (Morriss, Ely, & Frei, 2011). Under leadership like this, responsibility is shared, potential leaders are nurtured, and the organization becomes resilient enough to withstand personnel change.

There has been a tendency, particularly in schools in challenging contexts, to see the headteacher as the cornerstone of the success of a school. This is evident in the rise of the "super head": a previously successful headteacher who is brought in to a "failing" school in order to raise standards quickly. In their report "How to turn around a failing school", Hill and Laker reviewed the actions taken by the headteachers of 160 "failing" academies. While elements of this report were contested, the results were nonetheless interesting. They found that:

> Many academies parachuted in a "super head" from a successful school to turn themselves around. Although this had a positive short-term impact, it didn't create the right foundations for sustainable long-term improvement. These "super heads" tended to be involved only for one to two years and focused their changes on the school year (ages 15–16) and subjects (mathematics and

English) used to assess performance, so they could make quick improvements, take the credit, and move on. [Hill, Mellon, Laker, & Goddard, 2016]

Bringing a "super head" into a school is often a high-profile manoeuvre, reported on by local and even national press. While the rise of the "super head" appears to be waning, accounts and perspectives throughout this book highlight the pressure that is still exerted on headteachers and senior leaders to improve and maintain their school's performance. Under this much pressure, it is not surprising that some would focus on high stakes "quick wins" rather than on building the foundations for consistent and sustainable school improvement. Effective, high-quality leadership development provision can support school leaders to withstand this pressure through building their resilience, confidence, capability, knowledge, and skills, alongside providing access to a network of other school leaders.

In view of how transformational professional development can be for school leaders, this chapter draws on the author's experience of designing and delivering leadership development programmes with the aim of supporting providers of school leadership development to design and deliver effective programmes. The focus is on how providers can ensure that the programmes that they design are high-quality, adequately support those who participate in them, and have a positive long-term impact. Providers might include organizations that market their leadership development provision to schools, such as education charities or trusts and other not-for-profit organizations in receipt of funding to set up provision to develop school leaders or in-house leadership development programmes, particularly given the increase of Multi-Academy Trusts (MATs), Teaching School Alliances (TSAs), and Research Schools. In addition to offering a framework for how a provider might design a programme, this chapter can also be used to complement a provider's existing planning and design processes, and elements are transferable to those seeking to design and develop CPD on a smaller scale, such as within an individual school.

Other chapters in this book explore how our understanding of "leadership" has evolved over time and comment in more detail on the nature of effective school leadership. This chapter does not intend to contribute to that debate. However, it will highlight the parallels between effective "leadership" of an organization and effective "leadership" of a leadership development programme. Indeed, it is possible to consider Morriss' definition of leadership as being a test both of whether a leader is effective and of whether a leadership development programme is successful.

Stages of programme design

Ultimately, an effective programme will make those who undertake it "better" and have an "impact that endures" after the programme has ended. In order to achieve this, a provider needs to take a systematic approach to the design and development of their provision. This can be broken down into four stages:

» Stage 1: Knowledge gathering;
» Stage 2: Setting an overarching vision and strategy for programme design, delivery and evaluation;
» Stage 3: Designing the programme;
» Stage 4: Delivering and evaluating the programme.

This four-stage process aims to support providers to develop training that is not only of a high quality but is *consistently* of this high quality. This is important in the current landscape because while there exists some highly effective leadership development provision across the country, this is not universal. For example, the 2015 review into teacher professional development found that the three main barriers to teachers' engagement in professional development were "time, quality, and cost" (DfE, 2015c), with 56% of respondents (education professionals at all levels) highlighting quality of training as a specific barrier. While this report focused on professional development for teachers rather than school leaders, we see these concerns echoed by leaders in other sectors. In 2015, Korn Ferry, a global executive search firm and management consultancy, commissioned a worldwide survey about leadership development. On the basis of over 7,500 responses, they found that "more than half of executives rank their leadership development return on investment (ROI) as fair to very poor and [that] they would throw out and rework half of their current leadership development approach if they could" (Korn Ferry Institute, 2015). Finally, we can understand the need for better CPD across the country in the government's establishment of the Teaching and Leadership Innovation Fund (TLIF), a three-year investment of £75 million that aims to:

» improve the provision of teachers' continuing professional development (CPD) and leadership development in areas and schools that are facing challenges;
» stimulate the demand for provision of teachers' CPD and leadership development in areas and schools that are facing challenges;

» support the development of a sustainable market in CPD and leadership development that will be capable of becoming self-funding in the future.

(DfE, 2017c)

Stage 1: knowledge-gathering

The purpose of this stage is to ensure that a provider has all the necessary information in order to make informed decisions throughout the design and delivery process. This involves:

1. Deciding upon the intended audience
2. Understanding the context within which the intended audience works
3. Identifying the learning needs of the intended audience

The importance of this stage should not be underestimated and will therefore be considered in some detail. Here, the provider will lay the foundations for the three later stages of the process. Short-changing the investment of time and resources at this stage can increase the risk of avoidable problems down the line, undermine the quality of the programme and reduce its impact.

Deciding upon the intended audience

A provider should begin by considering the intended audience for their programme. The more specific a provider can be, the easier it will be to design the programme and develop relevant (and useful) content. However, any narrowing of audience must be balanced against thorough market research to ensure that it remains viable to market and deliver.

While a provider could "simply" decide that the audience will be deputy headteachers and move on to the next stage of the process, this would neglect the importance of participants' context and experience. Naturally, the lived experiences of deputy headteachers can vary considerably with respect to context and experience. In addition, they may have different opportunities to apply learning to the real-life context of their role through what Kolb would describe as a "concrete experience" (Kolb, 1984). For example, consider the leadership challenges that would be faced by these three individuals:

1. a deputy head in their first three months of post;

2. a deputy head of a school that has just received an Inadequate Ofsted rating;
3. an experienced deputy head of a school that has been Outstanding for eight years.

Therefore, a programme designed for deputy headteachers in general may not have equal relevance to each leader, as they would not all have equal opportunity to reflect on and apply any learning in their role.

Understanding the external context of potential participants

As highlighted above, the context within which a school leader works can affect the ways in which they engage with leadership development. Furthermore, professional development that is not relevant and transferable to the participants' context will be less likely to result in long-term, sustainable change[1]. Therefore, a provider should understand the wider educational trends that may affect what leaders need to know and how they need to behave in order to be successful. For example, "evidence-informed practice is now viewed by educational policymakers in England as a driver of school and system self-improvement" (Greany & Brown, 2017). This requires, according to Greany and Brown, the development of a set of knowledge and skills not previously required, including the following areas:

1. *Capacity to engage both in and with research evidence and data*
2. *Making research use a cultural norm*
3. *A learning culture: using research as part of an effective learning environment*
4. *Structures, systems, and resources*

The external context in which a leader works will also affect how any provision is perceived and what judgements are made about how it compares to other available programmes. For example, two topics currently dominating the headlines are the tightening of school budgets and teacher workload. Providers should therefore carefully consider the following two questions before they begin to design the programme in detail:

1. What is an affordable price point for schools/leaders to pay?
2. How demanding of participants' time can, or should, the programme be?

Conducting a learning needs analysis

A learning needs analysis is a systematic approach to understanding the learning and development needs of a group of individuals, used extensively by HR departments in large organizations. These can range hugely in scope, size, and cost, so an organization should consider what capacity they have and plan accordingly.

> Identifying learning and development (L&D) needs is based on an assessment of prevailing levels of skills, attitudes and knowledge, and on any current or anticipated gaps. This assessment can use formal and/or informal methods. Such an analysis will enable decisions about what learning provisions are needed at an individual, team or organisational level. [CiPD, 2017]

Before undertaking a learning needs analysis, a provider should take the time to build on existing knowledge about the needs and characteristics of the future programme participants through thorough research. This will have, in part, been completed through understanding the external context. However, it is also important to understand the requirements of the role. For example, when developing a senior leadership programme there are a number of useful sources, such as job descriptions and the National Professional Qualification for Senior Leaders (NPQSL) "content and assessment framework" (DfE, 2017a) which a provider should access. This research can be used to frame the foci of the learning needs analysis itself.

In addition to identifying the learning needs of a future cohort of participants—which can be used extensively in the planning of the training curriculum—undertaking a thorough needs analysis also protects the design process from being influenced by the bias or preconceptions of either individuals or the provider. The following case study exemplifies this in more detail.

Case study 1

A school leadership development provider reviews their portfolio of programmes and identifies that the programme it offers to assistant headteachers has not been recruiting well. In addition, there has been a higher than average number of withdrawals from the programme and some criticism of the content.

The programme leader meets with key team members to review the feedback from the training and reflect on the sessions they have attended. They conclude that:

- Some specific content is out of date, in particular the sessions on use of data (reflected in the feedback forms). These sessions will therefore be rewritten.

- The programme is too expensive (prohibiting sales) and they will reduce the cost by cutting one training session and one coaching session.

These changes may result in improved outcomes. However, it has not been possible for the programme leader to fully understand the issues which therefore prevents them from considering more innovative solutions. In fact, some of these ideas could be seen as "sticking plaster" solutions rather than getting to the heart of the issue.

An alternative approach would be for the programme leader to let go of any preconceptions about what is wrong with the programme. Instead, they would seek to understand the learning needs of this specific group. To do this, they research the educational context and the role of the assistant headteacher. They then hold a series of interviews and focus groups with headteachers, identifying what they perceive to be the skills gaps for assistant headteachers. Following this, they distribute a confidential survey to hundreds of assistant headteachers to find out what they struggle with in their roles. They follow this up with additional interviews and focus groups about the key themes to consolidate understanding.

This highlights a number of key themes:

- Assistant headteachers are increasingly expected to have knowledge of evidence-based approaches to improve teaching and learning and how these can be implemented across a school.
- Assistant headteachers tend to lack confidence and struggle to "step up" to senior leadership.
- Assistant headteachers feel that they want to spend more time focusing on the area of the school for which they have specific responsibility (e.g. literacy or assessment).

The programme leader is now in a position to consider a more radical overhaul, including:

- fewer face-to-face training sessions, replaced with some executive coaching sessions focusing on building participant's confidence;
- introduction of a whole-school improvement project as part of the programme where the requirements for success include engaging with research and evidence;
- inclusion of online modules that reflect the unique roles and responsibilities of different senior leaders (e.g. effective professional development for those in charge of CPD).

To undertake a learning needs analysis, the provider should first decide on which stakeholders they will involve. While it is important to include current post-holders, their views should not be considered in isolation. The provider should aim to gain an holistic view of how the role is perceived by post-holders as well as others who work in the sector. For example:

» line managers;
» direct reports, for example through 360° feedback tools;
» headteachers and MAT CEOs;
» sector experts (e.g. in the case of headteachers, representatives from the headteachers' union, etc.);
» those who have roles with significant responsibilities for improving leadership provision such as Specialist Leaders of Education (SLEs) and National Leaders of Education (NLEs).

Providers should also consider how to invite contributions from those with an up-to-date knowledge of leadership theory and best practice outside the education context. For example, large businesses typically invest considerable sums in leadership development, and can be at the forefront of new and innovative approaches. To elicit the views of these stakeholders, a provider might utilize focus groups, surveys, interviews, roundtables, etc. The techniques chosen will be dependent on the capacity that the organization has. For example, one-on-one interviews can provide rich data but take considerably longer to conduct. In all scenarios, care should be taken to ensure that stakeholders are able to share their perspectives and views openly. The areas for a provider to explore with stakeholders are suggested by the definition from CiPD: "Identifying learning and development (L&D) needs is based on an assessment of prevailing levels of skills, attitudes and knowledge, and on any current or anticipated gaps" (2017). For the intended participants of the programme, providers should seek answers to the following questions:

» What are the prevailing levels of skills, attitudes and knowledge?
» Where are the gaps in skills, attitudes and knowledge?
» What learning provisions are needed?

It is also useful to consider two further questions:

» What constitutes success in this role?
» What does "good" look like?

Understanding what success looks like for a given role helps to ensure that any training is pitched at the correct level and focuses on developing the knowledge and skills that are indicators of success. It is common for this to lead to the development of a "competency framework"—a tool that helps to clarify what different levels of performance look like in practice. Competency frameworks are often used as the basis for 360° feedback tools (described in more detail in chapter 11) and can help participants to conceptualize "success". However, the design and development of a valid and rigorous competency framework is a lengthy and resource heavy process and there are already useful frameworks in existence that providers may wish to consider, such as the NPQ "content and assessment frameworks" (DfE, 2017a) and the National Standards for Headteachers (DfE, 2015b).

Parallels between the effective "leadership" of a programme and good leadership can be drawn more broadly here. Other chapters explore the importance of leaders gathering good information, reflecting on their biases and preferences and using these to make good decisions. The process of conducting a learning needs analysis has a similar function because it helps to ensure that design decisions are rational, logical and reflect the needs of the leaders they seek to support, rather than the views of the provider. Furthermore, a good leader will invite challenge and fresh thinking and ask for feedback on actions, decisions and performance. Similarly, a provider should be open to challenge and prepared to question its own thinking, strategy and beliefs. A provider should plan for how it continues to invite constructive critique from a range of stakeholders—including the participants themselves—throughout the process, and for how it retains buy-in from those stakeholders who contributed to the design of the programme.

Stage 2: setting an overarching vision and strategy for programme design, delivery, and evaluation

In this stage a provider will define what they consider to be effective leadership development and use this to develop a vision for their provision that is distinct to that of the organization as a whole. The provider will subsequently consider how this vision relates to other elements of the strategy. As with the previous stage, this requires considerable thought and planning.

At the start of this chapter it was suggested that great leaders and leadership development programmes "[make] other people better as a result of [their] presence" (Morriss, Ely, & Frei, 2011). These improvements can be understood as creating *change* in others. A commonly utilized model of change management is that by Kotter (2012). In this eight-stage model, there is a clear focus on the importance of not only setting a vision, but on communicating that vision effectively. Similarly, it is important for leadership development programme to have a clear and well-communicated "vision". This vision needs to be understood by both those within the organization, as well as those who represent it, in order for the programme to function as intended. This is explored in the case study below.

Case study 2

A brand-new leadership development provider has designed a programme to deliver to headteachers in their first year in post.

The programme leader completed substantial research and a thorough needs analysis. In particular, their findings indicated that new headteachers can feel overwhelmed, leading them to lack confidence in their decision-making ability to make decisions. They received feedback that new headteachers benefit from having the space and time to reflect on their feelings and explore them in detail. In addition, they understood the need to create space for participants to reflect on the learning from the programme and apply it into their own practice. This research resulted in a programme that, alongside training sessions, invested heavily in executive coaching for each headteacher.

The programme leader had a clear vision for leadership development within this programme. The training sessions focused initially on the core knowledge and skills that new headteachers need to acquire quickly (HR, finance, governance, etc.) and then onto topics that would help to improve their leadership style. They would be required to work with a peer in another school to reflect on the training sessions, implement and review new learning and receive informal mentoring and support. Alongside this, coaching was offered to focus on building the confidence and self-efficacy of the headteachers through expert support and challenge.

In the first year, the provider recruited a small pilot cohort of headteachers. They also recruited a set of experienced executive coaches. To maintain quality, the programme leader ran all the training personally.

Feedback from the sessions and the coaching was positive, but a fuller evaluation demonstrated that there was no notable impact on the participants or the schools they were leading.

After significant further investigation, they realised that the vision for the programme, and therefore the purpose of the executive coaches and how they should support participants, had not been well communicated. This meant that, because of the pressures the new headteachers were under, the majority of the coaching relationships erred on the side of support, reassuring heads about their lack of confidence rather than supporting them to build it up. Participants were therefore not developing self-efficacy. Participants had rated the coaching highly because the conversations were comfortable, but their reported levels of confidence in their role had not changed.

In this case study, the provider discovered a mistake during the pilot, which would allow them to build in mechanisms to ensure the clear communication of their vision in the future. It is important for providers to remember that the more people there are involved in delivering a programme, the more it is necessary for them to understand what is happening and why.

The skills to implement the vision

In Kotter's model of change management (2012), step five is "Empowering employees for broad based action". This stage is focused on removing any barriers to the vision being implemented successfully, such as lack of skills or appropriate systems. Therefore, in addition to ensuring the vision is well understood, a provider should create a strategy for how they will *support* others to implement the vision through training and development. Alongside designing the programme, a provider should consider carefully the training and development it offers to those involved in its delivery; usually coaches, trainers, and facilitators. In addition, they should create clear policies that outline what will happen if individuals fall below the standards expected of them and processes to ensure the providers know if the standards have not been met. This can be difficult. With school budgets tightening, the pricing of a leadership development programme for leaders is, in many ways, a question of values and priorities as well as a practical one. The temptation to "cut" those things for which the return on investment is not easily quantifiable can be high. A programme that costs £1,500 and includes eight coaching sessions may look more attractive to schools than one that includes six coaching sessions, two supervision sessions for the coach and project coordination meetings between the programme team and the coaches. A provider needs to find a balance between what is financially viable and what will ultimately have more impact.

Working with the school as an organization

The stakeholders who need to understand and be bought into the "vision" for leadership development extends beyond those who work on the programme. Indeed, "professional development can be helped or hindered by school organisational context" (Avalos, 2011, p. 12). Therefore, a provider should consider:

» What mechanisms are in place to ensure alignment of vision between the provider and the school?
» What is the process for checking that the school's expectation for the outcomes of the programme is aligned to what the provider believes the programme can deliver?

Of course, it must be recognized that providers need to develop programmes that are financially viable, and that creating alignment may be easier for a large provider with a suite of programmes on offer. This may also be less relevant to MATs or TSAs that are developing programmes for schools with whom they work directly. However, without a strategy to ensure organizational alignment, there is a risk that the programme will not deliver what the *schools* expect and need. This can damage the reputation of the provider and prevent the programme from having its intended impact.

In order for professional development in schools to be effective it needs to be supported by school leadership and embedded within the school's culture (Cordingley, Higgins, Greany, & Coe, 2015). This is not always the case, and sometimes schools can invest in leadership development programmes for individuals without giving them the time, support or resources they need to fully engage with it. To help to prevent this, a provider might implement strategies such as:

» organizing training or induction sessions for school leadership teams;
» asking the school for a statement of support before the programme begins;
» requiring the headteacher or sponsor to "sign-off" on any tasks that are completed as part of the programme;
» providing guidance materials for the school detailing how they can get the most out of the programme;
» creating a specific role within the programme for the line manager or sponsor of the participants.

Finally, a provider should consider, and plan for, the resultant impact that a programme can have on the wider school community. For example, a programme that develops senior leaders can impact on the organization upwards (the headteacher) and downwards (middle leaders) as the senior leader starts to change their behaviours. In this scenario, a headteacher might be very supportive of senior leadership development in theory but in practice may struggle when senior leaders start to challenge their authority. This may lead the headteacher to be less supportive of the programme, even if unconsciously, affecting buy-in to the programme at a school level.

Planning to evaluate the programme

Schools, MATs and TSAs need to ensure that any professional development on offer for their staff is high quality. This is reinforced by the Ofsted framework which states that inspectors "will consider ... the quality of continuing professional development for teachers at the start and middle of their careers and later, including to develop leadership capacity and how leaders and governors promote effective practice across the school" (Ofsted, 2018). Schools are therefore becoming more discerning about the providers they choose and in particular, can be proactive in seeking evidence of impact from providers. It is important that schools are able to make a judgement about the quality and value for money of any provision they use.

Evaluating a programme will allow a provider to understand, and communicate to schools, the quality of the programme, and use this information to continually improve their provision. A provider should design a short and long-term evaluation strategy before the programme begins. The difference between these two types of evaluation is important as they serve different purposes. A short-term evaluation will focus on process, allowing the provider to understand how the programme feels to those who undertake it. Longer term, a provider is looking for whether the programme is achieving its intended impact, such as improving student outcomes.

Short term, there is significant value in gathering the initial thoughts and feelings of participants either immediately after training or periodically through the programme, usually through a feedback form. This can give an early indication of issues that might need to be addressed quickly, such as unclear guidance, unsuitable facilitators/coaches, or out-of-date content.

However, perceptions of the effectiveness of CPD at the end of a programme can be misleading since deep professional learning involves unlearning and re-evaluation of current practice, which is inevitably uncomfortable (Cordingley, 2015). Therefore, evaluation must go beyond a survey and ensure it monitors long- as well as short-term impact on practice, combining qualitative and quantitative tools.

Long-term, a provider could commission an external partner to design and run the evaluation. While this is likely to provide high-quality evaluation, it can be an overly costly investment and is not always practical. If a provider cannot commission an external evaluation, some useful techniques to evaluate in more detail include:

» measuring self-reported changes between levels on a competency framework;
» measuring line manager's and direct report's perception of change in a 360° feedback tool;
» detailed focused interviews with participants after the end of the programme in which they are asked about what behaviour changes they have seen in themselves;
» testimonies from the line manager or sponsor of the participants.

Schools, MATs, and TSAs often look specifically for evidence of impact on the outcomes of students as a measure of judging the quality of the professional development on offer. This has obvious benefits for schools, as it helps to ensure that they do not waste resources on provision that doesn't "work".

> The effect of leaders is largely *indirect*; what leaders do and say, and how they demonstrate leadership, does affect pupil learning outcomes, but it is largely through the actions of others, most obviously teachers, that the effects of school leadership are mediated. Nevertheless, school leadership influences outcomes more than any other factors, bar socio-economic background and quality of teaching, and whilst it is challenging to quantify the exact effect size or the precise combination of factors that lead to impact, the research evidence does largely reinforce the argument that "leadership matters". [Earley, 2016, p. 24]

In the complex and ever-changing world of schools, where external factors affect outcomes, it is difficult to isolate the impact of the actions of an individual or a group of leaders. It is even more difficult to ascertain whether those actions would have happened without the leadership development they have undertaken. Furthermore, it takes time for the impact of leadership development training to filter down through a school to student outcomes. Take the example of a group of senior leaders who, through a programme, have identified that the culture of their school did not foster trust in the staff. For this to change, it will require a shift in behaviour from the senior leaders, for the senior leaders to encourage similar behaviours in the middle leaders, and for the middle leaders to empower the teachers. In addition, the lack of trust may have manifested itself in the school policies and processes. This cannot be changed overnight: the senior leaders must work hard to get staff on board, communicate their vision, and implement changes steadily while providing the necessary support. It could easily take a year before teachers feel trusted to take on professional responsibility for their teaching and start to hone their craft. A year or two later, the school may begin to see the results of this change through improved student results. In this scenario, for a provider to measure impact, they would need to stay in touch with those whom they have trained long-term (making the measurement even more "indirect"). Even then, the provider cannot wait three years before publishing information on the impact of their provision, as it is likely to prevent them from marketing effectively. To counteract these challenges, a leadership development provider should consider developing a "theory of change" and using this to design their evaluation strategy.

Writing a Theory of Change

The development of a Theory of Change allows a provider to define the intended impact of a programme and to use this to develop a long-term evaluation structure.

> [A] Theory of Change is essentially a comprehensive description and illustration of how and why a desired change is expected to happen in a particular context. It is focused in particular on mapping out or "filling in" what has been described as the "missing middle" between what a programme or change initiative does (its activities or interventions) and how these lead to desired goals being achieved. [Center for Theory of Change, 2019]

This tool can be used, with increasingly levels of complexity, across a programme, a suite of programmes, or a whole organization. This can be a significant piece of work for an organization to undertake and requires detailed thinking and engagement with the process. This chapter provides a brief overview of the benefits for programme design, but it should be recognized that there is a wealth of available guidance and literature that an organization can, and should, access before undertaking a theory of change. An example of a theory of change is provided in Figure 12.1.

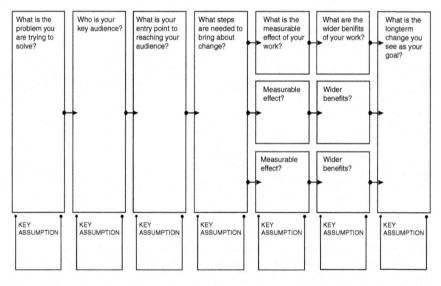

FIGURE 12.1

Theory of change (Nesta, 2014).

An organization starts by outlining the problem it wants to solve, being as specific as possible to increase the likelihood of more effective action. The template is then completed from left to right. At each stage an organization must consider the "assumptions" that they have made. They should note them and ensure that they are integrated within their programme planning. More complexity and detail could be added by:

» splitting measureable effects into short-, medium-, and long-term effects;
» considering barriers alongside "key assumptions" as a way of considering potential risks in more detail.

For example, having completed a theory of change, an organization might conclude that the measurable effects of a programme for head-teachers are:

» reduction in staff turnover;
» positive self and peer ratings in a 360° review;
» improved feedback in student and parent surveys;
» improved Ofsted grade after an inspection.

Once complete, a provider will have a clear understanding of the short- and long-term indicators that would demonstrate that the programme is working as expected. They can then put a plan in place to collect and measure these indicators, starting with gathering baseline data across all participants/schools. In addition, the provider should plan a programme review process into the delivery model, outlining where evaluation data will be collated and shared and when redesign of the programme will happen. This will ensure that:

1. the provider has a structure to evaluate whether the programme is working, and can therefore make changes where they are needed;
2. the provider has a wealth of data that can be used to demonstrate impact when marketing the programme to schools;
3. schools are able to use this data to justify their decision to invest in the programme.

Stage 3: design

Having completed Stages 1 and 2, the design of the programme will have already started to evolve. The provider will understand the learning needs of the participants, have articulated their approach to leadership development, and have developed the programme strategy. This will be the basis for developing the full curriculum. During the third stage, it is important to take time to consider the *learning journey* of participants on the programme. In part, this involves arranging the learning topics logically and planning for any inter-module activities such as tasks, readings, or coaching/mentoring sessions. In addition, a provider should consider how the curriculum sits alongside the typical responsibilities of the participant's role: for example, a programme heavy in face-to-face sessions during exam season is unlikely to be popular.

Alongside these practicalities, the curriculum should reflect the vision and strategy for leadership development that was identified in Stage 2. For example, if a provider's vision was focused on experiential learning, sessions might be organized to move through: "concrete experience; reflective observation; abstract conceptualization and active experimentation" (Kolb, 1984). While a full exemplar curriculum design is not feasible here, the Case study 3 does provide an example of how a provider might look to improve a specific leadership behaviour through an experiential approach.

Case study 3

A provider is designing a programme for newly appointed headteachers. Within the learning needs analysis, the provider identified the need to support them with how to "manage upwards" and to influence their governing body.

Rather than delivering a training session on the topic of "working effectively with your governing body", the provider chooses to structure the programme tasks through Kolb's experiential learning cycle as follows:

1. The participant attends a governing board meeting in their school (concrete experience).
2. At a training session:
    a. participants are placed into triads to reflect on the meeting, consider how it went and how it could be improved (reflective observation);
    b. theories about how to manage senior stakeholders effectively are introduced (abstract conceptualisation);
    c. participants are given an opportunity to practise key elements in a simulated meeting, thus trialling some new learned behaviours, and receiving feedback from peers (active experimentation).
3. The participants attend another governing board meeting, using this as an opportunity to embed some of the learning from the session (concrete experience).

4. Participants reflect on the process with their coach, identifying actions and next steps (reflective observation).

For some providers, this example might take too much professional autonomy away from the headteacher, and they may wish to give more scope for them to lead their own learning. The decision of where to position themselves along this spectrum should be made by the provider, guided by their vision and strategy for leadership development.

A provider should also consider how the programme will "encourage a sense of purpose and mission" (Korn Ferry Institute, 2015) in the participants from the start and how this will continue throughout the programme. It is believed that "achieving a shared sense of purpose [during CPDL] is an important factor for success" (Cordingley et al., 2015). In particular, it is important that the participants buy-in to the programme and its purpose, intended outcomes, and aims. To achieve this, a provider may consider:

» cohort induction session(s);
» relating a participant's personal learning needs (identified either through self-assessment or through the programme application process) to the outcomes of the programme, so that they understand what they will gain from the process;
» linking elements of the programme to the participant's professional development plan;
» short individual phone calls with participants before the start of the programme.

Finally, having developed a full curriculum, a provider should build in adequate time to test the final design, get buy-in, and—where necessary—secure sign-off from key stakeholders (e.g. board members, staff, etc.) before the programme is launched.

Stage 4: delivering and evaluating the programme

Delivery of the programme involves overseeing the programme, managing the logistics and participants, and so on. If adequate time and resources have been dedicated to the previous three stages of the design process, the provider will have increased the likelihood of a successful and effective programme. In an ideal world, the delivery of the programme would simply be a case of putting the plan into action. However, it is easy to be surprised by some of the difficulties that are encountered when the plan is put into action. Should this be the case, suggestions such as these could be considered:

1. Be transparent with evaluation data and the actions taken as a result

As previously explored, it is important to use a range of evaluation data to improve the programme. A short-term evaluation strategy is likely to ask participants for feedback after training sessions or events, which can provide useful insights into the programme (e.g. where those who deliver or manage your programme might need further training or some feedback).

Recently, there has been a trend in leadership development towards the idea of the "authentic leader" (George, 2004). In part, an authentic leader is one who allows their true self to shine through and who is transparent and honest—even when things go wrong. In a similar vein, participant engagement with the evaluation process is likely to increase when providers are more open in sharing elements of the feedback they received (good and bad) and what changes will be made to the participant experience as a result. This can further increase the participant's engagement with and trust in the *process* of evaluating the programme and can lead to them providing more valuable feedback, thereby supporting the programme development cycle.

2. Hold your nerve

Be wary of being too reactive to negative feedback. Criticism, in particular when it feels unfair, can be personally upsetting and can provoke snap decisions being made about programme design that are not sufficiently evidence-based. Negative feedback, particularly when received from a minority of participants, can be provoked by many things—such as a cold training room or low-quality catering. Furthermore, "deep professional learning … can be very uncomfortable", as it requires participants to change their own behaviours, which can "generate negative immediate feedback that translates into much more positive feedback once teachers have had a chance to reflect" (Cordingley, 2015, p. 6). Given that reactions such as these will be likely to manifest for some individuals, it would be beneficial to plan for what support might be offered to participants at times when the learning will be more challenging.

It is important to trust in the professional judgement of the programme design team. If the programme has been well constructed, they should have a clear understanding of the effectiveness of the learning experience. In addition, the provider should have systems and processes set up that enable them to sense-check negative feedback. For example:

» quality assure a proportion of the development opportunities (coaching sessions, training sessions, etc.), ensuring that a highly skilled professional can make a judgement about the quality of provision;

» ask those who deliver any development opportunities to share their feedback on the quality of the provision, so this can be compared with the feedback from participants;

» In some scenarios, it might be appropriate to conduct follow up calls with disgruntled participants, when some time has passed from the event, to delve further into their reflections and feelings about the experience.

3. Support and develop key personnel

Anyone who interacts with programme participants, such as coaches, facilitators, tutors, and staff, is central to the participants' experience and their perception of the programme. It is essential that a programme provider has a clear strategy to manage, quality assure, train, and support them.

4. Focus on participant experience

It is important not to forget the impact that participant experience can have on a programme. Therefore, it is vital to consider what it will *feel* like to undertake the programme. In particular, pay attention to the following:

» Are all events and materials provided in an accessible format?

» At events, are the participants comfortable and well catered for in terms of venue and food?

» Whom will the participant contact on a day-to-day basis, and to what extent is that staff member trained to support them effectively?

» How user friendly and intuitive are any digital or online materials, and what training is provided to support use of these materials?

» How much work is required of the participant outside their normal working hours, and is this a reasonable and realistic expectation?

» How frequent are the communications with participants?

» Do participants have access to all the information they need to complete the programme successfully, and do they know where to find it?

Final thoughts

This chapter has described the four stages of designing and managing a leadership development programme. However, it is important to emphasize here that reaching Stage 4 does not mean that the work is complete—even if the provider delivers a very successful programme. The core elements of each stage should be repeated as part of a planned cycle of continuous review and improvement. Through maintaining open lines of communication with stakeholders, keeping an eye on the policy horizon, and using evaluation data intelligently, a provider will be able to make better informed decisions about how the programme evolves over time. Naturally, the learning needs of leaders will not remain static, as the educational landscape shifts and as school structures evolve. Best practice in leadership development will move forward as we learn more about how people learn and what effective leadership looks like in different sectors. Methods of evaluating impact will change, and the need for evidence of impact is likely to increase as the sector moves towards more evidence-based approaches. If schools continue to feel budget pressures, providers will need to continue to balance their priorities between investing in quality delivery and training and offering good value for money provision to schools. A potential solution will be online and blended learning—as it evolves and improves. Whether a provider identifies changes in the policy landscape, in their evaluation data, or in the skills needed by their participants, they must continue to reflect deeply on how these changes should affect their provision, whether in structure, content, price, or delivery methods.

Note

1 See also Ben Bryant's chapter 8 in this book.

CHAPTER THIRTEEN

Lessons from "The London Challenge": a whole-system approach to leadership development

David Woods

Historically, London has had a mixed picture of educational success. In the early years of the twenty-first century, London was the worst-performing region in England, with too many schools failing to inspire and lead their communities and many areas where educational aspirations were too low. The government of the day decided to intervene and in 2002 began to develop what became known as the London Challenge programme through the Department for Education (DfE).

To my knowledge, it is the only government-led, one-city education reform initiative in the world to date. This was set out to be a five-year programme funded by central government (2003–2008), but it was so successful that it was extended until 2011.[1] Fortuitously, this bold step coincided with the ground-breaking establishment, in 2000, of the National College for School Leadership (NCSL). The NCSL was to be a centre of excellence for the training, support, and development of school leaders. Originally conceived as a non-departmental public body, independent of government, it had begun to research, collate, and disseminate the very best leadership and organizational development practice from different public and corporate sectors around the world.

London is a great world city that needs and deserves a world-class education system, ideally placed to test-bed and proselytize the NCSL's mission and strategy. Its education system should serve every community and enable every child and person in the capital to fulfil their creative potential—but it is a city characterized by diversity and extremes. These extremes of wealth, poverty, social capital, and social cohesion are contained within very limited geographical areas, across 32 boroughs and the City of London. In reality, there are multiple "Londons": not simply inner city and suburban and outer London, but many networks, urban villages, and communities. It is a kaleidoscopic mix of thriving local communities, each with their own history, culture, and connections—sometimes changing with dramatic rapidity. London schools typically have a diverse ethnic, social, and cultural mix, many with high proportions of disadvantaged children.[2]

These differences in social contexts and educational attainment presented challenges to developing a citywide approach, especially as the infrastructure of the former Inner London Education Authority no longer existed.

One of the biggest problems to overcome was that in certain communities and areas London schools competed against each other in terms of recruiting students and staff. This was partly solved by making sure that London schools supported schools outside their local boroughs. However, the real success was the growing belief that collaboration can deliver great benefits to everybody by "baking a bigger cake", so that all could take an increased share of success, particularly London's children and young people.

Successful system leadership required a change in the mindset of highly effective school leaders. In addition to the professional responsibility for the life chances of students at their own school, system leaders needed to accept that they had a shared and collective responsibility with other school leaders for the well-being of all students in their community. London's schools now collectively constitute the top-performing region in the country, with currently 92% of them judged to be "Good" or "Outstanding". This is testimony to the collective change towards "system leadership", demonstrating that collaboration works and that all schools can improve together rather than achieve success at the expense of others.

This chapter describes the strategies that worked—and continue to work—and both the challenges and opportunities for the leaders of some 2,600 London schools. For example:

» The ethnic and linguistic diversity of pupils offers the potential for enriching educational experience for all, but may also act as a source of tension.

» There is a complex and variable range of parental and community expectations, polarized from high engagement and involvement to antipathy, but ample opportunities for working with communities and other public services.

» There are great opportunities in London for teachers and leaders who can advance their professional learning and careers faster than elsewhere. However, the relative costs of housing and transport may act as a barrier to the recruitment and retention of appropriately qualified staff.

» There are some socially and culturally impoverished communities but also the greatest concentration of social and cultural resources anywhere, enabling schools to show their pupils "the very best that is".

» Poverty exists, with a high percentage of children receiving free school meals, especially in inner London. This is sometimes exacerbated by health and housing issues that can lead to excessive pupil mobility. However, no poverty of expectations and a rich and varied infrastructure ensure a highly diversified workforce and significant opportunities for employment and social mobility.[3]

From the outset, a key component of the Challenge was the development of the London Leadership Strategy to complement the other strategies that were designed to give a better deal to London teachers, students, and communities. This can be seen in Figure 13.1, which depicts the London Challenge Programme as a whole.

The London Challenge programme

Through the already established London Leadership Centre at the then London University Institute of Education (IOE) and the NCSL, the Challenge developed specific leadership programmes for London schools. The London Leadership Strategy (LLS) can best be described as a pan-London network of experienced school leaders. Over time, these leaders played a critical role in establishing the concept that, given the right policy conditions, practitioners could lead the system-wide transformation of schools. One of the key features of the LLS was that it was to be led by headteachers, working in partnership with London Challenge advisers, and with their own director. Headteachers had a mandate to improve and transform the leadership programmes, school-to-school support, and system leadership. In the beginning there was much debate and discussion about the scope of the strategy, influenced in particular by the writing and advocacy of Michael Fullan and David Hargreaves, and also by Tim Brighouse, who had been appointed as the first Commissioner of London Schools and the professional lead for the London Challenge. Tim Brighouse had previously been a very successful

FIGURE 13.1   The London Challenge Programme
(Woods & Brighouse, 2014, p. 25).

Director of Education in Oxfordshire and then Birmingham, the largest local authority in England. He worked closely with Michael Fullan, the Dean of the Ontario Institute in Education, University of Toronto, who is recognized as an international authority on educational reform. David Hargreaves was a former Chief Inspector for the Inner London Education Authority (ILEA), an influential thinker and writer on school improvement who acted as an early adviser to the Leadership Strategy.

From these early discussions and debate emerged a theory of action that would help to transform the education system in London. It was felt that London's leaders needed to be motivated and inspired by the idea of moral purpose—a collective belief that all London's children and young people deserved the best possible education, whatever the realities of ethnicity, poverty, and other social barriers. Although it was acknowl-edged that London's school leaders' first responsibility was to their own schools and communities, they should also contribute where possible to improving other schools in the capital. To do this effectively, there was a need to invest in leadership development at all levels, which, through training and coaching, would generate increased capacity both in indi-vidual schools and across the system as a whole. Through the Strategy there would be intensive leadership and management support for under-performing schools, but it was also recognized that there was a need to "grow the top", encouraging "Good" and "Outstanding" schools to take up a wider leading role in school improvement. To support this, London's leaders were to have access to the best possible pupil and school perfor-mance data and management information. This was benchmarked by putting schools into "families" based on socio-economic factors, which would guide intervention and school-to-school support programmes.[4]

There were, of course, some problems to overcome. Could the strategy attract enough of the best school leaders to act as system leaders while running their own school? How quickly could a critical mass of leaders be established to make a real difference? What would be the mechanism of pairing schools together? Would schools who were used to competing with each other be able to work together for the common good?

Relatively quickly, headteachers, with the backing of the London Challenge and the NCSL, agreed a programme of action based on a "Four Capitals Model" developed in particular by George Berwick (2010), one of the first Headteacher Directors of the London Leadership Strategy.

This was based on four "capitals" appropriate for the capital city.

» *Moral capital*: developing a moral purpose among all headteachers and school leaders that all students in London schools deserved the best possible education: a compelling and inclusive moral purpose based on equity, social justice, and unshakeable principles was to be shared and acted upon by everyone.

» *Knowledge capital*: identifying those with the knowledge of best school improvement practices, and capturing and disseminating this effec-tively.

» *Social capital*: helping schools and staff to develop the social skills to share their knowledge effectively through coaching and training.

» *Organizational capital*: setting up the organizational systems to share knowledge with those who need to learn, through leadership pro-grammes and school-to school support.

(Berwick, 2010)

Out of this model the London Leadership Strategy identified schools and school leaders who could demonstrate outstanding practice, who were motivated by moral purpose, and who could provide the organizational structure to match schools and leaders and disseminate the knowledge within the system. These were termed "London Consultant Leaders", and they were given training based on a rigorous coaching model, so that they could work effectively alongside colleagues in other schools. This pool of consultant leaders worked with a team of London Challenge Advisers who had a role to broker and commission bespoke programmes of leadership and school improvement based on an audit of need agreed with the school. The matching process for school-to-school support was critical, based on performance data, local intelligence, and the deployment of school leaders who had the ability to co-construct knowledge and develop better practice in difficult contexts. Underperforming schools, designated positively as "Keys to Success" schools, were all allocated a consultant leader, who provided both support and challenge for leadership teams. In effect they functioned as "tug boats". They were able to broker "Leadership from the Middle" training and development programmes, designed by the NCSL, arrange school visits for key leaders, and organize coaching for individuals or teams. In order to increase the momentum towards well-organized system leadership, the pool of consultant leaders met as a team to evaluate progress and change arrangements as necessary. The practice of using a collaborative decision-making process was crucial in the early years of the LLS, sharing issues and fine-tuning leadership support for school. A national evaluation team led by Peter Matthews and Pam Sammons concluded that there was an association between the degree of engagement in the leadership strategy's programmes and "both enhanced leadership effectiveness and differential improvement of results". The consultant leader programme was deemed to have been particularly effective. The impact of this programme was at three levels: first, with the headteacher at a personal level, building morale and confidence to lead change; second, through direct involvement with senior leadership teams; and third, through working with middle leaders. More generally, consultant leaders helped the head to focus on key issues amid a welter of demands, expectations, and interventions. Consultant leaders achieved this through "humility", winning the trust of headteachers through patience, courtesy, and empathy, and by demonstrating a commitment to an approach to teaching and learning that would increase opportunities and raise the achievements of students (Matthews & Sammons, 2006).

The Department of Education was so impressed with the LLS consultant leader programme and the effectiveness of school-to-school support that it decided in 2006, with the NCSL, to take the programme to scale across England. Leaders of "Outstanding" schools were given the opportunity to become "National Leaders of Education" (NLEs) and their schools "National Support Schools" (NSS), with a commitment to supporting other schools. In effect, this meant a commitment to outreach work of different kinds and at varying levels in other schools, according to need.[5]

The criteria used to select NLEs was based on the LLS selection criteria for consultant leaders and, in particular, a track record in working with other schools to secure improvement. In London the number of consultant leaders (now NLEs) increased considerably, including a pilot programme for primary schools in 2007, which was developed extensively until 2011. This provided a substantial resource for all London schools that needed support. When the programme first started in 2003, there was some doubt as to whether the best school leaders would reconcile their own and their school's interests with the demands of system leadership, and some governing bodies had to be convinced that their own school would not suffer. However, evaluations over time demonstrated that this was a "win–win" arrangement as the schools providing support sharpened their own leadership and school improvement methodology as well as the schools receiving support. In addition, there was a double lift in performance outcomes demonstrated in Ofsted inspection reports in these years, and this still applies today (Hill & Matthews, 2008).

Apart from this major programme of school-to-school support, the Leadership Strategy developed a number of programmes to enhance knowledge capital and share best practice effectively. As well as intensive support for "Keys to Success" schools, there were programmes for schools performing satisfactorily but aiming to become "Good" as judged by Ofsted, using some of the methodology applied to Keys to Success Schools. This was the "Gaining Ground" programme, which had the particular objective of improving the progress of pupils in secondary schools and closing attainment gaps, using partner school support and challenge. A "Leading from the Middle" programme continued to be offered, along with the development of specialist support networks for subject leaders as well as those leading English as an additional language (EAL). The "Inclusion Support" programme offered specialist support for Special Education Needs Co-ordinators (SENCOs). An important new programme was "Moving to New Headship", which was introduced in 2007. This gave an entitlement of coaching support to everyone in London starting a new headship, following their appointment, through the transition to their new post, and for the first four terms of headship. Although the majority of supported headteachers were in their first headship, the programme also supported colleagues in second headship, recognizing the different challenges that this may present (Woods & John, 2010).

The London Leadership Strategy was always aware of the need "to grow the top of the system" as well as support schools who needed help. From 2008, the secondary school programme was led by a serving head-teacher, Sue John, and a decision was made to invest in a "Good to Great" programme. This programme would enable "Good" schools to improve to "Outstanding", whose leaders would then be better placed to become system leaders themselves, adding considerably to the overall capacity of a school-led system of improvement. The aim of the programme was deliberately ambitious: to have at least 25% of London secondary schools rated as "Outstanding" by 2011, thereby making London's education sys-tem world-class. These schools had full access to a programme of support and resources, including conferences and publications, a knowledge-sharing network, and access to other LLS programmes. By 2011, almost 30% of all secondary schools were rated as "Outstanding", against a national average of 17.5%. This improvement rate amounted to a 50% increase from the start of the programme. While the programme itself cannot claim to be responsible for all of the improvements, a significant number of engaged schools moved from "Good" to "Outstanding", and the evaluation concluded that some of the key elements that contributed to its success were: the ambition and aspiration it generated; the multidi-mensional layers of support; and the provision of challenge and support from peer schools (Matthews & McLaughlin, 2010).

After a pilot year in 2007, the LLS developed a particular strategy to improve primary schools. The first wave of consultant leaders had already been deployed effectively, to be followed by many others, all with appropriate coaching and training. These leaders now were given the designation either as "Local Leaders of Education" (LLE) or as "National Leaders of Education" (NLE). There was also a headteacher director of the London Primary team with a reference group of primary headteach-ers. Bespoke programmes were developed to respond to specific needs. In particular, the primary strategy took advantage of the newly developed "Improving Teacher Programme" (ITP) and the "Outstanding Teacher Programme" (OTP) to build capacity for the leadership of teaching and learning. London Teaching Schools (TSAs), on behalf of the LLS, ran both of these, offering teachers the opportunity to improve their skills. The ITP aimed to improve the quality of teaching so that it was consistently good, and the OTP aimed to help teachers to understand and implement outstanding teaching. Both programmes required 10 days' attendance a term supplemented by action programmes in the "home" school. The programmes were hosted in London schools graded "Outstanding" and offered the opportunity for participants to observe real lessons taught by exemplary practitioners. By 2010, the LLS had developed, in partnership with the NCSL, some 20 London "Teaching Schools", based loosely on the Teaching Hospital model, to be hubs of teaching and leadership development. They would promote high-quality training as part of a collaborative, school-led system of improvement. This model was adopted nation-wide from 2011 on, and by 2016 there were over 500 Teaching Schools across England, with 93 in London. In December 2010, an Ofsted report about teaching schools in London stated that:

> Participants at all levels considered that this intensive approach— learning, discussion, practical exercise, and live teaching—was much more effective than a more traditional model of continuous professional development, such as an induction course. [Ofsted, 2010]

Because of the number of primary schools needing support, a new initiative of "Primary Challenge Groups" was developed. These were triads of schools, led by an outstanding school leader, working on key priorities for improving standards and funded to work collaboratively and share expertise. These groups resulted in growing sustainable improvement across the system.

After some five years of the London Challenge and the London Leadership Strategy, there was already a large pool of system leaders in London at different levels set to expand even further. A tipping point had been reached where there was enough growing capacity to provide support for all schools and leaders who needed it. There was now an increasing city-wide pride in the rapid improvement of London schools with significantly increased percentages of "Good" and "Outstanding" schools and collective performance data. From being the lowest-performing region, London exceeded national averages in 2007 and was, by 2009, the highest-performing region in the country—significantly closing gaps in the performance of groups of children from disadvantaged backgrounds. This still remains the case both in attainment and in significant rates of progress (GLA, 2017). Such was the success of the many leadership programmes and the growing number of outstanding schools and system leaders that there was a demand for a special programme for outstanding schools and leaders who had hitherto been providing support to other schools. They were also on a journey of continuous improvement, and so, in 2010, a "Going for Great" programme was launched for schools wanting to aim for an "Outstanding" Ofsted judgement—first with secondary schools, then primary, and with special schools joining several years later. The criteria for selection were as follows:

» currently an "Outstanding" school as judged by Ofsted inspection;
» making a significant contribution to system-wide school improvement (in London, but also nationally and internationally);
» evidence of a culture of research-based enquiry;
» commitment to becoming a "great" school.

The aims were:

» to encapsulate the features and qualities of schools that may be described as great;
» to share exceptional practice;
» to ensure that the best schools are engaged in making education in London world-class;
» to support schools in maximizing their impact on the education system through system and systemic leadership.

The methodology of this programme has evolved over the nine years of its existence, but the key elements are:

» exploring the nature of great schooling and researching this through a series of seminars led by guest speakers from a range of universities and organizations;
» participation in "excellence visits" to participating schools in groups of four and feeding back to the whole group;
» sharing specific issues and topics in depth together;
» preparing and writing a case study showcasing an area of great practice within the school; this has led to the publication by the LLS of nine volumes of case studies—some 168 in all—as a rich resource to London schools.

Most influential of all, successive cohorts of school leaders on this programme have defined and refined "The Nine Pillars of Greatness", which have become the ambition for all schools engaged in LLS programmes (Woods, Macfarlane, & McBeath, 2018). They are as follows:

1. A clear vision, a compelling and inclusive moral purpose, optimistic aspirations, forward thinking, and a commitment to excellence are manifested in the school's culture, structures, systems, and leadership.

2. Transformational and shared leadership embedding aspiration and ambition, building and sustaining high-quality relationships, a capacity for growth and adaptation to change extended, and system-wide leadership are widely practised by leaders at all levels.

3. The promotion of high-quality learning should be at the heart of the school. This includes: excellent classroom management skills; consideration of what constitutes effective learning; a varied personalized learning approach; and regular assessments, helping students to learn independently, develop self-esteem, and aim high.

4. A strong student voice is celebrated and young people are involved in leading, managing, and planning their educational experiences at all levels.

5. The school is a knowledge-creating and learning community with very effective staff development, including coaching, mentoring, and critical thinking. The school is enquiry-minded and geared to innovation and research in order to sustain high performance.

6. Considerable attention is paid to the whole school environment and the quality of the daily experience of those who work and learn in the school. This includes a high-quality infrastructure, a flexible design for personalized learning, the promotion of autonomous learning, and the development of mature citizens.

7. The curriculum focuses on the acquisition of knowledge and understanding, the development of learning skills, and the fostering of positive character traits that provide pupils with the opportunity to learn and practise skills that will prepare them for careers in a fast-changing world. Cultural opportunities, engagement in enrichment activities, content for moral learning, and cross-curricular links support pupils' enjoyment of learning.

8. The school recognizes its responsibility to support the education of young people beyond the school gates, engaging with parents and developing a system-wide contribution through a sustained and substantial contribution to the local, national and/or international community.

9. The school has a self-evaluation culture that builds time for collective enquiry, conducts regular and forensic analysis of performance data, and practises appreciative enquiry. There is a continuous process of reflection, in which schools ground self-evaluation in sophisticated, accurate, and open analysis, alongside seeking open and challenging feedback.

The London Leadership Strategy: 2011 to 2018

The London Challenge officially came to an end as a centrally funded programme in 2011. Such had been its success that the headteachers who had been the driving force behind the London Leadership Strategy were determined to continue this work. This needed a further culture shift towards a real school-led system of improvement. Support and challenge had to come from within the system, and school leaders would need to be given legitimacy by their peers, with schools choosing to participate. By 2012, the London Leadership Strategy had re-established itself as a not-for-profit trust with a Chair, Managing Director, and Board of Directors, all of whom were headteachers. There was a simple set of objectives:

» every child realizing their potential;
» a self-sustaining, world-leading city for education and creativity;
» effective school-to-school collaboration and support;
» enabling outstanding professional development and the sharing of best practice;
» world-class schools, systems, and leaders at the leading edge of achievement and innovation, able to drive forward system improvement.

As an organization born from the London Challenge, it continued to keep its mission and spirit alive. This included developing a website where school leaders, educationalists, governors, and parents alike can find reports and resources. The trust has been very successful in securing funding from the Department of Education, the London Mayor's office, and a range of other bodies to support knowledge mobilization across the capital and the best leadership practice. A range of new programmes for school leaders has been developed, such as "Securing Good" for schools requiring improvement. This retains the main features of all LLS programmes—support given by NLE/NSS to individual schools and leaders and school visits, but also a range of seminars mainly led by Her Majesty's Inspectors on aspects of the School Inspection Framework. For primary schools, there was a "Successful Teaching and Learning" programme, where teachers observe lessons and reflect on their own practice over an extended period of six weeks. This programme was supported by expert facilitators and school leaders and a primary hub model offering bespoke consultant headteacher and LLS support. Tailored packages for school improvement groups and individual schools could be put in place as required. In general, any London school, and in certain cases those outside London, could request bespoke support packages from a range of consultant NLEs working with senior leaders from their National Support Schools. A new Special Educational Needs and Disabilities (SEND) programme supported schools to raise standards for children with special needs through a bespoke package of support. This helped schools to identify areas for improvement in their provision, equipping practitioners to better review and create improvement and helping to embed a focus on SEND into normal school improvement practice. SEND reviews were offered and the best SEND Leaders, including Specialist Leaders of Education, offered support and advice. As from 2016, two new programmes were offered to meet particular needs. First, to meet the demands for new headteachers in London, a programme for aspiring headteachers to both inspire and equip them to be confident and successful. Second, because of the growth of Multi-Academy Trusts of schools, a programme to equip the very best school leaders to be Chief Executives of a group of schools while often retaining leadership of a specific school.

In total, there were 12 leadership programmes as well as bespoke school-to-school support offers. Almost all the Strategy Directors developed and ran specific programmes, something that has always been a feature of the Strategy.

Learning and reflections from the London Leadership Strategy

Over some 15 years of development, the London Leadership Strategy had developed a distinctive ethos and way of working. The foundation of its success were a robust sense of moral purpose, with an urgent and unswerving belief in the difference that education can make to children's life chances. This compelling and inclusive moral purpose drove the London school community forward, based on equity, social justice, and unshakeable principles. Leadership in London is the most powerful tool we possess to raise the aspirations and confidence of school communities. Allied to high expectations, this enables children and young people to achieve their potential. The Leadership Strategy has always had a clear focus on raising standards and closing attainment gaps between groups of pupils and schools. It had constantly developed programmes to address some of these issues, as well as engaged expert school leaders to design strategies and broker solutions. Perhaps the greatest feature of the strategy was the depth of system leadership, enabling highly effective school-to-school support to strengthen leadership, learning, and teaching in those schools that required support.

The London Leadership Strategy was well known for its partnership-working and practitioner networks, sharing best practice through joint practice development, excellence visits, peer review, and a range of activities and programmes. The Strategy has been able to mobilize intellectual, social, and organizational capital, therefore maintaining the vision, energy, depth, and staying power to sustain excellent education outcomes. It has done this through purposeful networking and influencing and by tailoring key messages to many different audiences in the capital city and in other regions in the country (Claeys, Paterson, & Kempton, 2014). It has also built alliances, invested in relationships, and worked through and with other partner agencies as a catalyst for leadership in London. The strategy has provided open and connected leadership and great opportunities for professional learning, as evidenced in The London Leadership Annual Prospectus. Through the moral purpose and positivity of the London Challenge brand originally, the London Leadership Strategy continued to work with a strong sense of optimism and coherence relating to the possibilities of change and improvement.

To be a London leader now, more than ever, is a special opportunity to work in one of the world's greatest cities with high levels of professional commitment and engagement. London's leaders have a particular sense of place that is more than a local community or borough but with a strong connection to the capital city as an entity. With this comes a sense of pride in being a leader of a London school and celebrating the collective achievement of London's schools, children, and young people. This demonstrates, in particular, that deprivation and disadvantage need not be destiny. Above all, London's leaders have a strong sense of purpose. They know that their service makes a huge difference to the life chances of their pupils, and they relish the pace, excitement, and intensity of working in such complex and diverse settings. They are sustained and supported by like-minded colleagues working in a partnership, with a real sense of collegiality. To complement a sense of place, pride, purpose, and partnership, London's leaders work with passion and pace so that they can make rapid progress and sustain momentum.

The London Leadership Strategy enabled a community of school leaders to come together and work together for the benefit of all children and young people, offering cross-connected leadership experiences in order to sustain transformation in the system so that progressive cultures flourish. It recognized that to be a London Leader requires enduring personal resilience characterized by optimism, determination, and commitment. The challenges are great, but the rewards are even greater. Leading a London school is an unparalleled opportunity to change thousands of lives, to lead a learning community that can take children and young people on a journey of discovery and development, and enable them to define their place in the world as global citizens within one of the world's greatest cities.

The London Leadership Strategy offered a great example of a school-led system of improvement where leaders, teachers, and schools learn from each other and from action research, so that effective practice spreads. The best schools and leaders extend their reach across other schools, so that all schools improve. There was a system focus on collaborative partnerships, sharing expertise and high leverage of best practice. Collective moral purpose was a value shared and enacted by all stakeholders, and social capital was high within and between schools. Joint practice development was well established, and evaluation, support, and challenge were practised at every level. All in all, the Strategy sought to inspire, creating idealism, confidence, and excitement about what is possible while also enabling and giving school leaders the scope to transform the system. It was a learning organization, believing always that learning and reflection are at the core of continuous improvement. Working originally as part of the London Challenge programme and then as a trust, the LLS played an important part in national education system reform and school improvement.[6]

Notes

1 For further details see two Education Department publications: *London Schools: Rising to the Challenge* (DfES, 2005) and *Vision for London, 2008–2011* (DCSF, 2008).
2 For a further discussion on the London Context, see Brighouse and Fullisk, 2007.
3 See also Woods and Brighouse, 2014.
4 For further information, see Fullan, 2003, 2005, and Hargreaves, 2003.
5 For further description see Brighouse and Woods, 2013.
6 There is a considerable literature on the London Challenge and London Leadership Strategy. Other sources include Baars et al. (2014), *Lessons from London Schools, Investigating the Success* (in particular, chapter 5 on leadership). Also see Fullan and Boyle (2014), *Big-City School Reforms: Lessons from New York, Toronto, and London,* and Elwick and McAleavy (2015), *Interesting Cities: Five Approaches to Urban School Reform* (chapter 3 on London).

PART IV

THE LAST WORD

CHAPTER FOURTEEN

Talking heads: the voice of school leaders

Andrea Berkeley et al.

In this chapter ten school leaders write about the central emotional and psychological challenges of their roles: how they have experienced and been affected by them; how they have met and overcome them; and what they have learned in the process. We asked them to reflect on their thoughts and feelings, their ideals and values, and their learning and development. Where relevant, they draw on the ways in which coaching and other approaches to leadership development described in this book have helped and supported them. They write from different contexts and years of experience and in different styles and forms, often colloquially and movingly—we gave them free rein to find their own voices. We have respected anonymity where requested and have not closely edited any reflections, wanting their voices to ring out with authenticity and freshness.

The purpose of the chapter is to offer some insights about the normal range of experience of life as a school leader. Although there are many common recurring themes, each voice reflects an individual and personal experience.

First 100 days: crossing the threshold

We begin with two secondary heads reflecting on their first one hundred days in post. Although already an experienced leader, *Sarah Creasey* describes her apprehension and anxiety in stepping up to headship in a London school with a strong reputation for academic excellence; how she found her own distinctive voice and authority, negotiated the inevitable "honeymoon period", and built a new senior team around her. Second, *Kate Williams* describes the impact of challenging encounters, from Day 1, at an underperforming school serving a diverse community, including the most socially disadvantaged part of Brighton. They describe some of the trials and surprises of the role and how they sustain themselves. Despite long hours, feelings of isolation, exhaustion, and "imposter syndrome" at times, their moral authority, hope, and optimism shines through.

Sarah Creasey, headteacher
Parliament Hill School for Girls (11–19), London

After being appointed as a new headteacher, I was repeatedly asked, "Are you excited?" Of course, the response had to be "yes". At the time, I was genuinely looking forward to taking up the role, but the truth was that I wasn't entirely sure that I'd made the right decision.

Many inspirational commentaries by headteachers focus on the moral purpose, the professional and personal fulfilment: being energized by a unique leadership opportunity to make a difference to children's lives. I've heard it described many times as "the best job in the world". A key element of leadership at this level is being able to articulate certainty, confidence, and optimism. However, when looking forward to the role, there are fears and anxieties beneath the surface—what if I fail? What if I'm not really cut out for this? 100 days into headship, these haven't magically disappeared. In my experience, they intensify with time. It's a bumpy ride. The most important question for me was whether I was going to enjoy the role—or whether the demands would be unsustainable. There were months of imagining myself as a head—some practice runs in summer term when recruiting staff, strategic planning, or welcoming the new Year Seven intake. There was lots of planning and much shaping of that all-important vision, but it wasn't until August, when the outgoing Head handed the keys to me and walked out through the school gates for the final time, that I really felt what I can only describe as a vertiginous sense of responsibility. It was when I was on my own that I started to find out whether I was really excited and whether I was really going to relish the responsibility.

The first half-term was a definitely a honeymoon period. I was pleasantly surprised by how much I was enjoying the role, including new challenges. I had taken on the position as an internal candidate at a high-performing school which enjoys a well-deserved reputation for excellence within the local and professional community. In a way, it felt like taking over a long-haul jumbo jet mid-flight, the controls set to autopilot and everything working smoothly and efficiently. There was work to be done immediately: a new team to build, new students and families joining us, and the start of a significant building programme. But the systems that were already in place helped to make the initial weeks feel exciting rather than stressful. Being internally promoted, I knew the school well and benefited from the speed of trust that comes from building relationships over a number of years. In the early days, I was vitalized by the buzz of doing something new.

The psychological challenge before starting—and in those first weeks—came from an acute awareness of the importance of finding my own voice and taking up my own authority. It's not the first time that I've experienced "imposter syndrome", but exposure in this role has a distinctively uncomfortable quality. Leading in the shadow of my highly regarded and experienced predecessor was always going to be difficult, and this was what I worried about most at the beginning. I had learned an enormous amount from working alongside her as a deputy, and my internal voice still asks what she would do when faced with a seemingly insuperable problem. I don't have a problem with that—I have benefitted from fabulous leadership role models. I enjoy being a magpie, learning from experience and, more importantly, from watching and listening, reading, collecting, and shelving away. However, I also knew that I needed to find my own distinctive way. So, much at the start was about communication: sharing, and setting the direction of vision with staff, presenting to new colleagues, meeting with governors, leading assemblies, responding to parents, speaking at open evenings, producing a new prospectus and website, and being interviewed by the local press. I learnt about the symbolic role of the Head in those first weeks. I'm an introvert and expected it to be draining, but, with crucial careful planning, it was an energizing part of establishing myself and crystallizing my priorities in role.

The first few weeks felt like a bit of a phoney war. Examination results had been generally good, and I felt that I knew what I was doing. But that didn't last—when you ultimately take over the controls, the workload is heavy and the hours are long. I accepted this, approaching the first year very much like being a newly qualified teacher (NQT). Induction is all about building professional experience and resilience. I knew that much would be completely new and that I would make mistakes. The reality of early headship is that you are frequently thrown into unfamiliar territory—the budget, asbestos management, catering contracts, building planning, complex human resource issues, confidential safeguarding referrals, critical incidents, "snow days", and boilers packing up. I vowed when I started that I would not allow myself to be distracted from the core business of delivering outstanding teaching and learning and that I would make time for strategic thinking. But that really is easier said than done.

Many early anxieties came from the feeling of being regarded as an expert while often not knowing the answers. Throughout my career, I've been fortunate to have had inspirational role models, and I'd like to think that I have good track record in developing others and leading high-performing teams. But when in the grip of a stressful situation, all that I know about the power of collaborative problem-solving and coaching styles of leadership goes out of the window, and I move more quickly into a directive mode than I would normally. I'm learning not to be forced into making snap decisions and to ask for time to think. Complex decision making has been much more effective when, as a leadership team, we've used structured tools like the Group Problem Solving Protocol (Easton, 2009) to help us think more creatively and avoid group think and premature consensus (a particular risk for a new team).

However, as an internally promoted head, there have been times when I haven't been directive or clear enough with my team—people do constantly want to know what you think and what you want. Recalibrating those relationships takes time. I guess the art is in remaining unafraid of creative conflict and challenge while also providing clear direction. One of the most useful pieces of thinking that we have undertaken as a newly formed senior leadership team has been around Tuckman's Team Development Cycle (Tuckman, 1965). Understanding that teams constantly evolve and surfacing the fact that that we were probably at the "storming" phase was important in order to interpret and frame how we were working and the reasons for some of our frustrations. Leading a new team comprised of both new and existing colleagues is challenging in itself. They are finding their way and so are you. It can be frustrating for everybody, particularly for those who have worked with the team in a previous incarnation when it's been at "performing" stage of the cycle. Keeping those people on board and utilizing their strengths is incredibly important. A team away day with an external consultant, using the Myers–Briggs Type Indicator psychometric to gain an understanding of our preferred ways of working individually and insight into our team dynamic, was helpful. We did this before beginning strategic planning work, and, although it initially slowed down the pace of this process, I think it has already made us much more effective and efficient as a team.

People often talk about how lonely the job of a head is. That's very true—there have been really difficult situations involving staff and students where only I've been able to make the final decision. Weighing up and taking responsibility for the consequences has been all-consuming, and I've learned that you sometimes need to protect staff from external pressures. While all the positive interactions with students and staff are rewarding, as headteacher you are also a receptacle for negative messages and complaints—about things that inevitably go wrong in a highly demanding professional organization.

It's hard not to take things that go wrong personally. I've learnt how important governors can be as a sounding board and a genuinely useful source of challenge and support (much more so that I expected) and being coached by an independent external consultant myself has been invaluable. These sessions have provided the confidential space to explore emotional, practical, and strategic challenges, but, most importantly, they have enabled me to step back, examine, and understand what is going on beneath the surface of complex organizational relationships and the impact of my own leadership within this.

Kate Williams, headteacher
Longhill High School (mixed, 11–16), Brighton

Emotional challenges

At the time of writing, I had been a headteacher for 66 days, during which period my emotions ricocheted from joy to sorrow and from hope to fear. I had accurately anticipated that my first headship would be an emotional and psychological roller-coaster. However, I underestimated the scale and the pace of a job that has completely consumed me. I consider myself resilient and pragmatic, with a plethora of relevant experience, but I have still found myself frequently tested by difficult situations and challenged by many people. Within weeks I had to call the police following an incident with the parents of a student suspected of criminal activity, whom I had temporarily excluded. Although the use of fixed-term exclusion is a neutral act, pending investigation, the student's parents reacted aggressively and placed an intimidating and abusive video on a public social media site. In view of the personal threat to me, the police became involved, and later the parent was convicted. While this experience was upsetting and difficult, a positive outcome was the respect I gained from staff in my first half term. Some thanked me for standing up to parents who had been abusive to staff over a number of years. However, the public attack felt personal. Although it was aimed at my authority, not me personally, I found it very difficult to separate my role from my personal identity. The attackers didn't "know" me, my values, morals, character, or history, and I had to work through the emotional turmoil that this invoked. I used sessions with a coach to help me analyse the incident and separate the personal from the professional. Since then, I have developed the "broad shoulders" of observational powers and the "armour" of objectivity.

Psychological challenges

I find that I am required to remain calm, positive, and solution-focused in challenging times and that others look to me for reassurance and support. The energy required for this daily cannot be underestimated. Whereas in my previous deputy role I could turn to my boss if I became upset or annoyed, now I have no container for my emotions. In order to survive I have developed coping strategies, turning to other colleagues for professional support. I spend more time in my own head, reflecting, questioning, analysing, scenario-running, and developing ideas. There is another layer of reflection required in headship that I had not previously needed—one of self-diagnosis, due to the isolation of the role. Previously I would reflect after a conversation with my principal about my work or development, but now I have to be self-sufficient and more self-aware. It is unlikely that staff who work for me will challenge my decisions, as my superiors would have done previously. This professional reflection can be missed, avoided, or half-heartedly completed, with no one to encourage or supervise, if you think you are doing a perfectly (or near perfectly) good job! I believe this reflection is a vital, healthy process that supports successful headship and can be developed through coaching.

I have actively engaged with coaching for several years, finding the process exceptionally rewarding and developmental. Since beginning my headship, I have enlisted the services of a coach to support me though the delivery of a staffing restructure and, as a result, felt able to support staff through an unsettling process. The emotional impact of making changes to the working lives of many staff in just a few months has taken its toll. I have had to make some difficult decisions, so I have learned to reflect on them and be flexible, in a constructive and positive way, while remaining true to my values. Although some decisions have been unpopular with staff, I have tried to be transparent and to articulate my rationale. I hope that in time they will understand. Staying true to my beliefs with regard to what is right for young people and high academic standards has been fundamental to my survival and has given me strength in difficult moments.

Political literacy

I have reacted both positively and negatively to the need to develop "political literacy" in my headteacher role. Although the school is my priority, I also have to engage at a local and national level in order to get the best for my stakeholders. People and organizations all around us have their own political agendas, and it takes some time to realize who wants what from whom—and why. For instance, on my very first day I was taken to a local council meeting by a prominent local figure without being told that I was expected not only to speak but to answer questions about my plans for the school. Naturally, this was also a public meeting, and, unknown to me, a local newspaper journalist was in attendance and I found myself quoted in a newspaper on the following day. Fortuitously, this had a positive outcome—but it could well have gone wrong for me and the school.

Legacy and culture change

Changing the direction and culture of an organization is a long process, but people usually want quick results, so managing people's expectations is challenging. Building trust is important, and, although time-consuming, I have introduced a system whereby staff need to meet with me personally to discuss any request for absence. Primarily intended to reduce staff absence, this also gives me the opportunity to get to know them on a personal level—their pressures and concerns, such as caring for sick children or elderly relatives. In this way, I gain insight and a connection with staff. I think it is important that they feel that I listen and support them, but they also need to understand that the education of young people must be our first priority.

What I have learned in a short amount of time

I have learnt to trust my instincts more and to develop my questioning and enquiry skills. I have been blessed with having worked with some great leaders in the past, and I have gained knowledge from them. I know that I will make mistakes and can accept that (as long as they are small). I know that I can't control everything all of the time. The way I relate to staff when there are problems is vital, so I model calm and clarity during critical incidents and hope that they in turn feel supported and empowered. I need to be quietly assertive, to direct staff so that students are safe and cared for, but at the same time begin to investigate so that decisions can be made around actions to be taken. Staff often see only the climax of student conflict, but there is always a lot more going on beneath the surface. They can be upset by dealing with student fights and conflicts, and my role is to de-escalate the situation, even when I have worries and concerns myself.

While it is possible to emulate ideal leadership, in the end we all have to find our own way of leading. Aiming for perfection in this demanding and pressurized job is not sustainable. I am glad that I realized this before I began my headship.

Headteacher as heart-teacher: leading from the heart

Next, two well-established primary school headteachers, with over seven years' experience in contrasting contexts, write heartfelt accounts of their emotional experiences of headship—the pressures and the pleasures, the highs and the lows—with compassion, common sense, and a little humour. *Denise Buckley* is now in her second headship, but here she reflects on formerly leading a challenging school in a disadvantaged coastal area and the toll on her wellbeing. *Yvonne Baron* is head of high-performing Jewish primary school in North London, which she had the rare privilege of founding, with a group of parents, as one of the first new "Free Schools" (state-funded and free to attend, but free from local authority control). Among many things, they write about the burden of containing the emotions of so many different stakeholders, parents in particular, from both sides of the social class divide. Their accounts contain sound advice for anyone embarking on headship, including a call to lead from the heart as well as the head.

Denise Buckley
experienced primary school headteacher

Leading a primary school is not just a job—it is a lifestyle choice. Nobody warned me that once you become a headteacher, your life changes. I dream of school every night. I can't sleep without checking emails one last time, in case some emergency may have to be dealt with. If I do get an email, there goes my night's sleep—as I know I will worry about it all night!

I work at weekends because there is never enough time during the week. Don't even get me started on Ofsted! As a leader, your focus is no longer on teaching—and not even on children! It is all about adults. Who knew that leading a primary school would not revolve around the children?

I began my career because I wanted to teach children. I had an idealistic view that I was going to change the world, like Robin Williams in "Dead Poets' Society", or be loved by all children, like Miss Honey in "Mathilda". Instead I became a cog in the government's wheel of never-ending bureaucracy and paperwork. The standard of my teaching is judged on what somebody in parliament—who has never taught in a classroom—has decided is "good". Conforming to this system, I am constantly trying to balance paperwork and actual teaching. I am under daily pressure from the government to provide written evidence of effective teaching: evidence of data analysis, plans and interventions for different groups of children, to tight deadlines. My problem is this: *while teachers are focused on paperwork deadlines, who is focusing on the children?*

Throughout my career, successive political parties changed the curriculum, assessment methods, and teaching standards criteria. It is difficult for me to advocate a system I do not believe in but have to adhere to. Does a detailed plan make you an outstanding practitioner? If you are so prescriptive that you have to write down every question you are going to ask, is that inspirational teaching? Some of the best lessons I have taught or observed have not necessarily provided too much written evidence of planning. The government does not understand this concept. All that seems to matter is written evidence.

Being a school leader is a multifaceted role. I have to be empathetic to staff, but not a walkover; have high expectations, but not too much, for fear that I burn teachers out. I have to be visible around the school at all times but still meet bureaucratic deadlines. I have a responsibility to ensure high-quality teaching, but it is difficult to recruit any teachers in my area, let alone high-calibre ones. I have to ensure outstanding lessons are being taught, but I cannot afford to resource them. I have to have open communications with parents but not allow them to take over. I am a juggler!

With little experience of human resources initially, I have had to find my own way to monitor and challenge under-performing teachers, trusting my instincts and learning from observation of experienced leaders. On occasions, I have had to show courage and determination to see things through, not getting too personally involved when holding a disciplinary hearing, for instance.

Former HMCI, Sir Michael Wilshaw, once stated, "If anyone says to you that 'staff morale is at an all-time low' you know you are doing something right" (*The Guardian*, 23 January 2012; see Abrams, 2012). I totally disagree with this statement. In my experience, staff do not perform to their best ability with low morale, which spreads quickly like a virus and permeates down from staff to students, creating a toxic climate for all. This is not an environment I want to create for the children in my school, and I am mindful of the part my behaviour plays in creating school culture. I need to remain outwardly calm in a crisis (even if I am dying inside!) and remain positive at all times (even when I feel like throwing in the towel), so that staff and children follow my example. My mood affects the atmosphere and dynamics of the whole school and how it works on any given day.

It is important that my staff trust me and feel they can come to me with a problem. They say that trust works both ways, but, in my experience, when I have taken it for granted that things have been done because I have asked for them to de done, I have often been disappointed. I have realized that even experienced staff need constant reassurance and reminding—but not in a patronizing way. Trying to develop emotional intelligence in order to empower staff and students while also ensuring that tasks are done to my standard requires a fine balance. Humour has got me through—and sometimes my senior team meetings turn into occasions where we can laugh or cry about an issue that we have had to deal with that day.

I have learned to build a wall around myself personally and to keep a professional distance from staff. This has been difficult for me, as I am a social person, and I have found the job quite lonely at times. I have discovered that I am quite resilient and have grown a thicker skin, especially when dealing with aggressive parents who have shouted at me, called me names, threatened me, and reported me to Ofsted. My job has taken its toll on my health: I had pneumonia after my first Ofsted, I often forget to eat (or do not have time to eat) or am sick when the holidays come around. I am in a constant state of anxiety about school and never fully switch off. Some days it has been difficult to continue, and I have shed a few tears in the safe haven of my office. However, I have always tried to be optimistic and persevere. Sometimes I ask myself why I carry on, but I know it is for the sake of the children.

Despite all of the above, I actually love my job! I have high expectations of myself and children academically, and I expect them to work hard to achieve their personal optimum. For me personally, the pressures are all worth it for precious moments, like when the child with attention deficit disorder, who struggles to concentrate in class, sings like an angel in the Christmas carol service; when the child who has struggled so much with maths that she has been making herself sick, finally has her light bulb moment with long division; when the boy who has been struggling with his behaviour realizes he is good at football and scores the winning goal; when the child who speaks five languages at home (none of which are English) reads his book aloud to me. These are the moments I carry with me.

I have realized that my dream of changing the world of education may have been a tad naïve. However, if I have made an impact on the lives of the children or staff I have encountered, or if I have inspired even one child to have the courage to pursue their dream, then it has all been worthwhile.

Yvonne Baron, headteacher
Etz Chaim Jewish Primary Free School, Mill Hill, London

Being a headteacher is the best job. The opportunity to create and steer a school in the direction that I totally and utterly believe in is exciting and extremely rewarding. Starting a completely new school eight years ago offered a unique opportunity to create and shape education provision and to make fundamental decisions about curriculum, staffing, and the learning environment. It is a real privilege, as there are few other jobs where you can make such a positive difference.

The sheer scale of the job is one of the biggest challenges, being responsible for staff recruitment, human resources, financial and site management, catering, installing alarm systems and telephone points, and supporting staff and families through challenging personal situations, as well as teaching and learning. The pressure is immense. I have never worked so hard, doubted myself so much, and yet, at the same time, felt such high levels of job satisfaction and pride. Every day is different, with its own challenges and surprises—I am never sure what or who might come through the door!

One reason why I think Headship is so challenging is having to meet the needs of so many different people—children, their families, staff, governors, local authority, Department for Education, the local community, and other organizations. Everyone wants a piece of you! They all make different demands and are blissfully ignorant of how many directions you are pulled in. It is important to have quality relationships with all these groups, but I give absolute priority to my staff, investing a huge amount of time and energy into them. Teams don't just happen, you have to create them. Staff who support each other, who are loyal to the school and me, have been key in challenging and stressful times. Building a relationship with each and every one of them has helped me to understand them, to know their strengths, likes, and motivations. This has enabled me to develop their skills, delegate effectively, and create capacity. It is impossible to do it all yourself, and acknowledging and celebrating this can also be very empowering for the staff team.

When times are really tough, there's no one better to turn to than colleague headteachers, as they understand and will help problem solve. I value their advice more than anyone else's and have armed myself with some fantastic colleagues whom I trust. Visiting other schools and talking to other heads about what they do has been hugely valuable. Their passion is infectious, creating new energy and enthusiasm to take back to your school.

I belong to a Work Discussion Group for headteachers, which provides an opportunity to discuss and share dilemmas and difficulties in a safe and supportive space. Although our contexts are different, everyone in the group can relate to and draw upon their own experiences to help think through individual issues and solutions. This not only brings clarity to an issue but is also calming and restorative and a great remedy for the emotional and psychological challenges of headship. They understand the real fear that all headteachers have, of what others may think of them and how they might be judged. There are higher levels of accountability than ever before which create high levels of stress. There are times when I have felt that Headship is professional suicide, and the pressure of living under the spotlight has taken its toll.

Regular coaching has given me strength and resilience and changed the way I approach my role. I have more clarity in decision making and more confidence in difficult situations. "What's the worst that can happen?" has been a significant question for me, helping me gain perspective when I've felt overloaded or am dealing with a difficult situation. "Good is good enough" is another phrase that has helped me to keep a clear head. It is not realistic to keep on top of everything in headship. There are too many plates to spin at any one time. If they drop, pick them up! There is no time to be precious, so understanding and accepting that the job is never finished is essential and realistic. An experienced head once told me that they plan only one task in their diary per day—a great piece of advice, as there are always unscheduled demands that are time-consuming and need to be factored in. "Only do what only you can do" is another phrase that I frequently say to myself. As a former teacher, I am still interested in the classroom, and it is not easy to let go, give up some control, and delegate to others. Over time, I have learned that when I delegate well, my time management and work life balance improve greatly.

Leading a new school, which opened in the first wave of Free Schools in September 2011, has particular challenges. Despite not playing any part in its application or opening, parents took a risk, choosing to send their children to a new Free School. As a result, some of our initial families feel that it is "their" school, expecting to be treated differently from other families who joined us later. Even after eight years, there are times when I still feel as if I have to prove myself to them, as their demands can be unrealistic at times. Creating some distance between myself and parents has been important: if the size of the PE bag is a parent's major worry, I delegate to one of my senior team, so that parents feel heard—but I haven't had to listen to them! Social media platforms also are increasingly used by parents to fuel complaints and campaigns against schools, and emails are often fired off by parents expecting an immediate response. Heads develop significant emotional attachment to their schools, so it is hard not to take every negative comment or complaint personally. I try to unpick what feelings and emotions might be underpinning a complaint before meeting or speaking to a parent. I once heard a head say that ten percent of parents make ninety percent of the noise. This is a hundred percent true! Most of the parents, most of the time, are supportive, but they just don't tell you. I try to regularly remind myself of this when a few parents are being vocal and difficult.

My leadership journey to date has been a rollercoaster ride that has challenged every part of me—but one that I don't want to get off. What has struck me is how many of my decisions are based on gut instinct. I just know whether or not something feels right, whether it aligns with my vision or not. I have come to realize that emotions are essential in leadership. There is no one way to lead. You can, and must, be yourself, with a core set of values and principles which help you develop and articulate your vision. My advice to other headteachers would be: listen to your heart, follow what makes you tick, and strive for what you truly believe in.

The road of trials: finding helpers

Writing from opposite ends of the experience spectrum, the next two school leaders chose to describe their emotional and psychological leadership challenges through the lens of their coaching journeys. First, *Ellen Clarke*, a London comprehensive deputy head, writes with immediacy about the trials often faced by young and aspirational leaders: work–life balance, acquiring gravitas when working with older and more experienced colleagues, and guilt that arises from the pursuit of perfection. *Sarah Pringle*, an experienced secondary academy principal much in demand as a mentor and consultant to other heads in her academy trust and local education authority, reflects on her leadership journey, including a crisis of confidence along the way, which will be familiar to many headteachers. They write with candour and wisdom about overcoming fears and anxieties, learning from mistakes, not taking everything too personally, and developing others. They describe how they systematically plan for school improvement and staff development, while remaining mindful of their own personal and professional growth—and how they found support to sustain themselves personally through challenging times.

Ellen Clarke, deputy head
Park View Secondary School (11–16 mixed), Tottenham,
North London

"I think you might benefit from some coaching", my headteacher suggested. He was right: I was a relatively new senior leader, and it had been a stressful couple of months, culminating in my dissolving into tears in front of a "mock" (mercifully) Ofsted inspector. My responsibilities included whole-school literacy, higher attaining pupils, assessment for learning, community links, and line-management of subject departments and a year team, and I was finding it difficult to balance all the different elements. There seemed to be a nagging sense of guilt at the back of my mind at all times. Why haven't you done this? Why can't you just make things happen? Why can't you do everything perfectly?

Coaching sounded useful, yet my initial reaction was an internal wince. I am a relatively private person who can overthink responses to even the most basic questions, and I was nervous about it. I had worked successfully with a coach at Teach First and gained a huge amount from the experience. This made my trepidation hard to explain, but it seemed to boil down to two things: first, if your boss suggests coaching, it must mean you are not doing a good enough job (guilt); second, this is going to cost some serious money, and you need to be worth it. It was important to try to reverse these thoughts in my head. They had to become "You are worth investing in."

I did need to be worth it, and that meant preparing, committing, and genuinely acting on everything we discussed. Across six sessions over eight months we tackled a whole range of topics, from line-managing year nine to whole-school literacy. By the end of each and every session, I'd had the opportunity to talk through my current approach, reflect on it, and, ultimately, improve on it. Increasingly, I came to realize that feeling guilty about what I hadn't achieved so far was unhelpful on a number of levels: it was making me feel bad when, all in all, I was doing a pretty good job; it was compromising my ability to think strategically and to prioritize what mattered; and, crucially, it was making me far too negative about my own and my teams' contributions to school life, when there was much to celebrate.

Coaching also provided an opportunity to reflect on and improve my work–life balance. I had increasingly resorted to working evenings and weekends in order to feel on top of work. Instead, coaching encouraged me to consider the key focuses in each of my remits and to look for specific actions as priorities, rather than attempting to do everything at once. Making time to step back, look at the whole picture, and pinpoint what would have the most impact also made me recognize how infrequently I had done this in the preceding few months. It was not difficult to see why I felt overwhelmed. In tandem, celebrating my successes meant I was able to see that I didn't have to be working constantly in order to be an effective senior leader.

The key breakthroughs came from "thinking" rather than just blindly "doing": my coaching provided me with a "thinking space" and the insight to focus more on the former and less on the latter. I therefore made a conscious effort to reduce my working hours, to have the self-belief to say no, and to acknowledge that doing a good job and being an effective leader is not about throwing more hours at the problem.

Another key moment was a conversation about gravitas. A sense that I was not quite inhabiting the "leader" role had been bothering me for a while, but I had been reluctant to raise it in the early stages of coaching. My thinking shifted in later sessions. Being brave enough to raise the issue led to an incredibly helpful discussion: what exactly is gravitas? How do you get it? Do I need to stop looking flustered? (Answer: obviously, yes). It helped me to re-appraise my behaviour around school, which, at the busiest times, had included too much rushing about and apologizing. Knowing the value of a good apology is golden, but frequently entering rooms or conversations with the word "sorry" is probably underselling my worth. I learned to slow down, take time over decisions, and to be confident without arrogance. I still have to catch myself at times, but it is a positive work in progress. Being able to come back to my coaching sessions and say "I've worked on this", increased my motivation to change.

Coaching allows space for thoughts to be fully developed without interruption. Initially, I found it hard to find space in my calendar for the sessions, but this soon turned into an eagerness for the next session and an attempt to top them up with structured hours of thinking in-between, almost like a conversation with myself. Strategic thinking has always been one of my strengths, and honing it was gratifying. At the time, I was leading on a number of whole-school policy changes, and discussing their implementation with my coach made me better able to pinpoint blockages around personalities or current structures that might previously have scuppered even the best laid plans.

An integral aspect to the success of coaching for me was accountability. There is a powerful sense of obligation to both your coach and to yourself, a sense that you need something to say when you return for the next session. It is very different to guilt though—the focus is on looking forwards rather than regretting that which remains undone. The feeling of progress is powerful. I reflected to my coach that I have a real "good girl" mentality, a nagging desire for a gold star! However, coaching builds a sense of self-affirmation alongside the spur of other people's praise. As a result, I have re-appraised my line management approach and have a greater desire to challenge those I work with, through projects that develop their own sense of accountability and achievement. Historically, I might have been worried about overburdening colleagues, but now I see the need to empower my team in just the same way that the coaching process empowers me.

The sessions also encouraged me to be more honest with myself. I was able to admit aspects of my role I was struggling with and to identify why I was struggling, rather than simply blaming myself or feeling that this was an admission of weakness. I can now focus on specific challenges and how to tackle them—and I feel in control, rather than guilty. Essentially, I beat myself up about things far less now than I used to, and, as a result, I am far better placed to lead other people effectively. I make a more conscious effort to isolate the negatives and celebrate the positives, and this has been good both for me and for my team.

Overall, coaching has increased my self-confidence and renewed my energy and enthusiasm for leadership in school. Any process that makes you feel lighter by the end of each session must be helpful, and any that encourages you to focus on controllable external factors rather than your own perceived failings is invaluable. Teachers and school leaders shoulder a great deal of blame from various quarters at present. Recognizing how one can change and improve, without feeling guilty, has been good for my sense of self-worth and must be good for our approach as a profession.

Sarah Pringle, Principal
Seahaven Academy (11–16, mixed) East Sussex

Initially, taking up authority in the top job is a gargantuan psychological leap—even after several years' leadership experience in deputy, associate head, and "head of school" roles. Our sense of self and how this is reflected in the way others see us can give rise to very complex, sometimes bemusing sensitivities. Without the comfort blanket of former support networks, carefully built up through mutual respect and collaboration, professional strengths can easily be lost and resilience eroded, simply through the process of starting again in a new role. However, I felt as prepared as I could possibly be. I wasn't expecting too many surprises, and, in one sense, I was correct—I have very rarely been faced with a situation I haven't met before—but, in another, totally unanticipated way, I was completely wrong. I was not prepared for some of the emotional, philosophical, and psychological challenges that come with such a high-profile, high-stakes, and high-reward job. I thought I knew who I was, what I believed in, and how I would translate my previous experience into school improvement. However, I wasn't prepared for how different the role of headteacher could be from one school context to another.

As I began to tackle the textbook challenges of establishing a vision, raising expectations, winning over staff who weren't keen on change, and trying to build leadership capacity, I began to acknowledge that I wasn't really sure where to start in trying to solve some of the problems I faced in this new role. I came to the conclusion that I just could not possibly be the omniscient being I needed to be and that working with a coach and consultant would give me some dedicated thinking time for discussing live problems. Working with an experienced practitioner helped me frame questions and investigate possible solutions, although at the time I often wondered whether I would have reached the same conclusion working alone as I did when working with a coach. A "lightbulb moment" came when I realized how the way in which I dealt with staff in different situations was communicating a significant message about my own character traits and values. For instance, it was pointed out to me by a close colleague that a somewhat obsessive regard for following procedure, for instance, indicated that I would take honesty and transparency very seriously. During this period, I enjoyed applying the theory and constructs we discussed and felt that I was constantly building my own capacity to tackle new questions. My senior team and I became involved in a series of training activities using psychometric tools such as the Myers–Briggs Type Indicator (MBTI) preferences questionnaires, team building sessions, and, for some, certified qualifications. Coaching at all levels swiftly became part of the culture and language of the school.

My circumstances—and my coaching—changed significantly at the start of my second year, as I faced the impact of significantly lower public examination results than anticipated, and the questions a downturn in school performance raises in terms of strategic, professional, and personal confidence. I was no longer new—and I was personally accountable. Having successfully redesigned my senior leadership team, I was now faced with the prospect of having to redesign myself after a six-month period, working alongside an executive principal who would eventually move on, leaving me to take sole responsibility for my school again. The process of re-inventing myself in order to regain my confidence after the fall in results took something different from a process-driven approach to coaching. It became less of an interesting and appealing vehicle for professional development and more of an essential tool for navigating the storms that inevitably follow such a change in fortunes— focused on emotional and psychological issues rather than concrete, solution-focused ones.

To begin with, I found this change slightly disconcerting, as I was more comfortable talking about the analysis of a problem than reflecting on the feelings this may have evoked. But it didn't take long before I understood that these aren't mutually exclusive conversations. My own traits and professional characteristics became more significant than in previous coaching sessions, but personal development was then also combined with practical strategies, such as how, when, and with whom to have key meetings. The result was a carefully planned start to the summer term and a relaunch of my vision for the school. Coaching gave me a new set of "lenses" through which to assess and solve a number of conundrums: for example, I soon realized that deciding when to use the experience and expertise of other staff rather than deliberately leading from the front to re-establish my own position (and vice versa) was made far easier by talking through different scenarios with my coach. Giving up classroom teaching, to become more strategic, was another example of this, and not a conclusion I would have reached on my own, for fear of losing credibility with staff.

I would not regard myself as a natural coachee. Despite having participated in many thought-provoking but rather superficial courses in the last 15 years, I don't think I fully understood the breadth, depth, and power of coaching as a tool for personal development, until I really needed it. Being encouraged to analyse every aspect of both your context and your leadership—in addition to day-to-day responsibilities—when faced with need for rapid change and progress is absolutely exhausting. In reality, however, it isn't in addition to the "day job". It underpins it, works alongside it, and ultimately drives what you do. Self-evaluation and reflection eventually just become part of what you do, because you start to use them more as lenses through which to see your role and vision, rather than tools for carrying it out. This stage of my headship was about transformation; rebuilding confidence, raising further (not lowering) aspirations in the wake of disappointment, and keeping personal values and integrity intact. Most of all, it was about translating and transferring this to the context I work in and the people around me—using the day-to-day scenarios we meet to work out who we are, rather than what we are like.

Becoming a headteacher means having a remarkably personal set of experiences played out in a very public arena. This in itself can be disorienting. When you add to this constant external challenges arising from examination result pressures, diminishing budgets, problems recruiting high-calibre staff, and the increase in the number of students suffering from the type of societal issues that put all of this back into context, it would be understandable if this did not look like a dream job. But it can be. You just have to find the right support and professional development to allow you to make it what it should be.

Leading from the edge: resilience and risk

The rollercoaster as a metaphor for the emotional experience of headship—as well as sporting analogies—recurs throughout this chapter, illustrating the courage, resilience, and risk required for leadership. The next two school leaders chose to use learning a new and challenging sport as an extended metaphor for reflecting on leadership. As Kilburg (2000. p. 181) has observed, metaphor can help us understand how assumptions, values, attitudes, beliefs, thoughts, feelings, defences, conflicts, and behaviours are shaped.

First, *Trevor North*, principal of a coastal primary academy for six years, likens headship to the exhilarating but risky sport of kite-surfing. He describes how he found his own authority and balance in an initially ambiguous role, resolving internal politics, balancing control and autonomy, and rescuing the school from falling standards. Second, professional riding coach *Sally Deverill*, together with a novice rider who is a long-standing secondary headteacher with 14 years' experience, reflects on equestrian metaphors, idioms, and proverbial sayings and describe how their conversations on horseback developed into a meditation on leadership.

Trevor North, Principal
St. Mary's Church of England Primary Trust, Folkestone, Kent

Standing in bare feet on a pebbled beach, littered with hazardous rocks and foot-shredding shells, on a cold winters' morning, I realized that I had no idea how the next few moments of my life were going to pan out. What made this more uncomfortable was the thin neoprene suit I was wearing and the small issue of being attached to a 12-metre square nylon sheet on 30-metre-long lines, waiting to launch a kite into a fairly strong 25-mph wind. The words of everyone I know and care for were ringing in my ears: "What were you thinking of?!" I had read the book, watched a few YouTube clips, and had a good friend telling me it was all going to be fine. "Just trust the science", he shouted, as I pulled on the line to raise the kite. My mouth dry with fear, my mind alert with anticipation, the kite filled, and the power of the wind surged through the lines and clutched at my harness, telling me something unexpected was about to happen.

Looking back on my start as Principal in a complex and challenging context, I can't help but compare the experience with my first day kite-surfing. I was confident I could do it, knew the risks and was prepared to take them. I guessed it was going to be hard, but I had read the books on school leadership and had just completed my NPQH. I considered myself well qualified. Just like YouTube videos on kiting, reading leadership theory makes leading a team and change seem all so very easy. In reality, you have to live with the consequences of decisions you make and the emotional ebb and flow of working with a wide range of personalities.

As the kite filled, it rose. As it rose, I glared at the kite, willing it to look after me. After a few glances to my good friend on the beach, who sent encouraging smiles and "thumbs-up" in return, I had the kite in the air. It was under control and steady. Slowly it pulled me to the water's edge, and then, as my fear drained and my confidence grew, a whole new world of excitement and challenge opened up before my eyes. For the next few weeks I spent hours being dragged around the sea, swallowing seawater and learning that every pull on the kite magnified reaction to painful levels. However, despite blows from the waves, I was eventually riding on them with complete control of my kite. I was kitesurfing, and I loved it!

There are parallels with emotions evoked by extreme sports and headship: the adrenaline of fear, moments of elation and supreme confidence, huge steps taken into the unknown, the big crashes, and humble pie to be eaten on many occasions. Standing in front of a new staff team full of hope and enthusiasm for change, I felt confident. However, as the role took me to the brink of the sea, I launched on a journey that was soon to consume all my energy.

I hadn't expected the overwhelming impact of the responsibility and expectations which chipped away at my self-confidence. Setting a vision, raising expectations, and modelling excellence takes an enormous amount of emotional energy and drive. No one can truly describe the roller-coaster of emotion—alternating waves of guilt, paranoia, confidence, insecurity, elation, and anger—washing over me like a winter sea.

Headship was like my first kiteboard ride—exhilarating. With the winter sun on my face, the spray behind me, powering along at 25 miles per hour, I couldn't have been happier. Elation soon turned to fear: I realized I had to turn the kite, control it, and make it work for me. Nothing else has ever come close to the joy and sense of freedom that follows mastering kite-surfing. Similarly, the reality of headship hit me hard—like crashing in the ocean with little shore to focus on, I found myself alone. Who could I talk to about the issues I was facing? Where was my safety jacket?

I was in a complicated situation, with the previous head still working in the school as Chief Executive Officer (CEO), responsible for finance and health and safety. How could I take up my own authority in a tactful and diplomatic way? We both started with good intentions but soon realized that our roles overlapped. Power struggles emerged as boundaries were crossed and expectations confused. Staff who were loyal to their previous headteacher grew frustrated with the confused dynamics and messages. In any extreme sport, particularly surf-kiting, taking one's eye off the goal or making an error of judgement can put one in danger very quickly.

Our kind of "joint leadership" was set to challenge us both, and it took a certain type of character to make it work. I had to focus on my goals: raising standards in teaching and learning. The CEO was a humble professional who supported me with patience and incredible resilience. However, it was difficult for me to feel in control, and there were times when positions and decisions taken by the CEO and the governing body knocked me off-balance—like being hit by a great gust of wind, with a hole in my surf-kite. The joint leadership roles of CEO and principal inevitably caused conflict, usually resulting from lack of clarity around decision-making and communications. This led to feelings of powerlessness, distrust, and self-doubt, a tangled ball of emotion and stress which was at times debilitating. I had never felt so alone.

Nevertheless, with the tenacity of an enthusiastic kiter, desperate to succeed and ride the waves, I pulled through these tough and dark moments. Kiting is a strange sport: you are on your own, smiling at the exhilaration of controlled risk, but scared about the consequences of it going wrong. Only other kiters truly understand the experience. If you practise in the right place, you will have other kiters around you and confidence in knowing that if something goes wrong, someone is there to help. In retrospect, the CEO role of the previous headteacher provided me with a leadership "life jacket"—great support and counsel, aligned with a long-established and well-formed governing body. No one could have anticipated that such a dual leadership role could succeed—but it has, giving me the capacity and freedom to focus on the main priority of improving standards in my own way.

Being passionate about high standards is not sufficient alone to change a culture of low expectations. I had learned as deputy that leadership needs to be devolved and distributed in order to be an effective agent of change. Taking up headship is a bit like looking at a tangled mess of kite lines. If you approach it with a robust tug on one particular line, you end up tightening everything and making it an impossible task. I wanted to focus on improving all areas. In order to de-tangle kite lines you need to create space, give a little shake, a few tweaks and soon you will identify the real problem. The right line is then gently moved, and more space is created. A slow methodical approach will soon have the lines free and fully functional. It became clear that I couldn't do this on my own: a kite will only spin in circles if on one line.

First, I built a team of phase leaders, focusing purely on raising the expectations of teachers. I modelled good practice and the importance of evaluation, challenge, and support. This gave me a solid foundation of excellent emerging leaders all enthusiastic for change and improving standards. I was beginning to detangle the web of a failing school. I had five lines flying a kite! Staff morale improved, and everyone was beaming with pride at the speed at which we were growing and achieving success. Kiting is amazing when it is all going smoothly, but, as in any extreme sport, there are huge risks. Putting yourself out there on your own in the middle of the sea with a kite powerful enough to lift you off your feet makes you vulnerable—yet you feel invincible. Were we strong enough to stay upright and floating when the wind had dropped? When the kite was beginning to deflate, was I prepared to fall?

Tackling the underperformance of teachers can be depressing and stressful. Was I prepared to challenge a popular member of staff who was performing way below standard? Was I going to rock the boat we had just steadied?

As head, you are never sure whether your own perception of events is accurate. Not being able to share self-doubt increases the stress. Do staff truly understand? Are they confident to say when things are not right? Do they just tell you what you want to hear? The paranoia grips you. It turns your stomach when you see bad practice, and lightens your soul when you see good. It was hard. There were extreme polarizations of my emotions every day. I could be hated one minute and praised the next. This spectrum of emotions was exhausting and remains so. My rock in the school is my leadership team, providing the strength to tolerate these emotions and model the excellence we need.

However, a strong team alone isn't enough to thrive. The complexities of headship are such that one needs space to think clearly and process emotions. If leadership is to be authentic, these emotions must be expressed, shared, and explored. Having a coach who was able to verbalize my feelings and contextualize dilemmas, who challenged my thinking and my doubts, was instrumental in keeping my head and keeping my team! The opportunity to be open and honest about the stress and anxiety of capability meetings, to test out my dilemmas and personal conflicts in a safe place, helped me to recalibrate my moral compass.

The challenge of leadership is to make tough decisions that are the right ones, at the right time. Without coaching I may have been overwhelmed in a fog of emotion and indecision, unable to overcome staff resistance to change. From tackling underperformance to strategic planning and the restructuring of leadership teams, coaching gave me clarity of thought. It enabled me to detangle the lines of governance, poor teaching, low morale, and team dynamics and to ensure pupils were at the heart of what was needed, just like my good friend on the beach guiding me to think clearly about the risks of kite-surfing, talking me through small technical mistakes, giving gentle prompts, and helping me find my own way of handing the kite. Support from a leadership coach, underpinned with my own grit and determination, enabled me to identify precisely my focus and style as a leader. At the time of writing my team has transformed a failing coastal school into one that has been deemed to be "Good" in all areas and is now well on its way to being "Outstanding".

Sally Deverill, equestrian, with a secondary headteacher

You can lead a horse to water ... ...

Most people living at the time will recall the moment of John F. Kennedy's assassination. One of the most striking images of Kennedy's funeral procession was that of the riderless horse, boots reversed in the stirrups, as an iconic symbol of a fallen leader.

Decades later, when my local education authority launched a "well-being initiative", urging headteachers to make time for themselves, take up a physical activity, learn something new, I decided to take up horse-riding, as a complete beginner. At first my worthy intention was to volunteer with a "Riding for the Disabled" group at my local partner special school. Little did I know that new, humbling—and at times painful—learning in later life, and conversations with my talented riding coach would result in a meditation on leadership.

It is not surprising that many leadership metaphors are equestrian, because riding a horse is a form of leadership, an intriguing idea that had not previously occurred to me. Whenever we *"take up the reins"* we physically declare our intention to be in charge. What the horse does next is simply a matter of cause and effect, depending a lot on our leadership skills. How headteachers lead students and staff—how they behave, what they say and do—are subject to daily scrutiny and reaction by those being led.

Straight from the horse's mouth

Leadership is about getting people to want to do what you want them to do. As I follow my riding coach's instructions and listen to her pedagogic analogies and observations, I cannot help but make connections with school leadership. *"Whenever time is spent with horses, they are influenced by their riders and will learn from that experience, whether positive or negative."* How often as school leaders do we reflect on our staff's feelings about previous experiences of leadership when there is a change of leader or strategic direction? What motivates them, and what they might fear or resist?

Horses are herd-living, social animals, some of whom have a strong motivation to dominate in the hierarchy of their social group. Even in a yard or stables, the "herd leader" will have the advantage of being able to access the best grass or hay, get to drink water first, benefit from the best shelter from the flies and the safest place from predators. Even a domesticated, quiet-natured riding-school horse has these basic survival instincts. In the analogous social setting of a school staffroom, it is easy to overlook the underlying, often unconscious causes of resistance to leadership. A new staffroom might not be welcomed if habitual seating hierarchies are destroyed in the process, even if better facilities are provided. A curriculum change might upset the balance of power between subject departments. A union representative on the governing body might be perceived as an alternative power base.

Have yourself a bit of horse sense

As we ride, my coach develops the leadership theme. *"It's about not only the rider, but also the horse, so I must invest in training my horses. This really is an infinite activity—you're never finished—there's always something more you can achieve. Whenever I take the horse out of the field and away from its herd I must take up leadership authority. I need to prove my skills to the horse—that I am not afraid to stand my ground, will protect them and be fair, be resilient and make quick decisions. Horses need to know that I will delegate responsibility, that I listen and give reward where it is due. This leadership deal between me and the horse isn't a signed contract: it has to be earned—through a series of very subtle behavioural "tests". Initially I attract their attention, then I will move into their space, next I gently touch them (not like a predator would!) and finally reward them for not moving away (food)."* I think of newly appointed heads, often struggling with taking up authority, establishing trust, appearing just, and delegating effectively. I reflect on the continuing challenge of these leadership competences. The most effective leaders are those who not only inspire but also value and empower others. They know how to pick and train good staff, nurturing and trusting them. They delegate and let others take the credit, and in doing so they command loyalty and respect.

Chomping at the bit

Much of everyday leadership is routine. However, headteachers must start each day with enthusiasm and determination. They are always on show, and their perceived moods will affect their followers. As my riding coach explains, "*I never, ever assume that my leadership status lasts forever—I frequently use body language to assess response-time, to ascertain any subtle challenges to my "authority". Without my leadership, the horse will believe that it is free to do as it wants—to explore, rest, eat, call out to others, or try to return to its field companion.*" I think of the frustrations of heads who need staff to adopt consistent approaches to behaviour management or formative assessment. It is not enough to have a fine new policy unless it is applied consistently, so vision and strategy need to be communicated and modelled daily.

Give someone a leg-up

With her decades of experience training horses and riders, my coach's understanding of human as well as equine behaviour is impressive. "*My role is to support my rider in acquiring skills that will enable them to be in control of their horse—in effect to become a leader. This training is very much 'on-the-job' because my rider will be sitting on a horse at the time, before any leadership negotiations have begun. Learning to control a horse within an enclosed arena, at various speeds, can take anything from 10–100 hours of practice, so I need to maintain my herd dominance for everyone to stay safe. It is important to stay quite close, within two or three metres to begin with, micro-managing the situation. As the rider begins to become competent (I assess the horse's reactions to the rider's requests—when the horse responds without hesitation I consider the rider to be in control) I gradually move away—up to 20 or 30 metres. If the horse shows signs of challenging the rider (these can be quite subtle so the rider may not notice) I will move closer to reinforce what they are asking the horse to do. Each lesson involves an ever-changing leadership triad of rider, horse, and coach, and, as the rider's skills improve, authority is taken up for longer and longer.*" A widely held view is that the most effective heads distribute leadership. This is a subtle art of developing, enabling, and empowering senior and middle leaders, so that they in turn can lead their teams. This means knowing when to let go of the power and authority invested in the top job. Many heads find this a challenge, especially in underperforming schools where improvement needs to be rapid. Looking back on my own headship, investing time and money in the development of middle leaders paid off in terms of bringing about rapid change in a failing school (although I did not trust many of them at the time!).

Don't put the cart before the horse

"When learning to ride, effective communication skills must be learned as a progressive structure of applied knowledge. Communicating with a horse has its own "language," involving body, mind, and all five senses—and even a "sixth sense': you'll learn a few simple words first, then sentences and paragraphs. A rider needs to use intelligence if they are to process thinking into doing. Methods of communication must be so well-rehearsed that the rider is able to use them under extreme pressure—for example, if the horse shies away from something fearful. If, in that situation, the rider finds that they have indeed done as they rehearsed, there is usually a great sense of euphoria at their success! However, it is not just understanding, memory, and practice that builds competence. Riding is an emotional sport: the thrill of going fast; experiencing harmony between rider and horse; enjoying the open countryside. And sometimes we can be just too thrilled or over-confident to stay focused (pride comes before a fall). The opposite end of the emotional scale is fear, by far the biggest barrier to learning to ride." Leading a school is also an emotional experience that many have described as veering from fear to exhilaration on a daily, even minute-by-minute, basis. As in any position of power, the rewards are great, but the risks are high. A steady pair of hands "on the reins" is needed where events can be unpredictable, even dangerous, especially in areas of social disadvantage. Well thought out, communicated, and rehearsed health and safety and safeguarding policies are essential when responsible for thousands of young people and hundreds of staff. They provide a framework and build the capacity of leaders to respond quickly and appropriately to critical incidents and unexpected risks—everyday accidents, extreme weather conditions—and also normal and abnormal adolescent risk-taking and suicides; external threats to the vulnerable, including violent attacks, substance abuse and child abuse or trafficking. Integrity, thinking on one's feet and making decisions under pressure depend not only upon courage and conviction but also the management of fear.

You have to get back on the horse

When riding a horse for the first time, feelings of vulnerability are inevitable. Challenges and trials are frequent, so we need to be honest with ourselves—be clear about what we are afraid of, and ask for help. True bravery means having a go, despite being afraid. Having a coach to support and keep you safe will give you courage to go on, to return to where you were and to give it another go, whether you are a novice rider or a beleaguered headteacher. *"Part of my role is helping riders manage their emotions"*, explains my riding coach. *"I ask my riders to see themselves being ruled by two forces—their heads and their hearts. If something frightens you and the horse, it is your responsibility (as leader) to calm the horse first, despite feeling afraid yourself. The rider must know themselves long before they can get to know the horse."* Similarly, in the complex role of school leader, it is important to have reflective time with others, to receive feedback on leadership behaviours and blind-spots, support the thinking through of dilemmas, to process ambivalent feelings and evaluate actions and plans.

Don't flog a dead horse

In riding, as in headship, if your plans are going wrong, change what you are doing. *"Apportioning blame to the horse, the rider, or the coach is not helpful. Spend time thinking about the events leading up to the moment you realised things weren't right. Sometimes it's the horse that isn't listening, preoccupied with the wind in the bushes, as though a wolf were there. There probably isn't, but instinct says there could be. Riders learn empathy and ways round seemingly impossible situations, reviewing each lesson. This measurement of achievement is always ipsative—it cannot be anything else."* Similarly, there is no one way to lead a school—all heads have to find their own way.

Never look a gift horse in the mouth

The addiction of struggling through difficulties to finally achieve harmonious control of a horse is always a delight—as is achieving a favourable Ofsted judgement after riding the long hard road of school improvement. However, this final phrase reminds riders and school leaders to be humble and to accept good things. Give praise where praise is due—horses are generally honest and will give immediate feedback to you, either by doing as you requested or by throwing you off, running away, or stopping and eating grass. Teachers and students also need praise and to feel valued, or their motivation and morale will decline and they will ultimately leave or seek to undermine you. When all the basic skills of riding have been acquired and when the conditions are right, riding coaches step away and let horse and rider go it alone, being mindful of not developing dependence. When a school is well led, both students and staff perform well—and the canny headteacher will allow them to take all the credit. *Success it is, when you take that horse to water and it does have a drink.*

Finding headspace

Finally, two headteachers with substantial experience leading schools in complex urban contexts reflect on what they have learned as leaders through both turbulent and satisfying times. They describe their strategies for school improvement and change management—and how they have "kept their heads" on the road to success. *Andrew Webster* illustrates how nothing really prepares one for the ultimate responsibility of headship, the importance of investing in people, and team development and building a supportive network. Finally, *Jerry Collins*, who has a decade's experience both of turning around a failing school and of starting a new one—with both judged by Ofsted as "Outstanding"—reflects on the maturing of his leadership over time, sharing learning, insights, and observations that will resonate with many school leaders.

Andrew Webster, headteacher
Park View Secondary School (11–16), Tottenham, London

Although now well established as headteacher of a diverse and fully inclusive mixed comprehensive in the West Green area of Tottenham in north London, I still believe that nothing truly prepares you for the challenges of Headship. While training and working as an assistant and deputy headteacher in challenging Newham schools, I was well supported by Ambition Institute (previously the Future Leaders Trust), an education charity experienced in developing headteachers and principals for the country's most disadvantaged schools. Having completed five years as a deputy head in an outstanding inner city school in Islington, my assumption was that I had it all under control: I would breeze into the role and immediately make a massive and lasting difference to the lives of young people fortunate enough to experience my leadership—a bit like a supercharged version of the film, "Dead Poets' Society". I was mistaken.

A question commonly asked in headship interviews is, "Can you explain the difference between being a deputy head and a head?" My answers would focus on strategic leadership, driving vision, values, ethos and budget control and that other classic answer of "having total accountability". I now realize that I did not have an idea of exactly what this last answer meant—until I was in post. I think that if headteachers or principals regularly took a step back and considered deeply the level of responsibility that they have, many might pick an alternative career. I would like to make very clear from the outset that this is not a grumble about headship. Every day I feel honoured that sensible people have trusted me with leading one of the most important assets in their community. Headship is a privilege, and anyone who questions that does not deserve the position. That said, it does not come without its challenges. My learning curve continues to be exponential—and not only in order to survive the job. More importantly, the young people in my care deserve to be safe and to experience schooling that suitably prepares them for the rest of their lives.

I will now outline some of the support strategies that my senior leadership team and I have used to move forward and stay (relatively) sane in what is a genuinely high-pressure and high-stakes environment. I was incredibly fortunate that, following my appointment, the governors commissioned a very experienced interim headteacher to support me for two terms. This is the first time that I have publicly acknowledged that I couldn't have done it without him. I was also very lucky to have been offered executive coaching throughout my time as a trainee headteacher on the Future Leaders programme, maintaining regular contact with highly experienced leaders. I was initially very sceptical of coaching. I believe my default position as a leader is edging towards "directive", and the idea of spending vital minutes and hours talking without finding a quick answer felt a waste of time. What could they possibly think of that I hadn't already tried? I have come to realize, however, just how important it is to structure time to be reflective of one's own and others' practice—although time-consuming, the rewards outweigh the risks.

The nature of headship requires the ability to manage a conveyor belt of contrasting challenges and decisions involving a wide range of stakeholders—pupils, parents, teachers, support staff, community leaders, politicians, press—on a daily, minute-by-minute basis. As I became more established, I worked towards developing my senior and middle leaders into teams who are confident in making effective leadership choices in the best interests of our pupils and the community. That said, I know that I will always be personally accountable for their decisions, good or bad.

I have invested heavily in a range of development activities to support reflective practice at all levels in the school, although my focus in writing here is on building my vital senior leadership team. The previous interim head shifted the culture of senior leadership from individuals working independently in silos—often oblivious to the "bigger picture"—to one of team cohesion and joint accountability. He had inherited a school where many leaders were not equipped with the skills or confidence to offer and receive criticism or feedback in a balanced and supportive manner. This had led to a culture of paranoia and resistance to constructive feedback that permeated the school. When senior leaders in a school don't trust and respect each other, this is soon reflected across the school. The previous headteacher and I have since observed that, while he had given the senior leadership team the confidence to open "cans of worms" across the school, it was my job to deal with the contents.

School improvement often involves changing organizational culture and raising expectations of staff. I recall one particularly challenging feedback session from a lesson observation. After a very positive first 20 minutes discussing the strengths of the lesson with the teacher, I commented that unfortunately there was no evidence that students had made much progress over time and that the level of challenge in the work was not sufficient to support this. What started as a very productive, almost jovial discussion shifted immediately into accusations against me of ignorance, misogyny, incompetence, stupidity, and racism. While this was indeed an extreme response, it highlighted that staff in the school were perhaps not used to receiving critical feedback on their practice and that this was something I should prioritize.

This experience, alongside several other very challenging first conversations, served as a catalyst to make the development of reflective practice a key priority across the school. I have introduced a 360° review process with my senior leadership team, followed by a session to compare team members' views of their own practice to the perception of others, facilitated by an experienced consultant. As part of this process, I volunteered to be interviewed in front of the rest of the team, discussing openly why I believed that others' perceptions of me as a leader were as they were. The team were then given the opportunity to work together to discuss their own findings, feelings, and aspirations for the school and themselves.

While it would be inaccurate to suggest that this one event was completely responsible for shifting the dynamic of our team, it certainly played a big part. Senior meetings are now open, honest, and (usually) very good fun. Everyone is confident to speak their mind, and it is rare that people take feedback or criticism badly. When things haven't been received well, we have worked together as a team to get back to a positive standpoint and regularly review our progress.

I have also arranged executive coaching for other members of my senior leadership team. When faced with school budget cuts, the idea of paying not insignificant amounts of money so that one or two people in a team have a level of personal attention may seem counterintuitive. I am now confident that it is not. People working in schools never have enough time to reflect. As mentioned earlier, my default position is to "tell" people how to fix issues, and rarely can I commit the time necessary in a working day to best support those who might need it most— even if I had the prerequisite skills. I am also their line-manager, and I have found from personal experience that admitting where you may be weakest to your boss is rather scary. Good coaches have the skills to focus and personalize issues while maintaining the position of "critical friend". This gives school leaders the confidence to be more honest and open about their situations and the emotions that these often arouse. In my experience, leaders who have benefitted from executive coaching are more willing to return to line management conversations that could otherwise have been perceived as challenging, with a renewed sense of confidence.

I believe that early intervention is best. Historically at Park View, fear of challenging poor professional conduct and low expectations over time had led to extended staff sickness, grievances, unfilled vacancies, breakdowns in trust and relationships, paranoia, compromise agreements, and staff shortages. If cost were a primary concern, these outcomes are all far more expensive and toxic than dealing with issues when they first arise. I have come to believe that giving people the skills to reflect and adjust in a structured and supportive environment will, in the long run, bring about the biggest gains for my school.

I accept that I am totally accountable for the outcomes of our young people, and this can be an intimidating prospect. However, I have realized that as I develop the skills of those around me and ensure that they are empowered to support their own development, the job may not be impossible.

Jerry Collins, North London Regional Director for Ark Schools former Principal of Pimlico and Ark John Keats Academies, London

I was a principal for ten years, a role that I found to be the most rewarding and invigorating since I entered the teaching profession. It is a role that shaped me professionally and personally, and it is one that, at times, I found hugely challenging. I believe there are common emotional and psychological challenges all leaders face, but there will be a multitude of responses to these challenges. Responses depend on one's own background, the quality of role-specific training, preparedness for leadership, emotional resilience, and the context of the organization and culture within which one is working. I have set out below some of the challenges I faced and my responses.

I think almost everyone who seeks a principal's position has a keen desire to lead and to shape the direction of their school. While this is a useful trait in school leaders, I believe it can also lead to significant emotional challenges. Until recently there was the much-espoused myth of the "principal personality"—the outgoing, confident, larger than life school leader. This put pressure on principals, and there was a startling lack of insight and guidance on how effective schools are run and led.

There was much on leadership traits and leadership outcomes but little codified best practice on leading a school that is highly effective in all aspects of its practice. I found the sheer volume of areas that I was supposed to lead on almost overwhelming at times. I was also weighed down by the fact that I simply did not have the requisite expertise to make confident decisions in these areas—building design, budgets, IT infrastructure, contracts, and other operational matters. While I had colleagues leading in these areas, final decisions rested with me, and I was often ill-prepared to make these. Finding time to develop expertise in these areas—which with some I never quite did—also added to the psychological burden of trying to turn around a school in a precarious position in my first headship.

The pressures of exam results and Ofsted inspections were significant emotional challenges for me during my time as a principal. The emotions generated by these were not always negative, as in some ways they were positive drivers for me and I was excited and motivated greatly by both. However, those sleepless nights before GCSE results and the sinking feeling when that "Ofsted call" came will live with me forever! My main psychological challenge with both exam results and Ofsted was to ensure I did not see them as personal reflection on me—if results were good and Ofsted Outstanding, I was not the greatest educator of the 21st century, or, if both were poor, I was not a failed principal who would be sacked and never lead a school again!

In many ways, I had a very fixed mindset when I first became a principal. I took things very personally and also felt personally responsible for every aspect of the school's performance. If a pupil behaved badly on the way home from school, I felt a personal failing. This impeded my ability to learn from mistakes and to see them as opportunities to learn and use my skills. Focusing on the negative led to poor thinking and reactive rather than responsive behaviours.

Leading change is emotionally and psychologically testing. In the face of all the challenges, I sometimes found it difficult to be that positive role model, leading change from the front.

There were no magic solutions to the challenges presented above. Undoubtedly experience helped and, in my case, enabled me to gain a better perspective and clarity in my thinking. Over the years, I developed a very clear vision for building highly effective schools, and this guided me in all key decisions. On operational issues, I sought to make appointments and create structures that meant little input was required from me. For my second headship I moved to a Multi-Academy Trust (MAT) that provided high-quality support in areas outside my expertise.

The MAT was also very values-driven, and this made it much easier for me to ask for help in areas where I required support.

Recruiting high-quality staff, aligned to my vision, was a hugely significant factor in helping me meet the emotional challenges of leadership. I did not compromise when recruiting staff, and this has meant I worked with highly educated colleagues who shared my vision and values. This made the working environment professional, supportive, mission-driven, less stressful, and eminently more enjoyable. Starting a school from scratch—as I did in my second headship—made this far easier than inheriting a fully operational school, as I did first time around.

When I first became a principal, a very helpful colleague told me it was the loneliest position in the world! For me, leading a school was a real privilege, as it enabled me to bring positivity, direction, and real hope to the day-to-day experiences of large numbers of people. However, there are issues that cannot be discussed with all staff and which can magnify and take up a lot of thinking space if not shared. In both my headships I had a vice principal who came with me from my previous school and whom I trusted implicitly. Having these colleagues had a significant impact on my ability to share my thinking and feelings and to negate my tendency to magnify problems or react impulsively. I also met with an experienced executive coach for a number of years, and I found those sessions helped move my thinking forward on particular issues. I would advise anyone going into headship to ensure they have a base of trusted and supportive colleagues both inside and outside the organization to share their thinking and emotions with.

Finally, developing my personal organization and theoretical knowledge helped me meet the emotional and psychological challenges of leadership. The very nature of working in a school means new and unforeseen challenges arise on a daily basis. I found that the better prepared I was for the routine and foreseeable, the less impact the unforeseeable had and the better I responded. I became much better at planning the year, the term, the week, and the day. I also became much better at leveraging my work on high-impact activities. I lost the need to be the big-personality principal and instead became determined to ensure that my colleagues and I left a legacy at our school, so that others could continue our work seamlessly. I read far more widely than I had when I first became a principal. A number of books influenced me and helped give me that sense of direction and clarity that lessens the emotional and psychological stresses of uncertainty. *Teach Like a Champion* (Lemov, 2010), *Leverage Leadership* (Bambrick-Santoyo, 2012), *Mindset* (Dweck, 2012), *Bounce* (Syed, 2010), *Switch* (Heath & Heath, 2010) and

The Seven Habits of Highly Effective People (Covey, 1989) are ones that were particularly helpful.

Leading schools undoubtedly presents emotional and psychological challenges, but this can also be seen as a motivating factor—good leaders accept these challenges and seek solutions. A strong personal vision, a network of trusted colleagues, coaching, good personal organization, and open-mindedness are, in my experience, very helpful in this and enable school leaders to feel a deep sense of personal contentment in doing a truly important job.

REFERENCES

Abrams, F. (2012). Is the new chief inspector of schools just an instrument of government? *The Guardian*, 23 January. Available at: www.theguardian. com/education/2012/jan/23/chief-inspector-schools-michael-wilshaw

Adams, M. (2012). Problem-focused coaching in a mainstream primary school: Reflections on practice. *The Coaching Psychologist*, 8 (1): 27–37.

Adams, M. (2016). Psychology in coaching. In: *Coaching Psychology in Schools: Enhancing Performance, Development and Wellbeing* (pp. 38–54). London: Routledge.

Allen, R. (2017). *Making Teaching a Job Worth Doing (Again)*. Caroline Benn Memorial Lecture, London, House of Commons. Available at: https:// socedassoc.files.wordpress.com/2017/11/caroline-benn-lecture-2017-by-rebecca-allen.pdf

Allen, W. (2009). *The Heart of the Headteacher: The Emotional Dimension of School Leadership*. Research Associate Report, National College for School Leadership, Autumn.

Ancona, D., Malone, T., Orlikowski, W., & Senge, P. (2008). In praise of the incomplete leader. *Harvard Business Review*, February.

Armstrong, D. (2004). Emotions in organizations: Disturbance or intelligence? In: C. Huffington, W, Halton, D. Armstrong, & J. Pooley (Eds.), *Working Below the Surface: The Emotional Life of Contemporary Organizations* (pp. 11–27). London: Karnac.

Armstrong, D. (2005). *Organization in the Mind: Psychoanalysis, Group Relations, and Organizational Consultancy*. London: Karnac.

Aurelius, M. (2015). *Meditations by Marcus Aurelius*. Sweden: Wisehouse Classics.

319

Avalos, B. (2011). Teacher professional development in *Teaching and Teacher Education* over ten years. *Teaching and Teacher Education*, 27 (1): 10–20.

Avolio, B. J., & Gardner, W. L. (2005). Authentic leadership development: Getting to the root of positive forms of leadership. *Leadership Quarterly*, 16 (3): 315–338.

Baars, S., Bernardes, E. Elwick, A. Malortie, A. McAleavy, T. McInerney, L., et al. (2014). *Lessons from London Schools: Investigating the Success*. Reading: CFBT Education Trust.

Balint, M. (1957). *The Doctor, His Patient and the Illness*. Tunbridge Wells: Pitman Medical.

Bambrick-Santoyo, P. (2012). *Leverage Leadership: A Practical Guide to Building Exceptional Schools*. San Francisco, CA: Jossey-Bass.

Bandura, A. (1986). *Social Foundations of Thought and Action: A Social Cognitive Theory*. Englewood Cliffs, NJ: Prentice-Hall.

Barber, M., Chijioke, C., & Mourshed, M. (Eds.) (2010). *How the World's Most Improved School Systems Keep Getting Better*. London: McKinsey & Company.

Barber, M., & Mourshed, M. (2007). *How the World's Best Performing School Systems Come Out on Top*. London: McKinsey & Company.

Barr, M., & van Nieuwerburgh, C. (2015). Teachers' experiences of an introductory coaching training workshop in Scotland: An interpretative phenomenological analysis. *International Coaching Psychology Review*, 10: 190–204.

Benington, J., & Hartley, J. (2009). *Whole Systems Go! Improving Leadership across the Whole Public Service System*. London: National School of Government.

Bernstein, B. (1970). Education cannot compensate for society. *New Society*, 15 (387): 344–347.

Berwick, G. (2010). *Engaging in Excellence, Vol. 2: Moral Capital*. London: Olevi Press.

Bion, W. R. (1961). *Experiences in Groups and Other Papers*. London: Tavistock Publications.

Bion, W. R. (1962). *Learning from Experience*. London: Heinemann. Reprinted London: Karnac 1984.

Bollas, C. (1987). *The Shadow of the Object: Psychoanalysis of the Unthought Known*. New York: Columbia University Press.

Briggs Myers, I. (2000). *Introduction to Type* (6th edition). Mountain View, CA: Consulting Psychologists Press.

Briggs Myers, I., McCaulley, M. H., Quenk, N. L., & Hammer, A. (1998). *MBTI Manual: A Guide to the Development and Use of the Myers-Briggs Type Indicator* (3rd edition). Palo Alto, CA: Consulting Psychologists Press.

Brighouse, T. M., & Fullisk, L. (Eds.) (2007). *Education in a Global City: Essays from London*. London: UCL Institute of Education.

Brighouse, T. M., & Woods, D. C. (2013). *The A–Z of School Improvement, Principles and Practice*. London: Bloomsbury Education.

Brown, C. (Ed.) (2015). *Leading the Use of Research and Evidence in Schools*. London: IOE Press.

Bubb, S., & Earley, P. (2007). *Leading and Managing CPD* (2nd edition). London: Sage.

Bush, T., & Glover, D. (2014). School leadership models: What do we know? *School Leadership and Management, 34* (5): 553–571.

Campbell, D., Draper, R., & Huffington, C. (1991). *A Systemic Approach to Consultation*. London: Karnac.

Campbell, J. (2016a). *Coaching and "Coaching Approach": What's the Difference?* Chatswood, NSW: Growth Coaching International. Available at: www.growthcoaching.com.au/articles-new/coaching-and-coaching-approach-what-s-the-difference

Campbell, J. (2016b). Coaching in schools. In: C. van Nieuwerburgh (Ed.), *Coaching in Professional Contexts* (pp. 131–144). London: Sage.

Canham, C. (2002). Group and gang states of mind. *Journal of Child Psychotherapy, 28* (2): 113–127.

Canham, H. (2000). Exporting the Tavistock Model to social services: Clinical, consultative and teaching aspects. *Journal of Social Work Practice, 14* (2): 125–133.

Cantore, S., & Hick, W. (2013). Dialogic OD in practice: Conversational approaches to change in a UK primary school. *OD Practitioner, 45*: 5–10.

Center for Theory of Change (2019). *What Is Theory of Change?*. www.theory-ofchange.org/what-is-theory-of-change

Chapman, C. (2013). Academy federations, chains, and teaching schools in England: Reflections on leadership, policy, and practice. *Journal of School Choice, 7* (3): 334–352.

Charan, R., Drotter, S., & Noel, J. (2001). *The Leadership Pipeline: How to Build the Leadership Powered Company*. San Francisco, CA: Jossey-Bass.

CiPD (2017). *Identifying Learning and Development Needs*. London: Chartered Institute of Personnel and Development. Available at: www.cipd.co.uk/knowledge/fundamentals/people/development/learning-needs-factsheet

Claeys, A., Paterson, C., & Kempton, J. (2014). *Regional Challenges: A Collaborative Approach to Improving Education*. London: Centre Forum.

Clutterbuck, D., & Megginson, D. (2005). The business case for creating a coaching culture. *Making Coaching Work: Creating a Coaching Culture* (pp. 1–13). London: Chartered Institute of Personnel and Development.

Clutterbuck, D., Whitaker, C., & Lucas, M. (2016). *Coaching Supervision: A Practical Guide for Supervisees*. London: Routledge.

Collingwood, H. (2001). Personal histories: Leaders remember the moments and people that shaped them. *Harvard Business Review, 79* (11): 1–23.

Conger, J. A., & Kanungo, R. N. (1987). Toward a behavioral theory of charismatic leadership in organizational settings. *Academy of Management Review, 12* (4): 637–647.

Connolly, J. A., & Viswesvaran, C. (2002). *Assessing the Construct Validity of a Measure of Learning Agility*. Presentation at the conference of the Society for Industrial and Organizational Psychology Toronto, Canada.

Cordingley, P. (2015). *A World-Class Teaching Profession: Response to the DfE Consultation*. Coventry: CUREE. Available at: www.curee.co.uk/files/publication/[site-timestamp]/A_World_Class_Teaching_Profession_Feb_2015-publish.pdf

Cordingley, P., Higgins, S., Greany, T., & Coe, R. (2015). *Developing Great Teaching: Lessons from the International Reviews into Effective Professional Development*. London: The Teacher Development Trust. Available at: http://tdtrust.org/wp-content/uploads/2015/10/DGT-Summary.pdf

Coughlan, S. (2017). OfSTED Warns Schools against "Disadvantage One-Upmanship". BBC News, 13 December.

Covey, S. R. (1989). *The Seven Habits of Highly Effective People: Restoring the Work Ethic*. Sydney: Simon & Schuster.

Covey, S. R. (2004). *The 7 Habits of Highly Effective People: Restoring the Character Ethic*. New York: Free Press.

Covey, S. M. R. (2006). *The Speed of Trust: The One Thing That Changes Everything*. New York: Free Press.

Craig, I. (2017). Toxic leadership. In: P. Earley & T. Greany (Eds.), *School Leadership and Education System Reform* (pp. 182–190). London: Bloomsbury.

Cranston, N. (2013). School leaders leading: Professional responsibility not accountability as the key focus. *Educational Management, Administration & Leadership, 41* (2): 129–142.

Creasy, J., & Paterson, F. (2005). *Leading Coaching in Schools*. Nottingham: National College for Teaching and Leadership.

Creissen, T. (2008). *The Impact of the Leadership Programme for Serving Heads*. Doctoral dissertation, The Open University, Milton Keynes. Available at: http://oro.open.ac.uk/59986/1/491166.pdf

Croft, J. (2016). *Taking a Lead: How to Access the Leadership Premium*. Research Report No. 9. London: Centre for the Study of Market Reform of Education.

Cunliffe, A., & Eriksen, M. (2011). Relational leadership. *Human Relations, 64* (11): 1425–1449.

Davies, B., & Davies, B. J. (2005). Strategic management. In: B. Davies (Ed.), *The Essentials of School Leadership* (pp. 13–36). London: Sage.

Day, C., & Sammons, P. (2013). *Successful Leadership: A Review of the International Literature*. Nottingham: CfBT Education Trust.

Day, C., Sammons, P., Hopkins, D., Harris, A., Leithwood, K., Gu, Q., et al. (2009). *The Impact of School Leadership on Pupil Outcomes: Final Report*. Nottingham: Department for Education.

Day, C., Sammons, P., Leithwood, K., Hopkins, D., Harris, A., Gu, Q., et al. (2010). *Ten Strong Claims about Successful School Leadership*. Nottingham: National College for Teaching and Leadership.

Day, D. V., Fleenor, J. W., Atwater, L. E., Sturm, R. E., & McKee, R. A. (2014). Advances in leader and leadership development: A review of 25 years of research and theory. *Leadership Quarterly, 25* (1): 63–82.

DCSF (2008). *Vision for London, 2008–2011: London on the Way to World Class.* Nottingham: Department for Children, Schools and Families. Available at: Nationalarchives.gov.uk

Deloitte (2014). *Global Human Capital Trends 2014: Engaging the 21st-Century Workforce.* www2.deloitte.com/content/dam/Deloitte/ar/Documents/human-capital/arg_hc_global-human-capital-trends-2014_09062014%20(1).pdf

Dewey, J. (1933). *How We Think: A Restatement of the Relation of Reflective Thinking to the Educational Process.* Boston, MA: D. C. Heath.

Dewey, J. (1938). *Experience and Education.* New York: Kappa Delta Pi.

de Shazer, S. (1985). *Keys to Solution in Brief Therapy.* New York: Norton.

DfE (2010). *The Importance of Teaching: The Schools' White Paper.* London: Department for Education.

DfE (2015a). *The Governors' Handbook.* London: Department for Education.

DfE (2015b). *Headteachers' Standards.* London: Department for Education. Available at: www.gov.uk/government/publications/national-standards-of-excellence-for-headteachers

DfE (2015c). *A World-Class Teaching Profession.* London: Department for Education. Available at: www.gov.uk/government/uploads/system/uploads/attachment_data/file/430227/150319_WCTP_response.pdf

DfE (2017a). *National Professional Qualification for Senior Leadership (NPQSL).* London: Department for Education. Available at: www.gov.uk/guidance/national-professional-qualification-for-senior-leadership-npqsl

DfE (2017b). *EduBase* [May]. London: Department for Education.

DfE (2017c). *Teaching and Leadership Innovation Fund.* London: Department for Education. Available at: www.gov.uk/guidance/teaching-and-leadership-innovation-fund

DfES (2005). *London Schools: Rising to the Challenge.* London: Department for Education and Skills.

DfES/DoH (2006). *Report on the Implementation of Standard 9 of the National Service Framework for Children, Young People and Maternity Services.* London: DoH.

Dinh, J. E., Lord, R. G., Gardner, W. L., Meuser, J. D., Liden, R. C., & Hu, J. (2014). Leadership theory and research in the new millennium: Current theoretical trends and changing perspectives. *Leadership Quarterly, 25* (1): 36–62.

Drath, W. H., McCauley, C. J., Palus, C. J., Van Velsor, E., O'Connor, M. G., & McGuire, J. B. (2008). Direction, alignment, commitment: Toward a more integrative ontology of leadership. *Leadership Quarterly, 19*: 635–653.

Drucker, P. (2011). Leadership quote. *Integral Leadership Review*, August. http://integralleadershipreview.com/3483-leadership-quote-3

Dweck, C. (2012). *Mindset: How You Can Fulfil Your Potential*. New York: Ballantine Books.

Earley, P. (1993). Developing competence in schools: A critique of standards-based approaches to management development. *Education Management and Administration*, 21 (4): 233–244.

Earley, P. (2013). *Exploring the School Leadership Landscape: Changing Demands, Changing Realities*. London: Bloomsbury.

Earley, P. (2016). Global trends and challenges for school leaders: Keeping the focus on learning. *Educational, Cultural and Psychological Studies*, 14: 21–33.

Earley, P., & Bubb, S. (2014). Data and inquiry driving school improvement: Recent developments in England. *Journal of Educational, Cultural and Psychological Studies*, 9: 167–184.

Earley, P., Higham, R., Allen, R., Allen, T., Howson, J., Nelson, R., et al. (2012). *Review of the Leadership Landscape*. Nottingham: National College for School Leadership.

Earley, P., & Weindling, D. (2004). *Understanding School Leadership*. London: Paul Chapman/Sage.

Easton, L. B. (2009). *Protocols for Professional Learning*. The Professional Learning Community Series. Alexandria, VA: ASCD.

Edge, K., Descours, K., & Frayman, K. (2016). Generation X school leaders as agents of care: Leader and teacher perspectives from Toronto, New York City and London. *Societies*, 6 (2, Article 8): 1–21.

Ehren, M., Perryman, J., & Shackleton, N. (2014). Setting expectations for good education: How Dutch school inspections drive improvement. *School Effectiveness and School Improvement: An International Journal of Research, Policy and Practice*, 26 (2): 296–327.

Elwick, A., & McAleavy, T. (2015), *Interesting Cities: Five Approaches to Urban School Reform*. Reading: CFBT Trust.

Fitzsimons, D., Turnbull James, K., & Denyer, D. (2011). Alternative approaches for studying shared and distributed leadership. *International Journal of Management Reviews*, 13: 313–328.

Fletcher, J. K. (2004). The paradox of post-heroic leadership: An essay on gender, power, and transformational change. *Leadership Quarterly*, 15: 647–6661.

Forde, C., McMahon, M., Gronn, P., & Martin, M. (2013). Being a leadership development coach: A multi-faceted role. *Educational Management Administration & Leadership*, 41: 105–119.

Francis, R. (2013). *Report of the Mid Staffordshire NHS Foundation Trust Public Inquiry*. London; Stationery Office.

Freud, S. (1901). *The Psychopathology of Everyday Life. Standard Edition*, 6.

Fullan, M. (2003). *The Moral Imperative of School Leadership*. Ontario: Corwin Press.

Fullan, M. (2005). *Leadership and Sustainability*. Ontario: Corwin Press.

Fullan, M. (2007). *The New Meaning of Educational Change*. New York: Teachers College Press.

Fullan, M., & Boyle, A. (2014). *Big-City School Reforms: Lessons from New York, Toronto and London*. New York: Teachers College Press & the Ontario Principals' Council.

George, B. (2004). *Authentic Leadership: Rediscovering the Secrets to Creating Lasting Value*. Hoboken, NJ: Wiley & Sons.

Gitsham, M. (2009). *Developing the Global Leader of Tomorrow*. Berkhamsted: Ashridge Business School. Available at: www.unprme.org/resource-docs/DevelopingTheGlobalLeaderOfTomorrowReport.pdf

GLA (2017). *Annual London Education Report*. London: Greater London Authority.

Goff, P., Goldring, E., Guthrie, J. E., & Bickman, L. (2014). Changing principals' leadership through feedback and coaching. *Journal of Educational Administration, 52*: 682–704.

Goffee, R., & Jones, G. (2000). Why should anyone be led by you? *Harvard Business Review, 78* (5): 62–70.

Golawski, A., Bamford, A., & Gersch, I. (2013). *Swings and Roundabouts: A Self-Coaching Workbook for Parents and Those Considering Becoming Parents*. London: Karnac.

Goldacre, B. (2013). *Building Evidence into Education*. London: Department for Education. Available at: www.gov.uk/government/news/building-evidence-into-education

Goleman, D. (1996). *Emotional Intelligence*. London: Bloomsbury.

Goleman, D. (1998). *Working with Emotional Intelligence*. New York: Bantam Dell.

Goleman, D. (2000). Leadership that gets results. *Harvard Business Review, 78*: 78–90.

Goleman, D., Boyatzis, R., & McKee, A. (2013). *Primal leadership: Unleashing the Power of Emotional Intelligence*. Boston, MA: Harvard Business Press.

Gorard, S. (2010). Education *can* compensate for society—a bit. *British Journal of Educational Studies, 58* (1): 47–65.

Gormley, H., & van Nieuwerburgh, C. (2014). Developing coaching cultures: A review of the literature. *Coaching: An International Journal of Theory, Research and Practice, 7*: 90–101.

Graen, G. B., & Uhl-Bien, M. (1995). Relationship-based approach to leadership: Development of leader-member exchange (LMX) theory of leadership over 25 years: Applying a multi-level multi-domain perspective. *Leadership Quarterly, 6* (2): 219–247.

Graham, G. (2013). A coach-therapy journey: Destination ICT with parents. *Association of Integrative Coach-Therapist Professionals, 6*: 16–20.

Grant, V. (2015). Stress, fear and tears—The truth about being a headteacher. *The Guardian*, 3 February.

Greany, T. (2015). How can evidence inform teaching and decision making across 21,000 autonomous schools?: Learning from the journey in England. In: C. Brown (Ed.), *Leading the Use of Research and Evidence in Schools* (pp. 11–29). London: Institute of Education Press.

Greany, T., & Brown, C. (2017). The evidence informed school system in England: Where should school leaders be focusing their efforts? *International Journal of Education Policy & Leadership*, 12 (3): 1–22.

Greany, T., Doughty, J., Earley, P., Farrar, M., Grainger, P., Hodgson, A., & Nelson, R. (2014). *Leading in Volatile Times: Learning from Leadership Beyond the Education and Training Sector*. IOE Report. London: Education and Training Foundation.

Greany. T., & Earley, P. (2017). Introduction. In: P. Earley & T. Greany (Eds.), *School Leadership and Education System Reform* (pp. 1–14). London: Bloomsbury.

Gu, Q., Rea, S., Smethem, L., Dunford, J., Varley, M., & Sammons, P. (2015). *Teaching Schools Evaluation: Final Report*. London: Department for Education.

Gurdjian, P., Halbeisen, T., & Lane, K. (2014). Why leadership-development programs fail. *McKinsey Quarterly*, January.

Handy, C., & Aitken, R. (1986). *Understanding Schools as Organisations*. London: Penguin.

Hargreaves, A. (1994). *Changing Teachers, Changing Times: Teachers' Work and Culture in the Post-modern Age*. New York: Teachers College Press.

Hargreaves, A., & Skelton, J. (2012). Politics and systems of coaching and mentoring. In: S. J. Fletcher & C. A. Mullen (Eds.), *The Sage Handbook of Mentoring and Coaching in Education* (pp. 122–38). London: Sage.

Hargreaves, D. H. (2003). *Education Epidemic: Transforming Secondary Schools Through Innovation Networks*. London: Demos.

Harris, A., & Spillane, J. (2008). Distributed leadership through the looking glass. *Management in Education*, 22 (1): 31–34.

Harris, M. (1968). Consultation project in a comprehensive school. In: M. Harris Williams (Ed.), *Collected Papers of Martha Harris and Esther Bick* (pp. 283–310). Strath Tay: Clunie Press, 1987.

Haslam, S., Reicher, S., & Platow, M. (2010). *The New Psychology of Leadership*. Hove: Psychology Press.

Hattie, J. (2015). *What Works Best in Education: The Politics of Collaborative Expertise*. London: Pearson.

Hawkins, P. (2012). *Creating a Coaching Culture*. Maidenhead: Open University Press.

Heath, C., & Heath, D. (2010). *Switch: How to Change Things When Change Is Hard*. New York:: Random House.

Heifetz, R. (1994). *Leadership Without Easy Answers*. Cambridge, MA: Harvard University Press.

Heifetz, R. (2002). *Leadership on the Line: Staying Alive through the Dangers of Leading*. Boston, MA: Harvard Business School.

Hersey, P. (1986). *The Situational Leader*. Englewood Cliffs, NJ: Prentice-Hall.

Higham, R., Hopkins, D., & Matthews, P. (2009). *System Leadership in Practice*. Maidenhead: Open University Press.

Hill, A., & Matthews, P. (2008). *Schools Leading Schools: The Power and Potential of National Leaders of Education*. Nottingham: National College for School Leadership.

Hill, A., Mellon, L., Laker, B., & Goddard, J. (2016). The one type of leader who can turn around a failing school. *Harvard Business Review, 20 October*. Available at: https://hbr.org/2016/10/the-one-type-of-leader-who-can-turn-around-a-failing-school

Hill, R., Dunford, J., Parish, N., Rea, S., & Sandals, L. (2012). *The Growth of Academy Chains: Implications for Leaders and Leadership*. Nottingham: National College for School Leadership.

Hirschhorn, L. (2003). *Politics, Strategy and Passion*. Paper presented at ISPSO Symposium, Boston, Massachusetts.

Hooijberg, R., & Lane, N. (2009). Using multisource feedback coaching effectively in executive education. *Academy of Management Learning & Education, 8* (4): 483–493.

Hooker, T. (2014). The benefits of peer coaching as a support system for early childhood education students. *International Journal of Evidence Based Coaching and Mentoring, 12*: 109–122.

Huffington, C. (2004). What women leaders can tell us. In: C., Huffington, D. Armstrong, W., Halton, L. Hoyle, & J. Pooley (Eds.), *Working Below the Surface: The Emotional Life of Contemporary Organizations* (pp. 49–66). London: Karnac.

Huffington, C., James, K., & Armstrong, D. (2004). What is the emotional cost of distributed leadership? In: C. Huffington, D. Armstrong, W. Halton, L. Hoyle, & J. Pooley (Eds.), *Working Below the Surface: The Emotional Life of Contemporary Organizations* (pp. 67–82). London: Karnac.

Jackson, E. (2002). Mental health in schools: What about the staff? Thinking about the impact of work discussion groups in school settings. *Journal of Child Psychotherapy, 28* (2): 129–146.

Jackson, E. (2005). Developing observation skills in school settings: The importance and impact of "work discussion groups" for staff. *International Journal of Infant Observation and Its Applications, 8* (1): 5–17.

Jackson, E. (2008a). The development of work discussion groups in educational settings. *Journal of Child Psychotherapy, 34* (1): 62–82.

Jackson, E. (2008b). Work discussion groups at work. In: M. Rustin & J. Bradley (Eds.), *Work Discussion: Learning from Reflective Practice in Work with Children and Families* (pp. 51–72). London: Karnac.

Jackson, E. (2014). Work discussion groups as a container for sexual anxiety in schools. In: D. Armstrong & M. Rustin (Eds.), *Social Defences against Anxiety: Explorations in a Paradigm* (pp. 269–283). London: Karnac.

Jackson, J. (1970). Child psychotherapy in a day school for maladjusted children. *Journal of Child Psychotherapy, 2* (4): 54–62.

James, C., & Connolly, U. (2000). *Effective Change in Schools*. London: Rout-ledgeFalmer.

James-Ward, C. (2013). The coaching experience of four novice principals. *International Journal of Mentoring and Coaching in Education*, 2: 21–33.

Janis, I. (1972). *Victims of Groupthink: A Psychological Study of Foreign-Policy Decisions and Fiascoes*. Boston, MA: Houghton Mifflin.

Jung, C. (1923). *Psychological Types*. Princeton, NJ: Princeton University Press, 1971.

Keohane, N. (2010). *Thinking about Leadership*. Boston, MA: Princeton University Press.

Kerr, J., & Toriello, M. (Eds.) (2012). *The State of Human Capital 2012: False Summit. Why the Human Capital Function Still Has Far to Go*. The Conference Board and McKinsey & Company. Available at: www.mckinsey.com/~/media/mckinsey/dotcom/client_service/organization/pdfs/state_of_human_capital_2012.ashx

Khan, W. A. (1992). To be fully there: Psychological presence at work. *Human Relations*, 45 (4): 321–349.

Kilburg, R. (2000). *Executive Coaching: Developing Managerial Wisdom in a World of Chaos*. Washington, DC: American Psychological Association.

Kipling, R. (1910). *Rewards and Fairies*. New York: Doubleday, Page and Company.

Klauber, T. (1999). Observation "at work": The application of infant observation and its teaching to seminars in work discussion. *International Journal of Infant Observation*, 2 (3): 30–41.

Klein, M. (1931). A contribution to the theory of intellectual inhibition. In: *Love, Guilt and Reparation and Other Works 1921–1945* (pp. 236–247). London: Hogarth Press, 1985.

Knight, J. (2007). *Instructional Coaching: A Partnership Approach to Improving Instruction*. Thousand Oaks, CA: Corwin.

Knight, J. (2011). *Unmistakable Impact: A Partnership Approach for Dramatically Improving Instruction*. Thousand Oaks, CA: Corwin.

Knight, J. (2018). *The Impact Cycle: What Instructional Coaches Should Do to Foster Powerful Improvements in Teaching*. Thousand Oaks, CA: Corwin.

Kolb, D. (1984). *Experiential learning: Experience as the Source of Learning and Development, Vol. 1*. Englewood Cliffs, NJ: Prentice-Hall.

Korn Ferry Institute (2015). *Real World Leadership: Develop Leaders Who Can Drive Real Change*. https://focus.kornferry.com/leadership-and-talent/real-world-leadership-develop-leaders-who-can-drive-real-change

Kotter, J. (2012). *Leading Change*. Boston, MA: Harvard Business Press.

Lacan, J. (1977). *Ecrits: A Selection*. London: Tavistock.

Ladkin, D. (2010), *Re-thinking Leadership: A New Look at Old Questions*. Cheltenham: Edward Elgar.

Lawrence, G., Bain, A., & Gould, L. (1996). The fifth basic assumption. *Free Associations*, 6 (1): 28–55.

Lawrence, G., & Robinson, P. (1975). *Innovation and Its Implementation.* Unpublished paper. London: Tavistock Institute.

Leach, C., & Green, S. (2016). Integrating coaching and positive psychology in education. In: C. van Nieuwerburgh (Ed.), *Coaching in Professional Contexts* (pp. 169–186). London: Sage.

Leadbeater, C. (2008). *What's Next? Twenty One Ideas for Twenty First Century Education.* Luton: The Innovation Unit. Available at: https://charleslead-beater.net/2010/01/whats-next-21-ideas-for-21st-century-education

Leithwood, K., Day, C., Sammons, P., Haris, A., & Hopkins, D. (2006). *Seven Strong Claims About School Leadership.* Nottingham: National College for School Leadership.

Leithwood, K., & Seashore Louis, K. (2012). *Linking Leadership to Student Learning.* San Francisco, CA: Jossey-Bass.

Lemov, D. (2010). *Teach Like a Champion: 49 Techniques That Put Students on the Path to College.* San Francisco, CA: Jossey-Bass.

Lencioni, P. (2005). *Overcoming the Five Dysfunctions of a Team.* San Francisco, CA: Jossey-Bass.

Lencioni, P. (2012). *The Advantage.* San Francisco, CA: Jossey-Bass.

Lombardo, M., & Eichinger, R. (1996). *The Career Architect Development Planner* (1st edition). Minneapolis, MN: Lominger.

Lombardo, M., & Eichinger, R. (2003). *The LEADERSHIP ARCHITECT® Norms and Validity Report.* Minneapolis, MN: Lominger.

Lord, R. G., & Hall, R. J. (2005). Identity, deep structure and the development of leadership skill. *Leadership Quarterly, 16* (4): 591–615.

Louis, K. S., Leithwood, K., Wahlstrom, K., & Anderson, S. (2010). *Learning from Leadership: Investigating the Links to Improved Student Learning.* St Paul, MN: University of Minnesota.

Lupton, R., & Thomson, S. (2015). *The Coalition's Record on Schools: Policy, Spending and Outcomes 2010–2015.* Social Policy in a Cold Climate, Working Paper 13, Joseph Rowntree Foundation/Nuffield Foundation/Trust for London. Manchester: University of Manchester.

Luthans, F., & Peterson, S. J. (2003). 360-degree feedback with systemic coaching: Empirical analysis suggests a winning combination. *Human Resource Management, 42* (3): 243–256.

Marzano, R., Waters, T., & McNulty, B. (2005). *School Leadership That Works: From Research to Results.* Alexandria, VA: Association for Supervision and Curriculum Development.

Maslow, A. (1959). *Motivational Personality.* New York: Harper & Row.

Matthews, P., & McLaughlin, C. (2010). *Up for It? How Good Schools become Great with a Little Help from Their Friends, An Evaluation of the Good to Great Programme.* Nottingham: National College for School Leadership.

Matthews, P., Rea, S., Hill, R. & Gu, Q. (2014). *Freedom to Lead: A Study of Outstanding Primary School Leadership in England.* London: Department for Education.

Matthews, P., & Sammons, P. (2006). *Supporting Leadership and Securing Quality: An Evaluation of the London Leadership Strategy.* Nottingham: National College for School Leadership.

Maxwell, B., & Greany, T. (2015) (with Aspinwall, K., Handscomb, G., Seleznyov, S. & Simkins, T.). *Approaches to Research and Development for "Great Pedagogy" and "Great CPD" in Teaching School Alliances.* Nottingham: National College for Teaching and Leadership.

McCall, M. W. (2010). Recasting leadership development. *Industrial and Organizational Psychology, 3:* 3–19.

McCall, M. W., Lombardo, M. M., & Morrison, A. M. (1989). *The Lessons of Experience: How Successful Executives Develop on the Job.* Lanham, MD: Lexington Books.

McCauley, C., DeRue, S., Yost, P. & Taylor, S. (2014). *Experience-Driven Leader Development: Models, Tools, Best Practices, and Advice for On-the-Job Development.* San Francisco, CA: Wiley.

Menzies, I. (1959). A case study in the functioning of social systems as a defence against anxiety. *Human Relations, 13:* 95–121.

Menzies Lyth, I. (1988). *Containing Anxiety in Institutions: Selected Essays, Vols. 1 and 2.* London: Free Association Books.

Micklewright, J., Jerrim, J., Vignoles, A., Jenkins, A., Ilie, S., Bellarbre, E., et al. (2014). *Teachers in England's Secondary Schools: Evidence from TALIS 2013. Research report.* London: Institute of Education, University of London.

Miller, E. (1993). *From Dependency to Autonomy: Studies in Organisational Change.* London: Free Association Books.

Miller, E., & Rice, A. K. (1967). *Systems of Organisation: The Control of Task and Sentient Boundaries.* London: Tavistock Publications.

Morriss, A., Ely, R., & Frei, F. (2011). Stop holding yourself back. *Harvard Business Review, 89* (1–2). Available at: https://hbr.org/2011/01/managing-yourself-stop-holding-yourself-back

Myatt, M. (2016). *High Challenge, Low Threat.* London: John Catt.

Nadler, D.A., & Spencer, J. L. (1998). *Executive Teams.* San Francisco, CA: Jossey Bass.

NCTL (2016). *Teaching Schools' Evaluation: Final Research Report.* Nottingham: National College for Teaching and Leadership. Available at: https://assets.publishing.service.gov.uk/government/uploads/system/uploads/attachment_data/file/503333/Evaluation_of_Teaching_schools_FINAL_FOR_PUB_25_feb_final_.pdf

Nesta (2014). *DIY Development Impact and You.* Available at: http://diytoolkit.org/media/DIY-Toolkit-Full-Download-A4-Size.pdf

Netolicky, D. M. (2016). Coaching for professional growth in one Australian school: oil in water. *International Journal of Mentoring and Coaching in Education, 5:* 66–68.

Northouse, P. G. (2009). *Leadership: Theory and Practice* (5th edition). London: Sage.

Obholzer, A. (1994). Authority, power and leadership: Contributions from group relations training. In: A. Obholzer & V. Z. Roberts (Eds.), *The Unconscious at Work: Individual and Organisational Stress in the Human Services* (pp. 38–48). London: Routledge.

Obholzer, A. (2004) (with Miller, S.). Leadership, followership, and facilitating the creative workplace. In: C. Huffington, D. Armstrong, W. Halton, L. Hoyle, & J. Pooley (Eds.), *Working Below the Surface: The Emotional Life of Contemporary Organizations* (pp. 33–48). London: Karnac.

OECD (2016). *What Makes a School a Learning Organisation? A Guide for Policy Makers, School Leaders and Teachers*. Paris: Organisation for Economic Co-operation & Development.

Ofsted (2010). *Report on the London Challenge*. https://webarchive.nationalarchives.gov.uk/20141107033128/www.ofsted.gov.uk/resources/london-challenge

Ofsted (2016). *Maintained Schools and Academies Inspection Outcomes as at 31 March 2016*. www.gov.uk/government/statistics/maintained-schools-and-academies-inspections-and-outcomes-as-at-31-march-2016

Ofsted (2018). *School Inspection Hansdbook Annual London Education*. https://assets.publishing.service.gov.uk/government/uploads/system/uploads/attachment_data/file/730127/School_inspection_handbook_section_5_270718.pdf

ONS (2006a). *Statistics of Education: Trends in Attainment Gaps: 2005*. National Statistics Bulletin. London: Office for National Statistics.

Osborne-Lampkin, L., Folsom, J. S., & Herrington, C. D. (2015). *A Systematic Review of the Relationships between Principal Characteristics and Student Achievement* (REL 2016–091).Washington, DC: U.S. Department of Education, Institute of Education Sciences.

Parker, S., & Gallagher, N. (2007). *The Collaborative State: How Working Together Can Transform Public Services*. London: Demos.

Passmore, J., & Brown, A. (2009). Coaching non-adult students for enhanced examination performance: A longitudinal study. *Coaching: An International Journal of Theory, Practice and Research, 2*: 54–64.

Passmore, J., & Jastrzebska, K. (2011). Building a coaching culture: A development journey for organizational development. *Coaching Review, 1*: 89–101.

Pendleton, D., & Furnham, A. (2012). *Leadership: All You Need to Know*. London: Palgrave Macmillan.

Peters, T., & Waterman, R. (1984). *In Search of Excellence: Lessons from America's Best-Run Companies*. New York: Harper & Row.

Petriglieri, G., Wood, J. D., & Petriglieri, J. L. (2011). Up close and personal: Building foundations for leaders' development through the personalization of management learning. *Academy of Management Learning & Education, 10* (3): 430–50.

Piaget, J. (1955). The construction of reality in the child. *Journal of Consulting Psychology, 19* (1): 77.

Pillans, G. (2015). *Leadership Development: Is It Fit for Purpose?* London: Corporate Research Forum.

Priestley, M., Biesta, G., & Robinson, S. (2015). *Teacher Agency: An Ecological Approach.* London: Bloomsbury Academic.

Primary School Headteacher's Blog (2012). *The Musings of a Head Teacher* [24 June]. https://themusingsofaheadteacher.wordpress.com

Quenk, N. (1993). *Beside Ourselves; Our Hidden Personality in Everyday Life.* Mountain View, CA: Davies-Black.

Quenk, N. (2000). *In the Grip: Understanding Type, Stress and the Inferior Function.* Mountain View, CA: Consulting Psychologists Press.

Roberts V. Z. (1994). The organization of work: Contributions from systems theory. In: A. Obholzer & V. Z. Roberts (Eds.), *The Unconscious at Work: Individual and Organizational Stress in the Human Services* (pp. 28–38). London: Routledge.

Robertson, J. (2016). *Coaching Leadership: Building Educational Leadership Capacity Through Partnership* (2nd edition). Wellington, NZ: NZCER Press.

Robertson, J., & Allan, R. (1999). Teachers working in isolation? Enhancing professional conversations. *set: Research Information for Teachers, 2* (Item 3).

Robinson, S. (2012). *School and System Leadership: Changing Roles for Primary Headteachers.* London: Continuum.

Robinson, V. (2011). *Student-Centred Leadership.* San Francisco, CA: Jossey-Bassey.

Rogers, C. (1961). *On Becoming a Person: A Therapist's View of Psychotherapy.* London: Constable & Robinson.

Rustin, M., & Bradley, J. (Eds.) (2008). *Work Discussion: Learning from Reflective Practice in Work with Children and Adolescents,* London, Karnac.

Ryan, R. M., & Deci, E. L. (2000). Self-determination theory and the facilitation of intrinsic motivation, social development and well-being. *American Psychologist, 55*: 68.

Salzberger-Wittenberg, I., Henry, G., & Osborne, E. (Eds.) (1983). *The Emotional Experience of Learning and Teaching.* London: Routledge & Kegan Paul.

Scheer, A., & Jensen, M. (2007). *A New Model of Leadership.* Harvard NOM Research Paper No. 06–10. Available at: http://papers.ssrn.com/abstract=920623

Scheerens, J. (Ed.) (2012). *School Leadership Effects Revisited: Review and Meta-analysis of Empirical Studies.* Utrecht: Springer.

Schleicher, A. (Ed.) (2012). *Preparing Teachers and Developing School Leaders for the 21st Century: Lessons from around the World.* Paris: OECD.

Schutte, N. S., Malouff, J. M., Hall, L. E., Haggerty, D. J., Cooper, J. T., Golden, C. J., & Dornheim, L. (1998). Development and validation of a measure of emotional intelligence. *Personality and Individual Differences, 25* (2): 167–177.

Seashore Louis, K. (2015). Linking leadership to learning: State, district and local effects, *Nordic Journal of Studies in Educational Policy*, 1: 1–10.

Seifert, C. F., & Yukl, G. (2010). Effects of repeated multi-source feedback on the influence behavior and effectiveness of managers: A field experiment. *Leadership Quarterly*, 21 (5): 856.

Seligman, M. E. P., & Csikszentmihalyi, M. (2000). Positive psychology: An introduction. *American Psychologist*, 55: 5–14.

Simkins, T. (2012). Understanding school leadership and management development in England: Retrospect and prospect. *Educational Management, Leadership and Administration*, 40 (5): 621–640.

Sims, H. P., Jr., & Lorenzi, P. (1992). *The New Leadership Paradigm: Social Learning and Cognition in organizations*. Thousand Oaks, CA: Sage.

Smythe, J., & Wrigley, T. (2013). *Living on the Edge: Rethinking Poverty, Class and Schooling*. New York: Peter Lang.

Southworth, G. (2009). Learning-centred leadership. In B. Davies (Ed.), *The Essentials of School Leadership* (2nd edition, pp. 91–111). London: Sage.

Spaten, O. M., & Flensborg, W. (2013). When middle managers are doing employee coaching. *International Coaching Psychology Review*, 8 (2): 18–39.

Stoll, L. (2015). Using evidence, learning and the role of professional learning communities. In: C. Brown (Ed.), *Leading the Use of Research and Evidence in Schools* (pp. 54–65). London: Institute of Education Press.

Sutton Trust (2009). *Attainment Gaps between the Most Deprived and Advantaged Schools*, London: Sutton Trust. Available at http://eprints.lse.ac.uk/23921

Sutton Trust (2011). *Improving the Impact of Teachers on Pupil Achievement in the UK: Interim Findings*. London: Sutton Trust. Available at: https://dera.ioe.ac.uk//30348/

Syed, M. (2010). *Bounce: The Myth of Talent and the Power of Patience*. London: Fourth Estate.

Tichy, N. M. (1989). GE's Crotonville: A staging ground for corporate revolution. *The Academy of Management Executive*, 3 (2): 99–106.

Timperley, H., & Parr, J. (2008). *Coaching as a Process of Knowledge Building and Self-Regulatory Inquiry. Paper presented at the British Educational Research Association Conference*, Edinburgh, September.

Tucker, S. (2010). An investigation of the stresses, pressures and challenges faced by primary school headteachers in a context of organisational change. *Journal of Social Work Practice*, 24 (1): 63–74.

Tuckman, B. (1965). Developmental sequence in small groups. *Psychological Bulletin*, 63 (6): 384–99.

Turquet, P. (1974). Leadership: The individual and the group. In: A. D. Colman & M. H. Geller (Eds.), *Group Relations Reader, Vol. 2* (pp. 71–87). Washington, DC: A. K. Rice Institute, 1985.

Turquet, P. (1975). Threats to identity in the large group. In: L. Kreeger (Ed.), *The Large Group: Dynamics and Therapy* (pp. 87–144). London: Maresfield.

Uhl-Bien, M. (2006). Relational leadership theory: Exploring the social processes of leadership and organizing. *Leadership Quarterly*, 17 (6): 654–676.

van Nieuwerburgh, C. (2012). Coaching in education: An overview. In: C. van Nieuwerburgh (Ed.), *Coaching in Education: Getting Better Results for Students, Educators, and Parents* (pp. 3–23). London: Karnac.

van Nieuwerburgh, C. (2014). *Introduction to Coaching Skills: A Practical Guide*. London: Sage.

van Nieuwerburgh, C. (Ed.) (2016a). *Coaching in Professional Contexts*. London: Sage.

van Nieuwerburgh, C. (2016b). Towards a coaching culture. In: C. van Nieuwerburgh (Ed.) *Coaching in Professional Contexts* (pp. 227–234). London: Sage.

van Nieuwerburgh, C., Knight, J., & Campbell, J. (2019). Coaching in education. In: S. English, J. M. Sabatine, & P. Brownell (Eds.), *Professional Coaching: Principles and Practice* (pp. 411–426). New York: Springer.

van Nieuwerburgh, C., & Tong, C. (2013). Exploring the benefits of being a student coach in educational settings: A mixed-method study. *Coaching: An International Journal of Theory, Practice and Research*, 6: 5–24.

Van Velsor, E., & McCauley, C. D. (2004). Introduction: Our view of leadership development. In: C. D. McCauley & E. Van Velsor (Eds.), *The Center for Creative Leadership Handbook of Leadership Development* (2nd edition, pp. 1–22). San Francisco, CA: Jossey Bass.

Vygotsky, L. S. (1978). *Mind and Society: The Development of Higher Mental Processes*. Cambridge, MA: Harvard University Press.

Waddell, M. (2002). *Inside Lives: Psychoanalysis and the Growth of the Personality*. London: Karnac.

Warman, A., & Jackson, E. (2007). Recruiting and retaining children and families' social workers: The potential of work discussion groups. *Journal of Social Work Practice*, 21 (1): 35–48.

West-Burnham, J. (2002). *Leadership and Spirituality*. Nottingham: National College for School Leadership.

Western, S. (2008). *Leadership: A Critical Text*. London: Sage.

Whitmore, J. (2009). *Coaching for Performance: GROWing Human Potential and Purpose. The Principles and Practice of Coaching and Leadership* (4th edition). London: Nicholas Brealey.

Wigdortz, B., & Toop, J. (2016). *The School Leadership Challenge: 2022*. www.ambitionschoolleadership.org.uk/documents/533/The_School_Leadership_Challenge_2022.pdf

Wiliam, D. (2014). *The Formative Evaluation of Teaching Performance*. CSE Occasional Paper No. 137. Melbourne: Centre for Strategic Education (CSE).

Wiliam, D. (2016). *Leadership for Teacher Learning: Creating a Culture Where All Teachers Improve so that All Students Succeed*. West Palm Beach, FL: Learning Sciences International.

Winnicott, D. (1949). Mind and its relation to the psyche-soma. In: *Through Paediatrics to Psychoanalysis* (pp. 243–254). London: Tavistock Publications, 1958. Reprinted London: Karnac, 1984.

Wong, K., & Nicotera, A. (2003). *Enhancing Teacher Quality: Peer Coaching as a Professional Development Strategy. A Preliminary Synthesis of the Literature.* Washington, DC: Institute of Education Sciences.

Woods, D., & Brighouse, T. (Eds.) (2014). *The Story of London Challenge.* London: London Leadership Strategy Publications.

Woods, D., & John, S. (2010). *Lessons Learned from London.* London: London Leadership Strategy and National College.

Woods, D., Macfarlane, R., & McBeath, D. (2018). *The Nine Pillars of Great Schools.* London: John Catt.

Wrigley, T. (2016). Not so simple: The problem with "evidence-based practice" and the EEF toolkit. *FORUM, 58* (2): 237–250.

Youell, B. (2006). *The Learning Relationship: Psychoanalytic Thinking in Education.* London: Karnac.

Yukl, G. (2002). *Leadership in Organizations* (5th edition). Upper Saddle River, NJ: Prentice-Hall.

INDEX

Abrams, F., 293
abstract conceptualization, 262
academy(ies), 17–21, 29, 50, 54, 214, 216, 224, 246
academy trusts, 17, 21, 32, 134, 201, 208, 210, 216, 224
accountability:
    collective, 33
    high-stakes, 39, 48
    increased/high, 7, 19, 28, 29, 38, 41, 224, 238
        climate of, 28
        as source of pressure, 19–21
    levels and patterns of, 29
        changes in, 47
        domino effect of, 29
    public, 20
accountability culture, 38
accountability model for schools, 50
accountability systems:
    centralized, enhanced, 47
    high-stakes, 48
acting out, 66, 70, 77
action learning, 155, 156
action-learning programmes at General
        Electric, 155
active experimentation, 262
Adams, M., 227, 229

administration, era of in school
        leadership development, 48
affiliative leadership styles, 33
Aitken, R., 26
alcohol abuse, 19
Allan, R., 242
Allen, B., 28
Allen, R., 29
Allen, W., 148
alliances of schools, 20
altruism, 35, 36, 77
Ambition Institute, 6
Ambition School Leadership/Future
        Leaders Trust, 201, 208, 312, 313
Ancona, D., 50
Anderson, S., 43
Andrews, J., 232
antagonists as sources of dissonance, 168
antisocial behaviour, 25
anxiety:
    container of, school as, 61–62
    containment of, 92–93, 110, 128, 131
    defences against, 68, 77
        social systems as, 79
Ark John Keats Academy, London, 315
Ark Schools, 315
Armstrong, D., 32, 38, 82, 117, 128, 130
attainment gap(s), 51, 52, 55, 273, 279

attention deficit disorder, 294
Atwater, L. E., 152
Aurelius, M., 199
authenticity, critical importance of, 234–238
authentic leadership, 46, 152, 264
authoritative leadership styles, 33
authority:
    from above, 83
    and power, use of, 123–125
    sources and use of, 83–85
autonomous learning, 277
autonomy, 48, 163, 184, 185
    forced, 35
    illusory, 35
    institutional, 47
    school, 55
    teacher, 50
Avalos, B., 256
Avolio, B. J., 152

Baars, S., 281
baF: *see* basic assumption fight–flight
Bain, A., 87, 90
Balint, M., 135, 140
Bambrick-Santoyo, P., 317
Bamford, A., 231
Bandura, A., 228
baO: *see* basic assumption oneness
baP: *see* basic assumption pairing
Barber, M., 28, 51
Baron, Y., 292, 295–297
Barr, M., 12, 226–245
basic assumption(s):
    dependency [*baD*], 87–88, 91, 148
        recognizing and responding to, 88
    fight–flight [*baF*], 87
        recognizing and responding to, 89
    functioning, 91, 148
    me-ness [*baM*], 87
        recognizing and responding to, 91
    mentality, 86–87, 92
    oneness [*baO*], 89
        recognizing and responding to, 90
    pairing [*baP*], 87
        recognizing and responding to, 88
    sophisticated use of, 90–91
Bay of Pigs invasion (1961), 89
BCYP: *see* Brent Centre for Young People
Belbin diagnostic tool, 153
Bell, J., 8, 57, 73–93
Bell, S., 243
bench strength, 200

Benington, J., 42
bereavement, 63, 195
Berkeley, A., 1–13, 17–40, 97–115,
        132–150, 199–225, 285–318
Bernstein, B., 51
Berwick, G., 271
Bickman, L., 229
Biesta, G., 234
Bion, W. R., 60, 61, 86, 87, 91, 135, 148, 180
Birmingham terrorist attack (2017), 35
Bollas, C., 105
boundary relationship with parents and
        carers, 22–25
boundary role of headteachers, 19–26
boundary spanners, 45
Boyatzis, R., 152
Boyle, A., 281
BP Azerbaijan, 200
Bradley, J., 135, 150
Brent Centre for Young People [BCYP],
        4, 5, 136
Bridge of Weir Primary School,
        Renfrewshire, 243
Briggs Myers, I., 126, 174
Brighouse, T., 269, 270, 281
British Council, 210
Brown, A., 231
Brown, C., 53, 250
Brown, G., 159
Bryant, B., 10, 151–170
Bubb, S., 49, 53
Buckley, D., 292–295
burn-out, 35
Bush, T., 46
business development, 54, 161
business management theory,
        commercial-sector, 48

Campbell, D., 75, 229, 241
Campbell, J., 226, 227, 229, 230, 232, 241
Canham, C., 86
Canham, H., 135
Cantore, S., 229
capacity-building, 44
Career Anchors, 153
career coaching, 242
centralized accountability systems,
        enhanced, 47
Challenge Partners, 212
change, continuous, 35
    as source of pressure, 19–21
change management, 222, 254, 256, 312
Chapman, C., 54

Charan, R., 203
charismatic leadership, 152
Chartered Institute of Personnel &
        Development [CIPD], 251, 253
Chijioke, C., 28
childhood obesity, 35
child protection, 19, 20, 36
CiPD: *see* Chartered Institute of
        Personnel & Development
circle of pairs, 130
Claeys, A., 280
Clarke, E., 297, 298–300
class group dynamics, 97, 136
classical leadership, 46
Clutterbuck, D., 231, 242
coaching (*passim*):
    approaches to, 99
    career, 242
    cognitive behavioural, 99
    eLearning, 243
    for leadership, 212–213, 242
    leadership pair(s), 3, 110, 116–131
    vs. mentoring, 213, 226, 227, 237
    parameters of, 109
    peer, 233, 242
        reciprocal, 243
    person-centred approach to, 227
    positive-psychology-based approach
        to, 228
    psychological theories and
        approaches informing, 227
    range of issues brought to, 100
    self-determination theory, 228
    self-efficacy theory, 228
    solution-focused approach to, 228
    systems-psychodynamic, 99
    technology, 242
coaching approach, 227, 229, 232, 237
coaching conversation(s), 18, 29, 33, 38,
        108, 232, 237, 241, 242, 244
coaching culture(s):
    in schools, 226–245
    whole-school, 12, 226, 229, 231,
        233, 243
coaching leadership styles, 33
coaching relationship, confidential, 37
coaching sessions:
    basic allowance for, 99
    one-to-one, 9, 98, 114
    structure and frequency of, 99–100
coaching skills, specific, importance of
        training in, 241
coaching supervision, 242

coaching way of being, 229
Coe, R., 257
coercive leadership styles, 33
cognitive behavioural coaching, 99
collaboration, inter-school, 22
collaborative models of school
        leadership, 117
collaborative professional learning, 242
collective accountability, 33
collective leadership, team dynamics
        required for, 130
Collingwood, H., 153
Collins, J., 312, 315
commercial-sector business
        management theory, 48
communication skills, 23, 30
community-based settings,
        psychoanalytic approaches in, 4
competency(ies), 48, 110, 148
    for assessment and development,
        214–215
    core, 216
    functional, 216
    general, 216
    leadership, 214, 216
competency framework(s), 216, 220,
        254, 258
conceptual thinking, higher-order, 30
concrete experience, 249, 262
confidentiality, 115, 121, 213
    client, 116
    in work discussion groups, 139
conflict management/resolution, 33, 37,
        141, 216
Conger, J. A., 152
Connolly, J. A., 148, 208
consultant leader programme, 272
container–contained, 60
container of anxiety, school as, 61–62
containment:
    concept of, 72
    emotional, 35
    layers of, 62
    maternal, 60, 61
    psychological and emotional, for
        students' anxieties, 35
    Russian Doll model of, 61
    in systems psychodynamic
        framework, 92
contextual intelligence, 46, 205
contingency or situational leadership
        theory, 46
contingent leadership, 46

continuing professional development [CPD], 12, 242, 247–249, 252, 258
Cordingley, P., 257, 258, 263, 264
core competencies, 216
corporate memory, school's, 237
Coughlan, S., 37
countertransference(s), 66, 147, 157, 161, 169
    concept of, 72
    and observation, 68–70
Covey, S. M. R., 239
Covey, S. R., 140, 318
CPD: see continuing professional development
Craig, I., 47, 49
Cranston, N., 47
Creasey, S., 285, 286–289
Creasy, J., 231
creativity, encouragement of, 128–129
Creissen, T., 212
crime, 19, 37
    knife, 35
criminal activity, 19
critical thinking, 277
Croft, J., 42, 43
cross-cultural competence, 205
Csikszentmihalyi, M., 228
cultural fit, importance of, 205
cultural plurality, 205
Cunliffe, A., 118
cyber-bullying, 36

data management, 29
data protection, 20
Davies, B., 45
Day, C., 28, 32, 42, 43, 49, 50, 132, 205, 224
Day, D. V., 152, 153
day conferences, 5
DCSF: see Department for Children, Schools and Families
decentralization, 47, 48, 55
Deci, E. L., 228
decision-making simulations, small-group, 155
deep professional learning, 258, 264
defence mechanisms, 157
defences against anxiety, 68, 77
    social systems as, 79
defensive behaviour, 77, 87, 91
defensiveness, 23, 166
Deloitte, 199, 200
democratic leadership styles, 33
demographic changes, 19

Denyer, D., 118
Department for Children, Schools and Families [DCSF], 150
Department for Education [DfE]:
    Innovations Unit of, 137
    national "Fast Track" recruitment scheme, 208
Department for Education and Skills [DfES], 136
Department of Health [DoH], 136
dependency basic assumption [baD], 87, 91, 148
    recognizing and responding to, 88
dependency culture, 27, 67
dependency group, 180
DeRue, S., 210
de Sauma, M., 4
Descours, K., 37
de Shazer, S., 228
development, Kleinian theory of, 60
development actions, 202, 218, 220, 223
development menus, 220
Deverill, S., 303, 307
Dewey, J., 151, 154, 155
DfE: see Department for Education
DfES: see Department for Education and Skills
diagnostic surveys, 153
diagnostic tool(s), 153
dialogic approach, 230
Dinh, J. E., 152
disadvantaged children/families, 51, 69, 209, 268
disciplinary procedures, 145
distributed leadership, 7, 18, 32, 46, 50, 117
dogmatism, 36
DoH: see Department of Health
dominant function, preferred mental process as, 174
Draper, R., 75
Drath, W., 118
Drotter, S., 203
Drucker, P., 55
drug abuse, 19, 35
Dunford, J., 54
Dweck, C., 38, 317
dynamics, group, unconscious, 86

Earley, P., 7, 8, 41–56, 259
Easton, L. B., 288
Edge, K., 37
educational outcomes and poverty, link between, 50

educational platform, 234
Education Endowment Foundation
        [EEF], 52, 53
Education Reform Act (1988), 26, 48
EEF: *see* Education Endowment
        Foundation
Ehren, M., 47
Eichinger, R., 202, 208, 216
eLearning coaching, 243
Elwick, A., 281
Ely, R., 246, 254
email, tyranny of, 26
emotional intelligence, 8, 38, 42, 82, 92,
        148, 152, 228, 294
emotional life of organization, 82
emotional literacy, 31
entity-based leadership, 118
envy, overcoming or tolerating, as early
        childhood task, 65
epistemophilic instinct, 60
equal-opportunities policies, 207
era of management, 48
Eriksen, M., 118
Etz Chaim Jewish Primary Free School,
        London, 295
evidence-based approach(es):
    to school-based decision-making, 53
    to teaching and learning, 252
evidence-informed culture, 52
evidence-informed practice, 250
evidence-informed profession, teaching
        as, 51
examination leagues tables, 21
excellence visits, 276, 280
exclusion(s), 31
    permanent, 19, 21, 29, 36, 63
exclusions appeal panel, 100
executive coaching, 5, 6, 137, 153, 252, 255
    for school leaders, 97–115
executive head, 22
executive learning, 10, 152, 157
    deeper, examples of, 158–163
    70:20:10 model for, 154
Executive Learning Disabilities, 151
executives, psychotherapy for, 154
existential task, 80
experiences checklist, 200, 209
experiential learning, 6, 10, 147, 262
    leadership, 151–171
    Piagetian view of, 156
experiential learning cycle, 262
experiential learning principles, 152
external "on the boundary" pressures, 19

external pressures on headteachers,
        19–26
Extraversion [E]:
    and Introversion [I], 177–182
    qualities of, 178

Facebook, trial by, 25
facilitation skills, 53
failure:
    externalization of, 166
    fear of, 39, 145, 166
fear of failure, 39, 145, 166
fear of success, 145
federations of schools, 20
feedback:
    mutual, 9, 116, 125, 129
    surveys, 360°, 153, 205, 217, 220, 221,
        253, 254, 258, 261, 314
Feeling [F]:
    preference, 177
    and Thinking [T], 73, 177, 187–192
feeling type, 177
fight–flight basic assumption [baF], 87,
        91, 148
    recognizing and responding to, 89
financial planning/management, 26,
        27, 217
financial processes, 29
Fitzsimons, D., 118
Fleenor, J. W., 152
Flensborg, W., 237
Fletcher, J. K., 117, 118
followership, 83
    cooperative and creative, 59
    role of, 29–31
Folsom, J. S., 43
Forde, C., 229
forgiveness, 77
Forster, E. M., 179
Four Capitals Model, 271
fragmentation, 110
Francis, R., 79
Frayman, K., 37
free-floating thinking, 129
Free School(s), 18, 20, 21, 32, 101, 292, 296
free school meals, 51, 52, 269
Frei, F., 246, 254
Freud, S., 59
Fullan, M., 133, 148, 269, 270, 281
Fullisk, L., 281
functional competencies, 216
Furnham, A., 26, 45
Future Leaders, 6, 220, 312

Gaining Ground programme, 273
Gallagher, N., 22
gang state of mind, 86
gap analysis, 215
Gardner, W. L., 152
gender stereotypes, 71
general competencies, 216
General Electric, action-learning
        programmes at, 155
George, B., 264
Gersch, I., 231
Gitsham, M., 200
GLA: see Greater London Authority
Glover, D., 46
Goddard, J., 33, 247
Goff, P., 229
Goffee, R., 153
Going for Great programme, 275
Golawski, A., 231
Goldacre, B., 53
Goldring, E., 229
Goleman, D., 33, 38, 82, 148, 152, 205
Gontier, F., 240, 241
Good to Great programme, 274
Google, trial by, 25
Gorard, S., 43, 51
Gormley, H., 226, 229
Gould, L., 87, 90
governance, 20, 74, 83
    and leadership, 116–131
governing body/board of trustees, chair
        of, and headteacher, relationship
        between, 9
Graen, G. B., 152
Graham, G., 231
Grant, V., 38
gratification, 36
gravitas, 297, 299
Greany, T., 7, 8, 41–56, 250, 257
Greater London Authority [GLA], 275
Green, S., 228
Gronn, P., 229
group discussion, 144, 145, 146, 147, 179
group dynamics, 8, 19, 33, 73–93, 99
    class, 97, 136
    unconscious, 86
Group Problem Solving Protocol, 288
group relations, 3
group-think, concept of, 89
GROW model of coaching and
        mentoring, 99
growth mindset, 29
Grubb Institute, 3

Gu, Q., 49, 54
Guedes, A., 238, 239
Gurdjian, P., 153
Guthrie, J. E., 229

Haileybury College, Melbourne,
        Australia, 240, 241
Halbeisen, T., 153
Hall, R. J., 152
Hammer, A., 126
Hampstead School, London, 2
Handy, C., 26
Hargreaves, A., 237, 269, 270, 281
Haris, A., 133
Harris, A., 50
Harris, M., 135
Harrison, S., 12, 246–266
Hartley, J., 42
Haslam, S., 44
Hattie, J., 44
Hawkins, P., 231
Hay Group, 212
headship:
    emotional challenges of, 289–290
    need for equilibrium, 17–40
    psychological challenges of, 290
headspace, finding, 311–318
Heads' Roundtable, 212
headteacher(s):
    and chair of governing body/board of
        trustees, relationship between, 9
    as heart-teacher, 292–297
    hopes and expectations of, 140
    isolation and loneliness of, 144
    pressure on, sources of, 19
    support for, 114–115
    work discussion groups for, 10,
        132–150
headteacher leadership, role of, 44
health education, targeted, 35
Heath, C., 317
Heath, D., 317
Heifetz, R., 46
helping relationships, 238
Henry, G., 135
Her Majesty's Chief Inspector [HMCI],
        37, 293
Her Majesty's Inspector [HMI], 149, 278
Herrington, C. D., 43
Hersey, P., 205
Hick, W., 229
Higgins, S., 257
high achievers, 204

Higham, R., 54
high-stakes accountability systems, 48
Hill, A., 33, 246, 247, 273
Hill, R., 49, 54, 55
Hirschhorn, L., 128
HMCI: see Her Majesty's Chief Inspector
Hogan diagnostic tool, 153
Hooijberg, R., 154
Hooker, T., 230
Hopkins, D., 54, 133
Hoyle, L., 141
Huffington, C., 5, 9, 32, 75, 116–131
human resources [HR], 26, 29, 167, 200,
       224, 251
   coaching function within, 212
Hunter, S., 241, 244

ILEA: see Inner London Education
       Authority
Imison, Dame T., 3
imposter syndrome, 27, 286, 287
impression management, 237
Improving Teacher Programme
       [ITP], 274
Inclusion Support programme, 273
independent schools, 20, 42
Industrial Society [Work Foundation], 3
in-group, 85
Inner London Education Authority
       [ILEA], 268, 270
innovation, encouragement of, 128–129
inspection regimes, 20, 29
institutional autonomy, 47
institutional stress, 65
instructional coach(es)/coaching, 12, 230
instructional mentoring, 214
intellectualization, defence of, 168
interim governing body, 22
international school chains, 224
internal pressures, 19
internet, 25, 165
interpersonal concepts, 134
interpersonal dynamics, 8, 98, 173
   inherent in school life, 1
interpersonal relationships, 19, 58, 147
interpersonal skills, 41
inter-school collaboration, 22
inter-school work discussion groups, 137
inter-team dynamics, 174
intra-personal dynamics, 8
intra-psychic concepts, 134
intra-psychic dynamics, of school life, 1
intra-team dynamics, 173

Introversion [I]:
   and Extraversion [E], 177–182
   qualities of, 178
Intuition [N]:
   preference, 177
   and Sensing [S], 177, 182–187
IOE: see London University Institute of
       Education
ITP: see Improving Teacher Programme

Jackson, E., 1–13, 76, 97–115, 132–150,
       157, 173–198
Jacques, E., 135
James, C., 148
James, K., 32
James-Ward, C., 229
Janis, I., 89
Jastrzebska, K., 231
Jensen, M., 44
job shadowing, 211
John, S., 143, 274
John Lyon Trust, 4
joint practice development, 280
Jones, G., 153
Jones, R., 233, 239, 243, 244
jouissance, 128
Judging [J]:
   and Perceiving [P], 177, 192–197
   preference, 177
Jung, C., 11, 174, 176

Kanungo, R. N., 152
Kempton, J., 280
Kennedy, J. F., 89, 307
Keohane, N., 44
Kerr, J., 199
key assumptions, 261
Keys to Success schools, 272, 273
Khan, W. A., 39
Kilburg, R., 303
Kipling, R., 17
Klauber, T., 135
Klein, M., 60, 65
knife crime, 35
Knight, J., 226, 229, 230, 238
knowledge sharing, 54
Kolb, D., 155, 249, 262
Korn Ferry Institute, 248, 263
Kotter, J., 254, 256

Lacan, J., 128
Ladkin, D., 118
Laker, B., 33, 246, 247

L&D: *see* learning and development
Lane, K., 153, 154
Lawrence, G., 80, 87, 90
Leach, C., 228
Leadbeater, C., 133
leader(s):
  identity and authenticity of, 153
  system, 50, 53, 54, 268, 271, 274, 275
leadership:
  authentic, 152
  charismatic, 152
  classical, 46
  definitions of, 26, 42, 44, 247
  distributed, 7, 18, 32, 46, 50, 117
  era of, in school leadership
      development, 48
  and governance, 116–131
  importance of, 43, 44, 224
  in non-educational organizations, 45
  organic, 46
  organizational, 9, 117
  as process, 46
  quality of, 43, 51
  reflective, 38
  responsive, 38–39
  shared, 122, 126, 129
  sustainable, 38–39
  system, 7, 42, 49, 54, 133, 137, 268, 269,
      272, 273, 279
  teacher, 46
  transactional, 46
  visionary, 46
leadership coaching, 3, 110, 242
leadership competencies, 214, 216, 221
leadership development (*passim*):
  aims and assumptions of, 199–201
  in business world, 199–225
  experiential learning in, 151–171
  learning methods for, 152
  models of, 201–203
  needs, 137, 217
  practices, 224
  senior, 10, 257
  70:20:10 model of, 202, 218
  theory and practice, 152
  traditions and practices, 152–154
  whole-system approach to, 267–281
leadership development design
      principles, 12, 223
leadership development programme(s),
      7, 13, 18, 133, 153, 155, 201, 205,
      216, 247, 254–257, 266
leadership development training, 223, 259

leadership pair(s), 6, 9
  coaching, 116–131
  senior, 118, 119
Leadership Pathways, 49
leadership pipeline, 200, 201
  model, 203–205
Leadership Programme for Serving
      Headteachers [LPSH], 6, 49
leadership roles, personal and
      professional authority in, 106
leadership strategy, coaching as, 237
leadership styles, 2, 41, 46, 70, 221
  affiliative, 33
  authoritative, 33
  coaching, 33
  coaching skills, use as part of, 205
  coercive, 33
  democratic, 33
  dictatorial, 84
  impact of, on organizational
      climate, 205
  intuitive leader's, 184
  laissez-faire, 84
  pace-setting, 33
leadership training, key elements of,
      221–223
Leading Edge Partnership, 137
Leading Edge school(s), 137, 149
Leading Edge status, 137
Leading from the Middle programme,
      49, 273
league tables, 35, 58
  public examination, 3, 21
learning:
  connecting to workplace, 222
  triggers for, 152, 164
  while leading, 156
learning and development [L&D], 13,
      227, 234, 251, 253
learning-centred leadership, 46
learning disablers, 152, 166
learning from experience, 60, 71, 78, 155,
      156, 208, 287
learning narratives, 157–158
learning needs analysis, 251–254, 262
learning organization(s), 53, 281
  schools as, 53
learning partnerships, 238
learning skills, development of, 277
learning through reflection, 155
le Blanc, F., 161–163
Leithwood, K., 43, 132
Lemov, D., 317

Lencioni, P., 30, 33
LIFO diagnostic tool, 153
line management relationships, 157
LLE: *see* Local Leaders of Education
LLS: *see* London Leadership Strategy
LMS: *see* Local Management of Schools
local authority, 10, 19, 48, 53, 58, 59, 114, 123, 214, 270
local education authorities [LAs], 7, 208
Local Leaders of Education [LLE], 133, 214, 274
Local Management of Schools [LMS], 26
Lombardo, M., 154, 155, 202, 208, 216
London Challenge programme, 3, 4, 12, 212, 267–281
London Consultant Leaders, 272
London Leadership Annual Prospectus, 280
London Leadership Strategy [LLS], 269–276, 278–281
London University Institute of Education [IOE], 210, 269
Longhill High School, Brighton, 289
Lord, R. G., 152
Lorenzi, P., 153
Louis, K. S., 43
Lucas, M., 242
Lupton, R., 52
Luthans, F., 154

Macfarlane, R., 276
Malone, T., 50
management, era of, in school leadership, 48
managerial leadership, 46
Martin, M., 229
Marzano, R., 42
Maslow, A., 36
MAT: *see* Multi-Academy Trust(s)
maternal containment, 60, 61
Matthews, P., 49, 54, 272, 273, 274
Maxwell, B., 53
MBTI: *see* Myers–Briggs Type Indicator
McAleavy, T., 281
McBeath, D., 276
McCall, M. W., 154–156
McCauley, C., 118, 210
McCaulley, M. H., 126
McKee, A., 152
McKee, R. A., 152
McKinsey's 7S framework, 33

McLaughlin, C., 274
McLeod, M., 233, 242
McMahon, M., 229
McNulty, B., 42
Mead, M., 225
Megginson, D., 231
Mellon, L., 33
member exchange, 152
me-ness basic assumption [*baM*], 87, 90
    recognizing and responding to, 91
mental health concerns/problems, 145
    among young people, 36
mentoring, 7, 12, 99
    vs. coaching, 213, 226, 227, 237
    instructional, 214
    in leadership training, 213–214
    programmes, 213
Menzies, I., 80
Menzies Lyth, I., 80, 135
Micklewright, J., 50
Mid Staffordshire NHS Trust, 79
Miller, E., 75, 80, 135
moral leadership, 46
Morrison, A. M., 154, 155
Morriss, A., 246, 247, 254
mother, "attuned", 66
Mount Scopus Memorial College, Melbourne, Australia, 232
Mourshed, M., 28, 51
Moving to New Headship programme, 273
Multi-Academy Trust(s) [MATs], 2, 7, 11–12, 18, 20, 29, 35, 42, 49–50, 53–55, 83, 111, 185, 187, 207, 247, 253–259, 279, 316, 317
Munro, C., 12, 226–245
Myatt, M., 45
Myers–Briggs Type Indicator [MBTI], 76, 126, 153, 288, 301
    background, 174–175
    and common reactions to stress, 196–197
    language of, 177, 181
    personality preferences, 11, 173–198
        Extraversion and Introversion, 177–182
        Judging and Perceiving, 192–197
        Sensing and Intuition, 182–187
        Thinking and Feeling, 187–192
    use of, with school leaders, 175
    uses and misuses, 175–176
    workshop, 175, 185, 186

Nadler, D. A., 119, 124
National College for School Leadership [NCSL], 3, 6, 48, 134, 205, 212, 267, 269, 271–275
National College for Teaching and Leadership [NCTL], 22, 201
National Curriculum, 50
national education policy agendas, 7, 42
national "Fast Track" recruitment scheme, 208
national framework for school inspections, 3
National Governance Association [NGA], 123
National Health Service [NHS], 79, 160
national initiatives, 29
National Leaders of Education [NLEs], 22, 54, 133, 214, 253, 273, 274, 278, 279
National Professional Qualification for Headship [NPQH], 6, 12, 17, 18, 22, 27, 49, 203, 208, 211, 304
National Professional Qualification for Senior Leaders [NPQSL], content and assessment framework, 251
National Professional Qualifications [NPQs], 11, 133, 201, 202, 204, 216, 220
   content and assessment framework, 254
National Standards for Headteachers, 254
National Strategies, 133
National Support Schools [NSS], 273, 278, 279
NCSL: see National College for School Leadership
NCTL: see National College for Teaching and Leadership
negotiation skills, 42
NEO diagnostic tool, 153
Netolicky, D. M., 233, 238, 239, 240
New Labour, 48
NHS: see National Health Service
Nicotera, A., 230
"Nine Pillars of Greatness", 276
NLE: see National Leaders in Education
Noel, J., 203
non-educational organizations, leadership in, 45
non-verbal communication, 135
normative task, 80
North, T., 303

North Berwick High School, North Berwick, Scotland, 233, 239, 243, 244
Northouse, P. G., 44, 45
NPQH: see National Professional Qualification for Headship
NPQs: see National Professional Qualifications
NPQSL: see National Professional Qualification for Senior Leaders
NSS: see National Support Schools

obesity, childhood, 35
Obholzer, A., 19, 30, 59, 83–85
observation, psychoanalytically informed, 68
occupational health, 110, 143
OECD: see Organisation for Economic Cooperation & Development
Office for National Statistics [ONS], 133
Office for Standards in Education, Children's Services and Skills [Ofsted], 3, 29, 35, 63, 78, 98, 102, 115, 224, 257, 273, 275, 312, 316
   inspections, 20, 28, 51, 61
Ofsted: see Office for Standards in Education, Children's Services and Skills
omnipotence, feelings of, 36
oneness basic assumption [baO], 87, 89
   recognizing and responding to, 90
one-to-one support, 6
ONS, 133: see Office for National Statistics
Ontario Institute in Education, University of Toronto, 270
organic leadership, 46
Organisation for Economic Cooperation & Development [OECD], 51, 53
organization:
   emotional life of, 82
   primary task of, 80
organization-in-the-mind, 38, 82, 83, 92
organizational design, 54, 55
organizational dynamics, 1, 8, 73–93
organizational leadership, 9, 117, 118
organizational management, 50
organizational pressures, 19, 26–33
organizational systems, unconscious processes as, 2
Orlikowski, W., 50
Osborne, E., 135

Osborne-Lampkin, L., 43
OTP: *see* Outstanding Teacher
　　Programme
outdoor exercises, 155
Outstanding Teacher Programme
　　[OTP], 274

pace-setting leadership styles, 33
pairing basic assumption [*baP*], 87
　　recognizing and responding to, 88
pairing group, 180
parameters of coaching, 109–110
parental authority, 27
parental choice, 23, 47
parental complaints, 23, 127, 129
parental contact, benefits of, 23
parental satisfaction, 23, 40, 224
parents:
　　hard-to-reach, 19, 24
　　hostile, 19
Parish, N., 54
Parker, S., 22
Park View Secondary School, London,
　　298, 312
Parliament Hill School for Girls,
　　London, 286
Parr, J., 241
participant experience, 264, 265
partnership principles, 238
passive aggression, 77
Passmore, J., 231
Paterson, C., 231, 280
Paterson, F., 231
PDPs: *see* Personal Development Plans
peer coaching, 230, 233, 242
　　reciprocal, 243
peer discussions, 205, 221, 233, 242
peer networking, 221
peer reflective practice, 242
peer review, 13, 211, 280
peer support, 13, 132, 211, 212
Pendleton, D., 26, 45
People Days, 206
people management skills, 205
Perceiving [P]:
　　and Judging [J], 192–197
　　preference, 177
performance data, 29, 271, 272, 277
performance management, 28, 29, 47,
　　105, 216, 237
permanent exclusion, 63
Perryman, J., 47

Personal Development Plans [PDPs],
　　206, 218–219, 222
personality preference(s):
　　inborn, 176
　　innate, 176
　　Jung's theory of, 174
　　MBTI, 11, 76, 173–177, 197
　　pairs of, impact of in school
　　　　leadership, 177–197
personality profiles, 217, 220
personality types, 76, 174
personal narratives, writing of, 10
personal trait leadership theory, 46
person-centred approach to
　　coaching, 227
Peters, T., 33
Peterson, S. J., 154
Petriglieri, G., 153, 154
Petriglieri, J. L., 153, 154
PGCE: *see* Post-Graduate Certificate in
　　Education
phantasies, unconscious, 23
phenomenal primary task, 81
phenomenal task, 80
Piaget, J., 151, 154
Pillans, G., 41, 46
Pimlico Academy, London, 315
Plato, 153
Platow, M., 44
police presence in schools, 142
political awareness, 42
political environment, increasingly
　　complex, 7, 41
political literacy, 8, 31
　　need for, 291
positional leadership, 117
positive mind-set, 38
positive psychology, 228
positive-psychology-based approach to
　　coaching, 228
Post-Graduate Certificate in Education
　　[PGCE], 115
post heroic leadership, 117
poverty, 19, 269
　　and educational outcomes, link
　　　　between, 50
power:
　　and authority, use of, 123–125
　　management of, 34–35
　　sources and use of, 83–85
power and influence leadership theory, 46

PP: *see* Pupil Premium
pragmatism, 36, 196
Preston Manor School, London, 3, 4, 5,
    136, 233, 242
Priestley, M., 234
Primary Challenge Groups, 275
primary task, 8, 28, 91, 156
    of organization, 80, 82
    phenomenal, 81
principal personality, 315
Pringle, S., 297, 300–303
problematic staff cultures,
    addressing, 140
process, leadership as, 46
professional development, 12, 52, 97,
    103, 104, 114, 188, 210, 247–252,
    256, 259, 263, 275, 278, 301, 303
    continuing, 22, 134, 207, 248, 257
    teacher, 248
professional mentoring, 12
projection(s), 58, 65–70, 77, 147, 157, 169
    of anxiety, 71
    concept of, 72
    cycle of, 111
    unconscious, 23
projective identification, 147
projective process, 77
project management, 29, 210
protainment, concept of, 128
PRU: *see* Pupil Referral Unit
psychoanalytically informed
    observation, 68
psychoanalytic approaches in
    community-based settings, 4
psychodynamic approaches, 227
psychodynamic concepts, 8, 157
psychodynamic thinking, 8, 74, 75, 99
psychological presence, 39
psychological type, Jung's theory of, 174
psychometric tests, 217, 220, 221
psychotherapy, 2, 5, 110, 139
    for executives, 154
public accountability, 20
public examination league tables, 3, 21
public examinations, changes to, 20
Pupil Premium [PP], 51–52
Pupil Referral Unit [PRU], 137, 146

Quenk, N., 126, 174, 196

racism, 35
rationalization, defence of, 168

Rea, S., 49, 54
reciprocal peer coaching, 243
reflective exercises, 221
reflective observation, 262, 263
reflective practice, 233, 313, 314
    peer, 242
reflective space, 3, 9, 92, 121, 129
Regional Schools Commissioners, 49
Reicher, S., 44
relational leadership, 117, 118
relationship distance and intimacy, 126
relationships:
    centrality of, 100
    effective management of, need for, 97
religious faith, headteachers', 33
representation, defence of, 168
research-based enquiry, culture of, 276
Research Schools, 12, 247
resilience, 9, 17, 38, 41, 98, 215, 228, 280
return on investment [ROI], 223, 248, 256
Rice, A. K., 75, 80, 135
Riding for the Disabled, 307
risk management, 54, 55, 136
Roberts, V. Z., 75
Robertson, J., 229, 232, 234, 242, 245
Robinson, P., 80
Robinson, S., 54, 234
Robinson, V., 50
Rogers, C., 227
ROI: *see* return on investment
role differentiation, 168
role-plays, 155
Russell Group universities, 201
Rustin, M., 135, 150
Ryan, R. M., 228

Sackson, E., 232
safeguarding, 20, 25, 27, 31, 287
Salzberger-Wittenberg, I., 135
Sammons, P., 28, 42, 132, 272
Sandals, L., 54
SATS: *see* standard attainment tests
Scheer, A., 44
Scheerens, J., 42
Schleicher, A., 47
school(s):
    alliances of, 20
    as container of anxiety, 61–62
    as learning organizations, 53
    as social institutions, internal
        dynamics of, 8
school autonomy, 55

school-based decision-making, evidence-based approach to, 53
school-based management, 48
school budgets, 224, 250, 256
    diminishing, 224
    tightening of, 250
school culture, existing, influence of, 239–240
School Inspection Framework, 278
school inspections, national framework for, 3
school leader(s):
    central emotional and psychological challenges of, 285–318
    coaching for, as duty of care, 113–114
    internal world of, 33–40, 70–71
    personal and professional development of, 103, 104
    personal histories of, 33–34
    serving, experiences of, 285–318
school leadership:
    changes in, 47
    complexities and emotional pressures of, 39
    contemporary, context and challenges of, 7–8, 41–56
    as crucial factor in school effectiveness, 42
    current and historical trends in, 6, 7, 42
    development of, 7, 12, 210, 247, 251
        eras in, 48
        five-stage career framework for, 48
        psychodynamic approaches, 9–11
    effective, 18, 247
    impact of, 43
    models of, 118
        collaborative, 117
        shared, 117
    moral imperative of, 148
    personality preferences, impact of on, 173–198
    successful, 49
    as work of passion, 56
school leadership programmes, 12
    design, management, and evaluation of, 246–266
school leadership teams, 257
school life:
    developmental stages of, 62
    unconscious dynamics in, significance of, 8
school management, 29

changes in, 26–27
school performance league tables, 35
school politics, 36
school staff:
    challenging, management of, 145
    dependency of, 146
    work discussion groups for, 136
school-to-school collaboration, 49, 278
school-to-school support, 52, 53, 269–273, 279
school uniform, 116
Schutte, N. S., 152
scrutiny, 7, 41, 307
    increased, as source of pressure, 19–21
Seahaven Academy, East Sussex, 300
Seashore Louis, K., 43
security cameras, 142
Seifert, C. F., 153
self-actualization, 36
self-awareness, 8, 41, 42, 164, 205, 208, 227
    training, 153
self-determination theory, 228
self-development orientation, 208
self-efficacy, 233, 234, 242, 255
    theory, 228
self-examination, resistance to, 169
self-harming, 36
self-identity, 39
self-improving system, 21, 133, 210
    school, 51–53
self-reflection, 153, 155
    critical, defence against, 165
    systematic process for, 155
Seligman, M. E. P., 228
SENCOs: see Special Education Needs Co-ordinators
SEND: see Special Educational Needs and Disabilities
SENDCO: see Special Education Needs and Disability Co-ordinator
Senge, P., 50
senior leadership team, 108, 109, 119–122, 129–132, 142, 143, 180, 183, 202
    development meetings, 130
    meetings, 206
sense-making, 11, 46, 152, 157
Sensing [S]:
    and Intuition [N], 177, 182–187
    preference, 177
sensing type, 177
separation anxiety, 63
Shackleton, N., 47

shared leadership, 46
  school, models of, 117
Simkins, T., 48, 49
Sims, H. P., Jr., 153
site management, 26
Situational Leadership, 205, 212
  theory, 46
Situational Leadership Model, 205–206
Skelton, J., 237
SLEs: see Specialist Leaders in Education
small-group decision-making
        simulations, 155
Smythe, J., 43, 50
social distance, senior executive's, 167
social identity, 157
social institutions, schools as, internal
        dynamics of, 8
social media, 45
  pressures of, 25–26
social psychology, 157
social science theory, 48
social systems, as defences against
        anxiety, 79
socio-technical systems, 75
Socratic dialogue, 167
solution-focused approach to
        coaching, 228
solution-focused therapy, 228
Southworth, G., 27
Spaten, O. M., 237
Special Educational Needs and
        Disabilities [SEND]
        programme, 279
Special Education Needs and Disability
        Co-ordinator [SENDCO], 4
Special Education Needs Co-ordinators
        [SENCOs], 273
Specialist Leaders of Education [SLE],
        210, 253, 279
special measures, 22, 133
Speirs, B., 11, 199–225
Spencer, J. L., 119, 124
Spielman, A., 37
Spillane, J., 50
spirituality, 33
  headteachers', 33
splitting, 65–67, 69, 70, 77, 147, 157,
        169, 261
staff cultures, problematic, addressing,
        140
staff development meetings, 206, 225
staff disciplinary issues, 36
staff restructuring issues, 31, 36, 290

staff retention, 214, 224
standard attainment tests [SATS], 61
standards-based agendas, 47
St Kevin's College, Melbourne,
        Australia, 241, 243, 244
St Mary's Church of England Primary
        Trust, Folkestone, Kent, 303
Stoll, L., 53
St Paul's School, Brisbane, Australia, 232
strategic thinking, 41, 55
Sturm, R. E., 152
style leadership theory, 46
success:
  fear of, 145
  inability to explore, 166
Successful Teaching and Learning
        programme, 278
succession planning, 11, 104, 127, 129,
        200, 206
suicide, 35
  teenage, 29
super head, 246, 247
suppression, defence of, 168
Sutton Trust, 51, 133
Syed, M., 317
systemic approaches, 227
systemic concepts, 73, 115, 134
systemic thinking, 99
system leadership, 7, 42, 46, 50, 53, 133,
        137, 268, 269, 271–275, 279
  early pioneers of, 54
  era of, in school leadership
        development, 49
systems psychodynamic approach/
        perspective, 74, 92
systems-psychodynamic coaching, 99
systems psychodynamic framework,
        containment in, 92
systems thinking, 8, 74
  application of, to organizational
        life, 75

talent management, 11, 127, 207, 222
Talent Review, 206
Tavistock Clinic, 3–5, 135
  Adolescent Department, 5
Tavistock Consultancy Service/
        Tavistock Consulting [TCS], 5, 6,
        137, 141
Taylor, S., 210
TCS: see Tavistock Consultancy Service
TCS executive coaching programme, 6
teacher autonomy, 50

teacher leadership, 46
teacher professional development, 248
teacher–student relationship, difficulties
        in, 136
teacher training, 22, 97, 148
Teach First, 201, 208, 212, 298
teaching:
    collegial culture of, 28
    as evidence-informed profession, 51
Teaching and Leadership Innovation
        Fund [TLIF], 248
Teaching and Learning Toolkit, 52
teaching hospitals, 52
teaching practice, 230
Teaching School Alliances [TSAs], 10, 12,
        22, 210, 214, 247, 257, 259, 274
Teaching Schools, 49, 51, 52, 54, 274, 275
team-building, 33, 140
Team Development Cycle, 288
team dialogue, 167
team dynamics, 98, 147, 149, 180
    management of, 145
    required for collective leadership, 130
technological system, 75
technology coaching, 242
teenage suicide, 29
terrorism, teenage, 35
test leagues tables, 21
theory, place of, within work discussion
        group, 147–148
Theory of Change, development of,
        260–261
Thinking [T], 177
    and Feeling [F], 73, 177, 187–192
    preference, 177
thinking space, 106, 299, 317
Thomas Carr College, Melbourne,
        Australia, 238, 239
Thomson, S., 52
Tichy, N. M., 155
Timperley, H., 241
TLIF: see Teaching and Leadership
        Innovation Fund
tolerance, 36, 77, 166
Tong, C., 231
Toop, J., 224
Toriello, M., 199
toxic leaders, 47, 49
toxins filter, headteacher's role as, 36
trait or "great man" leadership
        theory, 46
transactional leadership, 46

transference(s), 68, 71, 147, 157, 161, 169
    concept of, 72
    parental or grandparental, 67
transference assumption, 71
transference relationship, 68
transformational leadership, 46
transparency, 162, 206, 301
traumatic loss, 63
triggers for learning, 152, 164
TSAs: see Teaching School Alliances
Tucker, S., 76–77
Tuckman, B., 288
Turnbull James, K., 118
Turquet, P., 82, 87, 89, 135
Twitter, trial by, 25
type theory, 174

UCL IOE: see University College London
        Institute of Education
Uhl-Bien, M., 118, 152
unconscious, the, at work, recognizing
        and responding to, 81
unconscious communication(s), 68, 70, 72
unconscious dynamics:
    group, 86
    in school life, significance of, 8
unconscious mind, 59, 66
unconscious phantasies, 23
unconscious processes:
    functioning of, 78
    as organizational systems, 2
unconscious projections, 23
unemployment, 19, 81
United Learning, 201
University College London Institute
        of Education [UCL IOE], 3, 4, 6,
        28, 210

valency, 91, 148
van Nieuwerburgh, C., 12, 226–245
Van Velsor, E., 118
variance reduction, 165
visionary leadership, 46
Viswesvaran, C., 208
"VUCA" environment, volatile,
        uncertain, complex, and
        ambiguous, 41
Vygotsky, L. S., 154

Waddell, M., 93
Wahlstrom, K., 43
Warman, A., 136, 150

Waterman, R., 33
Waters, T., 42
WDG: *see* work discussion group(s)
Webster, A., 312
Wesley College, Perth, Australia, 233,
        238, 240
West-Burnham, J., 33
Western, S., 118
Whitaker, C., 242
Whitmore, J., 234
whole-school coaching culture for
        learning, 229–231
whole-system approach(es), 6
    to leadership development, 267–281
whole-system development, 7
whole-systems thinking, 42
Wigdortz, B., 224
Wiliam, D., 233, 234
Williams, G., 61
Williams, K., 286, 289–292
Williams, R., 292
Wilshaw, M., 293
Winnicott, D., 60
WomenEd, 212
Wong, K., 230
Wood, J. D., 153, 154
Woods. D., 12, 267–281
work discussion group(s) [WDG]:
    confidentiality in, importance of, 139
    in educational settings, development
        of, 135

evolution of, 135
facilitators' role, 139
format of, 141
ground rules for, 139
for headteachers, 10, 296
        inter-school, 132–150
history of, 135
inter-school, 137
location of, 138
model, 134–136
open vs. closed, 139
place of "theory" within, 147
presentation to, 140
for school staff, 4, 136
size of, 138
timing and duration of, 138
at work, 138–141
working method, 140
Work Foundation [Industrial Society], 3
work group mentality, 86, 91
work–life balance, 141, 213, 220,
        297, 298
workplace, connecting learning
        to, 222
work simulations, 217, 221
World Economic Forum, 200
Wrigley, T., 43, 51, 52

Yost, P., 210
Youell, B., 8, 33, 57–72, 74
Yukl, G., 44, 153

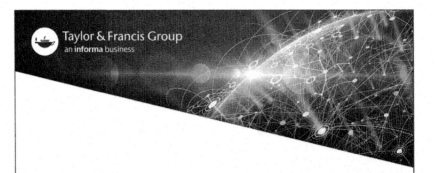